Enlightenment Biopolitics

the
LIFE
OF
IDEAS

SERIES EDITOR

Darrin McMahon, *Dartmouth College*

After a period of some eclipse, the study of intellectual history has enjoyed a broad resurgence in recent years. *The Life of Ideas* contributes to this revitalization through the study of ideas as they are produced, disseminated, received, and practiced in different historical contexts. The series aims to embed ideas—those that endured, and those once persuasive but now forgotten—in rich and readable cultural histories. Books in this series draw on the latest methods and theories of intellectual history while being written with elegance and élan for a broad audience of readers.

∴

Enlightenment Biopolitics

∴

A HISTORY OF RACE, EUGENICS, AND THE MAKING OF CITIZENS

William Max Nelson

THE UNIVERSITY OF CHICAGO PRESS

CHICAGO AND LONDON

The University of Chicago Press, Chicago 60637
The University of Chicago Press, Ltd., London
© 2024 by The University of Chicago
All rights reserved. No part of this book may be used or reproduced in any
manner whatsoever without written permission, except in the case of brief
quotations in critical articles and reviews. For more information, contact the
University of Chicago Press, 1427 E. 60th St., Chicago, IL 60637.
Published 2024
Printed in the United States of America

33 32 31 30 29 28 27 26 25 24   1 2 3 4 5

ISBN-13: 978-0-226-82556-4 (cloth)
ISBN-13: 978-0-226-82558-8 (paper)
ISBN-13: 978-0-226-82557-1 (e-book)
DOI: https://doi.org/10.7208/chicago/9780226825571.001.0001

Library of Congress Cataloging-in-Publication Data

Names: Nelson, William Max, 1976– author.
Title: Enlightenment biopolitics : a history of race, eugenics, and the making
    of citizens / William Max Nelson.
Other titles: Life of ideas.
Description: Chicago : The University of Chicago Press, 2024. | Series: Life of
    ideas | Includes bibliographical references and index.
Identifiers: LCCN 2023036607 | ISBN 9780226825564 (cloth) | ISBN
    9780226825588 (paperback) | ISBN 9780226825571 (e-book)
Subjects: LCSH: Sieyès, Emmanuel Joseph, comte, 1748–1836. Qu'est-ce que
    le Tiers-Etat? | Biopolitics—France—History—18th century. | Eugenics—
    France—History—18th century. | Eugenics—Philosophy—History—18th
    century. | Enlightenment—France. | France—History—Revolution,
    1789–1799.
Classification: LCC JA80.N45 2024 | DDC 323.0944—dc23/eng/20230826
LC record available at https://lccn.loc.gov/2023036607

♾This paper meets the requirements of ANSI/NISO Z39.48-1992
(Permanence of Paper).

Contents

Illustrations

Becoming Biopolitics

At some point in the last decades of the eighteenth century—possibly before he became one of the most important political thinkers of the French Revolution—a man put pen to paper outlining a plan to create, as he wrote, "a species between men and animals, a species capable of serving man for consumption and production."[1] This document—one of the strangest and most troubling fruits of the Enlightenment—went on to envision that "new races of anthropomorphic monkeys become your slaves."[2] The document's author, Abbé Emmanuel-Joseph Sieyès, made clear that "however extraordinary, however immoral this idea may appear at first glance, I have contemplated it at length."[3] Though it may seem surprising, there is nothing in the document, nor in the body of his writing, published or unpublished, that indicates he was being ironic or that his vision of anthropomorphic slaves was satire in the manner of Voltaire or Jonathan Swift.[4] In fact, based on Sieyès's body of work and an analysis of the scientific and political context, it appears that he truly believed the ideas expressed in this document.[5] He seems to have thought that these new slaves were the best means to reconcile the tension that existed between the educated citizens (those who could actively participate in politics and direct the work of manual labors) and the vast majority of people, whom he called the "human instruments of production," the simple "laborers who have only passive force."[6]

Sieyès believed that his plan could resolve this tension between active citizens and passive laborers, at once solving political economic problems of production and the problem of political participation by creating a new slave labor force of "a species that would have fewer needs and be less apt to excite human compassion."[7] It was as if Sieyès believed he had found a biological means of producing what Aristotle had called "natural slaves," people who were supposedly fit for slavery by their nature and, therefore, justifiably enslaved. Even more astounding is that he saw these new subjects as a means to facilitate democratic inclusion, since manual laborers burdened by an excess of work and a paucity of opportunities for improvement would be freed up so that they could be educated and made capable of active citizenship.[8] The fact that this proposal may appear to modern readers to be more like bizarre science fiction than something by a leading theorist of the French Revolution—one who had deeply engaged with Enlightenment thought—helps reveal how estranged we are from the emergence of biopolitics in the eighteenth century. It also suggests how much we can still learn about the Enlightenment and the Age of Revolutions.

When it emerged, biopolitics was more than population statistics, mortality tables, and public health matters. Building on Foucault, but revising his emphasis on the generative importance of these latter concerns, I argue that biopolitics emerged as eugenic plans and new ways of dividing up the population. Foucault characterized the emergence of biopolitics in the eighteenth century as "the entry of life into history, that is, the entry of phenomena peculiar to the life of the human species into the order of knowledge and power, into the spheres of political techniques."[9] I argue that life entered the sphere of political techniques through the concern with the qualities of individual and collective bodies and the conviction that it was possible to transform and improve these qualities. This focus on quality, as opposed to quantity, came to define biopolitics and differentiate it from more mechanistic approaches to studying population in the mercantilist political economy and political arithmetic that developed in the late seventeenth century and continued in the eighteenth century.[10]

This first took shape in France and its colonies in the second half of the eighteenth century as new understandings of nature and human bodies provided opportunities to address the perceived degeneration of the quality of the French population. Drawing on a new philosophy of vital materialism, some thinkers responded to the social and political context of the Old Regime and the French colonial empire by offering radical visions of the transformation of individual bodies and the population as a whole. Their ideas and proposals intertwined the biological and the political in new ways, making available new solutions to old social, political, and economic problems. The biological came to appear as a powerful, and sometimes necessary, means of affecting the political, and vice versa. But more than this, the biological and the political grew together until there was a reciprocal incorporation of the two of them in a way that resulted in ideas and practices that were not merely biological or political, but biopolitical.[11]

Throughout the book I use the term "biopolitics" to refer to the general constellation of interrelated ideas and practices of knowing, managing, fostering, and transforming the biological life of individuals and populations.[12] As it emerged, biopolitics was defined by two related procedures. The first one aimed to exclude groups of people from the collective body (whether conceived of as a social, political, or species body). The second aimed to transform the bodies of the individuals remaining within the collective body. This created two distinct, though related, strains of Enlightenment biopolitics that I identify for the purposes of clarity and convenience as "exclusion" and "breeding." Proposals of specific actions and administrative measures first emerged from these two strains, as opposed to the still rudimentary and haphazard attempts to gather and analyze vital statistics (such as birth and death rates), population statistics (such as the number of inhabitants of a territory or kingdom), and investigate the causes of epidemic and endemic diseases.[13] I focus, therefore, on these more activist and interventionist elements in the larger constellation of biopolitics, analyzing how these practices became conceivable and how they were first conceived.

Focusing on the emergence of these two strains helps gives a new perspective on the Enlightenment by elucidating how ideas of race, eugenics, and forms of exclusionary thought emerged along with inclusionary Enlightenment ideas of liberty, equality, rights, and reason. The coexistence of good and bad, emancipatory and discriminatory, is most commonly discussed in the contemporary scholarship of the Enlightenment in the analysis of ideas of race and slavery. The record is very clear: many Enlightenment thinkers wrote demeaning things about what they claimed to be the limited capacities and general inferiority of some racial and ethnic groups, particularly some of the peoples of Africa, the Americas, and the Arctic. It is widely recognized now that while central figures of the Enlightenment held some views that by today's standards might seem socially and politically progressive, they also expressed racial prejudice, sometimes even denying people of African and Arctic origins the status of being fully human.[14] This is true of "lesser lights" as well as luminaries such as John Locke, Voltaire, David Hume, Thomas Jefferson, and Immanuel Kant.[15] The record of philosophes endorsing the idea of a natural equality between men and women is perhaps even worse, with true egalitarians in this regard being extremely rare.[16] When scholars bring up the coexistence of emancipatory ideas and racial prejudice in the Enlightenment, the contradictory nature of these ideas is rightly emphasized.[17] But representing them as only logically and morally contradictory can obscure the way these ideas often stemmed from the same cluster of fundamental principles, concepts, and assumptions. It also obscures the fact that they developed in a complicated dialectic. The two poles that appear to be logically and morally contradictory often stemmed from the same historical and conceptual sources, reinforcing one another and pushing one another forward. The Enlightenment is not alone in demonstrating a paradox of this sort, but it was in the Enlightenment that inclusion and exclusion were heightened and interconnected in a way that first gave them a modern form.[18] The Enlightenment took on a particular shape because of the specific ideas of equality and inequality and the arguments for specific inclusions and exclusions.

More than just a dialectic or "co-occurrence" of inclusion and exclusion, the Enlightenment was characterized by the formation of new conceptual and practical foundations on which modern inclusions and exclusions were built.[19] This was nothing less than a shift in conceptual and practical conditions of possibility in the second half of the eighteenth century. A focus on this shift and the emergence of biopolitics reveals that a number of ideas and practices that are strongly associated with later time periods actually emerged in the eighteenth century. Furthermore, the conceptual and practical foundations of biopolitics in the Enlightenment, the formation of ideas of inclusion and exclusion on them, and their implementation and reformulation across subsequent centuries had great consequences for vast numbers of people, not just in Europe, but throughout the world, as European social and political ideas were adapted and translated, ramified and transformed, hybridized and appropriated, and in many cases imposed through imperial and colonial regimes, providing a bedrock for universalist emancipatory movements at the same time as they smuggled in and instantiated inequalities, exclusions, and qualifications to the professed principles of universalism. For this reason, I begin my narrative around 1750 and continue through the French Revolution, rather than starting with the Revolution and presenting its reimagining and contestation of citizenship, sovereignty, rights, and the idea of the nation as the birth of modernity.

"If it is good to know how to use men as they are," Jean-Jacques Rousseau wrote in 1755 in an entry on political economy in the *Encyclopédie*, "it is better still to make them into what one needs them to be."[20] Examples throughout this book demonstrate that many of Rousseau's contemporaries and immediate successors, such as Abbé Sieyès, agreed with him and that they envisioned this process of transforming people to be a question not only of education, moral formation, or the cultivation of civic virtue (as in the traditions of Lockean improvement or classical republicanism), but of the physical transformation of individual bodies and collective bodies.

In order to defamiliarize the story of biopolitics and the history of the Enlightenment, opening up the space in which to write a new history, I want to turn back to the strange vision of Sieyès. As bizarre as this brief and little-known archival document seems, perhaps the strangest thing about it is that it reflects many of the characteristics of the biopolitical thoughts and practices that first emerged in the eighteenth century and came to play a central role in the modern world. Analyzing Sieyès's proposal provides an opportunity to highlight several key characteristics of biopolitics as it took shape in the eighteenth century, which allows me to flesh out the general concept of biopolitics while also being more specific about what precisely its Enlightenment version entailed.

Chief among these representative characteristics is the fact that the plans were dramatically interventionist from the very birth of biopolitics.[21] For people to envision radically transforming human populations did not take until the development of the eugenics in the late nineteenth century, the global implementation of eugenic policies in the twentieth century, the horrendous employment of biopolitical projects under the Nazis, or genetic engineering facilitated by the development of molecular biology and technological advances in the late twentieth century.[22] Biopolitical thinkers in the eighteenth century were already proposing the massive transformation of large populations, as well as extreme transformations of individual human bodies.

Sieyès's plan also represents how biopolitics, from its emergence, aimed at recreating collective bodies through the linked processes of inclusion and exclusion. The creation of the new slaves is a particularly clear example of this link, since it was the creation of the slaves and their placement outside of the political body that was supposed to make it possible for many more people to be newly included as active members. By breeding humans with a variety of nonhuman primates, Sieyès envisioned producing three new intermediary species that would lift much of the labor burden off of manual laborers and domestic servants, enabling working people to receive an education and prepare for active political participation. Those in the first group of these new slaves would be large and strong, bred for manual labor. They would range in height from six to eight feet, being twice the size of those in the second group, who at only three to four feet would be created for domestic duties. The last group, of twelve to fifteen-inch anthropomorphic monkeys, would also be tasked with light domestic work "and amusement."[23] In Sieyès's vision, the promise of democratic inclusion seemed to rest on the creation of half-human slaves that would be excluded from the polity. The excluded anthropomorphic slaves were not, however, only a condition of possibility for the inclusion of more people as active citizens. Their existence and abjection was meant to play a vivifying role in the life of the collective; in this case, they were meant to contribute the labor that was necessary to meet the basic biological needs of the population, and to enable the body politic to thrive economically and hence to survive as a viable entity.

In another characteristic development, this excluded group was dehumanized so as to facilitate and justify their exclusion. In the case of Sieyès's slaves, the dehumanization was shockingly literal; the enslaved would have been less than fully human because they would have been hybrids of humans and animals. But often, symbolic dehumanization was attempted through implication and the analogical comparison of groups of people with animals. This bestialization of people was clearest in the biopolitical proposals drawing on the nascent theories of race, but they were also found in projects aimed at placing the poor and mobile working population of France into a form of slavery. It was not uncommon, for instance, to characterize so-called vagabonds as harmful swarms of insects or dangerous animals that were inherently violent and antisocial. As Sieyès stated explicitly about his proposed hybrid slaves, their status as less than human would mean that the subjects would be less likely to elicit compassion, and, implicitly, their exclusion from collective life in its social, political, and biological forms would therefore be easier.[24]

Another characteristic feature of Sieyès's plan was the intertwining of the life sciences and political economy. Again and again, biopolitical projects aiming at the transformation of collective and individual life were envisioned as solutions to the range of social, political, and economic problems that were within the capacious purview of eighteenth-century political economy. Sieyès was a careful student of the new political economy that had taken shape in the middle decades of the century, and he was also well acquainted with important new work in the life sciences.[25] Like Sieyès, with his vision of a variety of hybrid species bred for labor, several other of the theorists of Enlightenment biopolitics drew on new theories of animal generation and the hybridity of species to propose human breeding programs that would solve specific political economic challenges, whether they were related to ensuring an adequate supply of labor or cultivating the wealth of a nation through the improvement of the quantity and quality of its population. This was sometimes expressed, as in one subtitle, as a "project for enriching and improving the human species."[26]

Related to this intertwining of the life sciences and political economy was a more general intertwining of the biological and the political. In the second half of the eighteenth century in France a variety of problems that could be called political (in a broad sense) came to seem as if they were inseparable from the biological. They became entangled in a way that made them integral parts of a new whole. For a number of philosophes and a few government administrators and royal officials, the manipulation of biological life seemed to be a promising means of addressing various problems of the social, political, and economic realms. Sieyès, for instance, thought that the selective breeding of humans with various primates could help to solve fundamental social, political, and economic problems that resulted from the opposition between those whose lives were consumed by laborer and those who directed the labor of others. In fact, as he stated explicitly in the archival document, he believed this was the only way to resolve these problems. "You will not find other means," he claimed.[27] In addition to the biological providing new possibilities for solving political problems, an understanding of biological life provided a foundation on which many philosophes built their social and political theories. Visions of natural order had long provided foundations for visions of social and political order, but new ideas about the characteristics of nature and living beings created conceptual possibilities that were realized in the ideas and plans of Enlightenment biopolitics.

Another way that Sieyès's idea represents Enlightenment biopolitics is that it was not utopian in most of the senses in which scholars use this term, nor was it presented ironically or as satire. It might have been impracticable or appeared fantastical, but Sieyès did not propose the plan for some imaginary nonplace (as is the literal meaning of *u-topia*), nor did he present it as a thought experiment that offered a normative image from which to critique present circumstance.[28] It was also not utopian in the sense of envisioning an ideal society. Rather, he believed that it was scientifically possible and that it was politically and socially necessary. In terms of its morality (or immorality) and imagination, it is related to a group of "dangerous experiments" carried out in the eighteenth century (such as the public demonstrations of mass electrocution) and unrealized proposals for inhumane experiments (such as the vivisection of criminals, or the stranding of isolated children in uninhabited places), though it is important to recognize that the biopolitical proposals that I analyze were not just thought experiments or fictional proposals for some nonplace.[29] Most of them were proposals for specific actions to occur in specific places.

Sieyès's consideration of enslaved labor in the colonies was yet another representative feature of Enlightenment biopolitics. Slavery and colonialism often played an important role in the logic of biopolitical ideas and in the historical development of biopolitical practices. In fact, the role was so significant that the emergence of biopolitics cannot be adequately understood without considering both metropolitan France and the French colonies, particularly those in the Atlantic world, since biopolitics emerged, in part, out of the movement of people, practices, and ideas between France and its Atlantic colonies. The colonies were sites where a number of biopolitical theorists built proposals on the colonial precedents of controlling the lives of enslaved people, paying special attention to the questions of surveillance and working with new scientific ideas from the metropole to

reimagine features of colonial life while reentrenching slavery as an institution. Often these proposals built on nascent scientific ideas of race, occasionally even envisioning racial engineering as a fundamental tool for
reforming and securing the colonies.[30]

Although it was grounded in new scientific and philosophical ideas, the
biopolitics that took shape in the eighteenth century incorporated many
preexisting policies and administrative tools while responding to several
historical problems, economic developments, and social challenges. There
were, in fact, ancient precedents for numerous aspects of modern biopolitics. These ranged from the idea that animal breeding could act as a model
for human breeding, protoeugenic ideas such as those expressed by Plato
for the ideal polity in *The Republic*, and a wide variety of pronatalist policies
and laws created by the ancient Romans. Although some of these precedents were explicitly evoked in the seventeenth and eighteenth centuries,
particularly the Roman natalist policies, the biopolitics that emerged in the
second half of the eighteenth century differed in important ways largely
because of the general transformation of ideas about nature, vital materialist theories of the bodily "organization" of living beings, and the new understanding of human reproduction and human variation that developed
in the Enlightenment.[31] A new view of human beings and their relationship
to the rest of nature brought a biological character to modern biopolitics
that was absent from earlier ideas and practices. Although the term "biology" was not used to refer to a unified science of life until around 1800,
some Enlightenment figures working in natural history and the life sciences
had already developed an orientation that can properly be characterized as
biological.[32] This orientation was absent from earlier approaches to populations, whether in antiquity or in the early modern era.[33] For example, unlike the eighteenth-century proposals for the selective breeding of human
beings, the late seventeenth-century policy of encouraging intermarriage as
a means to assimilate and "Frenchify" (*franciser*) the native peoples of New
France was motivated by religious, social, and political concerns, not biological ones. Those advocating the mixing of peoples hoped to create social
and familial bonds that could help facilitate religious conversion and the
creation of political alliances.[34] The same could be said of the early modern
plans of forced migration that the Dutch, Portuguese, and English all hoped
would bring about an assimilation of colonial and metropolitan populations
through intermarriage.[35] The new biopolitics that emerged in the second
half of the eighteenth century in France was, therefore, not merely a combination of pronatalism, political arithmetic, and public health practices.[36]

It is unconventional to refer to ideas and practices of the eighteenth century as being "eugenic." The term, building on Greek roots implying a meaning of being well born, was not coined until 1883 by Francis Galton.[37] If the concept is invoked at all by scholars to refer to phenomena in the eighteenth century, it is usually qualified as "proto-eugenic" or "pre-eugenic."[38] But in the case of some of the biopolitical ideas and practices that I focus on in this book, this qualification is unnecessary and misleading. Some of them fulfill the fundamental criteria of eugenics, even if contemporaries did not yet have the term available to them to characterize their approach. Like later ideas of eugenics, the eighteenth-century proposals and suggestions were interventionist attempts to transform populations, focused on improvement through reproduction, often involving ideas of race, and concerned with the quantity and the quality of the population. Many of the eighteenth-century ideas envisioned large-scale projects to transform whole populations, or the entire human species, often through plans that were meant to be directed and executed by the state, but not always. They did not have a consistent position on the role of the state or the question of coercion, but neither did the eugenics movements of the twentieth century, which had advocates from all political ideologies, some who argued for coercion and strong state efforts and others emphasizing private initiative, persuasion, and incentives.[39]

In addition to fulfilling the major elements of the definition of eugenics, eighteenth-century ideas have an even closer conceptual relation to ideas of the nineteenth and twentieth centuries than is often, if at all, recognized. For example, even the idea that characteristics acquired by parents could be passed on to offspring, the main feature of the "Lamarckianism" that provided the theoretical justification and explanation of many nineteenth-century and twentieth-century eugenics, was already formulated by naturalists in the middle of the eighteenth century.[40] Although the concept of "the inheritance of acquired characters" is most associated with the name of the French naturalist Jean-Baptiste Pierre Antoine de Monet, chevalier de Lamarck, the idea was so common when Lamarck began to discuss it in the late eighteenth century that he did not feel compelled to name it or to provide evidence for the phenomenon. He was able to take it for granted that people like the famed naturalist Georges-Louis Leclerc, comte de Buffon, his mentor and patron, had long been discussing the reproductive inheritance of bodily transformations.[41] So while some scholars of nineteenth-century and twentieth-century eugenics argue that the idea of heredity played a central role in characterizing these later ideas and practices, it is important to note that in the second half of the eighteenth century savants began new types of inquiry into the phenomenon of the inheritance of characteristics.[42] Although they used the adjective "hereditary," rather than the noun "heredity," they developed new theories of the transmission of characteristics across the generations, arousing widespread interest in questions of generation and the similarity of parents and offspring.[43] As Carlos López-Beltrán, a scholar of the concept of heredity, explains, "a more or less general vision of hereditary transmission was shared by numerous savants of the eighteenth century."[44] These savants explicitly and repeatedly engaged in inquiries into the inheritance of characteristics and the relation of this inheritance to the processes of animal generation, human reproduction, and variation within the human species. In fact, some of the savants who were central to formulating the scientific ideas on which biopolitical plans were built—figures such as Buffon and Maupertuis—were among the most important to carry out experiments on hereditary transmission, popularize them in writing, and propose mechanisms that could account for reproduction and the inheritance of characteristics.[45]

An additional reason why I characterize some of the biopolitical projects envisioned in the eighteenth century as Enlightenment eugenics is that these biopolitical projects were both "positive" and "negative" in the technical sense employed by eugenicists in the twentieth century. There existed "positive eugenics" proposals for the encouragement of the reproduction of specific types of individuals or segments of the population, as well as "negative eugenics" that aimed to limit the reproduction of a segment of the population. Proposals for the selective breeding of human beings and large-scale projects of surveillance and policing that aimed to control the reproduction of segments of the population were the two most comprehensive and extreme forms of biopolitics that I identify in the eighteenth century. While both qualify as eugenic, it is important to recognize that the proposed programs of positive eugenics seem to have remained only proposals, whereas, in at least one case, a program of negative eugenics was implemented. As discussed in chapter 5, the biopolitical ideas of race and intervention in the reproduction of a part of the population developed into an actually implemented, though little enforced, policy of negative eugenics. This occurred in the late 1770s and early 1780s when a royal declaration and a series of legal clarifications established a set of laws and royal directives collectively known as the Police des Noirs. These laws and directives aimed at regulating the small population of African descent in metropolitan France.

Finally, supporting my claim that some Enlightenment ideas qualify as eugenic, it is worth distinguishing between the idea of eugenics and the historical phenomenon of the eugenics movement, which was located in specific times and places, coalescing at the dawn of the twentieth century and reaching its height between the two world wars. I do not argue that

Enlightenment examples of eugenic thought require a new chronology of the eugenics movement, since I do not think that they constituted a "movement." These Enlightenment ideas were too scattered and inchoate, too disconnected from widespread practices of governance, and they had no large "public" constituency or group of organized advocates. I do argue, however, these Enlightenment ideas of eugenics were clearly and publicly articulated in written works more than a century before Galton coined the term "eugenics." It is worth drawing attention to the fact that scholars of eugenics who focus on the late nineteenth century and the first half of the twentieth century also write about eugenics existing before Galton's neologism. In one of the first authoritative histories of eugenics, for example, Daniel Kevles observed that "Galton first published his eugenic ideas in 1865—well before he coined the word himself."[46] Other scholars have pointed to the fact that terms with similar meanings existed in languages other than English before Galton's coinage, that others had eugenic or "eugenical" ideas before Galton, and that one of the first experiments that could qualify as a systematic eugenic practice of controlled reproduction—what the participants referred to as "stirpiculture"—began in the Oneida community in New York in 1865.[47]

A number of long-term processes as well as a variety of immediate historical and intellectual conjunctions in the middle of the eighteenth century made the birth of biopolitics possible and helped shape its character. Major long-term processes like secularization, the development of capitalism, and the radical philosophical critique of traditional justifications of social and political order and authority that began in the seventeenth century all played an important role establishing the general conditions in which biopolitics emerged.[48] In addition to these very general and long-term processes, there were also four more immediate historical developments that made possible the reformation of a number of ideas and practices into the constellation of biopolitics: the emergence of a new type of dynamic, organic thought that produced new visions of nature and the place of humans within it; new attempts to ground social, political, and economic order in the natural order; an openness to social, administrative, and economic reform from within Old Regime absolutism; and a related, but distinct, openness to reform of the colonial order.[49] The combination of all these factors, and their location in France and the French Empire, helps explain why biopolitics emerged there and then.

The first two decades of the second half of the eighteenth century was a particularly intense period in the formation of Enlightenment biopolitics. The publication of the first three volumes of Buffon's massively influential *Natural History, General and Particular* (*Histoire naturelle, générale et particulière*) in 1749 is an important marker of the new dynamic vision of nature, the place of humans within nature, and the development of a new organic thought.[50] The end of the Seven Years' War in 1763 is an important marker in the establishment of the royal administration's openness to reform in the metropole and the colonies. This openness to reform and the search for means of countering what was perceived as widespread degeneration within France and its empire was one reason why so many of the people proposing biopolitical programs, particularly those involved in selective breeding, were employed or supported by the royal administration. While I analyze the historical circumstances in more detail in the following chapters, here I want to introduce more fully the most important and wide reaching of the intellectual transformations that made possible the formation of biopolitics. In addition to the development of the concept of organization, there was a more general transformation of the understanding of nature and the practices of natural history.

A new approach to the study of nature emerged from the endeavors of Buffon and a loose group of associates, friends, like-minded naturalists, and scientifically engaged philosophes. Together, from roughly the 1750s to the 1780s, they reconceptualized natural history and transformed its practice from a science that was consumed by extremely detailed observation and the categorization of natural objects, into a wide-reaching philosophical inquiry into the history of nature. This entailed the shift to an understanding of nature as a dynamic whole that was open to historical change and driven by immanent forces, which historians of science, following Phillip Sloan, have referred to as the "Buffonian revolution." This intellectual and scientific revolution saw ideas of static order and divine foresight replaced by ideas of eternal flux and complex historical development. This developed in tandem with new methodological approaches focusing on the identification of forces operating within nature in an attempt to explain immanent natural causes and to reveal the complex transformations of nature that defied rigid means of ordering, naming, and classifying.[51] The new understanding of nature that took shape in the middle of the century had ramifications far beyond the realms of natural history, the life sciences, and natural philosophy more generally.

The place of humans in this vision of nature played an important role in the formation of what became known in the second half of the eighteenth century as the "science of man." One important characteristic of this science was a new emphasis on understanding human beings as a biological species. That is to say, by roughly the middle of the eighteenth century, humans could be the scientific object of an inquiry into species, and they were reconceived according to Buffon's new definition of species as a group of similar individuals genealogically linked through reproduction. The human species became conceptualized as a new type of collective being: an imminent, historical, and dynamic whole, composed of individuals who shared interdependency and autonomy.[52] This shift is reflected in French in the second half of the eighteenth century as the naturalistic meaning of "the human species" competed with, and began to displace, the more general term *le genre humaine* (which can be translated as either "mankind" or "the human race"). This linguistic development appears to have corresponded with the conceptual development by which the unity of humans was rethought in terms of biological species. Both of these developments are evident in eighteenth-century biopolitical writing and related scientific work in natural history, the life sciences, and the science of man. This linguistic and conceptual shift was a part of a larger process through which human collective forms of existence were reimagined across the second half of the eighteenth century, as traditional accounts of natural order and hierarchy were challenged and various entities were reimagined in a way that allowed them to compete with metaphysical conceptions of absolutist political theology (such as the mystical body, the *corpus mysticum*) and the supposedly natural arrangement of corporate society in a hierarchy of social orders and estates.

New objects of social and political thought emerged, and old objects were rethought, as people began to question the very foundations of social and political order. For most of this process, from roughly 1750 until 1789, people reconceived of collective bodies in a disparate and loose fashion. It was a time of transition, as new ideas were being formed and new relationships imagined. The names "social body," "society," "body politic," "the human species," "race," and "population" were still used in inconsistent ways that sometimes overlapped with one another, but that, importantly, began to appear as different aspects, or different parts, of a living collective whole. In other words, they were used as different expressions of collective existence that placed more or less emphasis on social, political, biological, and economic aspects of collective life.[53]

The coming into being of the human species as an object of scientific knowledge was also a long and complex process that did not have a single decisive development, though an important series of conceptual developments, shifts in method, and syntheses of empirical evidence occurred around the middle of the century.[54] A marker of this development was the Swedish naturalist Linnaeus classifying humans among other animal species in his *Systema naturae* (1735), though the understanding of humans as a species was most influentially expressed and enacted in Buffon's long analysis "Varieties of the Human Species" in the third volume of *Natural History* (1749).[55] This work is a striking demonstration of how the Enlightenment formation of the science of man was characterized by the simultaneous assertion of the unity and variety of the human species. At the same time as the similarity of humans was rethought in terms of biological species, new types of biological differences within the species were identified and multiplied. Buffon argued for human unity and common origins without recourse to theological explanation, relying only on naturalistic explanation and a series of mechanisms and forces inherent in nature. At the same time as he formulated this secular theory of monogenesis, he synthesized the observations of bodily difference in the work of travelers, missionaries, and naturalists, creating the longest description and analysis of the "races" of the species to date.[56] "Everything therefore comes together to prove that humankind is not composed of essentially different species," Buffon concluded, "but to the contrary there was originally only a single species of men, which having multiplied and spread across the surface of the earth, underwent different changes by the influence of climate, differences of food, way of life, epidemic illnesses, and by the infinitely varied mixing of individuals more or less alike; that at first these alterations were not so marked and produced only individual varieties; that they then became varieties of the species, because they became more general, more noticeable, and more constant by continued action of these same causes."[57] Building on this foundation, the second half of the eighteenth century proved to be a formative time, in which the biological unity of and the biological differences within the species were thought through together. Unity was reimagined in scientific terms, and differences were located in the body, explained through the theories of the life sciences, and reified in a literature that increasingly took differences of race and sex to be real, embodied, and self-evident.

There were many ramifications of this development for both the breeding and the exclusion strains of Enlightenment biopolitics. Within the breeding strain this meant that the unity of the species (reformulated and turned into an empirical question through Buffon's assertion of the interfertility criterion) ensured that all varieties of human could reproduce together. This created a new scientific way to understand commonality, while it also theoretically enabled the manipulation of differences through the controlled crossbreeding and selective breeding of humans. It made possible new ideas about eliminating racial differences and homogenizing the species, while it also made possible ideas about reproducing and increasing the differences. It made possible, therefore, both the elimination of racial differences and the creation of more distinct "races." Its ramifications were profoundly ambivalent, enabling and encouraging proposals for "improvement" through

racial crossing and proposals for breeding out differences, while also enabling and encouraging proposals to make the biological differences associated with race more extreme and therefore more able to reinforce existing
social and legal hierarchies or to be harnessed for new social and legal hierarchies. Among the most important ramifications for the exclusionary
strain of biopolitics was the manner in which this simultaneous fashioning
of unity and variety, sameness and difference, introduced a new biological
foundation for social and political thought relating to the conceptual pairs
of equality/inequality and inclusion/exclusion. The new conception of the
unity and sameness of humans as a biological species provided a foundation
to reconceive social and political equality (which in turn grounded new arguments for inclusion) while at the same time variations and biological differences provided a foundation to reconceive social and political inequality
(which in turn grounded new arguments for exclusion). As I demonstrate
in this book, these possibilities were recognized and realized in biopolitical
proposals that drew on the new conception of the human species and its
place in the work of the Enlightenment science of man.

In France, the science of man was particularly bold and influential because many of its leading practitioners broke free from theologically based
explanations, such as physicotheology, that attempted to demonstrate divine creation and predetermined natural order through empirical evidence.
This was one of the primary reasons that biopolitics emerged at this time
in France and the French Empire, as opposed to other times and places.
French savants, such as Buffon and his friend and intellectual interlocutor
Pierre-Louis Maupertuis, were among the most important Enlightenment
savants to form naturalistic explanations that avoided recourse to super-
natural forces and divine agency in order to explain the characteristics of
the natural world. The practitioners of this Enlightenment science of man
aimed to find ways to "improve" and "perfect" people, both individually and
as a species. They were haunted by a concern that the species was degenerating, and they observed and speculated about the *mélange* (mixing) or
croisement des races (crossing of the races). The creators of biopolitics drew
on this same language and wrote of wanting to *améliorer* (improve) and
perfectionner (improve or perfect) people; they were concerned with *perfectibilité* (perfectibility) and *régénération* (regeneration), and with making
people *bien faits* (well made), *plus grands* (larger), and *plus robustes* (more
robust). Repeatedly, they aimed at the species and wrote of "improving the
human species."[58]

Investigating the birth of biopolitics helps reveal how the coexistence
of these ideas took on a particular modern form in the Enlightenment.

Two concepts that can help bring this into focus are what I call the equality of malleability and the paradox of Enlightenment. One of the widely agreed-on features that defined the Enlightenment was the development of a number of arguments about forms of social, political, and natural equality. One form of equality that has not been identified before is a type of physical equality between people. This was not the notion that all bodies were of equal size, strength, or vigor. Instead, it was a new recognition that all bodies were malleable, and equally so. Whether through the effects on the body of food, weather, physical activity, or mental activity, all bodies were prone to be transformed in their very structure and functions. Furthermore, these influences could create permanent, or semipermanent, changes in "organization" of individual bodies, which, crucially, were believed capable of being passed on from parents to children in reproduction, enabling the amplification and acceleration of bodily transformation across the generations and throughout populations. This malleability and transmission of bodily changes meant that individual lineages and whole populations of individuals appeared to be more susceptible to degeneration as well as to improvement.[59]

For its adherents, the equality of malleability was truly universal. It held true of every human, other than those individuals, perhaps, who fell into the early modern category of human anomaly, usually referred to as "monsters."[60] Man or woman, European or African, rich or poor, old or young, every person was susceptible to alteration. Every person was also a part of the transformation of the species over time; each individual was a part of the succession of like individuals linked through reproduction. This meant that there was a fundamental instability in the natural bodies of individuals, as well as in the collective bodies of populations and the species as a whole. The equality of malleability offered peril and promise. In its positive dimensions, the equality of malleability ensured that all people could be improved, since, to use the contemporary term popularized by Rousseau, all people possessed the faculty of "perfectibility" (*perfectibilité*).[61] But changes to the body were not always improvements, and they could degrade the physical and moral qualities. The equality of malleability, therefore, was a lurking threat as well as a reason for possible hope. The idea of race and the equality of malleability emerged together, and they combined to heighten some people's concern with the supposedly degenerative effects of the mixing of races while raising other people's hopes that a controlled crossing of the races could be a means of improvement. Malleability could be exploited to make people more alike or more different. It could be utilized in attempts to homogenize humanity or to reinforce existing differences that were believed to be racial. In short, malleability could be used to create "race" or to attempt to eliminate human variation. Not coincidentally, the primary theorist of malleability, Buffon, was one of the naturalists in this period most concerned with degeneration and race, doing the most to establish the scientific principles and the orientation on which the Enlightenment approach to biopolitical improvement was based.

The equality of malleability and the example of race can help reveal the paradox of Enlightenment. By calling it a paradox, I am not using the term in its most common contemporary usage. I do not mean an irresolvable contradiction. Instead, I am using a less common sense of the term: an apparent contradiction that illuminates a truth. In this case, the truth is that many Enlightenment exclusions were inextricably intertwined with Enlightenment inclusions, while many arguments for inequality developed out of arguments for equality. Conceptually and practically they depended on each other, implied each other, and developed together. More than coexisting in the Enlightenment, they were coconstitutive of the social, political, and intellectual orientation of the Enlightenment.[62] They expressed something fundamental about it and help illuminate an internal logic.

These features of the birth of biopolitics help reveal the paradox of Enlightenment even though biopolitical exclusions and the breeding of human beings were not major topical concerns of the philosophes in terms of the amount of written discussion that they inspired. Passages in which people in the eighteenth century explicitly discussed human breeding (in a nonsatirical fashion) or biopolitical exclusions were often short and sometimes just a small part of a large body of work. Whole books focused on the biopolitical refashioning of populations, such as Charles-Augustin Vandermonde's *Essay on the Manner of Improving the Human Species* (*Essai sur la manière de perfectionner l'espèce humaine*), were the exception.[63] Nevertheless, the very existence of these explicit discussions of human breeding, and forms of biopolitical exclusion, such as refashioning collective bodies through internal exclusion, helps reveal a fundamental paradox at the core of Enlightenment thought. Although some eighteenth-century biopolitical practices and ideas might appear unsavory, or even repulsive, from our contemporary vantage point, they were characteristic of the Enlightenment, for better or for worse. They helped established many of the questions, problems, and tensions that we still grapple with today, even if they do not provide us with simple moral exemplars or historically transferable ethical imperatives. Historically, they are of great importance because they established an approach to knowing, managing, and intervening in the life of populations that only became more significant with the continued development of racism and eugenics in the nineteenth century, the genocide and genetics of the twentieth century, and the manifold possibilities of genetic engineering that have emerged in the twenty-first century.

In order to illuminate the foundations of Enlightenment biopolitics and demonstrate some of the reasons how and why it developed in the second half of the eighteenth century, primarily in France and its Atlantic colonies, in chapter 1 I analyze how a group of philosophes developed an "organic world picture" based on an approach to nature that was both vitalist and materialist. Through the concept of "organization" and theories about the "organized bodies" of living beings, they established the conceptual foundations for Enlightenment biopolitics and laid the foundation for the modern concept of organism. They also developed a new mereology (a philosophy of part-whole relations) that I call "relational holism." I use examples from Buffon, Rousseau, and the physiocrats to demonstrate that these philosophes developed an organismic approach to entities such as the human species, the economy, and the body politic. Chapter 2 then focusses on the development of eugenic ideas that built on the revolution in the life sciences carried out by Buffon and his associates. New ideas of race, reproduction, malleability, and selective breeding provided a conceptual foundation for new experiments in animal breeding and new ideas about the possibility of improving human beings through selective breeding. Building on this revolution in the life sciences, Vandermonde presented the first modern eugenic vision addressed to rulers and proposing specific and extensive actions to take in order to improve the human species. Chapter 3 focusses on two proposals from around 1776 to racially engineer the population of the French colony of Saint Domingue (current-day Haiti). These proposals are shown to build on metropolitan ideas of human variation, bodily malleability, and experiments in animal breeding. The authors of the proposals adapted new ideas about race, reproduction, and selective breeding to propose biopolitical solutions to existing social, economic, and military concerns of colonial administrators, with the aim of stabilizing the colony and ensuring the continuation of slavery. I also situate these proposals in the history of ideas of race and other examples of biopolitics in the French colonial context and the anglophone Atlantic.

In chapter 4, I shift focus to the exclusionary strain of biopolitics, demonstrating how three categories of people (vagabonds, women, and people of African descent in France) were reconceived as people who should be internally excluded, those who "live amid society without being members of it," as Guillaume-François Le Trosne wrote in 1764.[64] First, a new campaign against people with no fixed home, property, or employment resulted in new policies that treated "vagabonds" as less-than-human enemies of society who should be put into forced labor camps. Second, the new set of laws and ordinances known as the Police des Noirs created a new regime of surveillance that aimed to biologically safeguard the white French population by forbidding marriage with people of African descent. Third, a new science of sexual difference cast women as distinct from men in every element of their body. This theoretical development, grounded in theories of organization, was used to justify social and political exclusions of women, particularly after the significant social gains of the French Revolution.

In the next chapters I connect Enlightenment biopolitics with ideas and events of the French Revolution. Chapter 5 focusses on the most important political theorist of the French Revolution, Emmanuel-Joseph Sieyès. I argue that he was a thoroughly biopolitical thinker whose ideas emerged from an engagement with Enlightenment biopolitics. I analyze his famous and influential pamphlet *What Is the Third Estate?*, his consequential ideas of nation, and his suggestion that breeding a new species of anthropomorphic slaves in the colonies could foster democratic inclusion in metropolitan France. Chapter 6 argues that leading intellectuals and political leaders during the Revolution envisioned biopolitical projects for regenerating the population of France. These leaders believed that changing people's everyday structures and practices would bring about changes in their habits, which would in turn create changes in the organization of their bodies and minds. Crucially, these changes were thought to be heritable, so that small transformations could add up over time and spread throughout the population. I give special attention to the work of the marquis de Condorcet and the physician-philosophe Pierre-Jean-Georges Cabanis, arguing that in articulating these ideas they developed a novel existential concept of habit that emphasized ways of being rather than repetition and its dulling effects.

In chapter 7, I discuss several ways in which Enlightenment biopolitics established new questions, tensions, problematics, and themes that continued to animate political, social, and biological thought around the time of the French Revolution and into the nineteenth and twentieth centuries. I conclude the book by returning to the question of how this history of biopolitics enables a reappraisal of the Enlightenment and demonstrates the need for an interpretive approach that does not reduce the Enlightenment to being either emancipatory or totalitarian but instead is attuned to the conceptual and practical connections between inclusion and exclusion, equality and inequality, rights and race, the "improvement of the human species" and practices of dehumanization.

CHAPTER ONE

Organizing the Swarm of Being

Over the course of a few weeks in the summer of 1769, when Paris was swel-
tering and his friends and family had retreated from the city, a lonely Denis
Diderot wrote one of his most imaginative and brilliant works, a group of
three interconnected dialogues known by the title of the middle dialogue,
D'Alembert's Dream (*Le rêve de d'Alembert*). Using himself and three of his
acquaintances as models for the characters, Diderot constructed one of the
most successful philosophical dialogues of the century, at turns bizarre and
insightful, obscure and direct. One of the characteristic features of the work
is the use of evocative images of vibrating strings, spiderwebs, and swarms
of bees to explore complex philosophical and scientific ideas. Ranging
widely, the discussion touches on topics such as the nature of consciousness
and the transformation of species, with occasional cosmological tangents
and grand metaphysical statements. "There is only a single great individual,
and that is the whole," pronounced the character of d'Alembert in a daring
outburst of monist philosophy that was quite uncharacteristic of the real-
life mathematician.[1]

The middle dialogue finds Mademoiselle de Lespinasse, the noted *sa-
lonnière* and companion of d'Alembert, reading out notes she had taken
the night before as d'Alembert spoke in his sleep, in an almost "delirious"
philosophical fever dream. One of the centerpieces of the dialogue is the
introduction of a swarm of bees as an illustration of how a "living point is
joined to another, and another again, and from these successive combinations there results a single unified being."[2] The image of the bees coming
together in a swarm and then forming a cluster at the end of a tree branch
is used to suggest how a new being could emerge from tiny parts joining
together. The bees can connect to each other by their feet in a way that
creates one continuous body that has its own unity and therefore exists as
a new whole. The bees move from a state of physical contiguity to one of
organic continuity.[3] As they cling to one another at the end of a branch,
"this cluster is a being, an individual, a kind of animal."[4] As it emerges

and becomes clearer through a series of discussions in the dialogue, the cluster of bees, like the dialogue itself, is a whole that is greater than the sum of its parts. Both the dialogue and the bees become more than simple aggregates.

While Diderot's use of the image of the bees was a powerful expression of organic unity, it was much more than this. Throughout the dialogues, Diderot introduces a series of analogies in relation to the bees, comparing them to the organs of the human body, freshwater polyps with their extraordinary means of regenerating a whole body from a severed part, and a monastery that maintains its identity over time as monks are gradually replaced. Through these analogies, Diderot reached out beyond the question of organic unity to fundamental questions in the philosophy of nature, probing the elusive relationship between being and becoming, part and whole, life and emergence. This was also the case with several of Diderot's contemporaries who employed the image of the swarm of bees in their writing to elucidate the emergence of life, the composition of bodies, the nature of reproduction, and the existence of collective beings. In addition to comparing the bees to polyps, human bodies, and monasteries, they also evoked flocks of birds and marching armies to extend and explore the image. Many of the questions that these images evoked in the second half of the eighteenth century coalesced in the theory of organization and the discussion of "organized bodies" and "organized beings."

Organization was a powerful concept with many implications.[5] Although the term might strike us today as innocuous and less than philosophically promising—more redolent of twentieth-century managerial thought than heterodox philosophy—in the technical sense used in the Enlightenment, organization implied nothing less than a turn away from divine design and an embrace of a thorough naturalism that saw living beings as self-organized and interconnected holistic entities that could not be reduced to their parts nor understood exclusively through analyses based on the principles of mechanical philosophy. Importantly, this not only took form as a body of abstract philosophical thought but also was grounded in the actual bodies of all living beings. In this conception, all living beings were organized bodies that were self-generating and self-organizing (requiring no outside agent to function or reproduce). They were integral wholes in which parts were interconnected and interdependent (meaning that parts communicated and influenced one another, contributed to the life of the whole while also depending on it, and the parts existed in a circular relationship in which they functioned as both cause and effect, means and ends). Organized bodies had hierarchical internal structures, levels of life, and emergent properties (meaning that they were wholes that were more than the sum of their parts in that they had properties and functions possessed by none of their constituent elements).

In this chapter, in addition to analyzing this new vision of nature and the new understanding of human beings that emerged with the theory of organization, I demonstrate that biopolitics in its modern interventionist form was enabled by these developments and that it established a line of thought that would develop into the full-blown organicism of nineteenth-century social and political thought. After giving a fuller description of the theory of organization, I will turn to several examples of what I call relational holism, a special type of holism developed by Enlightenment theorists of organization. I argue that organization and relational holism were important in the emergence or transformation of forms of collective existence such as "species," "society," "population," "the body politic," and "the nation." Buffon's important reimagining of the category and concept of species is an example of the ways that organization thinkers directly engaged with the questions of the general and the particular in order to illuminate the nature or life and collective forms of existence. Another form of collective existence analyzed will be the physician and political economist François Quesnay's reimagining of the economy as a holistic entity whose forms and features could be expressed in the graphic form of an "economic picture," the *tableau œconomique*. The school of political economy that Quesnay founded, which eventually became known of as physiocracy, had moments of great popularity and influence in administrative policies in the 1760s and again briefly in the 1770s. A number of members of the school employed ideas of organization in their political writing, particularly in proposals for provincial representative assemblies that aimed to animate and organize the social and political body. Jean-Jacques Rousseau's work was the most consequential and sophisticated example of Enlightenment political theory that tried to understand the body politic as a form of organized body. Although often overlooked, ideas of organization were central to Rousseau's political vision in *The Social Contract*, as I will show in the final section.

As a way of proceeding through these large historical developments, it might be best to ground the discussion in the particular, turning back to the swarm of bees and looking at the ways that Diderot and three of his contemporaries employed the image. In *D'Alembert's Dream*, shortly after Mademoiselle de Lespinasse reads the notes about the swarm of bees, the character of Dr. Bordeu, who has been called to attend to d'Alembert, praises the beauty of this vision and tells her that he could "almost" say what comes next in the notes. To her amazement, he then proceeds to actually do so. Comparing the bees to the organs of the human body, he finds d'Alembert's ideas perfectly sensible, and he is able to continue the line of thought because, in one of the subtle ironies of the dialogue, the comparison of the human body to a swarm of bees was first made by the real-life Dr. Bordeu in a medical treatise almost two decades earlier.[6]

In the realm of philosophical medicine, Bordeu provided the most developed Enlightenment vision of the human body as an organic unity composed of semiautonomous organs, each demonstrating its own "particular life" (or "simple life") and having its own sphere of influence (it's "department" or "district") while also playing a role in the life of the whole.[7] It was a vision of complex and dynamic bodily interconnection in which the parts and the whole were influencing and being influenced by one another. Bordeu's use of the image of the bees and his vision of the organic unity of the human body was captured well by a younger philosophical physician whom Diderot commissioned to write on medical topics in the *Encyclopédie*. Acknowledging Bordeu's use of the image, and referencing the use by the famous natural philosopher Pierre-Louis Maupertuis, with whom Diderot had engaged in an ambiguous polemic, the Montpellier-trained physician Jean-Jacques Ménuret de Chambaud asserted the importance of understanding the relationship between the parts of the body and the whole body.[8] Invoking the bees, with a vitalist emphasis on life, Ménuret wrote, "one sees them pressing together, supporting each other, forming a type of whole in which each part lives in its own manner while contributing, through the correspondence and direction of its movements, to upholding a sort of *life* of the whole body."[9]

An important feature of the image of the bees used by Diderot, Bordeu, and Ménuret, whether as a swarm or a cluster (an *essaim* or a *grappe*), was that there were no mentions of a hive or its monarch, whether envisioned as a queen or a king (as many had claimed in the early modern era).[10] They did not follow the monarchical characterization of bees created in the "absolutist entomology" of some prominent early modern naturalists.[11] The new being created by the collective of bees was a decentered and federated system, not a centralized system like a monarchy or a hive. As Bordeu put it, the human body, like the new being formed by the bees, was a federation of organs, each with their own "department."[12] The unity of the parts was not established, as it was traditionally explained, through the action of an immaterial soul, a substantial form, or some other central mechanism of unity.[13] An organized body was characterized by the relationships between the parts and the whole, as well as the relationships between the parts themselves. This reflects one of the key features of the unity of organized beings: that their unity was a distributed one where the features and the functions of the whole were distributed throughout the parts that composed it. This was a relationship between the parts and the whole in which neither could be reduced to, nor explained by, the other. Both the parts and the whole were necessary for the composition and functioning of the organized body. They were interconnected and interdependent. For these reasons, a study of both registers, that of the parts and that of the whole, was necessary in order to understand the body.

Implicit in the theory of organized bodies was both an ontological and an epistemological holism of a variety that I call relational holism. This philosophical position emerged out of a more general holistic disposition of thought that began to form in the sporadic challenges to mechanical philosophy in the late seventeenth century and the early eighteenth century. This disposition coalesced in work in a number of fields, including chemistry, physiology, politics, aesthetics, and natural history, taking shape as a coherent philosophical position as thinkers began to connect ideas from these seemingly disparate fields. On occasion, this synthesis can be seen in the work of a single individual, such as Diderot, who drew on ideas from all these fields and eventually wrote works in all of them.[14] Relational holism coalesced into a position between traditional holism and atomism as theorists of organization attempted to account for the part-whole relations of living beings. In opposition to traditional holism, they argued that the whole did not simply determine the properties and functions of the parts. In opposition to traditional atomism (like that expressed in mechanical philosophy), they argued that the whole demonstrated properties and functions that did not exist in any of the individual parts; that is, a whole could become something greater than the sum of its parts. Demonstrating a basic sense of emergent properties arising from the act of union and the resulting structure of the united parts (organization in the case of living beings), relational holists held that it was the relation between the parts and the relation of the parts to the whole that created the additional properties and functions.[15] This is one of the reasons organization theorists privileged relations in their epistemology and often emphasized the importance of the comparative method.[16] They repeatedly wrote of "relations" (*rapports*), "liaisons" (*liaisons*), and "links" (*liens*) existing between parts.

As it emerged in the middle of the eighteenth century, the theory of organization, with its distinctive relational holism, was an antireductionist alternative to mechanical philosophy. It opposed mechanism's treatment of objects as if they were only the sum of their parts. It also opposed the idea that all wholes could be understood through a process that successively isolated each part, analyzed them individually, and then brought them back together to create a comprehensive knowledge of the whole. While not rejecting the applicability of mechanical philosophy for the study of some elements of nature, organization theorists developed a philosophy of relational holism because they did not believe mechanism was adequate to explain a variety of phenomena, particularly those related to questions of life and living beings. They retained some minimal role for mechanism, even in the life sciences, but they emphasized that savants had to move beyond mechanism and develop new approaches to living beings.

Identifying the special part-whole relations of organized bodies allows us to understand how they became so important as a conceptual tool in the second half of the eighteenth century, and it allows us to better appreciate the scope of the intellectual transformation that occurred. It helps us see what was an unnoticed philosophical revolution of the Enlightenment: a new mereology (a philosophy of part-whole relations) that was found in a wide variety of domains of thought.[17] Although this transformation can be put in the abstract philosophical terms of part-whole relations, it found expression in many readily graspable images, such as the swarm of bees, and it had widespread intellectual ramifications through its formalization in the theory of organization, its foundational role in the historical development of the human sciences in the second half of the eighteenth century, and its practical applications in domains such as biopolitics.

The topic of organization emerged in the conceptual space where many of the most important, and most controversial, philosophical and scientific topics of the day converged. As it took shape from the late 1740s, organization touched on a series of interrelated questions about the soul, creation, divine design, vitality, animation, and the adequacy of mechanical philosophy, as well as the possible implications of naturalism, materialism, and atheism. One of the important works to popularize the concept of organization was one of the most controversial and infamous works of the century, Julien Offray de La Mettrie's *Man, a Machine* (*L'homme machine*) of 1747, a work whose seemingly mechanist title obscured the challenging provocations of the author as he groped for a coherent vision of a vital materialism.[18] The titles of other works by La Mettrie, *Man, a Plant* (*L'homme plante*) and *Animals, More Than Machines* (*Les animaux plus que les machines*) were probably less misleading expressions of the organicism and vital materialism that allowed Diderot to have La Mettrie in the place of the Dr. Bordeu character in a draft of *D'Alembert's Dream*.[19] Partially because of La Mettrie's polemical style and courting of controversy, his work ended up being most successful as a provocation that brought the question of organization to the forefront of the attention of the reading public at the same time as a number of natural philosophers and philosophical physicians were formulating and beginning to publish the fundamental ideas of organization theory. These midcentury efforts to form a new concept of organization built on a long history of philosophical and scientific thought, receiving immediate stimulus from three scientific phenomena that were observed in a roughly ten-year period from the early 1740s to the early 1750s: Abraham Trembley's observations of the regeneration of freshwater polyps; new microscopic observations made by John Turberville Needham, seemingly demonstrating spontaneous generation; and Albrecht von Haller's empirical investigations of involuntary reactions of muscles, and subsequent physiological debates about this property of "irritability" and its similarities and differences with the "sensibility" of the nervous system.[20] All these phenomena raised questions about the relationship of parts and wholes in animal and human bodies, particularly the regeneration of whole polyps from severed parts of a polyp, since this seemed to demonstrate that the whole was in each of the parts that composed it, reversing the intuitive relationship between part and whole, which in turn raised questions about human and animal generation.

Some writers who explored these topics employed the concept of organization in an attempted to either retain or defend the idea of the immaterial or immortal soul, arguing that it animated matter and formed bodies. This included writers as different as the widely read Swiss naturalist Charles Bonnet, who was motivated by religious belief and inspired by ideas of Gottfried Wilhelm Leibniz, and the aspiring man of science, and future radical journalist of the Revolution, Jean-Paul Marat.[21] It also included the best-selling author Louis-Sebastien Mercier and a group in the late eighteenth century who were captivated by the magnetic therapies of Franz Anton Mesmer.[22] This dualist strain of spiritualized vitalism played a relatively minor role in political and social theory, particularly in attempts to revise Rousseau based on the idea that humans were not embodied souls, as traditionally believed, but "ensouled bodies," as Johann Gottfried Herder put it.[23] The theorists of organization that I focus on were more subversive and ultimately more consequential in their vision of nature, as well as their model of the human, and the implications of both of these for social and political thought. The group that I have in mind is composed of people that were in general agreement with La Mettrie's critical take on Leibnizian attempts at "spiritualizing matter, rather than materializing the soul."[24] These figures were at the center of forming the theory of organization in a way that either materialized the soul or distributed its functions throughout the body in a fashion that had made moot questions of the relationship of body and soul.[25] This type of antidualist organization theory was central to the fashioning of a vital materialism in the second half of the eighteenth century.[26] In their attacks on Cartesian dualism, these vital materialists collapsed older questions of body and soul, animation and matter, into a monist conception of organization. "Life and animation, rather than being a metaphysical attribute of beings," Buffon repeated several times in *Natural History*, "is a physical property of matter."[27]

In addition to questions of body and soul, these theorists also recast questions of the relationship of body and mind, arguing for a new perspective on the continuity between what they called "the physical" and "the moral" dimensions of the human.[28] The relationship between the physical and the moral remained important to Enlightenment organization theory from Louis de La Caze's 1755 *The Idea of Man, Both Physical and Moral* (*Idée de l'homme physique et moral*) to Pierre-Jean-Georges Cabanis's 1802 *Relations of the Physical and the Moral in Man* (*Rapports du physique et du moral de l'homme*).[29] Organizational thinkers routinely claimed that "*le moral* is bound and governed by *le physique*," the former being "no more than the specific effects" of the latter.[30] The physical dimensions of the human are relatively self-explanatory, but the moral encompassed the dimensions of thought and feeling, in the sense of both basic sensations and things such as consciousness and higher-order moral judgment. "Sensibility" was a highly charged and somewhat amorphous concept that seemed to bridge the two realms, allowing an understanding of how the physical could affect the moral and, possibly, vice versa. Sensibility was often understood as the means by which physical stimulus became sensations. It was, in this sense, the medium through which the physical and the moral communicated. It was also the means by which the outside world was connected to the inner realm of sense impressions, or "sentiments." Sensibility, like organization, became a key word and a key concept in the Enlightenment science of man.[31] While sensibility was important, it must be remembered that it was often understood by vital materialists as a property that was activated or actualized through the organization of matter. For these vital materialists, sensibility was a property of organized matter.[32] Much of the writing on sensibility was, therefore, also about organization, even if only tangentially or implicitly.

Whether coming at the question of organization more from the perspective of the life sciences, aesthetics, epistemology, or politics, organization theorists worked with an ontological image of nature that was like the swarm of bees. This ontological image functioned like a normative understanding of nature—describing and prescribing, reflecting and revealing.[33] It was an image of dynamic and organic nature, a new "world picture," that emerged in contrast to the "mechanization of the world picture" that had taken shape with the development of the mechanical philosophy and the application of mathematics to the study of nature in the sixteenth and seventeenth centuries.[34] It was an image that allowed for, and incorporated, the emergence of new beings, the continual flux of forms, and complementary coexistence of extremes such as variety and unity. This understanding of nature, and the approach to studying it, was one characterized by an emphasis on grasping things coming into being and transforming. Yet, while it placed an emphasis on change, it maintained the tension between being and becoming, unity and variety. This orientation resulted in an epistemology and a methodology of harmonic oscillation (or "harmonic mediation" in Peter Reill's terminology) in which the particular was not absorbed or subsumed by the general, the part was not reduced to the whole, and apparent opposites could be taken to complement one another in a way that led toward the truth, rather than obscuring or obstructing it.[35] This was a relational form of thought and practice in which analyzing the bees, the cluster, and the transitional stage of the individual bees swarming together could help reveal the nature of nature.

The most concrete and identifiable contribution of this orientation to the history of ideas was the image of the organized body that enabled a modern concept of the organism and offered a new articulation of organic unity. The concept of the organized body was a mediation of things that seemed like they should be separate and contradictory, as if they could not exist in the same entity, yet were nonetheless found together as properties or characteristics of one and the same thing. Organized bodies were embodied mediations of a set of oppositions: difference and sameness, unity and variety, part and whole, being and becoming, cause and effect, ends and means.[36] It was out of this mediating theory that the organism as a concept began to take its modern shape and that humans began to be understood as a literal embodiment of this concatenation of mediations. This concept of the organized body was not, however, the only major contribution of this body of thought. In fact, the organized body was the centerpiece of a whole new vision of the structured interconnection of different domains of nature, which at times people extended to the social and political domains as well.

To understand this new vision of nature, and its social and political implications, it is necessary to be clear about the conceptual innovations of the "organized body." In the most general sense, the core of organization theory was the conviction that all organized bodies demonstrated a few basic properties, most of which could be put in the mereological terms of parts and wholes. Organized bodies were self-generating and self-organizing; they did not necessitate any outside agent to reproduce or function. Most of the organization theorists that I am focusing on believed in epigenetic generation of some sort, thinking that wholes came into being through the reproduction and combination of parts and their development in succession. As whole organized bodies came together through the processes of reproduction, growth, and assimilation, the parts became interconnected and interdependent. They contributed to one another's existence, contributing "life" to the whole and creating a circular relationship where individual parts functioned as cause and effect, means and ends. Diderot expressed this when he wrote of the body as a "prodigious chain of causes and effects" and "a system of actions and reactions."[37] With an eye toward the Hippocratic tradition and the persistence of ancient notions of circular interconnectivity in the human body—one that persisted even through some forms of mechanist physiological thought—the vitalist physician La Caze argued that "circle of action" within the body undermined the applicability of mechanistic explanations.[38] Buffon argued that the body of an animal was composed of such interconnected and interdependent parts that the alteration of even a single part would be reflected in the whole, which was true for external qualities such as size, shape, and color, as well as for instinct and "the most internal qualities."[39]

This circularity was important, yet difficult to explain, a problem that received its most penetrating and canonical philosophical articulation in the second half of Immanuel Kant's third critique, *Critique of the Power of Judgment* (1790).[40] But organization theorists before Kant were very interested in the question. There were several different solutions posed, but in general they all believed that there was some means of communication whereby the parts could affect one another and register effects on other parts that were not contiguous. This realm of "sympathy" was uncertain and highly contested because it was unclear how many types of communication there were in organized bodies.[41] It was also unclear whether the action was direct or indirect, that is, whether the action was physically linked through a mediating element, such as the nervous system, or whether it was action at a distance attributable to some type of force not unlike gravity. Kant's teleological solution was one of the most sophisticated responses to the problem of how an organized body seemed to be its own cause and effect, while also being composed of parts that seemed to be both cause and effect. His creative definition of purposiveness and his articulation of this organismic problem in terms of natural purposiveness was an important moment in the development of modern philosophy and biology, but it needs to be emphasized that organization theorists, with whom Kant was deeply engaged, had already developed their own quasi-teleological interpretations.[42]

Although the theory of organization implied analogical connections between the human body and larger bodies like the body politic, it did not partake in the idea that elements of the macrocosm were mirrored in the microcosm of the human body, as was predominant in much of early modern Europe.[43] Instead, for the theorists of organization, the human body became an object in a different type of network of analogically linked objects. The human body was an organized body, and in this respect it shared features with other organized bodies, large and small. While these bodies could be compared to each other through analogies, as they often were, they were also directly linked, or theoretically could be, through causal connections.

The connection between organized bodies at different scales, therefore, went beyond analogy. It was not only the case that these bodies at different scales shared the feature of organization and the many characteristics that follow from this (such as organic unity, interconnectivity, relationality, sympathy, etc.). It was also the case that organized bodies were seen to be connected in causal terms because they were implicated in each other's existence, either as constituent parts or as compound objects made up of smaller constituent parts. This meant that human bodies, for example, were composed of smaller organized bodies, while also being parts of larger organized bodies like the social body or the body politic. This conception created the idea of a new causal interconnectivity of the scales of being. In theory, microscopic bodies were implicated in the structure and function of human bodies as well as larger collective bodies, whether these collective bodies were viewed from the social perspective ("the social body"), the political perspective ("the body politic" or "the nation"), the biological perspective (a "race," "variety," or "species"), or a perspective that combined these perspectives (a "population").

The idea of the causal interconnection of the scales of organized being was long in formation, coming together in the coherent formalization of ideas of organization. Many of the constituent ideas about "organization," "organized bodies," and their relations had ancient precedents, and they began to be developed in important ways in the seventeenth century, even if they did not come together into a form that created an alternative to the mechanical philosophy and the mechanization of the world picture. One of the important developments that began in the seventeenth century, building on microscopic observation, was the shift from seeing smaller organic bodies inside a larger body, not as inhabitants, but as constituents.[44] The German philosopher and polymath Leibniz, in his idea of monads and the related image of a fish pond full of fish that were made up of small fish that were themselves made up of yet smaller fish, was particularly important in providing an image of nesting individuality in which organic beings nested in one another at various scales all the way down, infinitely.[45] In addition to Leibniz's fertile ideas, other visions of nested beings can be found scattered throughout the work of seventeenth-century philosophers and naturalists, including Benedict Spinoza, Blaise Pascal, and Marcello Malpighi.[46]

The philosophes knew Leibniz's vision of nested individuality. "Each organized body," as Abbé Étienne Bonnot de Condillac wrote in the section on Leibniz in his work on seventeenth-century philosophical system builders, "is composed of organized bodies."[47] Bonnet, the Swiss naturalist and an admirer of Leibniz, wrote that animals were "composites of animals," and that each organized body of an animal was "a world inhabited by other animals." But Bonnet was uncertain about the number of levels of life within an individual animal body. He did not know, as he wrote, "where organization ends, nor what is its smallest term."[48] In his discussion of organization, Jean-Baptiste-René Robinet, the philosophical man of letters who wrote several popular works on nature that helped disseminate the idea of organization in the 1760s, sometimes with his own unusual interpretations and additions, argued that even "the most simple Being of nature is a composite of similar Beings" so that "an organ is composed of smaller organs, and those, in turn, of even smaller organs."[49]

Although writers like Robinet and Diderot sometimes incorporated ideas of organization and nesting into strange metaphysical reveries, nesting was not just a theory, a metaphysical speculation, or an imaginative fancy. It was also a subject of intense empirical inquiry. The controversial experiments on spontaneous generation carried out by John Turberville Needham (alone and in collaboration with Buffon) seemed to provide empirical evidence of nesting, among other things.[50] As the Scottish philosopher Thomas Reid put it, commenting on the microscopic observations of rehydrated wheat blight reported in Buffon's *Natural History*: "Paste made of Flour engenders little Eels which seem onely to be sacks full of other little eels as appears upon opening them with a lancit."[51] This nesting did not only apply to plants and animals.[52] The same was true of humans as organized beings. In *D'Alembert's Dream*, Diderot had the character of Dr. Bordeu state that although a person could not be divided up and resolved into a multitude of little people, a person could be divided up into a multitude of microscopic creatures (*animalcules*).[53] For Buffon, the individual human or animal was composed of "little individuals" or "little organized beings," which were in turn composed of tiny organic parts called "organic molecules."[54] As Buffon argued, from the perspective of organization and reproduction, an individual polyp or oak tree "is only a whole, uniformly organized in all its interior parts; a compound of an infinity of resembling figures and similar parts."[55]

This nesting of organized bodies implied different levels of organization and life within organized bodies. Although there was not widespread agreement about the number of levels, or exactly how far down they went, most organization theorists recognized at least three levels of life within individual humans or animals. As Diderot wrote in *Elements of Physiology* (*Éléments de physiologie*), there are "certainly two very distinct lives, perhaps three: the life of the entire animal; the life of each of its organs; the life of the molecule."[56] There was no specific terminology for nesting or the conception of levels of life in the eighteenth century, but organization theorists clearly worked with these ideas, and they described the different levels. Physicians often envisioned the most detailed and numerous series of levels, some arguing for "systems" or "departments" of organs that existed above the level of organs, with many recognizing the existence of "tissues," "membranes," "vesicles," "globules," and "fibers" below the level of the organs.[57] Whether endorsing three levels, or more, many theorists of organization came to settle on Buffon's "organic molecules" as one of the basic units of human and animal bodies.[58] Some organization theorists explicitly synthesized medical vitalism and Buffonian ideas in creating accounts of the levels of life, arguing that it was not merely life that existed at various levels within the body, but "particular life" (invoking Bordeu's terminology). For example, the vitalist physician Grimaud invoked organic molecules to extend the idea of particular life down to the organic building blocks of organized bodies, arguing that "the life of each organ of the animated body is not only a simple life, but it is really the product of as many particular lives as there are organic molecules that enter into this organ's constitution."[59]

Some theorists recognized that the ideas of nesting and levels of life meant that the traditional conception of the great chain of being would need revision, since, apparently, the great chain not only extended outward, linking the space between different forms of beings, but it also reached inward through the hierarchical scale of nested organized bodies. This was not a topic of extended discussion, but Diderot acknowledged it when he suggested that perhaps comparative anatomists in the future could fill the apparent gaps in the great chain of being by considering the beings within beings. "Form is often only a misleading mask," he wrote; "the link of the chain that appears to be missing perhaps resides in a known being."[60] We can, therefore, revise A. O. Lovejoy's classic account in *The Great Chain of Being* to include the vision of the nesting of organized bodies at different levels of life.[61] This newly identified idea of the chain of being might best be characterized as the scale of organized being, a name that draws attention to the vision of nature, including humans, as interconnected in a new manner that was causal and constitutive, not merely metaphysical or ontotheological. With the levels of life and nesting of organized bodies, humans became more than the sum of their parts in a new sense that differed from traditional spiritual accounts of the role of the immaterial soul being superadded to the material body. The human became more than the sum of its parts, but not in the sense of having an immaterial soul in addition to its material body. In the vision of the organization theorists, the human became a complex assemblage of vital parts and wholes that existed on various hierarchical levels interconnected by a vast network of circular causation. Humans came to be an irreducible organic whole that was the result of numerous smaller organic wholes; the human body was composed of smaller organized bodies. Furthermore, they were interconnected to larger organized bodies like the collective body of the species, while also being connected to the many small bodies that helped constitute them. This was the new object that became enshrined in the Enlightenment birth of the science of man. For some, the human was now understood to be a "harmonic compound," as Ménuret de Chambaud put it, or a "harmonic combination," as Abbé Sieyès wrote.[62] This new understanding of the human body as a federated republic provided new resources for conceiving of the body politic.[63] The direction of the metaphors and the formation of the concepts of the human body and the body politic went both ways.

For most eighteenth-century philosophers of nature, it was a truism that everything in nature was interconnected. With the theory of organization, the philosophes of the second half of the century gave particularity to this general claim. Over the course of the second half of the eighteenth century as this vision of interconnection was fleshed out it was increasingly applied to the social and political dimensions of existence. The theory of organization created a coherent and compelling account of "organized bodies" that furnished people with a new means by which to conceive of the social body and the body politic. The novelty of thinking about the body politic as an organized body can be seen through the contrast with the political theories of the preceding century, in which, as Annabel Brett has succinctly put it, "the commonwealth or state is constructed as a union of human beings in a moral, juridical, and artificial body, the being of which is by definition different from that of the individual human beings by whom it is made or who constitute its matter."[64] In the political theories of organized bodies, the body politic (and similar forms of collective existence such as the state, the nation, and the social body) came to be conceived as being a natural body of the same sort as the individuals who composed it. Collective bodies and human bodies may have been different in some ways, but both were organized bodies, demonstrating all the fundamental characteristics of organization. Even if they could not self-generate, they might become self-reproducing. Collective forms of existence might still have been "artificial bodies" in the strict sense that they were not completely self-generating or self-organizing (they required human artifice to come into being), but people came to think that if the collective bodies were organized properly, they could have all, or almost all, the properties and functions of a natural body. This meant that the body politic could exist in either an organized or a disorganized form, as was reflected in the discourse of the French Revolution when the French word *désorganisation* (disorganization) was coined at the same time as the political sense of "organization" became explicit and widespread.[65] Since both organization and disorganization were possible, and humans had the ability to influence collective organized bodies, it was, therefore, up to people to bring about the organization and animation of these bodies. With this new naturalistic version of political voluntarism, making the body politic into an organized body became both a possibility and a responsibility.

Even before the midcentury synthesis of organization theory became available to political theorists, the philosophes already lived in a world of collective bodies in which people were united in collective forms of existence that were distinguished conceptually and legally. The social and political order of the Old Regime was composed of many corporations, orders, and estates that each gave a singular collective form to their constituent members. Although each collective form was singular and had its own particular identity, forms could overlap, since someone could, for instance, be a member of a professional corporate body as well as the corporate body of a city.[66] These various collective forms were arranged in a series of legal and normative hierarchies and networks that were, nonetheless, united by the singular power of the king in his twofold existence as both a physical and a metaphysical being. According to early modern political theology, the "natural body" of the king lived and died like all other natural bodies, while his *corpus mysticum* (mystical body) was immortal and imperishable. This second body accounted for the persistence of the royal *dignitas* (even upon the expiration of a king's natural body), and it united all the king's subjects in one collective body. This notion of the corpus mysticum, which derived from notions of the Christian community embodied in Christ and from explanations of the presence of the body of Christ in the Eucharist, came to provide the conceptual bedrock of absolutist political theology.[67] It even found expression in unusual forms of embodiment in which the metaphysical body of the king was literally incarnated in a physical form other than his natural body. These included the use of royal effigies representing the mystical body in royal funeral rituals, and a eucharistic understanding of the king's image, whereby even paintings of the king were treated as if they contained some element of him, much as the bread and wine of the Eucharist was said to contain the "real presence" of Christ.[68]

The experience of corporate society and the concept of the corpus mysticum, in both its theological and its political theological forms, provided the primary models for thinking about collective forms of existence before the formulation of organization theory and the model of the organized body at the middle of the eighteenth century. With their new naturalistic understanding of collective entities, however, the philosophes began to form alternative visions of social and political life based on the understanding that social and political bodies were themselves organized bodies, or at least had so many of the characteristics of organized bodies that they could be treated as if they were functionally identical. These ideas about collective bodies continued to develop across the last decades of the Old Regime so that by the time of the French Revolution, when ideas and practices of incarnating the nation and popular sovereignty gained a new urgency, revolutionaries had new models to draw on. The transfer of sovereignty from the king's bodies to the body of the people was not attempted, of course, in a philosophical or theoretical void, nor was it, I would argue, a process of political theology whereby a theological concept was transmuted or sublimated into a form that partially or completely effaced its religious origins.[69] This alternative form of political incarnation grounded in the understanding of organized bodies provided a way for the theorists of the Revolution to go about constructing a new politic body to fill the "empty place" left by the removal of the king's two bodies.[70]

Although this mode of organizational thought developed across numerous sites and through the work of many Enlightenment thinkers, it can be seen clearly in the most prominent and consequential examples of fully developed organizational ideas being utilized in Buffon's reconceptualization of species, the physiocrats' reconceptualization of the economy, and new ideas about the body politic that took shape in the work of Rousseau and the physiocrats. These new visions of collective bodies played a crucial role in biopolitical proposals about including or excluding some individuals, or groups of individuals, from the collective body.

While the naturalists and philosophers developing organization theory explored the new part-whole relationship of organized bodies in the case of individual bodies, they also did so in the case of species. Buffon was the most significant of these theorists, and his approach to species is one of the most important in the history of the species concept and the emergence of modern biological thought.[71] Buffon's work presented a new perspective on a number of fundamental and perennial questions about what exactly species were, many of which questions reached back to the canonical formulations of Aristotle. Were they atemporal logical universals, unchanging categories of nature, fixed units of divine design, groups of like individuals, arbitrary (and perhaps meaningless) epistemological projections, or some combination of all, or some, of these?

Buffon's reliance on the criterion of fertile interbreeding to determine biological species set the terms by which most of his contemporaries understood species as a scientific concept and a natural object. It was included in important *Encyclopédie* articles, and it was repeated in the writing of countless naturalists and philosophers, becoming one of the most repeated and consequential elements of Buffon's work.[72] More than a logical universal, or a combination of individuals that resembled one another, species for Buffon was also the historically unfolding succession of similar individuals linked through reproduction.[73] This immanent and historical approach to species was an important development, yet, I would argue, Buffon never resolved the exact relationship between species as an unchanging and essential category of nature and species as a chain of linked and similar individuals changing and unfolding in time.

While he may not have formed a coherent and comprehensive concept of species, he did form a relational epistemology and ontology of species that presented a unique understanding of species as a complex and irreducible object that could be grasped best through a new harmonic understanding, recognizing the distinct aspects of species, as well as the relations between these aspects. Buffon did not consistently argue that species was one specific and reducible thing. Instead, he recognized it as a relational whole that could be grasped only as the relation between the whole and its parts, changing form and unchanging identity, abstract category of nature and imminent succession of like individuals. For him, species was something that must be grasped in both its being and its becoming. In short, like an organized body, species was to be understood from the perspective of relational holism. While he articulated propositions about species in various articles in *Natural History*, he did not present this idea of species as a relational whole in the form of propositions. Instead we must look for this idea of species embodied in the formal structures and imaginative prose found in the second of two synthesizing "views of nature" that he published in the 1760s.

In writing the "Second View," Buffon developed a highly creative and innovative form of natural philosophical writing that best reveals the complexity and character of his thinking on species.[74] He drew on intellectual and formal precedents reaching back to antiquity, refashioning them into an unusual new amalgam. At the heart of his philosophical fiction was the idea that the members of a species could be considered together as if they were but a single individual. But instead of merely considering the human species as if it were a single human, as had already been suggested, for example, by

Blaise Pascal in the seventeenth century, Buffon attempted to get readers to "see" nature from the perspective of this compound individual, as if readers were actually embodying this impossible species-being.[75] This is what it means to think the individual and the species. You must see the individual from the perspective of the species and the species from the perspective of the individual, in a very imaginative way where you must be able to imagine yourself as a species that is a single being. The individual reader must become like a species that is an abstract, yet embodied, collective being.

While the shifts in perspective of the "Second View" were one of the more imaginative ways in which Buffon expressed the harmonic relations, establishing reciprocal relations between parts and wholes, the general and the particular, was the foundation of Buffon's epistemology and his method. As he explained, the study of nature requires the combination of "two qualities of the mind that appear opposed."[76] The naturalist must demonstrate "the great views of an ardent intellect that embraces everything with one glance, and the careful attention of a laboring instinct that concentrates only on a single point."[77] Although these contrasting qualities of the mind would be difficult for the naturalist to develop and maintain, it would also be difficult, but necessary, to hold on to the distinctness of these two perspectives while drawing comparisons and establishing relations between bits of evidence drawn from them. The views of nature must be kept separate, yet be brought into a harmonic relationship. This is precisely what Buffon attempted to achieve in the "Second View," drawing the reader into seemingly opposing perspectives from which to view species.

In order to achieve the imagined embodiment of the species in the "Second View," Buffon drew on a tradition of philosophy reaching back to forms of ancient Greek and Roman thought experiments that were formalized in the exercises of the Stoics and Epicureans before being adapted into the Christian tradition in the form of "spiritual exercises."[78] These exercises and thought experiments usually entailed practitioners attempting to see the world, or some element of it, from an unfamiliar perspective that would facilitate them having a new appreciation of the familiar. At times, these attempts to cultivate wisdom through seeing the world anew required complex moral defamiliarizations; at other times they simply required practitioners to look at purple fabric as if it were nothing but animal hair dyed in fish blood, as Marcus Aurelius put it in one example from his famous notebook of exercises. Sometimes, as in the Stoic practice of adopting a cosmic view, practitioners were required to adopt a view that was impossible for them to actually experience in their lives other than through an imaginative leap. It was this later kind of defamiliarization that Buffon attempted to narratively embody in his work. Although this type of philosophy, with its emphasis on forming as much as informing, is not often discussed in the context of the eighteenth century, these forms of spiritual exercises were still a living tradition, if in a modified form, in Enlightenment philosophy as well as in the Christian educational practices that characterized the primary education that many of the philosophes received.

In addition to inviting readers to see nature from the perspective of an imagined species-being, at the end of the "Second View," Buffon made another strange shift of perspective, arguing that individual human beings actually were something like the embodiment of the entire species, particularly if they were well educated and well read. When the collective knowledge of the species was transmitted from parents to a child, and this was combined with the collective knowledge passed on through writing and printing, the "reunion of centuries of experience in a single man, expands the limits of his being to infinity."[79] In Buffon's complex defamiliarization, seeing from the imaginary perspective of the species-being was actually to see from a perspective that was like the real viewpoint of a person, since "man, particularly educated man, is no longer a simple individual. He represents a great part of the whole human species."[80]

A different example of the way that relational holism and ideas of organization played a role in Enlightenment thought about collective forms of existence can be seen in creation of the first economic modeling device in history. François Quesnay created this unusual graphic arrangement of numbers, text, columns, and dots. He called it the *tableau œconomique* (economic picture), and he placed it at the center the political economic system that eventually became known as physiocracy (see figure 1).[81] The tableau has had a long and complicated history as an economic modeling device because of the difficulties that both contemporaries and subsequent commentators have had in interpreting its novel and complex form and function. It must be admitted that the tableau is difficult to make sense of, and even more difficult to resolve into some completely coherent and settled interpretation, since there seem to be inconsistencies and gaps in its representational work. The tableau, however, was not intended to present a final and complete argument, nor was it meant to simply embody propositional knowledge. Instead, as is very clear from Quesnay's written explanations and his correspondence with the cofounder of physiocracy, the marquis de Mirabeau, the tableau was meant to bring about a revelatory flash of insight into the nature of the economy, showing rather than telling.[82] It was intended to render the diffused abstraction of economic activity into a readily graspable entity that could be perceived in an image before one's eyes.

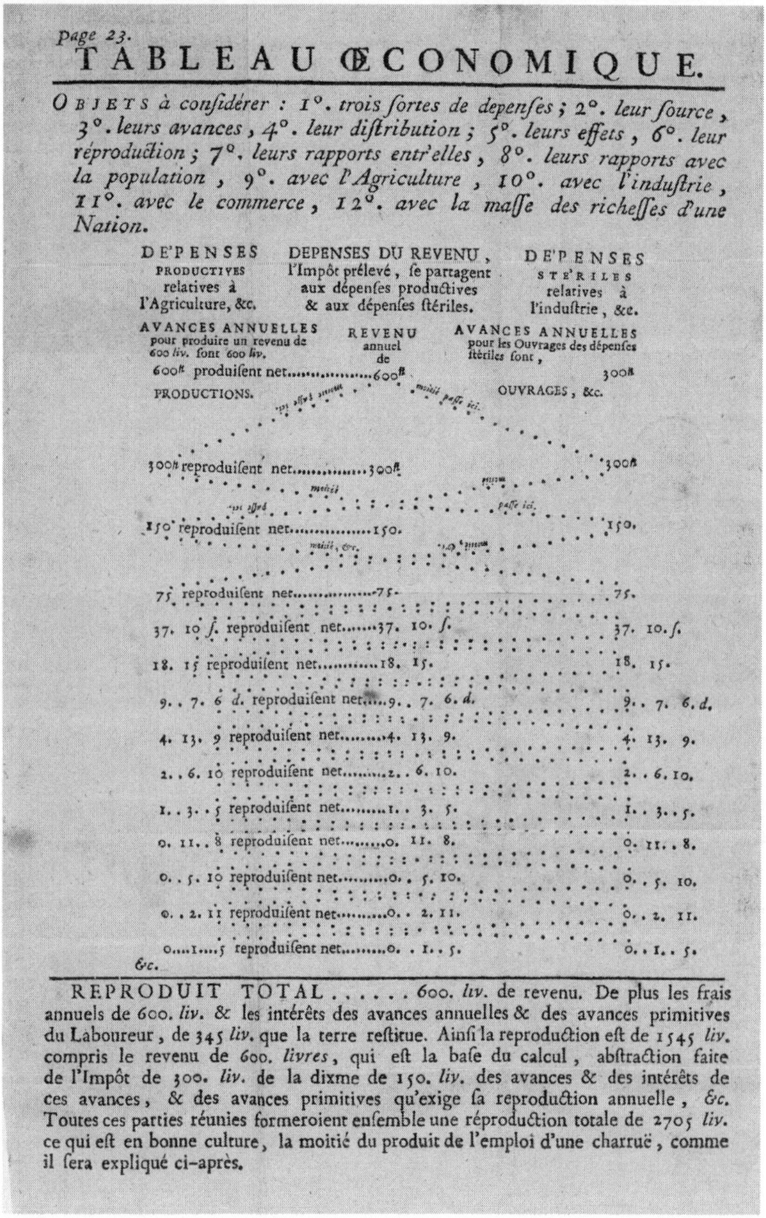

page 23.

TABLEAU ŒCONOMIQUE.

OBJETS *à conſidérer : 1°. trois ſortes de depenſes ; 2°. leur ſource, 3°. leurs avances, 4°. leur diſtribution ; 5°. leurs effets, 6°. leur réproduction ; 7°. leurs rapports entr'elles, 8°. leurs rapports avec la population, 9°. avec l'Agriculture, 10°. avec l'induſtrie, 11°. avec le commerce, 12°. avec la maſſe des richeſſes d'une Nation.*

DE'PENSES PRODUCTIVES relatives à l'Agriculture, &c.	DEPENSES DU REVENU, l'Impôt prélevé, ſe partagent aux dépenſes productives & aux dépenſes ſtériles.	DE'PENSES STE'RILES relatives à l'induſtrie, &c.
AVANCES ANNUELLES pour produire un revenu de 600 *liv.* ſont 600 *liv.*	REVENU annuel de	AVANCES ANNUELLES pour les Ouvrages des dépenſes ſtériles ſont,
600ᶫᵗ produiſent net	600ᶫᵗ	300ᶫᵗ
PRODUCTIONS.		OUVRAGES, &c.
300ᶫᵗ reproduiſent net	300ᶫᵗ	300ᶫᵗ
150 reproduiſent net	150.	150.
75. reproduiſent net	75.	75.
37. 10. *ſ.* reproduiſent net	37. 10. *ſ.*	37. 10. *ſ.*
18. 15 reproduiſent net	18. 15.	18. 15.
9. . 7. 6 *d.* reproduiſent net	9. . 7. 6. *d.*	9. . 7. 6. *d.*
4. 13. 9 reproduiſent net	4. 13. 9.	4. 13. 9.
2. . 6. 10 reproduiſent net	2. . 6. 10.	2. . 6. 10.
1. . 3. . 5 reproduiſent net	1. . 3. 5.	1. . 3. . 5.
0. 11. . 8 reproduiſent net	0. 11. 8.	0. 11. . 8.
0. . 5. 10 reproduiſent net	0. . 5. 10.	0. . 5. 10.
0. . 2. 11 reproduiſent net	0. . 2. 11.	0. . 2. 11.
0....1....5 reproduiſent net	0. . 1. . 5.	0. . 1. . 5.
&c.		

(moitié paſſe ici.)

REPRODUIT TOTAL . . . . . . 600. *liv.* de revenu. De plus les frais annuels de 600. *liv.* & les intérêts des avances annuelles & des avances primitives du Laboureur, de 345 *liv.* que la terre reſtitue. Ainſi la reproduction eſt de 1545 *liv.* compris le revenu de 600. *livres*, qui eſt la baſe du calcul, abſtraction faite de l'Impôt de 300. *liv.* de la dixme de 150. *liv.* des avances & des intérêts de ces avances, & des avances primitives qu'exige ſa reproduction annuelle, *&c.* Toutes ces parties réunies formeroient enſemble une réproduction totale de 2705 *liv.* ce qui eſt en bonne culture, la moitié du produit de l'emploi d'une charruë, comme il ſera expliqué ci-après.

FIGURE 1. François Quesnay, the "zigzag" version of the physiocrats' *tableau œconomique* (economic picture), from Mirabeau, *L'ami des hommes* (1759). Used by permission of the Bibliothèque nationale de France.

It did not present the economy as a completely separate sphere of activity, distinct from politics (it was still an image of political economy), but it did represent a novel holistic vision of the economy.[83] Building on aesthetic and organizational understandings of relational holism, Quesnay created a representation in which the wholeness of the economy could be easily grasped in a single picture, as could the interconnected relationship between constitutive parts of the economy, which included classes of people, agricultural production, artisanal production, investment, return on investment, production, and the circulation of money and goods.

Particularly in its first incarnations, the tableau was a beginning, an entrance into a "natural" understanding of the economy. Seeing the tableau in this light, and appreciating its relationship to theories of organization, results in a new understanding of the tableau, while also giving us a new perspective on physiocracy as a school. In short, an organizational reading of the tableau helps show that physiocracy was a political economy of relational holism that attempted to form the economy into a natural body that could be left to function on its own, reproducing and self-generating like an organized body. This gives us a new perspective on the ideas and logics behind laissez-faire economics and the more general development of laissez-faire ideas in classical liberal political economy. One of the reasons that some people began to argue that the economy might function best if it were left alone—as expressed in the summative phrase *laissez-faire, laissez-passez*—was that they believed that the economy was, or could be, formed into an organized body, with the specific properties that this entailed. Although there were flaws in their arguments, and in the very idea of treating the economy as if it could exist like an organized body left largely alone to self-organize and self-generate, they did create a new approach to political economy that was a central part of the formation of liberal political economy in the eighteenth century, whose consequences can be seen in the long history of laissez-faire economics and economic modeling, which the tableau, in fact, began.

The first version of the tableau, which Quesnay sometimes referred to as "the zigzag," was created to provide a simplified and reduced picture of the vast complexity of nature and the economic processes that both represented and conformed to its laws: "You must recognize, my friend, that everything is intermingled in nature, that everything moves through circles interlaced with one another. . . . Objects may be traced, distinguished, and considered only through abstract ideas that neither alter nor disrupt anything in the physical realm."[84] Quesnay attempted to find a visual arithmetic model that could be employed to adequately represent the complexity of the interconnections of what he called the "economic circle."[85]

In an early letter attempting to convince Mirabeau of the tableau's advantages over written arguments, Quesnay stated very clearly that these advantages derived from the fact that it was a visual image. "The well-conceived zigzag," Quesnay wrote, "effectively abridges many details and depicts the closely interconnected ideas that the intellect alone would find very difficult to know, untangle, and reconcile through discourse."[86] In his letter, he continued by explaining that "these ideas themselves would be quite elusive if they were not assured a place in the imagination by the tableau.[87] All means of visual representation, however, were not alike, and in order to create the clearest and most precise ideas through images, "the eyes must be spoken to with the support of a language appropriate to the understanding."[88] If this is done properly, an image of economic activity such as the tableau "makes all the rules of order and all their consequences sensible, almost palpable."[89] In creating this visual neologism, Quesnay likely drew on his experience as an apprentice engraver and on his prolonged engagement with visual artists.[90]

After his early training in printmaking, Quesnay became a surgeon, before eventually gaining a medical degree and practicing as a physician. There have long been naturalistic interpretations of the tableau that attempt to relate it to various scientific ideas and physiology models of the body that Quesnay would have known as a trained surgeon and physician.[91] Most of these interpretations have run into difficulties by drawing too strict of a dichotomy between mechanical and vitalist understandings of the body.[92] Quesnay developed his physiological ideas at a time when the dominant mechanical understanding of the body (iatromechanism) was being questioned and undermined, though it was not yet overturned or displaced by a comprehensive or consistent vitalist understanding.[93] This is reflected in numerous books and essays on physiology and medicine where Quesnay expressed his doubts about the adequacy of mechanical explanations of the body without adhering to a thorough vitalism. In *Essay on the Animal Economy* (*Essai physique sur l'œconomie animale*), for example, Quesnay discussed the vivifying properties of "ether" in the body, and he formulated a critique of mechanist theories of generation and the idea of infinitely divisible matter that lay at the heart of theories of preformation.[94] The transitional character of Quesnay's ideas was also reflected in correspondence with François Boissier de Sauvages de la Croix, one of the most important figures in French medicine to have drawn on Stahlian animism to critique purely mechanical understandings of the functioning of human bodies.[95] Boissier de Sauvages was one of the most important physicians teaching at the University of Montpellier, helping to transform the medical faculty in a way that allowed it to become a center of vitalist medicine and organic thought by the middle of the eighteenth century.[96]

Although Quesnay was of a slightly older generation than most of the theorists of organization, by the 1750s, when he lived in Versailles, he was nonetheless at the center of organization theory, both socially and intellectually.[97] Living at court through the 1750s and 1760s as a royal physician and the private physician of the king's mistress Madame de Pompadour, he worked with two royal physicians, Bordeu and La Caze, who had studied in the medical faculty of Montpellier and who in fact became the primary theorists of vitalist medicine in the Montpellier tradition. Quesnay was also a contributor to the *Encyclopédie* and friends with both Diderot and Buffon, sharing the patronage of Pompadour with the latter. While Quesnay had written about organization in the physiological sense before his collaboration began with Mirabeau in 1757, Mirabeau had already written about it in the political sense. In fact, Mirabeau had titled a work of his on provincial assemblies *Precis on Organization, or Memoir on Provincial Estates* (*Précis sur l'organisation, ou Mémoire sur les états provinciaux*).[98] As soon as they began collaborating, they wrote of the body politic being an organized body, with Quesnay seeming to bring greater rigor and scientific specificity to Mirabeau's use of the language of organization.[99]

By 1763, in their major collaborative work *Rural Philosophy* (*Philosophie rurale*), Quesnay and Mirabeau consistently employed the language of vitalism and organization to write about the nature of the economy and the necessary form of politics. They wrote of "vivifying reactions" and the need to analyze the economy like an organized body. "It is a question," they wrote, "of dissecting it and discovering the organization of it by an anatomical demonstration of all the parts and by the development of their intertwining, of their connection and the concurrence of their mutual action."[100] In addition to endorsing the relational epistemology of organization, they endorsed its relational ontology, arguing, "everything works in nature only by relations."[101]

In *Rural Philosophy*, they characterized governance as the art of maintaining the health of both the collective body and individual bodies.[102] Casting rulers as doctors, they argued that the collective body must be "subjected to a regime prescribed by nature and conducted by the Doctor."[103] People straying from the prescribed rules of nature were "sick and corrupt limbs" that were to be "cured or amputated."[104] In order for the doctor to properly conduct this health regime, it was necessary for him to study the constitution of the collective body, "for this constitution is not the work of the Doctor; it is a physical organization."[105] In some sense, rulers just had to get out of the way and allow the collective body, the economy, to function on its own. According to Quesnay and Mirabeau, the other primary tasks of a ruler were minimal. The most general and important task was to ensure that the "positive laws" (actually existing, written laws) were in accordance with the immutable and immortal "natural laws." In addition to this, the most important tasks of rulers were to collect taxes, preferably in the form of a single land tax since the physiocrats believed that the land was the only true source of wealth, and punishing those who transgressed the natural laws and interfered with the "natural" functioning of the economy.

Quesnay and Mirabeau were not the only physiocrats to directly invoke theories of organization in their political economic works. In addition to presenting a new vision of the economy as an organized whole, a number of physiocrats argued that the social body and the body politic each must be organized and animated. This was particularly true of those physiocrats who wrote about the importance of provincial assemblies, including Mirabeau, Dupont, and Guillaume-François Le Trosne.[106] In the famous memoir on municipalities that he drafted as the personal secretary of the reformist comptroller-general Anne-Robert-Jacques Turgot, Dupont wrote that France at the time was "a society composed of different orders, poorly united."[107] The French made up "a people with few social ties between its members."[108] At the root of the problems was the fact that the nation lacked a constitution and that the king often had to act through particular acts of will instead of through general laws. But, Dupont argued, addressing the king, "if the integral parts of Your empire had a regular organization and known relations," then "You might govern, like God, through general laws."[109] That is, if the political body were organized properly, the king would not need to intervene extensively in its functioning. Any intervention would only be in order to return the proper balance to the parts and allow the organized body to function as it should in a healthy state.

When Le Trosne wrote in the 1770s about the need to reorganize the political structures of the Old Regime so as to transform the collective body of the people into a truly living and united nation, it was also the vitalist and relational language of organization to which he turned. "The whole Nation," Le Trosne wrote, "which today seems deprived of life and action, having only a type of passive existence, must become animated and organized in all its part in order to form a true social body."[110] Le Trosne also wrote of animating and organizing the political body, pointing to the crucial role that provincial assemblies could play in transforming "the nation" from "nothing" into "a true living and organized political body."[111] This emphasis on the animated and organized collective forms of existence as more "true" or "real," and certainly preferable, can be found throughout Le Trosne's political economic writing. Elsewhere for example, he made similar vitalist comments about the body politic, claiming that the political existence of the nation must be "a real civil body, endowed with life, movement, and action," demonstrating "a common will."[112] While the physiocrats provided important arguments of political and social organization, the most brilliant, developed, and significant articulator of a political theory of organization in the eighteenth century was certainly Jean-Jacques Rousseau.

One of Rousseau's most important conceptual contributions to political thought was his reformulation of the ancient analogy between the body politic and the human body. Rousseau was the first to demonstrate how the body politic could be made into an organized body (in the sense that this term took in the second half of the century), though he obscured this feature of his political thought, keeping it from being recognized by scholars until recently. David Bates has analyzed the role of the physiological ideas of the nervous system and the common sensorium in Rousseau's political thought, and while I agree with many of Bate's insights, I believe Rousseau worked with the more general concept of the organized body as his model for the body politic.[113] Rousseau used many of the ideas and terms of organization theory, though he choose to refrain from specifically writing of "organization" and "organized bodies" in his most important and developed political treatise, *The Social Contract, or Principles of Politic Right* (*Du contrat social, ou Principes du droit politique*).[114] Nonetheless, these concepts were central to his political theory, and there is ample evidence of them throughout his wide-ranging writings. Though Rousseau did not share some of the philosophical and scientific commitments of the primary theorists of organization in the middle of the century, he did share their ideas about the fundamental properties of organized bodies.[115] Interpreting *The Social Contract* through this fact provides a new understanding of Rousseau's "organicism" and helps realign larger narratives about the development of organic thought in modern political theory. In contrast to earlier accounts that analyzed organic metaphors in *The Social Contract* as a sign of a quasi-totalitarian "extreme collectivism" in which collective life subsumed, absorbed, or determined the life of individuals, a proper understanding of eighteenth-century ideas of organization reveals that Rousseau attempted to envision a body politic that had true unity and existed as a single collective individual while still allowing constituent individuals to retain a form of particular life and a type of relative autonomy that can be characterized as freedom in association.[116] In short, Rousseau employed the unique mereology of organization in an attempt to demonstrate that the body politic could exist as a single living organized body made up of vital parts that contributed to the collective life while they retained their own individual properties, functions, and partial life. The body politic of *The*

Social Contract was an attempt to conceive a relational form of collective existence in which neither the parts nor the whole subsumed or determined the other, but instead, existed in a state of organic unity, interconnection, and interdependence.

Rousseau first wrote about the body politic as an organized body in a long essay on political economy that was published in the *Encyclopédie* in 1755.[117] While drawing readers' attention to the fact that the comparison was "in some respects inexact," Rousseau wrote, "the body politic, taken individually, may be considered as an organized, living body resembling that of man."[118] He then described a body politic where the parts were not envisioned as individuals, but as various social, administrative, and economic elements, for instance, as judges, magistrates, laws, agriculture, industry, and citizens, all of which were united by the sovereign as the head. This image fundamentally conforms to the traditional body politic metaphors reaching back through the early modern era to medieval articulations, such as that of John of Salisbury, which analogized elements of the state and society with organs of the body.[119] While Rousseau did not yet fundamentally change the metaphor, as he would in *The Social Contract* when he asserted that individuals were the parts that composed the body politic (as opposed to groups, orders, estates, or institutions), he began to ascribe some of the properties of the organized bodies, claiming the body politic was possessed of a "general will" and a "reciprocal sensibility and internal correspondence of all parts."[120]

In *The Social Contract*, Rousseau made it clear that he was deeply unsatisfied with previous theoretical accounts of how the body politic was formed. The transition from a disassociated collection of individual parts, which Rousseau called an "aggregation," to a truly unified and living whole, which he called an "association," was central to his concerns. He criticized previous political theorists for creating systems that first analytically dismembered the body politic and then employed conjuring tricks to supposedly recompose the parts as a single, living body. The sleight of hand made these theorists like the "charlatans of Japan" who were said to dismember a child, throw the parts into the air one by one, until, finally, the child fell back to earth "alive and whole."[121] For Rousseau, creating a truly living and animated body politic was a mysterious thing, but it was not magic. It did not require conjuring tricks, nor sleight of hand. The atomistic mechanical explanations of the social contract, such as that of Thomas Hobbes, were inadequate to explain how a living body politic could be formed. Rousseau attempted to show that there were naturalistic means of explaining and facilitating the transition from aggregation to association, from the will of all to the general will. The model of the organized body provided Rousseau a natural model for understanding and explaining the formation of the body politic.

Determining the precise genealogy of organizational thought in Rousseau is difficult, but it is clear that he had numerous social and intellectual connections to the theorists of organization. He was a close friend of Diderot (for a period), a great admirer of Buffon, a student of the chemist Guillaume-François Rouelle, and a personal acquaintance and admirer of the Montpellier vitalist Gabriel-François Venel, and shortly after *The Social Contract* he was an enthusiastic reader of the botanical writing of the Montpellier vitalist physician Boissier de Sauvages.[122] Rousseau also had many encounters with Montpellier physicians throughout his life.[123] By the time he began writing about the body politic as an organized body in the 1750s, he had already studied chemistry and written a book-length introductory work on the subject. Rousseau also brought an engagement with questions of aesthetic holism to his thinking about organized bodies. As the composer of several operas, the creator of a system of music notation, and an author of numerous reference works on music composition, Rousseau was deeply embedded in both the practical and the theoretical questions of aesthetic unity in music.[124] In his writing about harmony and the "unity of melody," for example, Rousseau was concerned with how a composition could create a complex relationship between various parts that would result in the parts maintaining their distinctiveness while working together as a single whole, producing neither a jumble of simultaneous "songs" nor dull unison.[125] Rousseau emphasized that, based on certain principles of harmony, a type of aesthetic unity-in-multiplicity could be achieved whereby each of the numerous parts within a composition "seems to have its own Song" while one hears "only one and the same Song."[126] The individual songs and the unified song exist together, without enfolding or smothering each other, but rather animating and energizing one another, making a whole that is greater than the sum of its parts.

In addition to his musical interest, we can also understand Rousseau's ideas about unity, collectivity, and the general will in light of the relationship scholars have pointed out between Rousseau's ideas and the concept of the divine "general will" as it was articulated in seventeenth-century Augustinian theology, as well as the ideas about ecstatic self-abandon and unity with the divine as expressed in the mystical religious thinking of quietists such as Jeanne-Marie Guyon and François de Fénélon.[127] Rousseau's interest in issues of aesthetic holism, theological ideas of generality, and mystical ideas of unity through self-abandon were presumably important elements of a holist disposition of thought that probably coalesced with the relational holism of theories of organization that Rousseau would have encountered through Diderot, Rouelle, and Buffon. In *Chemical Institutions* (*Institutions chimiques*), the book on chemistry that Rousseau wrote in the late 1740s but that remained unpublished during his lifetime, he argued that mechanical philosophy was not adequate to explain the construction of an organized body.[128] Echoing many eighteenth-century chemists, Rousseau argued that chemistry was a distinct discipline dedicated to explaining "the composition of bodies," "the development of organized bodies," and "the construction of an organized body."[129]

Rousseau wrote about organized bodies in various works throughout his life, often emphasizing the special unity that characterized them in ways similar to how he emphasized the unity that characterized his vision of the body politic. For example, by writing of organized bodies as being "rigorously one," Rousseau drew attention to the difference between an aggregate and an association, that is, between a mere combination of disunited parts and an association of living parts forming a truly unified whole.[130] Once the theory of organization is taken into account, the apparent redundancy of qualifying "one" with "rigorously" appears as a meaningful distinction between different types of collective objects. In a fragment written after *The Social Contract*, when Rousseau became increasingly absorbed in botany, he again expressed some of the specific properties of organized bodies. Contrasting the study of living flowers to dead, dried samples, Rousseau claimed, "to the eyes of the botanist, vegetables are organized beings, [and] as soon as the vegetable is dead and ceases to vegetate, its parts no longer have the mutual correspondence that enables it to live and that makes it one; it is no longer in the realm of the botanist; it is a simple substance, matter, an element, dead earth, which no longer belongs to the vegetable kingdom but to the mineral."[131]

Rousseau's writing about organized bodies, and their correspondence to his writing about the body politic in *The Social Contract*, helps explain some of the more enigmatic ideas and descriptions in the latter work. For example, understanding the body politic as a form of organized body helps explain the double aspect of the body politic, as well as the double aspect that each individual member of the body politic had. By saying that the body is called sovereign when active and state when passive, while individual members of the body are called citizen when active and subject when passive, Rousseau expressed the circular causation of an organized body in which the whole is both cause and effect of itself, with each part also being both cause and effect.[132] This double aspect can also be seen in the act of association in which "each individual, one might say, contracts with himself, and is bound in a double relation" since he is both a citizen/subject and an indissoluble part of the sovereign/state.[133] Keeping in mind the relations between parts and the whole in an organized body helps us understand how Rousseau conceived of the act of association being a "total alienation of each associate, together with all his rights, to the whole community."[134] The fact that the parts of an organized body maintain their "particular life" while contributing to the life of the whole helps make sense of Rousseau's claim that "each person, in giving himself to all, gives himself to nobody, and as there is no associate over which he does not acquire the same right as he yields to others over himself, one gains an equivalent of all that one looses, and gains greater force for conserving what one has."[135]

In *Émile*, published in the same year as *The Social Contract*, Rousseau gave a similar account of the relative and partial existence that an individual gains through becoming part of a truly unified whole. In contrast to people living in society, "natural man is entirely for himself: he is numerical unity, the absolute whole that has a relation only to itself or its kind."[136] Once people enter society, they become "civil man" with "only a fractional unity dependent on the denominator, and whose value is in his relation to the whole, which is the social body."[137] Rather than being a problem, this "fractional unity," somewhat like "particular life" within an organized body, is a new communal existence that creates new opportunities for sympathetic feeling and consideration for others. Rousseau claimed that "good social institutions are those that know how to denature man the best, to take his absolute existence from him in order to give him a relative one and transport the *I* into the common unity, with the result that each individual believes himself no longer one but a part of the unity and is no longer sensible except within the whole."[138]

Rousseau was famously critical of the effects of civilization and the supposed transition from the isolated and happy existence of humans in a state of nature to denatured life in society. Yet he also wrote that "our sweetest existence is relative and collective and our true *self* is not entirely our own."[139] Once humans had emerged from the state of nature, if they ever actually lived in such a conjectural past, it was important to organize the social and political body well in order to ensure individual and collective happiness. In his first draft of *The Social Contract*, Rousseau highlighted the unpleasant state of living in a form of collective aggregation, as opposed to the true wholeness and happiness of association. People living in an aggregation would have no true connections (*liaisons*) and, therefore, would have little communication with others and would think only of themselves. In a distinction similar to the one Diderot made between the swarm of bees moving from a state of physical contiguity to one of organic continuity, Rousseau argued that in a state of aggregation, people would merely make contact "without becoming united." This would be an unhappy condition in which people lived together, yet alone. They would be "isolated among others," Rousseau wrote.[140]

An association, on the other hand, would result in a collective "public felicity" that was greater than the sum of the happiness of individuals. Rousseau argued that a true association did not yet exist in actuality, only in the work of philosophers, but if a true association existed it would be a collective being with its own special qualities.[141] To described how the whole could have properties that would be greater than the sum of its parts, and in fact have qualities that were different from those of any individual part, Rousseau resorted to the composition of organized bodies in chemistry. The new type of collective being that Rousseau envisioned would, as he argued, have "its own qualities distinct from those of the particular beings who constitute it, in the same way that chemical compounds have properties that they do not obtain from any of the components that constitute them."[142] In this analogy, we can see Rousseau directly drawing on the relational holism of organization theory to explain the ontology of the body politic he envisioned. In this passage, Rousseau also characterized good and evil in the terms of relational ontology, claiming that public good and evil would not exist in the individuals, instead that "it would reside in the liaisons that unite them."[143] This relational ontology might provide a way to understand the classically enigmatic "general will" in *The Social Contract*. The general will might best be thought of as an emergent property, developing when the aggregation becomes an association, that is, emerging only once relations are established between people with particular wills.

Rousseau used the relationship between the parts and the whole in organized bodies as a model for theorizing the formation of the body politic and the properties that emerged along with the whole. He also used it as a way to envision maintaining individual liberty in communal life, creating an entangled political ontology in which neither individualism nor collectivism reigned. In this form of political life, people lived in double relations. They were both distinct individuals with relative independence and indissoluble parts of the whole. One of the interesting signs of the harmony between Rousseau's conception of the organized body politic and physiological idea of organized bodies was that some of the later generation of Enlightenment organization theorists gave descriptions of organized human bodies that had a new inflection of Rousseau. In fact, Charles-Louis Dumas, the *médecin-philosophe* who coined the term "vitalism" in 1800 in his attempt to consolidate and defend the Montpellier school, gave the key Montpellier concept of "particular life" a Rousseauist sense of communal alienation and self-abandon, in effect, merging Bordeu's idea of "particular life" and Rousseau's idea of the partial life and relative autonomy of individuals in a true political "association."[144] Sounding more like Rousseau than like Bordeu, Dumas wrote that in the human body, "each element loses its own life in order to live with the whole and contribute . . . to support the total life."[145] One of the ironies of this Rousseauist vitalism articulated by Dumas is that no part of the human body actually loses its life to be a part of the whole. Rather, like Rousseau's subject-citizen, it loses a portion of its autonomy and enters a state of collective existence characterized by partial life and "relative existence."

Although the nineteenth and twentieth centuries have rightly been characterized as "an age of organization" in political and social thought, the term "organization" was used in a political sense only after the physiological sense of the term was well established.[146] The 1762 edition of the *Dictionaire de l'Académie française*, for example, defined organization only as "the manner in which a body is organized," giving the example of the phrase, "the organization of the human body."[147] In a volume of the *Encyclopédie* published in 1765, the term is defined in a similar manner, as the "arrangement of parts that constitute animated bodies."[148] The political sense of the term began to appear in dictionaries and encyclopedias only after this basic physiological sense had appeared. In the *Dictionaire de l'Académie française*, for example, it was only by the fifth edition of 1798 that the dictionary mentioned that one could figuratively say "*the organization of the body politic* to signify the constitution of a State."[149] The popularity of the political sense of the term occurred so quickly and became so associated with the revolutionary reorganization of society and state that in 1798, the same year that the French Academy first included the political use of organization in its dictionary, the freethinking Welshman David Williams, a theorist of political organization, a close reader of Rousseau, and a disillusioned supporter of the French Revolution, claimed that since the outbreak of the Revolution, "Europe has been sickened with the words *organizing* and *organization*."[150] The words had become so ubiquitous, and had been attached to such calamities, in the estimations of some, that Williams could claim a common fatigue or dissatisfaction with them. Yet Williams did not give up on the terms, nor did he give up on making Enlightenment theories of organized bodies useful to political reformers. In fact, his own political writing became even more focused on organization and the conceptualization of the political body as a kind of organized body.[151] He, like a number of others throughout the nineteenth century, continued to pursue a political physiology—a biopolitics—based on the Enlightenment theory of organization.

Enlightenment visions of social and political order that built on ideas of the organization of nature and properties of organized bodies were important in the development of biopolitics because they created a new way of thinking about individuals and collectives, as well as about the *relationship* between individuals and collectives. Through the relational holism of organization theory, individual bodies and collective bodies were linked in new ways as parts of a hierarchy of levels of life in the scale of organized being. This created a new sense of the causal connections between individuals and collective bodies, whether the collective body of the species or the collective body of a particular population. The organization of the whole was built on, and in ways dependent on, the organization of the integral parts. Since it was composed of individual organized bodies, a collective body like the "population" was dependent for its existence and its functioning on the organization of individual organized bodies. If individual human bodies were not constructed well or not functioning in a proper "healthy" manner, the collective body would be affected.

Just like an individual body could be thrown into ill health through inflammation of an organ, the collective body could be significantly affected by an organizational problem in one of the constituent parts. Thinking of collective bodies as if they were interconnected wholes, locked in complex and close relations of cause and effect with their constituent parts, created the possibility that a small number of diseased, unhealthy, or weak individuals could cause a general state of disease or ill health in the collective body. Conversely, relatively small "improvements" of individual bodies could have wide-reaching effects, transforming the organization, vitality, and health of a collective body. Furthermore, it was not only the organization of individual parts that affected the whole, but also the organization of the whole that affected the parts. Causation could, in a sense, move both up and down the scale of organized bodies, from the general to the particular and from the particular to the general. Theorists and statesmen, therefore, needed to be concerned with the organization of each individual body as well as the overall structure and function of the collective body. If the parts were not brought together properly, or not allowed to communicate in the right way, the collective body could be imperiled, no matter how well organized the individual bodies were.

While discourses employing sociobiological ideas and metaphors of pathology and improvement existed in various forms before organization theory, they gained a new naturalistic foundation that many people in the late eighteenth century found compelling.[152] In fact, enough people found organization theory compelling that it became the foundation for many of the proposed Enlightenment plans of biopolitical improvement. It also played an important role in a number of new conceptualizations of society, the economy, the human species, and the body politic that later biopolitical programs of organic transformation were built on. In fact, the concept of organization and its eventual transformation into the concept of organism was central to European social and political thought of the nineteenth century.[153] It has not been widely noticed, however, that this concept did not originate in the philosophy or the aesthetic sensibility of Romanticism, nor did it emerge from a rupture in "the classical episteme" around 1800 that Foucault argued was a necessary condition that made modern biological thought conceptually possible.[154] The concept of organization emerged out of the Enlightenment body of theory that took shape in a number of fields of thought and coalesced in ideas about life and organized bodies, providing biopolitics with one of its foundations.

CHAPTER TWO

Enlightenment Eugenics

In the late 1770s, the French writer Jean-Baptiste-René Robinet turned from publishing two successful multivolume philosophical books about nature and the scale of organized being to other, even grander, publishing ventures. Robinet had become relatively well established within the republic of letters for his books *On Nature* (*De la nature*) and *Philosophical Considerations of the Natural Gradation of Forms of Being* (*Considérations philosophiques de la gradation naturelle des formes de l'être*), which daringly reimagined and expanded on many of the most important ideas about organization, generation, and the great chain of being.[1] After the success of these books, he collaborated with the famous publisher Charles-Joseph Panckoucke, taking on several large editorial projects, including the supplemental volumes to Diderot's *Encyclopédie*. He also turned his attention to politics at the time of the American War of Independence. He helped edit a fifteen-volume account of the relationship between England and America and then undertook a thirty-volume work published shortly after the fall of Turgot that attempted to compile everything that future enlightened statesmen would need to know in order to achieve the reforms that Turgot was unable to see through in his brief term as the chief financial minister, the comptroller-general. The possibility that a minister like Turgot could bring about enlightened reform of the administration was one of the great hopes of the philosophes, and Robinet set out to prepare future enlightened ministers. Included in his "universal dictionary" for statesmen was an article on the causes of the degradation of the human species. "Unfortunately the species of men is totally neglected, at least in Europe," wrote the anonymous author, possibly Robinet. "No law, no administrative measures among us have yet favored or encouraged the means of making [men] better built, larger, and more robust."[2] The author invoked the example of animal breeding, arguing that if people could improve horses and sheep through careful breeding, something could be done to improve the human species. This rhetorical move from animal breeding to human improvement was not new. In fact, it can be found in texts from antiquity and early modern Europe, such as Plato's *Republic* and Tommaso Campanella's *The City of the Sun* (1623).[3] What was new in Robinet's publication was that the call to physically improve human beings was included in a work aimed at would-be enlightened men of state. In the language of the article, countering degeneration and improving bodies should be a matter of "law" and "administration." Furthermore, the improvement of humans was presented as a practical and realizable goal, rather than an element of a utopian vision intended primarily to stimulate and provoke, as it was in writing before the eighteenth century. Finally, the author presented the means of improvement as essential knowledge for the statesmen. By the time Robinet's book appeared in 1781, the physical improvement of human bodies was a scientific possibility, and it could be a political issue, not merely a rhetorical gesture. Though the author did not directly say that human beings should be bred like animals, a number of naturalists and physicians opened up and popularized this possibility in the decades before this article appeared.

This chapter analyzes suggestions for human breeding in the second half of the eighteenth century, while also analyzing the scientific ideas on which these suggestions rested. I argue that animal breeding was the fundamental model for developing eugenic ideas about breeding humans. It was also the primary realm of inquiry in which naturalists and philosophers working in the life sciences developed the set of concepts, hypothesis, empirical examples, modes of inquiry, and explanatory strategies on which ideas of human breeding were built in the second half of the eighteenth century. This work on animal breeding revealed two things that were very important to the development and deployment of ideas of human breeding. The first was that the transformative effects of climate on animal bodies could be compounded and accelerated through sexual reproduction. The second was that humans might be able to control this process through the systematic selection of mates. When these two realizations were extended to humans—as they often were—they revealed the radical malleability of human bodies across generations. These developments came out of the work being done by a group of French savants organized around the central figure of Buffon. In addition to revolutionizing natural history and transforming it into a new science focused on nature as a dynamic and historical whole, Buffon and his collaborators and successors transformed the understanding of the human ability to control nature and remake living beings through reproduction. Theories of climate were important and widespread in eighteenth-century social, political, legal, and scientific discourses as it was widely believed that climate could affect the moral as well as the physical characteristics of human bodies—particularly over the course of generations. It was also widely believed that such changes were part of natural processes largely occurring beyond the reach of human agency.[4] By pushing beyond basic climate theory and showing that human intervention through selective breeding could accelerate, retard, or even reverse the influence of climate, Buffon and his peers radicalized the understanding of human malleability.[5]

These observations about the radical malleability of human bodies were picked up and developed by a number of naturalists, physicians, and philosophers attempting to counteract what they perceived to be the widespread degeneration of humans, in terms of both the quality of individual bodies and the quality and quantity of the population. To contemporaries in midcentury France, the problem of degeneration seemed particularly acute. To contemporaries in the colonies, colonial administrators in the metropole, and those who had scientific interests in the human variation, the problem of degeneration often took on racial dimensions and raised questions about the degenerative effects of the *mélange* or *croisement des races* (the reproductive mixture of people who were thought to be of different races). These concerns about the colonies and race often folded back into debates about how human bodies could be improved. New ideas about human breeding arose in the metropole from these scientific, intellectual, and social contexts in the 1750s and 1760s, finding their fullest articulation in Charles-Augustin Vandermonde's two-volume *Essay on the Manner of Improving the Human Species* (*Essai sur la manière de perfectionner l'espèce humaine*). Vandermonde turned to animal breeding as a model for human improvement: "Since we have succeeded in improving the race of horses, dogs, cats, chickens, pigeons, and canaries, why should we not make any attempt on the human species?"[6] In Vandermonde's *Essay*, this was not a rhetorical question, nor a vague and implicit suggestion that more attention should be paid to human improvement. Vandermonde argued that humans should be bred on the model of animals and that there were a number of guidelines that could be followed so as to improve people through directed breeding.

Vandermonde consolidated the conceptual and empirical developments of the Buffonian revolution, built on the new conditions of possibility established by Buffonian natural history, and applied its insights to the improvement of humans. Vandermonde developed an approach to the eugenic breeding of humans that built on ideas of crossbreeding and a more particular vision that employed particular criterion of to select potential partners whose reproduction would result in specific goals. Some of these goals were aesthetic (beauty), some of them were taken as general markers of health (size, strength, and robustness), and some of them were capacities or traits that related to ability (such as singing or dancing well). These achievements of Vandermonde were not lost on his contemporaries. The *Essay* was reviewed widely in the periodical press, and subsequent theorists of biopolitics acknowledged his work, including Abbé Henri Grégoire, Abbé Sieyès, and Joachim Faiguet de Villeneuve. After analyzing Vandermonde's *Essay*, I look at ideas about human breeding articulated by Faiguet de Villeneuve, Antoine Le Camus, and Maupertuis, before briefly touching on the more playful and ambiguous employment of eugenic ideas about human breeding in the fiction of Diderot and Restif de la Bretonne. I conclude the chapter with an analysis of subsequent developments in the anglophone Atlantic, exemplified by the writing of the Scottish physician John Gregory and the American professor Samuel Stanhope Smith. I show how these later examples from the anglophone Atlantic built on a similar foundation of Buffonian ideas, though they developed in different contexts with different aims.

The controlled propagation of animals had been practiced since antiquity, and in early modern Europe and the Americas it was practiced both by agriculturalists and by breeders of pets. By the middle of the eighteenth century, however, selective breeding was only beginning to be undertaken and observed in a systematic manner that aimed to integrate theory and practice. This occurred primarily among savants such as Buffon, his friend and scientific colleague Maupertuis, and the famed and influential naturalist René-Antoine Ferchault de Réaumur, who were attempting to understand the mechanisms that could account for the apparent heritability of certain physical characteristics.[7] Maupertuis played a vital role in initiating this new line of inquiry, but Buffon was the most noteworthy of the savants.[8] This followed from the manner in which he situated questions of animal breeding as the nexus in a sprawling network of interrelated epistemological questions, theoretical claims, and empirical investigations that included his attempt to reconceptualize species; his emphasis on the criterion of interfertility for empirically determining species; his use of a theory of epigenetic generation to build an innovative secular monogenetic theory of race, asserting that all peoples were of one species and one common origin; his conviction that crossing varieties within a species "ennobled" the species; and his integration of the results of breeding experiments and microscopic investigations with his innovative theories of generation and variation within species. His importance and reputation as a natural historian (rivaled only by the Swedish naturalist Carl Linnaeus) and the fact that his *Natural History* was one of the most popular and best-known works of the French Enlightenment, combined with his unprecedented integration of theory and practice to give his work an unapparelled position in the naturalistic discourse of animal improvement and the nascent biopolitical discourse of human improvement.[9]

One of the single most important conceptual innovations of Buffon was his creation of a theory of generation that provided a naturalistic account of reproduction. In fact, Buffon was the first to introduce the term "reproduction" into the life sciences, and he fashioned it into an account of how the bodily organization of each parent was combined and reproduced in the body of offspring. Although the mechanisms that Buffon theorized to account for reproduction—the "organic molecules" and "internal mold"— were difficult to grasp and they proved controversial, Buffon's transformation of a theory of generation into the concept of biological reproduction had a profound impact.[10] The theory of "organic molecules" was more widely embraced than the "internal mold," but it is an interesting historical case in which many people who openly doubted key elements of a scientific theory nonetheless ended up accepting and building on much of the conceptual architecture and the new possibilities that the theory created. The implications and possibilities opened up by Buffon in this regard were summarized well by Jacques Roger: "Buffon's theory allowed the problem of 'animal generation' to escape from the impasse where it had been stuck, by giving a natural and physical origin to the order of living beings. This order no longer had to come directly from divine creation, nor was it imposed on matter by some mysterious power: it came directly from the organization of the parents, who 'reproduced themselves' in the embryo. By thus introducing the new concept of 'reproduction,' Buffon changed the meaning of the phenomenon. He also made many other new ideas possible, which he either developed himself or left to others."[11] Organization took on a new importance through this theory, since it was the organization of the parents' bodies—which included any changes that occurred to the organization of the bodies before reproduction—that combined to constitute the offspring. This made the inheritance of acquired characteristics theoretically possible and explicable, which in turn gave a new importance to animal breeding. Experiments in breeding then became a means to develop knowledge of how to transform organized bodies, in addition to being an empirical inquiry into the boundaries of species.

Buffon conducted and documented an extensive array of breeding experiments from the late 1740s until his death in 1788.[12] Discussions of interbreeding appeared from the first volumes of *Natural History*, and archival manuscripts show that Buffon and his assistants carried out breeding experiments on Buffon's estate at Montbard.[13] He also provided the most-developed and most-sustained arguments for how and why humans could and should "change, modify, and improve species with time."[14] He lent scientific authority to the long-held view that because of nature's tendency toward balance, the crossing of different varieties of the same species would produce "improved" individuals, since some of the faults of the parents would cancel each other out in the offspring.[15] Importantly, however, Buffon added to the belief in the benefits of crossbreeding the idea that humans could control the specific characteristics that would result. Through the judicious selection of mates, an entire population, such as all the sheep in France, could be bred so as to produce certain characteristics, such as greater height and strength and extremely fine and bountiful wool.[16] In fact, Buffon argued that it was possible to selectively breed animals so as to bring about combinations of traits that had never previously existed, hence, altering populations in novel ways. Given these new possibilities of alteration, Buffon hoped that humans might transform domestic animals as dramatically as they had when they "transformed a sterile grass into wheat."[17]

Buffon developed his ideas primarily in his works on animals and animal generation, but he also addressed them directly in his writing about the "races" of the human species. For example, he suggested one of the most infamous human experiments of the Enlightenment, hoping to shed light on the effects of climate on human variation over an extended period of time. Climate, Buffon claimed, produced changes in humans so slowly and gradually that it was only over long periods that the differences became recognizable; thus it would probably take "a great number of centuries" for people with black skin to become completely white "through the influence of climate alone."[18] Buffon argued that the only way to find out how long it would take for climate alone to "reintegrate" the races of the human species into their original form (which at that time he believed to be blond-haired, blue-eyed people with white skin) would be to take people from somewhere like Senegal and move them to a place such as Denmark, where they would be isolated and not permitted to reproduce with the Danes.[19]

In contrast to the slow effects of climate, Buffon argued that the "mixing of races" could bring about changes "more quickly" than climate alone. In fact, it was only through sexual reproduction that changes to human and animal forms could be effected quickly and that they could be passed on to future generations, accumulating into dramatic transformations. Through sexual reproduction, Buffon argued, black skin could be changed to white in only four generations.[20] In theory, roughly half a century of racial mixing could bring about changes that would take centuries for climate alone to do. While climate was the initial cause of the alteration of human bodies (and therefore of variation within the human species), once these transformations had been realized, he believe that they could be manipulated to produce new combinations of characteristics. Despite the directness of

Buffon's statement, even some of the best accounts of his ideas of degeneration and race overlook or ignore this dimension of his writing.[21] Buffon may have even put these ideas into practice through his involvement arranging marriages. The editor of Buffon's published correspondence, his great-nephew Henri Nadault de Buffon, claimed that Buffon was "the greatest matchmaker of his time" (*le plus grand marieur de son temps*).[22] No details about Buffon's matchmaking were provided, so it is impossible to know whether he employed physical criteria in his process of selecting suitable mates or whether his matchmaking had any relationship to his ideas of animal improvement. There were, however, places in his published work in which he drew together the issues of animal breeding and human variations. In his writing on the human species in the third volume of *Natural History*, for example, right before observing the necessity of crossbreeding horses, Buffon discussed the appearance and physical makeup of French peasants, differentiating between poorer and better-off villages and between people who live at high elevation and those who lived in valleys.[23]

Buffon's ideas about animal breeding were quickly taken up and popularized by his contemporaries in works of natural history, as well as in a new wave of publications aimed at informing agriculturalists of these new ideas and implementing them in actual breeding practices.[24] At times in the second half of the eighteenth century, Buffon's ideas about the improvement of animals were also translated by savants into particular projects of improvement that attempted to practically realize the theoretical potential for improvement. A noteworthy example of the Buffonian approach to the improvement of species arose when the French state enlisted Buffon's longtime collaborator Louis-Jean-Marie Daubenton to lead a state-sponsored project to improve the quality of French wool.[25] Daubenton established an experimental farm in 1766 to improve this important commodity. Over the course of a decade, Daubenton carried out experiments with sheep that included altering many factors of their environment such as diet, temperature, and shelter.[26] He also imported varieties from all over the world in an attempt to crossbreed them to produce the best possible wool. In addition to the many memoirs he presented and published, his work culminated in the popular *Instruction pour les bergers et pour les propriétaires de troupeaux* (1782), which in various editions and abridgements circulated widely.[27]

Daubenton's experiments fulfilled some of Buffon's early observations about crossbreeding. "It seems that the model of beauty and good is dispersed over all the earth," Buffon wrote; "in each climate there resides a portion that always degenerates unless it is reunited with another portion taken from far away." A type of general mixing and crossbreeding was then needed to revive and improve the quality of domestic animal species. "To have beautiful horses and good dogs," Buffon observed, "foreign males must be given to our females and reciprocally foreign females must be given to our males." This was because "in mixing contrary races, and above all in renewing them often with foreign races, the form seems to improve itself and Nature revives herself in order to produce all that she might of the best."[28] In addition to confirming some of Buffon's observations about crossbreeding, Daubenton's experiments demonstrated that a general project of crossbreeding could lead to the improvement of specific traits, such as the quality of wool, as Buffon had suggested. The experiments also demonstrated that improvements could be made quickly, in a generation or two. This was recognized by metropolitan observers such as the comte d'Angevillier, as well as colonial administrators such as Gabriel de Bory, who argued that Daubenton's animal breeding experiments provided a model for carrying out a project of selective breeding that could racial re-engineer the sugar colonies, as I demonstrate in the following chapter.[29]

While the possibility of rapid transformation within a few generations, as discussed by Buffon and reinforced by Daubenton's experiments, presented great potential for improvement, it also posed a great danger of decline. Numerous people saw that this was as true of human bodies as it was of animal bodies. It meant that bodies could be improved, but if the proper attention was not given to ensuring this, a whole population could be ruined within a few generations. The physical transformation of the bodies of individuals composing populations became something that had to be actively resisted through discrete practices, and it also became something that could be exploited by administrators. This specter of corporal instability was particularly apparent in considerations of human variation in the second half of the eighteenth century. Repeatedly, naturalists as well as political economists, government administrators, and colonial commentators raised fears about the rapid transformations that could occur through intermarriage between people of European, African, and Native American descent. It was a widespread belief that the characteristics distinctive to each group could be effaced through the *mélange* (mixing) or *croisement des races* (crossing of the races) within four or five generations, possibly fewer. This concern could be found in the prominent writing of Buffon and the Dutch naturalist Cornelius De Pauw, who took up many of the questions Buffon raised about degeneration in the New World.[30] These concerns also found expression in the *Encyclopédie* and numerous popular works by people engaged with colonial questions such as Abbé Raynal, Hilliard d'Auberteuil, and Moreau de Saint-Méry.

Some, like Jean-Baptiste-Christophe Fusée Aublet, a French naturalist trained at the Jardin de Roi, believed that the transformation could be very rapid, occurring within fewer than four generations.[31] Fusée Aublet maintained intellectual and social connections with figures in Paris, including philosophes at the salon of Baron d'Holbach and naturalists at the Jardin de Roi, such as Buffon and Bernard Jussieu.[32] As a botanist, Fusée Aublet traveled to the Isle de France in the Indian Ocean in the 1750s as an employee of the Compagnie des Indes, before traveling to Guiana in the 1760s and briefly to Saint Domingue. In 1760, he became the enslaver of a woman named Armelle, with whom he had three children and whom he eventually married in 1775 when he became dangerously ill.[33] Based on his experience in various colonies, his study of the mélange of people of European and African descent in Guiana, and presumably the consideration of his own children, he claimed that when a mulatto and a white person had a child, though the skin was not yet white, "the traits and the hair are totally European." If this offspring in turn had a child with a white mate, the child was "a true White that has lost all resemblance with the Black." Furthermore, Fusée Aublet believed that "if, in these different marriages, the man is always of the white race and the woman is always of the black race, the change is quicker."[34] In Fusée Aublet's account, two or three generations were all it took for the appearance of racial difference to be completely eliminated. This type of specter of rapid transformation hung over much of the theory and practice of colonial biopolitics, and, as we will see with the creation of regulations to control the population of African descent in metropolitan France in the late 1770s, this specter also figured prominently in the formation of metropolitan biopolitical programs.

One reason why the Buffonian approach to corporal instability and its dual emphasis on degeneration and decline made such an impact in the period between the publication of the first volumes of the *Natural History* in 1749 and the 1770s was that it resonated with more general fears of degeneration and the hope for a means of recuperation and improvement. Although decline and degeneration were ancient concerns repeated in time-tested tropes, concerns with decline reached a critical mass in France in the period from the 1740s through 1760s as signs of decay and exhaustion seemed to appear in numerous realms of French life. In the 1750s there was great political, social, and religious instability: the monarchy was involved in prolonged clashes with the Paris Parlement and with the religious sect known as the Jansenists; a politically complicated regicide was attempted (the Damiens affair); a reversal of international diplomatic alliances occurred (the so-called Diplomatic Revolution); an expensive war fought across several continents and oceans (the Seven Years' War) resulted in defeat, and this not long after defeat in the Austrian War of Succession; a financial crisis developed, resulting largely from these wars; and censorship and suppression of radical works such as Claude-Andre Helvétius's *De l'esprit* (suppressed in 1758) and Diderot and d'Alembert's *Encyclopédie* (suppressed in 1759) increased.[35] The uneasiness generated by this widespread instability could be seen in the monarchical administration itself, where the crucial position of the comptroller-general, the most influential economic administrator in the government, changed five times between 1754 and 1759.[36] People also became widely concerned with the supposedly plummeting size of the metropolitan population; the apparently lagging agricultural productivity and its troubling effects on an economy buckling under military expenditures and war debts; the weakening vigor and virtue of the nobility; the diminishing clarity and precision of the French language; a proliferation of libertinage and a general moral erosion; and even signs that people's bodies were shrinking and becoming weaker with each generation.[37] Many French elites felt that wherever they turned there were signs of stagnation, if not terrible decline. Rousseau's first and second discourses criticizing the deleterious effects of civilization were some of the most popular and best remembered articulations of the concern with humanity's role in contributing to its own degeneration, but these concerns went far beyond Rousseau's powerful polemics.[38]

In light of this general concern with degeneration, the element of Buffon's work that was the most appealing to many savants was his radical approach to animal degeneration and the possibilities of countering it. Central to his project was the task of opening people's eyes to their own productive power, attempting to reveal to humans their ability to regenerate nature through thoughtful interventions.[39] If people respected the laws of nature, they could work with nature—"seconding" and "embellishing" it—to produce results that would not appear without human intervention.[40] As Buffon wrote, "nature alone cannot do as much as nature and man together."[41] Through wise and active human intervention, Buffon believed that it was possible that "a new nature will come from our hands."[42] In his attempt to "undo with time what time had done," Buffon helped create the means to go beyond nature's original forms.[43] Buffon reiterated this in many parts of *Natural History*, and as his work progressed, he became even more confidant in the degree to which humans could bring about new forms of animals. By the 1770s, he argued that humans, with time, could "bring to light an infinity of new beings that nature alone could not have produced" since "the seeds of all living matter belong to her and she forms all the germs of organized beings, but the combination, succession, assortment, reunion, and separation of each of these beings often depends on the will of man."[44]

This approach to countering degeneration and bringing about new animal forms was seized upon immediately because it provided a powerful model to direct projects of the physical regeneration of both animal and human bodies. In 1753, in the *Correspondance littéraire*, the newly printed fourth volume of Buffon's work was extravagantly praised. The entries on the horse, the donkey, and the cow were identified as being particularly worthy of emulation.[45] Charles-Augustin Vandermonde, a young Parisian doctor of the Paris Faculty of Medicine with ties to the Jardin de Roi, where Buffon was the chief administrator, apparently shared this opinion.[46] In 1756, Vandermonde published a bold two-volume work on "improving" the human species that drew directly on many of Buffon's insights in the first four volumes of *Natural History*, even borrowing unacknowledged passages from chapters like that on the horse.[47] Vandermonde's father had died while he was still coming of age, and the young Vandermonde sought advice from the famous botanist Bernard de Jussieu, one of his father's good friends. Jussieu, like Buffon, held positions at both the Jardin de Roi and the Académie des Sciences.[48] Vandermonde finished his education under Jussieu's guidance, and it is likely that he became acquainted with Buffon's work, and possibly knew Buffon personally, in the late 1740s and early 1750s.[49] Although in his *Essay on the Manner of Improving the Human Species* Vandermonde did not mention a personal relationship to Buffon, he was explicit in acknowledging his intellectual debt to him, repeatedly invoking him and his distinctive concepts, such as the internal mold (*moule intérieur*).[50] While he also drew on Maupertuis for inspiration, the debt to Buffon was primary. Vandermonde acknowledged this explicitly, tactically drawing on Buffon's stature and authority, while correctly asserting that the *Essay* was still innovative. It contained, he claimed, "some absolutely new materials, some presented in new combinations, and many taken solely from the natural history of Buffon, whose experience and enlightenment guarantee my principles."[51]

Vandermonde's work was innovative in several regards. First, he built on the new theory of reproduction to prescribe actions to improve humans through breeding. Second, he drew on the example of animal crossbreeding, while conceptually developing it and applying it to humans. Third, in addition to a vision of widespread and controlled crossbreeding, Vandermonde provided even more detailed and specific guidance on how humans should selectively choose mates. Fourth, as Anne Carol has argued, Vandermonde's essay was different from early modern guides to mate selection that preceded it because, in addition to giving guidance that individuals could use, Vandermonde also took into consideration improvement on the larger scale of the species.[52] I agree with Carol's point and would also argue that Vandermonde's work was new in that he drew together ideas about crossbreeding and selective breeding with the aim of improving the species, while also arguing that this provided the means of improving the quality and quantity of the population of a state. The target was not only the vague totality of human beings, therefore, but also specific populations. Though he did not address any states or sovereigns by name, he made it explicit that these biological prescriptions were for states.

In his most general and broad visions of improvement, Vandermonde called for the creation of "a type of general commerce among all the beings of the universe."[53] He developed the Buffonian claims that a natural "commerce" (an exchange of characteristics through breeding) was necessary to counter degeneration and that humans could "modify," "embellish," and "improve" the works of nature, "waking" and "renewing" nature, "reviving" its works.[54] For Vandermonde, humans had a privileged position in the commerce of beings since they were both its administrators and its most malleable object. Of all the natural beings, humans were the most susceptible to modification. Empowered by the theoretical insights of Buffon, humans emerged in Vandermonde's work as the extremely malleable objects of their own manipulations. Writing of "man," Vandermonde claimed that "it is himself, therefore, that he must improve. . . . We must reshape our organs, change, fortify, and improve all the springs of our machine."[55] "If chance can degenerate the human species, art can also perfect it," Vandermonde argued; "nature contains all sorts of varieties, [so] it is up to us to disentangle them from the chaos where they are, to create [something new] by putting our industry to good use, and by intelligently combining the various productions of nature."[56] The goal was nothing less than "perpetuating beauty, force and health in the human species." But, in addition to this general improvement of the species, Vandermonde was also much more specific in his prescription. He was himself the "handsome" product of the crossing of the Portuguese and French "races," as one eulogist put it, and he placed great hope in the ability of crossbreeding and selective breeding to improve all dimensions of humans, including their fertility, beauty, health, intelligence, skin color, and even ability to dance and sing.[57]

"Most men marry out of convenience, unite by necessity," Vandermonde claimed. This means that "we are born by chance."[58] Instead, he wanted reproduction to be carried out in a more considered and controlled manner. He wanted people to consider the physical organization of their partner so that they could select an appropriate mate and produce children that have an improved organization. Because a child was understood to be the combination of the organization of the parents, it was essential that the parents be well formed. "It is necessary above all," Vandermonde wrote, that the parents "have no vice of conformation, either in the parts essential to the two sexes, or in the organization of the rest of the body."[59] He gave a number of general rules for mate selection: neither partner should be too tall or too short; they should not be overweight; neither should have hollow eyes or sunken clavicles; they should not be "blind" or "deaf and mute"; they should be free of disease and "hereditary illnesses"; the fathers must not be libertines; and men are at their prime age at twenty-five, while women are ready at eighteen.[60] In addition to these general guidelines, there is another level of attention to particularities of the bodies of potential mates that needed to occur in relation to the specific form and qualities of both bodies of the pair. "It is necessary to give great attention to the difference or the reciprocity of the figures of the man and the woman, and to correct, if possible, the defects of the one with the perfections of the other."[61]

In one of the more unusual claims of the text, Vandermonde also argued that very specific traits, such as a good singing voice, could be selected for and perpetuated within a lineage. Mentioning the improved birdsong that resulted from mixing a canary and a goldfinch, Vandermonde suggested that "if marriage had brought together two of the most beautiful voices of the century, or if a skillful French male singer had been matched with some Italian woman with a distinguished voice, their children would probably have admirable [vocal] organs."[62] He claimed, in a similar manner, that excellent dancers from different countries might also be able to raise an excellent dancer: "It is probable that if one of our best male French dancers were matched with an Italian or English female dancer, they could easily raise their children to the highest degree of their art." The specificity of these selections, and the ideas that they could result in improvements that could be perpetuated, is a clear example that Vandermonde believed in more than simply a general crossbreeding of people from different countries or climates.

One of the other innovative elements of Vandermonde's work was the manner in which he recast crossbreeding, giving it an even more productive and positive role in the creation of improved people. Like Buffon, Vandermonde argued that climate produced differences between organized bodies and that this effect of climate could be manipulated instrumentally in reproduction. But going beyond Buffon and animal breeders, Vandermonde argued that differences of climate could be used to produce major differences of quality between generations. That is, in Vandermonde's view, the bodily difference resulting from the climates from which parents came could be intentionally combined in a manner that produced differences between the qualities of the parents and their children. In other words, crossbreeding people or animals from different climates was not merely a process of balancing or homogenizing. It did not have to be done in a way that merely corrected weaknesses or minimized faults. That is, it did not have to be a process of negation in which bad properties or traits were cancelled out, nor a process of limited productivity in which one parent's positive qualities lifted up the bad qualities of the other parents, producing some kind of neutral, or minimally improved quality in offspring. Instead, crossbreeding could be a productive process that resulted in new and significantly improved combinations. If done with attention to the particulars of specific climates and how they affected bodies, the crossing of people from different climates could produce children with qualities that were not seen in either parent. Because the right combination of climates could help produce a marked improvement in the quality of offspring, Vandermonde envisioned a time when the proper pairing of unexceptional parents could produce improved children. In that case: "one would cease to be surprised to see a father and a mother, who would have neither intelligence [*esprit*] nor beauty, make beautiful children full of intelligence, since the difference of the climates of the parents would suffice to give reason for the difference that would be found between them and their children."[63] This novel argument about differences of climate being employed so as to create differences in quality between generations reflects the holistic disposition of thought characteristic of organization theory. One of the primary characteristics of organized bodies was that they were wholes that were more than the sum of their parts, in that they had properties that were not found in any of the individual parts of the body. Since organized bodies could be wholes that were greater than the sum of their parts, so to could children, who were after all organized bodies. In Vandermonde's account, because of the specific selection and combination of the organization of both parents, the bodies of children could have qualities of mind and body that were found in neither of the parents.

Another new element of Vandermonde's work that successors built on was the treatment of the quality of the population (not just its quantity) as a political matter that should be addressed holistically with interventionist actions by the state. In Vandermonde's approach, the entire population needed to be considered and targeted for improvements to be made. Without directly addressing the king of France or any specific sovereign, and softening his prescriptions with the conditional tense, Vandermonde described what sovereigns should do to improve the quality and quantity of a population: "The example of all nations is more than sufficient to prove the necessity of crossing the human races to prevent them from degenerating. The most politically astute sovereigns should attract foreigners with the lure of rewards. By gratifying them, they [the sovereigns] would enrich themselves, and by depopulating other countries of the most beautiful men and the greatest geniuses they would repopulate their States with subjects capable of defending them and of making the arts and sciences flourish."[64] Although he prescribed a systematic crossing of people from different places, often drawing on exotic examples from Persia and the Caucuses, he did not limit his prescriptions to crossbreeding with foreigners from distant parts of the world, or even from other countries. In fact, "without leaving their country, without crossing the seas, people of a certain state can find great resources in the countryside."[65] Productive differences could be found within a single realm, Vandermonde argued, observing that "stronger and more beautiful children" more reliably result from matches of a city dweller and a country dweller than those who marry someone from their own city or village.[66] In the next sentence, he drew in a specific example from animal breeding, before turning back to human improvement and making it explicit that he intended these prescription to provide useful guidance for the state to bring about changes within the population: "Thus, among animals, it is normal to see a [male] horse and a Norman mare give birth to inferior horses compared to those of a Norman male and a mare from the Limousin. This would be the true means of populating the State with good subjects (as much for war as for the sciences and arts), rendering strength and beauty hereditary, and drawing models copied from wise and beautiful nature [*la belle nature*]."[67] Within three sentences he draws together animal breeding, human breeding, and state initiative, moving back and forth between them in a manner that represents this concatenation as providing the route to "populating a state with good subjects" and rendering "strength and beauty hereditary." While some figures of the Enlightenment rhetorically invoked animal breeding as a model for human breeding, Vandermonde invoked animal breeding as a true and direct model for human breeding, not just for individuals considering the choice of potential mate, but as Vandermonde's language makes clear, even as an issue of state action.

Although Vandermonde died at age thirty-five, he left enough of a mark on the medical profession for the reformist *médecin-philosophe* Pierre Roussel included him as one of the enlightened doctors who helped to transform medicine at midcentury.[68] Although there does not seem to have been extremely widespread commentary on the *Essay*, it was discussed by a number of Vandermonde's contemporaries, and there is evidence that, as a review in the *Journal encyclopédique* put it, "this important title has piqued the curiosity of the public."[69] The book received a number of long reviews that summarized, analyzed, and extensively quoted from the book, appearing in francophone periodicals such as the *Journal des sçavans*, the *Journal de Trévoux*, *L'année littéraire*, and the *Journal encyclopédique*.[70] In addition to these more substantive reviews, there were also brief mentions of the book in the improvement-oriented *Journal œconomique*, a short review in the British periodical the *Critical Review*, and in books such as one by the Prussian savant Johann Heinrich Samuel Formey, the latter of which brought Vandermonde to the attention of Abbé Sieyès in the 1770s.[71] In addition to Sieyès's taking note of the book, others who laid out biopolitical ideas about human breeding cited the *Essay* and referred to Vandermonde as an authority. Joachim Faiguet de Villeneuve, for example, referred to Vandermonde by name in his biopolitical writing of the 1760s that developed ideas of human breeding and other means of improvement.[72] Abbé Henri Grégoire invoked Vandermonde in his book on the physical regeneration of the Jews of France published in 1788, in which Grégoire suggests systematic intermarriage of Jews and Christians as a means of physically improving the Jews.[73] Vandermonde also was mentioned by the creator of the first biopolitical program in the German lands, Johann Peter Frank. Inspired by Vandermonde and another French physician, Antoine Le Camus, Frank adapted some of their ideas to the Cameralist tradition of German statecraft. His multivolume book on "medical police" began to appear in 1779, followed by many editions, commentaries, and adaptations, exerting a considerable influence on both public health policies and medical education in the German lands.[74]

One of the eighteenth-century individual authors in addition to Vandermonde to have proposed a specific eugenic program, addressed to someone in a position to carry it out, rather than merely as a general call for selective breeding, was one of Vandermonde's intellectual inspirations, Maupertuis. It seems that while in Prussia as the president of the Academy of Science under Frederick II, Maupertuis may have proposed that the king carry out a eugenic project in part of his territory. According to Immanuel Kant, Maupertuis proposed a program to improve humans in their moral and intellectual characteristics. It appears that this program qualifies as being a plan of "negative eugenics." Although no trace of this proposal has been found in Maupertuis's writing, published or unpublished, Kant reports that Maupertuis suggested "raising in some province a naturally noble sort of human beings in which understanding, excellence and integrity would be hereditary." This would be achieved "by means of careful separation of the degenerative births from the consistent ones." While Kant deemed the proposal feasible, he doubted the desirability of the results, since "the intermingling of the evil and the good" are what "set into play the sleeping powers of humanity and compel it to develop all its talents and to come nearer to the perfection of their destiny."[75] Like most of the figures of the Enlightenment, Kant did not denounce the eugenic project on moral grounds but rather argued about the feasibility or practicality of achieving the goal of improvement. Kant's account—and the fact that the proposal was probably directly addressed to King Frederick, Maupertuis's benefactor and protector—is plausible in light of some of his published ideas about human and animal breeding.

Although the details of this proposed eugenic plan are limited and some facts about it are unclear, it is another sign of Maupertuis's involvement in topics related to human breeding. By the early 1750s, in his written work, Maupertuis had already called on rulers to support large-scale and systematic animal breeding experiments, and he had observed that since pet breeders were able to create new varieties of animals, perhaps the same type of selective breeding could be carried out by some bored sultans in their seraglios.[76] Maupertuis played an important role in the formation of some of the ideas that were important to Enlightenment biopolitics, even though many of his most daring ideas were presented under the ambiguous cover of being nothing more than curious questions, or offhanded fleeting suggestions, often in the flippant style of the salon rather than the more sober register of scientific discourse. His more serious scientific work was also important in the early development of ideas related to selective breeding, although his exact intellectual contributions are, at times, difficult to establish.

In addition to making important early contributions to the theory of organization, Maupertuis was the first person since William Harvey to revive the epigenetic theory of generation. He incorporated it into his adaptation of Leibnizian ideas, resulting in a physical monadology that many of his contemporaries, such as Diderot and Buffon, found highly suggestive and stimulating, if not entirely convincing. In his writing, Maupertuis also wondered about the possibility of creating new animal species through breeding, inquired into the causes of albinism, and reported on his innovative research on the inheritance of sexidigitism (the formation of extra digits on hands or feet), showing how this condition was most likely passed on from parents to children, as opposed to being an anomalous "monstrosity." Buffon and Maupertuis were friends and intellectual interlocutors, and they seem to have developed many of their ideas about generation, animal breeding, the inheritance of characteristics, and organization in private conversations, of which we know little, other than their existence and the probable importance in the mutual development of ideas.[77] They acknowledged the innovativeness of each other's ideas in print, and they made gestures toward the significant role that their friendship played in the development of their scientific and philosophical perspectives. In addition to sharing ideas, Buffon and Maupertuis shared books and even animals that they used in experiments. Maupertuis, for example, gave Buffon one of the Icelandic dogs that Maupertuis had used for breeding experiments relating to his research on the inheritance of characteristics.[78]

Ideas of countering degeneration and bringing about improvement in the human form through selective breeding or systematic crossbreeding were focused on the physical qualities of individual bodies, in terms of racial difference as well as general strength, size, beauty, and fitness. This is true even of the wave of pronatalist writing that emerged in the 1760s. A number of the authors of biopolitical projects directly addressed this issue of quality versus quantity. In a work suggesting ways that the state could influence and intervene in reproduction, the minor royal official and contributor to the *Encyclopédie* Joachim Faiguet de Villeneuve observed in the 1760s, "if it is of great importance to increase" the population, "it is of even greater importance to regulate and improve" it.[79] This idea can be found in much of the biopolitical writing about the role of breeding in the development of population. This emphasis on population as a question of more than simple addition and subtraction reflects the underlying role of organization theory and vitalist thought in biopolitics. The holism and the concern with the idea of populations as wholes that are more than the sum of their parts differentiated biopolitical ideas about breeding from much of the mainstream writing about population, which advocated a more quantitative pronatalism that was concerned with population growth and conformed to the mechanistic approach of mercantilist political economy.[80]

Like many authors who called for human breeding, Faiguet invoked the trope of complaining about attention to animal breeding alongside the unfortunate oversight of the benefits of human breeding.[81] He argued that indifference to the issues of improvement and human reproduction were "a great political evil" and that it was highly problematic for weak and poorly made men to reproduce while well-formed men in the army, the religious orders, and domestic service remained celibate.[82] Faiguet invoked the name of Vandermonde, while also advocating several negative eugenic measures. He suggested introducing measures to make it more difficult for the feeble and disabled to reproduce and creating other laws and incentives to make it easier and more desirable for the able and healthy to marry.[83]

Similar ideas and calls to action were published in the late 1750s and the 1760s by a variety of authors of medical and political economic treatises that often drew directly on the naturalists' discourse of bodily degeneration. One of Faiguet's sources of inspiration was the prominent physician Antoine Le Camus, who railed against celibacy as the primary cause of a "degenerescence of the species" that "is unknown to all time."[84] He identified the "voluntary eunuchs" of the military and ecclesiastical orders as primary causes of the degeneration of the population. To the great detriment of the nation, these institutions kept many of the strongest and most vigorous men—*les hommes bien faits*—from reproducing.[85] Le Camus drew on organization theory and its ideas about the relationship of the physical and the moral, arguing that humans could affect the moral through interventions in the physical. In fact, controlling generation was one of the most promising means of altering the mind.[86] Not everyone working in these areas agreed with this optimist view of improvement, as evidenced by Diderot's dissent, but Le Camus's bold ideas inspired a number of authors to hope for extraordinary improvements through breeding.[87]

Enthusiasm and heightened rhetoric was also a feature of some of the writers warning against the decline of the size of the population and the deterioration of the strength and robustness of French bodies. This concern with bodily degeneration was often captured in provocative images, such as the marquis de Mirabeau's claim in the popular work of political economy that he began to publish before becoming a physiocrat, *The Friend of Mankind* (*L'ami des hommes*). In the second volume of this work, he argued that his contemporaries were mere "pygmies" compared to the men of the sixteenth century: "I ask if our polished and decorated apartments would have been able to contain men of moral fiber like those of yore. The tip of Balafre's sword would still be in the third antechamber, while the other end would be breaking the mirror over the couch in the boudoir."[88] With Balafre's sword reaching the boudoir, Mirabeau's double entendre got to the heart of the matter, making it clear that this was a problem of the utmost severity. Everything of man's was shrinking, even the most intimate of body parts.

In the 1760s and 1770s, a number of minor works continued the biopolitical approach to improving the strength and vitality of bodies through human breeding. These works rarely made original arguments or provided new terms for thinking about the population or its improvement, yet the contributions of writers like Pierre Fabre, Jacques Ballexserd, the Chevalier de Cerfvol, Abbé Romans de Coppiers, and Jean-Charles Desessartz propagated biopolitical ideas of human breeding.[89] In general, they demonstrated a relatively consistent body of discourse that built on the Buffonian concerns with degeneration and improvement, drew on Vandermonde's ideas of human breeding, and echoed Le Camus's concerns with the deleterious effects of the celibacy of well-made men in the army, the monasteries, and domestic service. The trope of the applicability of the model of animal breeding for humans continued and was often repeated, even in works that gave no real attention to the development of biopolitical ideas. For example, in 1763, when Louis-René de Caradeuc de la Chalotais, a royal prosecutor in the Parlement of Brittany, published a plan for national regeneration based on educating the young, he invoked the trope of animal breeding: "there is an art of changing the races of animals; would there be none for improving those of men?"[90]

In addition to the well-developed versions of these ideas of human breeding in the writings of naturalists and physicians, and scattered and relatively undeveloped expressions of them by others, another means by which these ideas permeated the culture was in imaginative literature. One of the most respected philosophes to partake in this kind of work was Denis Diderot. Although he never made an unambiguous endorsement of eugenic breeding, it was a topic that he explored in more than one of his fictional works, as well as in several nonfiction works. After the explorer Louis-Antoine de Bougainville returned from his high-profile journey to the South Pacific, publishing a popular account, Diderot took advantage of the great interest in Tahiti and prepared a dialogue that he presented as a supplement to Bougainville's written work. Diderot had the Tahitian character Orou recount his people's voluntary eugenic experiments.[91] Kathleen Wellman has noticed the intriguing similarities between the approaches to breeding in Vandermonde's *Essay* and in the writing of Diderot. "Vandermonde's text raised similar questions to those addressed by Diderot," she observed, concluding that "Vandermonde's premises might have inspired Diderot."[92] This is possible, though there is no direct evidence of a connection between Vandermonde and Diderot.[93] Given that Diderot was well acquainted with the natural historical work on breeding by Buffon and Maupertuis, he could have developed his thoughts on selective breeding without consulting Vandermonde.[94] Without new archival evidence, the question appears undecided, and we can only conjecture, noting the similarities. But it is worth pointing out that Diderot also had a number of passages about human breeding in the fictional dialogues that made up *D'Alembert's Dream*, and some of his contributions to later editions of the best-selling *History of the Two Indies* (published under the name of Abbé Raynal, known as the *Histoire des deux Indes*) discussed the "mixing of the races."[95] Given Diderot's central position in the development and popularization of theories of organization and Buffonian ideas of natural history and the life sciences, it is not surprising to find him include these ideas in his work, though it problematizes the narrowly positive portrayal of him as one of the principal architects of an emancipatory Radical Enlightenment.[96]

The most popular author, and the one with the most developed, extensive, and imaginative takes on ideas of human breeding, was the wild and prolific Nicolas-Edme Restif de la Bretonne. He was an eccentric figure, a self-educated master printer, an author of imaginative utopian fiction, and a creator of elaborate projects for social reform, as well as a libertine whose ribald works earned him the title "Rousseau of the gutter."[97] Restif, however, also considered himself to have something of the quality of an overlooked Buffon.[98] He had a great love of natural history, and he wove its details and questions into his fictional works, much as he did references to Buffon and his ideas.[99] He created fictional characters that were themselves hidden Buffons (such as Noffub, a reversal of the letters in the name Buffon), and in one of his works, he even had the community gathered on Sundays to listen to the priest read out of Buffon as well as the Bible.[100] Biopolitical ideas about human breeding were most developed in his novel about the voyage of a flying man to the Southern Hemisphere, where he encountered a variety of human-animal hybrids (see figure 2). Revolving around the character of the flying man and the engagement of his two sons with these fantastical hybrids, the bizarre tale also includes marriage with giants, the founding of an ideal community, the colonization of islands, the attempt to capture and civilize young hybrids, and ideas about the mixing of the races and intermarriage between humans and different varieties of the hybrids.[101] He also presented a detailed and extensive plan for the regulation of marriages along eugenic lines in his *Andrograph* (*L'Andrographe*). In his vision of a highly regulated society, all healthy and able-bodied people would have to marry, while the infirm would not be allowed to marry, and "the deformed" would be allowed to marry only widows over the age of thirty-five.[102] He also envisioned ceremonies in which young men and women would be ranked on general merit, and those men higher up in the ranks would receive priority in matching with a highly rated spouse.[103]

Outside of France and the French colonies in the late eighteenth century, there seem to have been only a few instances of people developing ideas about human selective breeding of which we have any indication or evidence. Within the context of natural historical thought and ideas of race within the British and British Atlantic world, for example, rather than an emphasis on rapid transformation through breeding, there was an emphasis on the role of climatic influence on the body, with many people arguing that the effect was slower and more gradual than previously thought. This resulted in a more gradualist body of thought and a "weak transmutationist argument."[104] This seems to have had direct influence on the development of biopolitics in the British and British imperial contexts. There were, however, two notable exceptions, John Gregory in Scotland and Samuel Stanhope Smith in the new United States. While these two men were in circumstances where they would have had access to the same ancient texts

Les Hommes-ours.

FIGURE 2. "Bear-men" (*les hommes-ours*) and flying men in Nicolas-Edme Restif de la Bretonne, *La découverte australe par un homme-volant, ou Le dédale français* (1781). Used by permission of the Bibliothèque nationale de France.

mentioning human breeding, and while they could have observed the successes of animal breeders, one of the noteworthy things about these two individuals is that there are indications that they were stimulated and informed by the vital materialism of organization theory, as well as Buffon's work on animal breeding, generation, and human variation. In essence, they seem to have built on the same theoretical foundation as French theorists of biopolitics. Before turning in the next chapter to the question of how French colonial proposals for racial engineering built on the French metropolitan ideas of Buffon and others that I have analyzed in this chapter, I want to analyze the anglophone examples of ideas of breeding to show they built on a foundation that was generally Buffonian, while developing these ideas in contexts that were different from those in France and the French Empire.

The first person in the British context to write about the possibility of improving people by breeding them like animals was the Scottish physician John Gregory in his *A Comparative View of the State and Faculties of Man with Those of the Animal World* (1765).[105] Gregory was trained as a physician in Leiden and Edinburgh, where he eventually returned as a professor.[106] For a time, he practiced medicine in London and became a member of the Royal Society, before moving back home to Aberdeen, where he taught medicine and cofounded the small, but important, Aberdeen Philosophical Society, also known as the Wise Club. The members of the learned society were pious and concerned with establishing a firm philosophical foundation for moral, social, and religious order.[107] They were disturbed, therefore, not only by what they took to be the morally destabilizing implications of the philosophical skepticism of their fellow countryman David Hume, but also by challenging scientific and philosophical ideas emerging from France. Buffon was one of the figures that seemed to most fascinate and trouble them. While they were unsettled by the implications of materialism and atheism that they found in some of his ideas, several members of the society nonetheless drew on a number of Buffon's ideas, even while strongly criticizing others.[108] For example, Gregory's cousin and fellow founder of the society Thomas Reid, though best known as a moral philosopher of common sense, criticized much of Buffon yet spent twenty-five years developing his own theory of generation after his close reading of Buffon's work. Reid adapted Buffon's theory, turning the organic molecules into "organized atoms" in a manner that clearly and explicitly retained a role for God as the creator, eliminating some of the ambiguity of Buffon's articulations.[109]

In the 1760s, at the same time that Gregory wrote and delivered the lectures that became *A Comparative View*, a fellow cofounder of the society, who had studied medicine in Edinburgh and Leiden and natural history at the Jardin de Roi in Paris, David Skene, delivered a series of natural history lectures. Having lived in Paris from 1751 to 1753, soon after the first three volumes of *Natural History* were published, and as Buffon worked intensely, carrying out breeding experiments and preparing future volumes, Skene was well positioned to give an inside account of Buffonian natural history. In Skene's lectures to the Aberdeen Philosophical Society, touching on various ideas of Buffon's, he discussed the interbreeding experiments, praising them for their "exactness and precision," and he echoed Buffon's emphasis on the criteria of fertile reproduction in determining species.[110] Recounting a series of experiments with dogs, foxes, and wolves, and another series with hares and rabbits, Skene concluded that "the only [interbreeding] experiments with which I am acquainted, that deserve to be mentioned or from which any just conclusion can be drawn, are those of M. de Buffon."[111]

In the first section of *A Comparative View*, after criticizing Descartes's mechanical understanding of the body, and expressing the type of qualified praise of George Ernst Stahl that was common among organization theorists, Gregory turned to the trope of animal breeding and its applicability to human improvement. "We should," Gregory claimed, "avail ourselves of Observations made on tame Animals in those particulars where Art has in some measure improved upon Nature."[112] He believed that the model of animal improvement through breeding had been shamefully ignored as a means of bringing about the improvement of people. This was true even of people who paid great attention to animal breeding. "We every day see very sensible people, who are anxiously attentive to preserve or improve the breed of their Horses," Gregory complained, "tainting the blood of their Children."[113] Gregory thought that selectively breeding human beings could bring about an improvement in physical constitution and that "a certain character or constitution of mind can be transmitted from a Parent to a Child."[114] The idea that changes to the body and the mind could be passed on to offspring was one argued for by French Enlightenment theorists of organization and biopolitics like Buffon, Vandermonde, and La Camus. It was also echoed in the early stages of the French Revolution by Condorcet, and it was articulated in an even stronger version of the argument by Pierre-Jean-George Cabanis and other French savants in the later stages of the French Revolution as there was a new attention after the Terror to finding ways of transforming people so as to bring about "the new man" and complete the process of wholesale "regeneration" (social, political, physical, mental, etc.) that had been promised since 1789. In character and intellectual foundation, Gregory's observations fit comfortably alongside the French discourse of biopolitics.

After the first edition of the book in 1765, Gregory made revisions and published many editions, reaching an eighth edition by 1778. The book gained him fame, and it eventually helped him attain a professorship at the University of Edinburgh. In the subsequent editions of the book, Gregory drew out the Buffonian foundations of his approach by adding material from *Natural History* and indicating Buffon as the source.[115] While Gregory's ideas about human breeding were not original or unusual in comparison to the French ideas that had already been articulated, they were likely one of the means by which ideas of organization and selective breeding spread through the anglophone Atlantic. They were also a sign of the ways that biopolitical ideas moved in circular flows between sites in the Atlantic world, as Gregory, responding and building on ideas expressed by French theorists, created the first English-language expression of the basic argument about human selective breeding, which then returned to France in a translation by none other than Jean-Baptiste-René Robinet, the editor, and possibly the author, of the article on countering human degeneration that was directed at future enlightened men of state, discussed in the introduction to this chapter. Although there is no indication that this translation circulated widely in France, it was prominent enough that in the early 1770s the young Abbé Sieyès, future theorist of biopolitics and important political philosopher of the Revolution, put it on the list of books that he would like to acquire.[116]

Gregory's teaching in Edinburgh, one of the most important medical schools in Europe and a popular destination for American students, may have been another means by which nascent biopolitical ideas circulated. For example, the second person in the anglophone Atlantic to express ideas about human breeding, and the first one to do so at length, Samuel Stanhope Smith, was a very close friend of the most distinguished physician of the early republic of the United States, Benjamin Rush, who had studied with John Gregory at the University of Edinburgh.[117] Gregory was just a part of the illustrious faculty teaching medicine and sciences at Edinburgh, which was already a center of organization theory and vitalist medical ideas thanks to the teaching of Robert Whytt and William Cullen.[118] Smith never traveled abroad, but he engaged with a broad range of scientific and philosophical questions, often in close consultation and dialogue with Rush.

Smith distinguished himself as the author of one of the most thorough and accomplished works on human variation to appear in English by the late eighteenth century. In his oration to the American Philosophical Society in 1787, which was published as *An Essay on the Causes of the Variety of Complexion and Figure in the Human Species* in the same year, Smith refuted the well-known polygenist Lord Kames, offering a naturalistic account of monogenism drawn primarily from Buffon.[119] The *Essay* was republished the following year in Edinburgh and then again the next year in London.[120] The second edition of the *Essay* in 1810 was much enlarged, refuting new polygenetic arguments with new observations drawn from his own anatomical measurements of people of African descent in Princeton and based on subsequent developments in the Buffonian approach to race, such as those that were made by Johann Friedrich Blumenbach and Immanuel Kant.[121]

Smith was a Presbyterian minister and learned figure of the American Enlightenment, becoming president of two colleges (one of them, the College of New Jersey, would become Princeton University), and a member of the American Philosophical Society.[122] Throughout his career he found no necessary contradiction between Christian beliefs and philosophically sound naturalistic explanations of natural phenomena, even many of those that were developed by French thinkers of dubious piety like Buffon. In the *Essay*, for example, he affirmed the biblical account of the common origin of humankind by drawing on, and rearticulating, the secular explanation of monogenesis and human variation developed by Buffon. "The most accurate investigations into the power of nature," he held, "serve to confirm the facts vouched by the authority of revelation."[123] In his Christian version of Enlightenment, "a just philosophy will always be found to be coincident with true theology."[124] In this spirit, Smith, like his close friend Benjamin Rush, was not afraid to engage with the materialist implications of theories of organization, nor did he shy away from the assertion of the intimate relation and "mutual influence" of body and mind.[125]

In the *Essay*, Smith wrote that "the human constitution is the most delicate of all animal systems: but it is also the most pliant."[126] This pliancy could be exploited through the modification of the environment, the state of society, and breeding. Endorsing Buffon's belief that blackness could be completely effaced in four or five generations of the interbreeding of people of African and European descent, Smith stated that, "by a proper mixture of races, and by the habits of civilized life, the black tinge may be entirely effaced."[127] In fact, he went even further, suggesting that an experiment combining transplantation to Europe and the selective breeding of humans like animals could bring about the racial "improvement" of Native Americans and Americans of African descent. "Carry the native of Africa or America to Europe, and mix the breed, as you do that of horses," Smith wrote, "and they will acquire in time, the high perfection of the human form which is seen in that polished country."[128] In another passage, Smith pushed the idea of selective breeding still further, beyond questions of race, arguing that if rulers could create a program of controlled selective breeding, they might be able to bring about almost any type of human form. "If men in the affair of marriage," Smith wrote, "were as much under management as some other animals, an absolute ruler might accomplish, in his dominions almost any idea of the human form."[129] Although this reference to an absolute ruler seemed to rule out the possibility of this kind of population management in the United States, twenty-five years later Smith suggested a different version of human breeding that reflected the specific political and social structures and historical circumstances of the early republic of the United States.

In 1812, when he published his biopolitical approach to resettling in western territories people freed from enslavement, Smith looked to enact a gradual emancipation, to reduce racial animosity, and successfully include formerly enslaved people in the polity. By the time that Smith published his suggestion for western colonization, others had already suggested removing enslaved people to western territories, though for most of them this was a way of isolating people of African descent and thereby reducing or eliminating intermixture.[130] Early ideas of resettlement focused on questions of security (of people of European descent resident in the eastern part of the country) and socialization (how to "civilize" people who had been enslaved). The ideas of people like the French Huguenot convert to Quakerism Anthony (Antoine) Benezet focused on creating new settlements that could function as experimental sites of social assimilation, allowing formerly enslaved people the opportunity to develop, and eventually, perhaps, integrate with the remaining population to the east.[131] Smith shared these concerns, but working from a Buffonian position on human variation and assimilation, he introduced biological assimilation as an additional means to bring about the "amalgamation" of the races.

In an unusual blend of exclusion and inclusion, Smith believed that a type of spatial exclusion was a necessary step toward the eventual inclusion through biological assimilation. In order to eliminate racial difference (or at least the outward appearance of bodily difference) and the attendant racial prejudices, Smith suggested that people freed from enslavement could be given "a certain portion of land in absolute property" in the "large district" carved out of the western "unappropriated lands of the United States."[132] The government would then establish a system for motivating and rewarding marriages between black people and white people, so that "every white man who should marry a black woman, and every white woman who should marry a black man, and reside within the territory, might be entitled to a double portion of land."[133] While Smith formulated this plan within the specific political and historical circumstances of the early republic of the United States, there was also a deep Atlantic background. Smith's understanding of racial variation and the potential biological benefits of intermarriage was a product of his involvement in the Buffonian scholarship on natural history and the life sciences. Building on this interest in the transformative effects of selective human breeding, Smith's resettlement project for the western territories also reflected the changing social and political circumstances of the early nineteenth-century Atlantic world, in which the successful revolution of those enslaved in Saint-Domingue (which became the Haitian Revolution and resulted in the founding of the Republic of Haiti) had given questions of emancipation and assimilation a new relevance and urgency—as Smith explicitly acknowledged.[134]

To return to the French Enlightenment and the most important figure in establishing the scientific ideas on which Enlightenment proposals for human breeding built, Buffon published the last of his major works included within the thirty-six volumes of *Natural History*. In *The Epochs of Nature* (*Des époques de la nature*), published in 1778, Buffon began openly to wonder how much the human species would be able to improve itself if it turned the practical and theoretical knowledge gained from improving animals onto the human species itself. He never wrote that humans should be bred in a systematic and controlled way as animals were—or that humans should be bred at all—but he did harness the analogy between the human ability to create new varieties of animals and the possibility of making physical and moral improvements to the human species. In the last pages of his final grand vision of nature—one that combined cosmology, a theory of the origins and transformation of the earth, a radical new account of the age of the earth, and a panoramic vision of natural history—Buffon brought to a close the seventh and final epoch of nature, "when the power of man has seconded Nature" and humans had come to realize their ability to work with the forces of nature to cultivate and alter its forms to such an extent that they could create new forms of living beings. "In the species of the chicken and the pigeon alone, we recently have made a great number of new races," Buffon claimed, and "in other species, every day we elevate and ennoble the races in crossing them."[135] Humans had come far in realizing their powers to modify nature, improve species, and make new races, but Buffon saw reasons to wonder if humans could go further, better realizing their own powers of modification and directing them with intelligence back onto themselves, not only with regard to individual reproduction but in a systemic fashion that improved the entire species. Buffon argued that awareness of this power was recent and that much more could be done to develop knowledge to harness its potential. "All these modern and recent examples [of new and ennobled races] prove that man has only lately come to know his power, and even that he does not yet know enough; it depends entirely on the exercise of his intelligence."[136] Then in the next paragraph—the last of the book—as he looked to the future, Buffon inquired into the limits of the possible, asking of "man": "And what could he not do to himself, that is to say his own species, if the will were always directed by intelligence? Who knows to what point man could improve either his moral or his physical nature?"[137]

Fifteen years before Condorcet went into hiding during the Terror and wrote his celebrated essay that similarly probed the limits of progress and the human ability to bring it about, Buffon wrote these lines, which represent both the intellectual developments of the previous decades and the sense that there was much more that could be achieved. This was both a summation of a life's work and a prospective vision of what might come—a reflection on Enlightenment biopolitical ideas of species improvement and a question of what more could be made of them. In the same years that Buffon was writing this final account of the human ability to transform nature, make races, and improve the species, two of the most specific and unprecedented proposals for human breeding drew on the conceptual and scientific conditions of possibility that the Buffonian revolution had made possible. The content and context of these two plans for the racial engineering of Saint-Domingue is the subject of the next chapter.

CHAPTER THREE

Making Men in the Colonies

A minor nobleman from Alsace, traveling in French colonial Saint-Domingue (present-day Haiti) on the eve of the French and Haitian Revolutions, expressed surprise that "it has not already occurred to some ingenious speculator to monopolize . . . the fabrication of all mulattoes."[1] Perhaps no one had embarked on this endeavor, the Baron de Wimpffen speculated, for fear that the metropolitan government would "take advantage of this bright idea to incorporate even the manufacture of the human race into its exclusive privilege."[2] While Wimpffen was clearly satirizing the *Exclusif*—the much-hated metropolitan monopoly on the trade and manufacture of natural resources and goods from the colonies—his comments indicate something that is not widely recognized about the eighteenth century: the "fabrication" or "manufacture" of human beings was conceivable.[3] His comments raise questions about whether this manufacture was believed to be possible, not just conceivable, and whether this production of new people would have been desirable to some. Wimpffen's words are jarring, not only because they raise the prospect of human beings being manufactured, but also because they do so in an offhand manner, presenting it as a whimsical observation or a delicate joke rather than as a ghastly vision of control and production in which human beings are merely another raw material to be transformed. Sexual relations between people of African and European descent were not an uncommon topic in eighteenth-century writing about Saint-Domingue, where it was generally agreed that they were more prevalent than in other French colonies; Wimpffen's comments, however, pointed beyond the usual tropes invoked against the social and moral ramifications of colonial "mixing" of the races and *libertinage* (the debased pursuit of sensual pleasure).

Although some enslavers profited from the sale of their own mulatto children, Wimpffen was presumably correct in believing that there were no actual businesses in Saint-Domingue that aimed to monopolize "the manufacture of the human race."[4] A decade earlier, however, two men with connections to the colonial administration—former governor-general Gabriel de Bory and a lawyer named Michel-René Hilliard d'Auberteuil—had published works calling for a kind of "manufacture." In *Essay on the Population of the Sugar Colonies* (*Essai sur la population des colonies à sucre*, 1776) and *Considerations on the Present State of the French Colony of Saint-Domingue* (*Considérations sur l'état présent de la colonie française de Saint-Domingue*, 1776–77), respectively, Bory and Hilliard d'Auberteuil sketched out separate plans for the large-scale selective breeding of enslaved people, free people of color, and the white residents of the island.[5] Neither viewed his project as a potential business venture; instead, each plan was envisioned as a solution to some of the colony's most significant social, political, and military problems. Neither proposal was highly detailed, nor was either of them the focus of the book in which it was included. Yet these works remain of great historical importance because they appear to have been the first suggestions for large-scale selective breeding of humans that were meant to be carried out in a real time and specified place (rather than the fictional nowhere of utopias). They were also distinguished by being suggestions for human breeding in which the intention of creating a new racial hierarchy was explicit and central.

The existence of these plans raises new questions regarding the relationship between the development of ideas about the selective breeding of human beings and the development of ideas of race. Throughout the second half of the eighteenth century in Europe and the Atlantic world, a fundamental idea was emerging of race as a heritable and inescapable way of being that encompassed physical, moral, intellectual, and psychological characteristics and provided a basis for hierarchical differentiation.[6] There was a considerable amount of fluidity and ambiguity within the new ideas and nomenclature, but people were gradually establishing and stabilizing many of the terms, concepts, and scientific questions that would lay the foundation for the more elaborate attempt to create a science of race in the nineteenth and twentieth centuries. Yet even as modern ideas of race were being formed, some people apparently believed that human beings could be constructed to fit within narrowly defined categories based primarily on skin color and civil status. The possibility of a dynamic circularity in the eighteenth century between making men and making race seems not to have been previously recognized by scholars.[7]

Analysis and contextualization of these racial engineering plans can contribute to the growing body of work arguing for the significance of the French Atlantic world in the development of ideas of race.[8] In fact, it suggests the value of utilizing an Atlantic framework for the study of the ideas of the Enlightenment more generally, since the plans that Bory and Hilliard d'Auberteuil proposed for Saint-Domingue were not merely metropolitan or colonial; they were Atlantic hybrids that drew on metropolitan science and colonial ideas of social, political, and racial order, as well as actual social and political circumstances in the metropole and the colonies. While there is not yet any evidence that these proposals had a direct impact on either colonial or metropolitan discourses on breeding and race, they are dramatic and little-known examples of the extremes to which ideas on race and the reconstruction of populations had developed in the Enlightenment. They stand as the most extreme manifestations of Enlightenment ideas of racial engineering, but as the previous chapter demonstrates, they were part of a larger discourse that has not been fully recognized in its breadth, its interconnections, or its relation to the "Buffonian revolution" in Enlightenment natural history. After contextualizing these plans in relation to both the Buffonian revolution and colonial concerns with the special political and economic circumstances, I analyze the plans at length, briefly touch on several other colonial plans for racial engineering, and then reflect on the role of the Bory and the Hilliard d'Auberteuil plans in the development of ideas of biopolitics as well as race.

The plans conceived by Bory and Hilliard d'Auberteuil represented a historically unprecedented and distinctive approach to the transformation of populations. They shared characteristics with, but differed significantly from, the long line of utopian protoeugenic visions of re-creating populations through selective breeding, the early modern discourse focusing on the selection of properly matched mates, the eugenic discourse in Enlightenment France focusing on the size and strength of individuals and the population, and the development of sexual regulations in the Atlantic world intended to influence the formation of colonial populations. Unlike the utopian visions that had existed since antiquity, Bory's and Hilliard d'Auberteuil's proposals were centered on a real population that actually existed in the world. They were directly and explicitly prescriptive plans for re-creating the population and not thought experiments intended to facilitate the reevaluation of sociopolitical formations, standards, and goals. They differed from the early modern discourse on individual mate selection in looking primarily at the possibility of selectively transforming specific characteristics of individuals as well as the population as a whole, as opposed to ensuring the general health and fitness of the offspring of a marital match.[9] They were less about the improvement of the population through an improvement of health and strength of individual bodies than they were about transforming the racial characteristics of populations based on specific strategic goals. Unlike the eugenic discourse developing in metropolitan France, Bory and Hilliard d'Auberteuil focused on what they believed were racial characteristics (primarily skin color) in their consideration of selective breeding. Their formulations also went beyond previous attempts to shape colonial populations through the creation of laws and regulations pertaining to sex and marriage; rather than merely suggesting a ban on sex, marriage, or concubinage between people of European descent and people who were deemed to carry "an indelible mark" (*une tache inéfaçable*) of slavery and blackness (or who were Native Americans), Bory and Hilliard d'Auberteuil envisioned a role for the government in actively directing reproduction by selecting mates according to specific criteria.[10]

While there were significant differences between their plans, Bory and Hilliard d'Auberteuil had the same main goal: to create a new type of male "mulatto" soldier who would address the three primary threats to the colony. These soldiers would provide security against a British or Spanish invasion, ensure white domination through the policing of the enslaved majority, and foster the white colonists' loyalty to the metropolitan authorities by allowing for the elimination of mandatory militia service. The mulattoes of Saint-Domingue, and those to be created in the future, were presented as human instruments of empire who could be used to strengthen the valuable French colony. Although eugenic projects to transform the racial composition of populations are primarily associated with the nineteenth and twentieth centuries, there were well-developed proposals for this type of biopolitical racial engineering in the colonial endeavors of the French Enlightenment. It is important to recognize that Bory and Hilliard d'Auberteuil were figures of the Enlightenment, and that their plans fit within its broad boundaries, even though—to invoke Kant's famous distinction—they were far from enlightened. Bory was a scientifically minded reformist who proposed numerous military and administrative reforms and drew directly on new Enlightenment understandings of nature, race, and the experimental approach to "improvement" through selective breeding.[11] Hilliard d'Auberteuil was a legally minded reformist who drew heavily on Montesquieu's legal and political ideas, opposed the metropolitan ancien régime hierarchy and its enshrined special privileges, articulated liberal economic arguments that were consistent with the new Enlightenment political economy, and implicitly built on the new approaches to nature, race, and breeding.[12]

Bory's and Hilliard d'Auberteuil's proposals were reactions to the problems that arose from the imperial struggle for Saint-Domingue and the social tensions inherent in colonies built on enslaved labor, but they were not merely this. They were also responses to the possibilities opened up by recent scientific developments in metropolitan France, particularly in relation to animal breeding, human breeding, and the concepts of species and race. This was an important period in the development of modern understandings of race because it was the time when—in the wake of the Buffonian revolution and the secular theory of monogenesis—the characteristics of individuals (physical, moral, intellectual, and temperamental) came to be seen as heritable and alterable, and therefore manipulable by others. The belief in the innateness and immutability of human qualities was being questioned and partially undermined, as were traditional explanations of mutability that focused on the influence of celestial bodies or the maternal imagination during pregnancy. Because of developments in theories of generation, new attention directed toward breeding experiments, and new ideas about species and varieties, the conditions of possibility were transformed, and it became possible to think that the development of whole populations and "races" could be affected through selective breeding. The realization that individual human bodies as well as whole populations were not only mutable but also controllable through selective breeding introduced a new conceptual and social instability. Some, including Bory, wanted to exploit this mutability to bring about "improvements" through selective intermarriage. Hilliard d'Auberteuil's work demonstrates a different type of reaction, an attempt to exploit this very mutability and controllability in order to reintroduce stability and fixity into human types and, in a sense, create "races." Hilliard d'Auberteuil wanted to exploit the Buffonian revolution to reassert the fixity of human types, or rather, to create a new type of fixity.

Bory's and Hilliard d'Auberteuil's plans were each conceived as a solution to what emerged from the Seven Years' War (1756–63) as one of Saint-Domingue's most contentious social and political problems among the free population: providing for the internal and external security of the island. Internal security was a constant concern for the whites and free people of color, who were both vastly outnumbered by enslaved people. The precise number of enslaved people, free people of color, and whites living in Saint-Domingue in the eighteenth century is uncertain. The last official census of Saint-Domingue in 1789 almost certainly underestimated the numbers of free people of color (and possibly enslaved people as well), registering 424,000 enslaved people, 30,000 whites, and 24,000 free people of color.[13]

The problem of internal and external security was most clearly manifest in the issue of militia service, which before the war had theoretically been mandatory for every free man on the island between the ages of fifteen and fifty-five. There was particularly strong resistance to this involuntary duty from the white population, who sometimes characterized it as white slavery.[14] Those whites and people of color who were wealthy enough to own slave plantations were also resentful about the loss of productivity their plantations suffered while they were fulfilling their militia obligations and the loss of labor they experienced on the occasions when enslaved people whom they owned were made to perform labor related to military defense, such as the construction of installations. While militia service had long been a point of conflict between the government and the free people of the island, the war changed the landscape in several ways. The animosity toward compulsory service reached new heights in the 1760s as it became invested with greater symbolic significance. It was increasingly viewed as a sign of the despotic constraint on the people, to the point that, as one governor-general complained, "the name alone of the militia creates an idea of constraint."[15]

But reforming the militia was not only a politically expedient means of fostering white creole allegiance; it was also seen as a military necessity in the struggle for the Americas. The loss of several Caribbean islands to the British during the Seven Years' War highlighted both of these issues. Much as the surprising loss of Havana played an important role in the militia reforms within the Spanish Empire, the loss of the French Caribbean islands triggered a series of events that would lead to significant changes in French colonial militias.[16] A more specialized and better-trained militia was clearly needed if the French were going to maintain long-term control of their colonies. The problem was particularly pronounced in Saint-Domingue because it was the most valuable colony in the region and was known to have a poorly trained and unenthusiastic militia. In the later stages of the war, as everyone waited for the island to be invaded by the British, Bory, then governor-general, wrote a letter to the minister in charge of the colonies, Étienne-François, duc de Choiseul, predicting that the militia would provide insufficient defense against a British attack. As he dryly noted, "The English do not attack our Colonies with their militias."[17] There would have to be significant reform of the militia if Saint-Domingue was to remain French. It was a question of assuaging the dissent of the white creole elite and creating a military force that could ensure the long-term viability of the colony. Surprisingly, more than a decade later, Bory would turn to science for help in solving the problem. His *Essay on the Population of the Sugar Colonies* would prove to be a stunning combination of colonial administration and Enlightenment science.

Excited by new scientific experiments being conducted on animals in the metropole, specifically the work being carried out by Daubenton, his fellow member of the Académie Royale des Sciences, Bory suggested in his *Essai* that a "new improved race" (*cette nouvelle race perfectionnée*) could be produced if the island's people were selectively bred like sheep.[18] Focusing on "the race of mulattoes," he proposed "trying the experiments of M[on-sieur] Daubenton on this portion of the human species," adding, "this clever naturalist [*physicien*] has made a great number [of experiments] on sheep."[19] By sanctioning marriage between mulatto women and white men, banning marriage between mulatto women and black men, and enforcing criteria of selection, administrators could "improve the race of mulattoes" and pro-duce a new group of men who would be well suited to take a greater role in fulfilling the military and policing duties of the colony.[20] "Nature and art offer us a new means of population [*un nouveau moyen de population*]," Bory wrote; "why not take advantage of it?"[21] As shocking as Bory's suggestion was, it has gone practically unnoticed by historians.[22]

Bory was an officer-philosophe who maintained an involvement in scientific work throughout his life. After rising through the ranks of the navy to become a ship captain in 1757, he assumed the governor-generalship of Saint-Domingue in 1761, serving until near the end of the Seven Years' War. He was relieved of his duties in 1763 and returned to live in France.[23] Less than three years after his arrival in the metropole, the most exalted scien-tific body in ancien régime France, the Académie Royale des Sciences in Paris, named him a free associate (an *associé libre*), a position that gave him the freedom to work in any area of the sciences. He subsequently achieved the high naval rank of *chef d'escadre* in 1766 and became a member of the scientifically oriented Académie de Marine in Brest in 1769, a naval adviser during the French Revolution, and a member of the National Institute of the Sciences and Arts (the institution that replaced the Académie Royale des Sciences) in 1796. While Bory did not achieve great success in the sciences with any specific discovery, creation, or analytical skill, he was a respected member of the scientific elite who was well enough established and promi-nent enough by the 1780s to be named to the famous committee assigned to judge the legitimacy of the magnetic therapies and theories of mesmerism (which also included scientific luminaries such as Benjamin Franklin and Antoine Lavoisier).[24] Though he wrote on a variety of issues, in the great majority of his work he pursued subjects related to naval concerns, colo-nization, and the sciences, such as the mapping of coastlines, introducing the reflecting octant to France, carrying out astronomical observations to improve navigation, determining the exact position of islands such as the Azores, and evaluating the different means of improving the quality of air below the decks of ships.[25]

Bory served as governor-general for only two years—during which time he even saw his control of the military transferred to a more experienced commander of ground troops, Armand, vicomte de Belzunce—but he had a considerable role in initiating some of the reforms that would transform the structure and composition of the militia and policing corps of Saint-Domingue between the Seven Years' War and the Haitian Revolution. Bory was aware of the unpopularity of militia service among white planters, and he also recognized the need for a more experienced and dedicated military force.[26] He wrote to the minister suggesting that white militia service should be abolished and that more free blacks and mulattoes should be enlisted to form a new corps. In the spirit of these suggestions, in April 1762 he ordered the creation of a new corps of "archers" or "hunters" composed of free blacks and mulattoes.[27] The ministry approved the organization of the Chasseurs volontaires d'Amérique, but it would not immediately approve the elimination of mandatory militia service for whites.[28]

Bory went beyond arguing for the creation of black and mulatto forces to replace white militia service, suggesting that all enslaved mulatto men of arms-bearing age should be freed so that they could be enlisted in military service.[29] As he would again in the *Essay on the Population of the Sugar Colonies* in 1776, he argued that all mulattoes "born and to be born" should be freed; sometimes he also included the *sang-mêlé* (mixed-blood), a loosely defined group of people of mixed African and European descent who generally had a larger proportion of European ancestors and lighter skin than most of the people designated as *mulâtre* (mulatto).[30] The many people of Saint-Domingue who were of mixed African and European descent were referred to by a great variety of names in the second half of the eighteenth century. Although usage was unsystematic, many of the names carried implications and particular meanings. The term *mulâtre* (mulatto) could be used to refer to a person who was equally of African and European descent, or nearly so. Along with *sang-mêlé*, the term *gens du couleur* (people of color) was the most general term, and *affranchis* (freed people) was a general term used for free people of color that emphasized their genealogical ties to enslavement. There also existed a number of terms with no exact translation, such as *griffe* and *marabou*, to refer to the people of mixed mulatto and African descent. While there was a long tradition of free black and mulatto military and police service in Saint-Domingue and the region, it was an unusual idea for mulattoes to become a special class of people who would be the only group responsible for the military service and policing of the island. To be more precise, it was not unusual for colonial administrators and planters to think about the free people of color as social intermediaries between whites and the enslaved, people who could also provide military or police service, keep enslaved people from fleeing plantations, and return those who had succeeded in fleeing. But the idea that mulattoes would be the only group responsible for these duties and that these duties would be their sole responsibility (except for a few white commissioned officers) was

not common.[31] While free people of color made up the majority of the police force (the *maréchaussée*) and the militia force of Saint-Domingue by the
later part of the eighteenth century, the size of those forces was woefully
inadequate to ensure lasting security for the colony or even to carry out
normal security duties. As one scholar has written, "a lot of the security
functions just did not get done."[32] Bory envisioned enlarging the militia,
giving it a greater role in policing, and filling all the positions, except for
those of the few commissioned officers, with people of color, thus creating
a large and separate soldier class.

During the war, Choiseul summarily rejected Bory's proposal to end
mandatory white militia service, and he seems to have simply ignored the
proposal to free all mulattoes.[33] When the war ended in 1763, the metropolitan government initiated militia reforms and briefly abolished mandatory service, but by the end of the decade the issue had become even more
contentious than it had been before the war. The strong resistance to the
militia developed into a full-blown revolt in 1769, and even though it was
put down relatively quickly by the government, the question of militia service was still central to the politics of the island when Bory and Hilliard
d'Auberteuil wrote their works in the 1770s.[34] The militia was still the most
potent symbol, along with the *Exclusif*, of white colonists' displeasure with
the metropolitan government. The disputes over the militia were also an
acknowledgment on the part of the white community of their precarious security. They were well aware that they were vastly outnumbered by people
whom they kept subjugated by threat and force, and that Saint-Domingue
was a valuable colony coveted by rival imperial powers.

Bory's *Essay* was an extension of the various military and militia-related
reforms that he had attempted to bring about, with varying degrees of
success, as governor-general. But now he could justify his arguments for
the creation of a mulatto and sang-mêlé militia through references to new
science that had recently received significant financial and logistical support from the government and that had been greeted enthusiastically by savants in Paris. He gave particular attention to Daubenton's state-sponsored
sheep-breeding experiments.[35] Unlike some previous and contemporary
experiments with controlled breeding, Daubenton integrated theory and
practice. He carried out the longest, the most extensive, and probably the
best-financed and most controlled selective breeding experiment in history
up until that point.[36] Not only was the project of great scientific interest, but
it offered the possibility of providing the nation with tremendous financial
gains. "The experiments of M. Daubenton have shown the way," enthused
the marquis de Condorcet, secretary of the Académie Royale des Sciences.
Condorcet saw much work to be done, but he believed that it held the

potential for a "treasure, more substantial than the Golden Fleece that the Argonauts set out to conquer."[37]

This breakthrough was not lost on the French government or on Buffon's collaborator Daubenton, whose thorough and meticulous style had first been demonstrated in the anatomical contributions to the *Natural History* and could also be seen in his experiments with sheep. There were two specific elements of that research that made it particularly appealing for Bory and his purposes in Saint-Domingue. Daubenton was interested in crossing the "races" of sheep that had the greatest demonstrable differences between them.[38] In pursuit of this goal, and with the considerable financial support of the government, he obtained a wide variety of sheep from as far away as Morocco and Tibet.[39] He claimed that with these exotic animals, he had produced a new type of French sheep that rivaled the famous Merino variety in the quality and quantity of their wool. This gave further validation to the idea that a "race" could be improved through crossbreeding. It also may have demonstrated to Bory that if the pairs being crossed were extremely different (as people of African and European descent were thought to be), this was not a liability, but instead could be utilized for "improvement."

Another important aspect of Daubenton's work was his claim that the characteristics of the male animals were reproduced more strongly in the offspring. In bringing together two animals of different quality, therefore, it was important to ensure that the male was the "better" of the two. This idea was common in early modern discussions of animal breeding as well as human reproduction, and it was a central element of the early modern discourse of noble blood and noble "race" (understood as lineage).[40] Beyond a general misogyny, this prejudice derived from—and was reinforced by—a complex of social, legal, and political concerns that were well beyond the narrow limits of the biological, chief among these being issues of the inheritance of property, noble titles, and offices. Daubenton's "scientific" finding surely reflected these preexisting prejudices about the dominance of male character in maintaining good lineage, but Daubenton's presentation of his findings separated ideas about the importance of male character from any explicit relation to the social world and presented them as pure and disinterested facts of science. Bory took up this idea and recounted it in aesthetic terms—as was common in writing about race—claiming that the "beauty" of an individual was particularly dependent on the beauty of its father.[41] In this way, he reinforced the taboo on sexual relations between men of color and white women and was able to conserve the sexual dynamics of society in Saint-Domingue.

As is clear from the examples in the previous chapters, Bory was not the only one to wonder about the applicability of animal-breeding experiments to humans. Along with Hilliard d'Auberteuil, Bory was the first to propose that specific breeding plans be carried out in a specific human population. They went even further than people like Vandermonde, suggesting that the reproduction of large groups should be regulated so that entire populations could be transformed on the basis of certain predefined goals. While Vandermonde tried to show that it was possible for the human species to be improved through selective breeding of individual humans, Bory and Hilliard d'Auberteuil accepted that it was possible to transform a large group of people (whether this large group was a species, race, or a population of a colony); argued that highly controlled selective breeding should be carried out on a large scale on a real (and specific) population; and focused on bodily characteristics associated with the new ideas of race as the primary criterion of selection.

While Bory explicitly referenced the writings of the metropolitan savants on animal breeding, Hilliard d'Auberteuil's debt to this work was less direct. His vision built on possibilities that had emerged only with the Buffonian revolution. Hilliard d'Auberteuil did not articulate the theoretical (biological) underpinnings of his plan, but whether or not he had direct knowledge of the work of Buffon, he based his proposal on several assumptions that were central to, and characteristic of, the Buffonian approach to selective breeding and human variation. Hilliard d'Auberteuil assumed a theory of secular monogenesis, epigenetic generation, and the implicit belief in the interfertility of human varieties or "races." These assumptions provide the basis for his conviction that human varieties as apparently different as people of African descent and those of European descent could produce fertile offspring without any sign of decreasing fertility through a lineage (as opposed to the many theorists who believed that mulattoes were infertile or of a very limited fertility that would keep them from creating a self-sustaining lineage). Furthermore, these assumptions also implied that both parents contributed physical characteristics to offspring and that acquired characteristics (such as skin color, which was initially acquired through the influence of climate) could be inherited. Most importantly, Hilliard d'Auberteuil's plan was not based on some vague idea of the "improvement" or "perfectibility" of the human form, but rather the conviction that humans could be selected and bred (like animals) to produce changes to specific characteristics such as skin color.

Born in Rennes in 1751, Hilliard d'Auberteuil set off for Saint-Domingue when he was only fourteen, finding work as a legal clerk.[42] Not much is known about his youth there, but he eventually became well known in colonial circles as a man of "violent temperament" who either had trouble restraining himself or repeatedly chose not to.[43] This "enemy of all subordination," who often wrote with "too much fire and freedom," frequently found himself in trouble because of his provocative rhetoric and his critiques of the established order.[44] But as a yet unknown and unpublished man in his early twenties, he began writing the two volumes of *Considérations*, which appeared in 1777 and would prove to be one of the most vituperative published critiques of French ancien régime colonial policy.

In *Considérations*, Hilliard d'Auberteuil developed an eclectic and energetic critical style that addressed a variety of topics and groups. He criticized the administrators in the metropole as well as those in the colonies, the philosophes as well as the planters, slave owners as well as the enslaved. In retrospect, he looks like an unlikely candidate for involvement in colonial administration, but at the time he was seen as a talented young prospect with legal training and the reforming spirit necessary to take on the entrenched problems of the colonies. While Hilliard d'Auberteuil never achieved as high-ranking an administrative position as did Bory, he did have many direct engagements with the colonial administration, including several significant positions in the legal apparatus.[45] In 1776, when he returned to France seeking publication of his long manuscript, he found support in the Bureau des Colonies of the Ministry of the Marine. After a favorable report from the physiocrat and former colonial intendant Pierre-Paul Le Mercier de la Rivière, publication of the book was supported by the ministry, which ended up paying some of the debts that Hilliard d'Auberteuil incurred in publishing *Considérations*. The book appeared with the *approbation & privilège du Roi*, although the book was suppressed quickly after publication in response to complaints from the planters and administrators of Saint-Domingue.[46] The suppression did not stop *Considérations* from becoming a significant work in French colonial discourse. Médéric-Louis-Élie Moreau de Saint-Méry would discuss it in his own influential book on Saint-Domingue, characterizing *Considérations* as "a great sensation in Saint-Domingue."[47] The book met with a book-length published refutation and a qualified defense within a few years, and ten years after publication Julien Raimond was still complaining to the minister of the marine about Hilliard d'Auberteuil's characterization of the gens de couleur.[48] The book was translated into German, and it found its most significant reception in metropolitan France in the work of Abbé Henri Grégoire, who discussed Hilliard d'Auberteuil and cited *Considérations* in several of his works.[49]

The argument of *Considérations* is difficult to characterize because as a denunciatory critique it enumerated many things that it was against while often remaining vague about what it supported. It was also full of ambiguity and apparent contradiction, including Hilliard d'Auberteuil's criticizing the baseness of the enslaved while also claiming that "no species of men has more intelligence."[50] Nonetheless, it can be said that Hilliard focused on describing the current problems of the colony and showing that reform needed to be effected through new policies on trade and taxation, the elimination of the military from governance, greater involvement of white creoles in government, and a new code of laws based on firsthand knowledge of the island.[51] He emphasized that it was only through living on the island over a long period of time that one could understand the unique *mœurs* (customs and disposition) of the people of Saint-Domingue and how they reflected the local climate. Such intimate knowledge was necessary if one was to achieve the all-important harmony of laws and mœurs. Although Hilliard d'Auberteuil had strongly worded criticisms for white creoles, his arguments generally reflected the nascent creole identity, generally advocated the empowerment of the colony in its relations with the metropole, and reinforced white supremacy on the island.[52] According to Malick Ghachem, *Considérations* "did more than any other single work of the colonial Enlightenment to advance a jurisprudence of *créolité*."[53] While many of Hilliard d'Auberteuil's jurisprudential ideas about the interaction of laws and mœurs echoed Montesquieu—sometimes merely copying from *The Spirit of the Laws*—he went beyond Montesquieu and almost all contemporary jurists in asserting that not only were the mœurs of a people made by laws, but so too were their bodies, or at least they could be. In chapters analyzing the population of Saint-Domingue and the class of *affranchis* (freed people, i.e., free people of color at least partially descendant from enslaved people), he argued that the government should literally and physically make men. These later chapters gave a new and more expansive meaning to the claim that "men are what the Government make them."[54] In the context of Hilliard d'Auberteuil's book, this phrase was not only an echo of the republican idea that a government and its laws could affect the moral character of a people; it was also a biopolitical claim about refashioning individual bodies and the collective body.

Hilliard d'Auberteuil developed his ideas about human breeding in the second volume of *Considérations*, in a chapter that focused on the affranchis.[55] He expressed his desire to see the creation of "an intermediary class between the slaves and free [white] people."[56] This class would need to be "absolutely distinct" from enslaved people, and this distinction had to be reflected through "external signs" that corresponded to the different civil statuses of whites, affranchis, and slaves.[57] Skin color was the only external sign that he discussed; in fact, his entire plan revolved around transforming the skin color of free people of color into a homogeneous "yellow." Hilliard d'Auberteuil wanted to reduce the diverse society of Saint-Domingue to three distinct groups, whose differences in civil status would be visibly apparent: blacks, who would be enslaved; whites, who would have full civil status; and the middle group, "yellow" mulattoes, who would have their freedom but would be subject to a number of segregationist laws and would be burdened with the special duty of providing security for the island and policing the enslaved majority.[58] In the new tripartite social and civil hierarchy intended to replace the metropolitan hierarchy of the three estates, Hilliard d'Auberteuil wanted to create a rigorous correspondence between skin color and status (both social and civil).

Hilliard d'Auberteuil's plan also would have enacted a ban on marriage between white men and any woman who was deemed to be black or within six generations of "la race des Noirs," since they would have still carried "an indelible mark" (*une tache inéfaçable*) of the contempt for blackness and slavery heaped on them by white society.[59] Like almost all his contemporaries who wrote about intermarriage and mixed coupling, Hilliard d'Auberteuil addressed sexual relations between women of color and white men but did not entertain the possibility of white women having sexual relations with men of color.[60] His aim was to stop white men from marrying "Négresses, Mulâtresses & Quarteronnes," but he acknowledged that such a ban could not be enforced for anyone from the sixth generation of descent from a black relative, because by that point it would be impossible to visually distinguish such a person from someone of exclusively European descent.[61] This call to prohibit intermarriage was not exceptional for the era or the region—a formal ban on marriage or concubinage between blacks and whites had been enacted in Louisiana in 1724, and a variety of ordinances to criminalize or discourage such relationships were in place across the Atlantic world.[62] Hilliard d'Auberteuil's plan, however, was unusual in its focus on free people of color and his suggestions about what needed to be done to make these people a homogeneously pigmented intermediary group.

The first step toward producing this middle group was for all free black men to be married to mulatto women, and for mulatto men to marry free black women.[63] Hilliard d'Auberteuil did not indicate how long he believed it would take for all the varieties of color of the affranchis to be balanced out into a relatively homogeneous "yellow." Presumably this would have been a long-term project spanning numerous generations. He aimed for the near-complete elimination, presumably within several generations, of the various peoples who fell in between the extremes of black, white, and "yellow." His second step was intended, among other things, to make the class of slaves more consistently black by granting freedom to all mulatto children—or as he referred to them euphemistically, those born from the "weakness" of the white colonists.[64] He did implicitly acknowledge that not all enslaved people would be of purely African descent; for instance, griffes and marabous (the offspring of one black and one mulatto parent) would continue to be born, but he regarded these people as "les négres" and re-iterated that they needed to "remain" in slavery.[65] He presumably believed that even though they were not strictly of African descent, their skin would be dark enough that they would be easily differentiated from the newly ho-mogenized, free "yellow" mulattoes.

Hilliard d'Auberteuil did not discuss the military role he envisioned for the new mulatto class as extensively as Bory did, but he made it clear that they would have a special role to play in providing external security from imperial aggression and internal stability. Furthermore, their internal role would be twofold, as they would provide a social buffer separating white people from enslaved black people, and they would also compose the po-lice units responsible for maintaining general order and hunting enslaved people who had fled plantations or otherwise escaped the control of their enslavers. Hilliard d'Auberteuil did not go into detail about the role the gov-ernment would need to play in carrying out his vision, but it is obvious from the scope of the proposal that it would have had to be a major role. In fact, it would have been well beyond the means of government. In terms of the large number of people who would have been directly affected, the substan-tial number of administrators and enforcers who would have been needed, the significant amount of money it would have required, the extraordinary amount of work and resources it would have taken to gain the consent or submission of the wealthy and powerful free people of color, and the long period of time that would have been needed to bring the plan to fruition, Hilliard d'Auberteuil's plan would have been a massive undertaking.

Among the white population of Saint-Domingue in the 1760s and 1770s, there was a growing concern with white purity that was reflected in new segregationist laws aimed primarily at containing the power and social sta-tus of free people of color.[66] At the same time, there was a growing concern about status deception and "passing." Hilliard d'Auberteuil was not the only one who offered a plan to ensure that no enslaved people could pass as free people and that no free people of color could pass for white. The archives of the Ministry of the Marine contain another such *mémoire* by a high-ranking official responsible for maintaining public order in late eighteenth-century Saint-Domingue, the seneschal and lieutenant of the Admiralty of Cap Français, Jean-Baptiste Estève.[67] Estève feared that through mixed mar-riage, some people of color were coming dangerously close to "our species," and that it would eventually become impossible to detect that these people were not of purely European descent.[68] It was therefore necessary to find means of creating greater differentiation between free people of color, the enslaved, and white people. He believed that regulating the free people of color was key to maintaining general order and the racial hierarchy, and to "ensur[ing] the quality of the mixed-blood race in the future."[69] He thus wanted to conduct a census to determine the size of the population of free people of color and then create a registration system to keep track of their numbers and locations. Estève also raised the long-standing suggestion that freed men of color should be given "a distinctive and external mark of their liberty."[70] While he believed that no one failed to find this idea promising, he acknowledged that it was not practical because there was no reliable means of ensuring that the enslaved could not escape and illegitimately acquire the mark. Although there is no sign that these ideas were put into practice in Saint-Domingue, they were a part of a larger development of heightened concern with identifying and tracking the movements of the enslaved in both the colonies and metropolitan France. For example, the metropolitan regulations from the late 1770s and early 1780s known as the Police des Noirs (analyzed in chapter 4) had some features that were identical to some of those in Estève's proposal. Colonial programs of population monitoring during the Revolutionary period also shared certain features, as when administrators of the French Caribbean colonies such as Victor Hugues and Léger-Félicité Sonthonax attempted to enact new racially based practices of surveillance.[71]

Unlike Estève and others who fantasized about creating an external mark to be placed on people, Hilliard d'Auberteuil wanted to change the people themselves by transforming their appearance until their bodies were immutable and transparent signs of their social and civil status. He did not merely want to change them by branding them (the common manner in which enslaved people were marked).[72] Nor did he want to force them to wear clothing that identified their position within the sociojuridical hierarchy, as was done to a degree in metropolitan France and more dramatically in the imaginary society of François de Salignac de La Mothe Fénelon's popular book *The Adventures of Telemachus, Son of Ulysses* (*Les aventures de Télémaque, fils d'Ulysse*) of 1699.[73] Hilliard d'Auberteuil wanted to literally change who they were, so as to bring their physical appearance in line with the newly transformed social and civil categories. He was not merely attempting to change the skin color of the people of Saint-Domingue. He had a more radical vision of a new colonial hierarchy for the island that would replace the three estates of ancien régime France. He was surprisingly explicit and direct about this. "Between white men," he wrote, "there should be no other distinctions than those of employment and personal merit; in the Colony, there should be neither grand men, nobles, nor corporate bodies; there should be only free people, freed people [*affranchis*], slaves, and the law."[74]

The project of human breeding that he proposed was an integral aspect of creating and maintaining this new hierarchy. He described his chapter on the affranchis as a discussion of "the means of preventing the confusion of ranks and the mixing of classes" of free white people, freed people of color, and black enslaved people.[75]

Hilliard d'Auberteuil's work provides a unique glimpse into the dynamic process through which the modern idea of race came into being in the eighteenth century. He recognized that the empirically evident differences between people were not signs of absolutely essential and fixed differences, but were merely unstable differences that needed to be actively stabilized, homogenized, and reproduced if they were going to provide the foundation for a new type of durable social hierarchy. In order for the newly developing racial categories to provide a basis for a sociojuridical hierarchy, external signs of difference needed to be manipulated and maintained. In other words, producing a more thorough and consistent racial hierarchy required that differences be reconstructed as well as reproduced. At times, Hilliard d'Auberteuil expressed within a single sentence this relation between human malleability and a type of contingent fixity, as when he reflected on the possibility of effacing the characteristics of people who embodied what he called "the natural and organic character of *la race negre*" (*le caractere naturel et organique de la race negre*).[76] He had already argued that whites, blacks, and "yellow" mulattoes should be made to be more consistently uniform in their skin color and that this should be reproduced over time so that it could act as a means to enforce civil and social differences. Then referring to the diminishment of blackness through a lineage in which each successive generation reproduces with a white mate, Hilliard d'Auberteuil argued that at some point there would no longer an identifiable and meaningful racial difference, which in turn made research into a family's racial lineage unnecessary. Through this crossing and whitening, "when the natural and organic character of *la race negre* is absolutely effaced, there is no longer any reason to maintain differences that no longer have anything real [about them]: there is a term beyond which one should not make any research, where they would even become absolutely useless."[77] The posited racial character was not absolutely essential nor fixed, yet it was "natural and organic." It could be reproduced and maintained with human actions, yet it could also be "absolutely effaced." It could diminish until it became undetectable and, in a sense, nonexistent, yet for it to disappear it had to have existed. This juxtaposition of fixity and contingency, existence and nonexistence, social construction and biological manipulation, reveals how race came into being as a transitional idea in the late eighteenth century. It is telling that it is through a claim about the effacement of race that Hilliard d'Auberteuil wrote of the supposedly natural and organic character of a race. In this case, the negative image throws into relief his assumptions and beliefs.

Hilliard d'Auberteuil wanted to change people to make them fit within the boundaries of racial categories, but in specifying what such people would be like, and suggesting how they could be made to better fit within these categories, he helped give meaning to the categories and therefore the very idea of race. His plan was an extraordinary example of the social application of the "metaphysics of presence," which was such an important element of French Enlightenment thought. Much as Condillac, Rousseau, Diderot, and other metropolitan philosophes desired to find a clear and immediate means of communication that could express the true nature of things, making them manifest and present, Hilliard d'Auberteuil wanted to create a transparent social order by making human bodies representative of their social position, primarily through skin color.[78] This overburdening of skin color as the ontological representation of human difference was a significant development in the "epidermalization" of race, whereby the external marker of skin color came to be seen as the primary marker of racial difference. Hilliard d'Auberteuil's vision of creating classes of homogeneously colored people seems to have gone beyond any of the practices of external marking and identification practiced in early modern Europe or the Americas.[79] Furthermore, there do not appear to have been any practices or proposals in the early modern Atlantic world or in Europe that went as far as his vision for the large-scale reconstruction of a population.

Hilliard d'Auberteuil's plan was also a clear demonstration of the links between ideas of inclusion and exclusion in Enlightenment biopolitics. His arguments, based on notions of equality and inequality, proposed the elimination of social and legal distinctions among white residents of Saint-Domingue as if it were contingent on the creation and entrenchment of a new hierarchy based on racial difference. In fact, Hilliard d'Auberteuil's radical argument for absolute equality between whites in the colony fit within a larger campaign to repress and transform the free people of color on the island. Saint-Domingue was one of only three large and economically dynamic slave societies of the region to have a large and successful population of free people of color by the late eighteenth century, yet it was the only of these three slave societies to have a swift and widespread campaign in which whites attempted to differentiate themselves and to use the law to economically, socially, and symbolically subjugate this group.[80] In the 1760s and 1770s, local officials and colonial administrators created a variety of laws and regulations to achieve these goals. In 1773, for example, free people of color were required to have a family name of "African" derivation, even if they had a greater number of European ancestors than they did "African."[81] At the same time, segregationist laws were put into place that barred free people of color from sitting with whites in public places like cafés and theaters. Later in the 1770s, sumptuary laws banned free people of color from wearing clothing made from some expensive fabrics, and they were banned from carrying swords, which were, of course, symbols of nobility in addition to being weapons.[82] A decade earlier, free people of color were banned from employment in some of the professions of status and power, such as medicine, surgery, pharmacy, the law, and the notarial services.[83] Throughout the 1760s and 1770s there were also a number of disparate attempts to shift the burden of proof of legitimate freedom onto free people of color. This included increases in the amount of evidence necessary to prove legitimate manumission, as well as various attempts to require free people of color to carry notarized manumission papers or similar proofs of freedom with them at all times.[84]

In light of this concerted efforts to change the social and economic structures of the colony along new racialized lines, we can see that Hilliard d'Auberteuil's vision of a new equality between white people was grounded in a new vision of the inequality between white people and free people of color. One of Hilliard d'Auberteuil's goals was to limit the considerable social and economic power of some free people of color by finding a way to raise the so-called *petit blanc* (the lower-status whites) above free people of color. Hilliard d'Auberteuil's book was, therefore, a part of the general campaign to subjugate the free people of color, and it became a primary target for those wealthy free people of color, such as Julien Raimond, who attempted to resist these efforts and appeal to the colonial officials in the metropole.[85] The racially based inequality of Hilliard d'Auberteuil's vision of a new hierarchy, with its exclusion of free people of color from the highest strata of social and civil status, was the condition of possibility for the newly envisioned equality between white people. The newly broadened inclusion of white people was based in the new exclusion of free people of color.

While there is not evidence of a large number of biopolitical projects aimed at the racial reconstruction of the colonies in this time period, there are a several breeding proposals that demonstrate that Bory and Hilliard d'Auberteuil were not alone in their vision of strategic racial engineering. When the military man Louis-Henry Laurent de Fayd'erbe, the comte de Maudave, proposed a new French colony in the wake of the Seven Years' War, he envisioned a permanent and productive French colony in the Indian Ocean that would compensate for the French losses in India suffered during the war. The new colony would supersede the underdeveloped colonial outposts on the Île de Bourbon and the Île de France. Years before the Kourou expedition set out for Guiana in hopes of establishing a new type of colony without enslaved people, Maudave proposed a colony in Madagascar where French settlers would mix with free indigenous peoples.[86] Maudave believed that bans on intermarriage were proper for established slave colonies that were already divided into populations of enslavers and enslaved. But in order to establish new colonies, like Madagascar, the population being free and having the freedom of marriage would produce a useful intermixing, resulting in the desired incorporation of the indigenous people into the colonizing population, improving the indigenous and the settler population.[87] In some ways, Maudave's proposal revisited the type of colonial mélange that was briefly advocated, though practiced in a limited fashion, during Colbert's term as minister under Louis XIV at the end of the seventeenth century. Unlike the assimilationist attempts to "Frenchify" (*franciser*) the native peoples of the Americas, Maudave's idea of mélange focused more on civilizing and "improving" the Malagasy than on the desire to create social, familial, and religious bonds.[88]

Another proposal for systematic mixing or crossbreeding aimed at transforming the physical and "racial" characteristics of a colonial population was formulated by Jean-Samuel Guisan, a Swiss engineer who was employed by royal administrators in the French colony of Guiana in the 1780s. Like Bory and Hilliard, Guisan was someone involved in the French colonial administration who participated in many typical activities of a figure of the colonial Enlightenment, such as projects of improvement (draining swamps and building canals), natural historical study and experimentation (writing works on electric eels and the acclimatization of clove plants in the Antilles), the policing of the enslaved (the taking of slave inventories), discussions with philosophes and naturalists while visiting Paris (including Buffon), and involvement in colonial reform (assessing the causes of death on the Kourou expedition).[89] In Guiana, a decade after the failed experiment to settle Kourou without enslaved people, Guisan sent a *mémoire* to the colonial officials in the metropole advocating a program of large-scale crossing between white settlers and a community that had been established by people who had escaped slavery, the "maroon" population known as the Boni. Guisan presented the reproductive mixing of the populations as the central means of transforming the supposedly barbaric and combative Boni into a civilized and productive colonial population of mixed people that could play an integral role in finally establishing Guiana on a firm footing.[90]

During the early stage of the French Revolution in 1789, a pamphlet was published in France by someone fashioning himself "J. M. C. Américain, sang-mêlé." The document bore the title *Precis on the Groaning of the Sang-mêlés in the French Colonies* (*Précis des gémissemens des sang-mêlés dans les colonies françoises*). Published by the printer of the National Assembly and addressing the representatives of the nation, the text focusses on *sang-mêlés* children in the French colonies in the Caribbean. The author claims that "it would be fitting to establish there a respectable asylum, under the name of [the House of] Order, for gathering and raising all the *sang-mêlés* who will be born in slavery."[91] The author is particularly concerned with the illegitimate children of white men, clarifying that he uses the term *sang-mêlés* in the broad, generic sense that includes "all mulattos, quarterons, *métis*, *tiercerons*, etc."[92] Regardless of the civil status of the mother or the position of the father, the state would seize all *sang-mêlés* children born into slavery, raise them in the newly established institution, and train them for useful work in the colonies. Appraising their maturation, the author turns an eye to their eventual social position and their biological reproduction: "the students, and those dependent on this establishment, could only exercise subordinate positions among themselves; they could only ally themselves with *sang-mêlés*."[93] These prescriptions would ensure a racial and social frontier separating enslaved black people and free people of color.

Advocating the breeding of humans was not the only way in which some people in the colonies envisioned racially engineering the population through biopolitical interventions. It is worth analyzing the work of a prominent colonial figure who had a biopolitical vision that also built on a Buffonian perspective, not as an advocate of selective breeding, but as someone working to reduce reproductive mixing in the colonies, particularly between people of European and African descent. Médéric-Louis-Élie Moreau de Saint-Méry was a French colonial jurist who worked to reduce racial mixing and to protect the "purity," distinctness, and supremacy of whiteness through measures that were both epistemological and practical. In his most important epistemological intervention, he attempted to create the most extensive and systematic series of tables representing possible racial mixtures so as to furnish an epistemic tool for those planters and colonial administrators who were interested in limiting reproduction between white people and people of African descent.[94] In addition to this epistemic tool, Moreau also recommended action to the royal administration. In a reflection sent to colonial administrators in the 1780s, he suggested the physical removal of all "mixed blood" people from the small French colony on the Indian Ocean island of Île de France (now Mauritius) so that they could not possibly reproduce with white colonists.[95] While it was not uncommon for someone who both was a member of the white planter class and was involved in colonial administration to want to eliminate or prevent peoples of European descent from reproducing with people of any degree of African descent, this little-known archival document of Moreau's demonstrates that

he thought that biopolitical interventions by the government were necessary and achievable, even if they entailed the forcible removal of a segment
of the population to another island. Rather than a biopolitical intervention
to produce a hybrid group, it was a biopolitical intervention to ensure a
hybrid group was not produced. Moreau's proposal, therefore, reflects a different dimension of racial engineering, revealing how much the biological,
the political, and nascent ideas about races were intertwined and mobilized
in colonial biopolitics.

Moreau had moved back and forth across the Atlantic several times since
first traveling to Paris as a young man to continue his legal education.[96] A native of Martinique who established his career as a lawyer in Saint-Domingue
in the 1770s. Before he married a white woman in 1781, Moreau fathered
a daughter, Jeanne-Louise (also known as Aménaïde), with a free person
of color, Marie-Louise Laplaine, who was identified in notarial records as
a housekeeper living with him since 1776. Upon ending the employment,
Moreau gave Marie-Louise and Aménaïde two enslaved people and a siz-
able amount of money to pay for a third enslaved person.[97] Later, Moreau
became the legal guardian of Aménaïde and made references to her as his
daughter.[98] As with many men in the white planter class, Moreau's connections to people of color in the colonies seems to have mixed exploitation
and intimacy, being at once social, economic, administrative, legal, familial,
and sexual. As is also clear from his written work, particularly on topics of
race and the sexuality of women of color, Moreau was caught up in what
Doris Garraway has characterized as a "colonial family romance" replete
with overburdened symbolic representations, complicated relationships,
and psychosexual fantasies, all of which was riven with unequal power and
a foundation of violence.[99]

Moreau caught the eye of metropolitan administrators, who enlisted him
to create a massive compilation of colonial law as a part of a larger process
of codifying colonial laws in a single, coherent body, a reformist goal that
was never realized for the Old Regime colonies, nor for the metropole.[100]
This work sent Moreau back and forth between the colonies and metropole,
and his access to ministerial archives provided him the opportunity to begin researching another massive work that he hoped to be something like
a colonial version of Diderot and d'Alembert's *Encyclopédie*. Moreau never
realized this latter goal, though he did use this material to publish a large
book of unprecedented detail about Saint-Domingue, the manuscript of
which he took with him from Saint-Domingue to France and then to the
United States, publishing it only in 1796 after setting up his own printing
press and bookshop in Philadelphia. In this book, *Topographical, Physical,
Civil, Political, and Historical Description of the French Part of the Island of*

Saint-Domingue (*Description topographique, physique, civile, politique et historique de la partie française de l'isle Saint-Domingue*) and in smaller works published in Philadelphia, Moreau expressed his ideas of race, breeding, colonial order, and the necessity of administrative vigilance, along with an extreme fear of what he understood to be racial mixing.[101] These works, and their analytical contextualization, gives new meaning to the archival report of suggesting racial segregation in the Indian Ocean colony.

In general terms, Moreau's approach to nature, and the place of humans within it, was built on Buffonian foundations and informed by vitalist theories of organization that dominated among colonial physicians.[102] For example, when he published a pamphlet on improving American horse breeds, he emphasized the importance of the proper "mix of the race," not only drawing on Buffon's ideas but also quoting and paraphrasing from his writing.[103] In his work in Saint-Domingue, Moreau also drew on Buffon's arguments that domestication could improve animals. Writing about enslaved people who were born in the Americas being superior to those born in Africa, Moreau concluded that "domestication has improved the species."[104] The Buffonian understanding of race and breeding is particularly evident in Moreau's writing about racial groups within the French colonies. He is an example of someone who combined his lifelong experience of Caribbean slave colonies with a deep involvement in the scientific, legal, and philosophical currents of thought coming out of metropolitan France. Moreau was one of the relatively rare individuals who seemed to fully embody an Atlantic permutation of the Enlightenment, bringing together experiences, ideas, and concerns that might seem disparate or incompatible at first.[105] In July 1789, for instance, while living in Paris, he was elected as the primary local representative of the Third Estate of Paris, a position in which he functioned like a mayor until the new governmental position was created. Following that briefly held position, in which he briefed the king on the fall of the Bastille, he became a prominent representative of colonial interests as a representative of Martinique in the Constituent Assembly, fighting doggedly to maintain slavery, publishing many pamphlets with this purpose, and eventually, once in Philadelphia, publishing one of the most extreme works on racial classification ever to have been published.

This latter work on racial classification is in a chapter of his *Description of the French Part of Island of Saint-Domingue*, which Moreau claimed he finished writing even before departing Saint-Domingue for France in 1783. In a chapter on racial mixing, Moreau attempted to codify the terminology of the different degrees of racial mixture, while also attempting to create a racial calculus of unprecedented exactness, revealing his concern with identifying even the smallest traces of African descent (see figures 3 and 4).[106] By

Combinaiſons du Blanc.

D'un Blanc & d'une	Négreſſe, vient	un Mulâtre.
	Mulâtreſſe,	Quarteron.
	Quarterone,	Métif.
	Métive,	Mamelouque.
	Mamelouque,	Quarteronné.
	Quarteronnée,	Sang-mêlé.
	Sang-mêlée,	Sang-mêlé, qui s'approche continuellement du Blanc.
	Marabou,	Quarteron.
	Griffonne,	Quarteron.
	Sacatra,	Quarteron.

FIGURE 3. One of the tables attempting to fix racial nomenclature and identify all mixtures of people of European and African descent. It is titled "Combinations of White" and gives an ordered and sequential table of mixtures and racial terms for the resulting offspring. For example, a white man and a black woman produce a *mulatto*, while a white man and a mulatto woman produce a *quarteron*. The table also shows the number of generations it takes to go from a parent of African descent and a parent of European descent to the important colonial category of *sang-mêlé*, which is represented as being someone who is 1/128th (or less) black. Médéric-Louis-Élie Moreau de Saint-Méry, *Description topographique, physique, civile, politique et historique de la partie française de l'isle Saint-Domingue* (Philadelphia, 1797), 1:71. Courtesy of the John Carter Brown Library.

Combinaiſons du Quarteronné.

D'un Quarteronné & d'une Blanche, vient,		un Sang-mêlé.
	Sang-Mêlée,	Sang-Mê'é.
	Mamelouque,	Quarteronné.
	Métive,	Mamelouc.
	Quarteronne,	Métif.
	Mulâtreſle,	Quarteron.
	Marabou,	Quarteron.
	Griffonne,	Quarteron.
	Sacatra,	Mulâtre.
	Négreſſe,	Mulâtre.

FIGURE 4. Table of racial nomenclature and mixtures representing the offspring produced by various types of women with a *quarteronné*, a man considered by Moreau to be 1/64th black. Médéric-Louis-Élie Moreau de Saint-Méry, *Description topographique, physique, civile, politique et historique de la partie française de l'isle Saint-Domingue* (Philadelphia, 1797), 1:73. Courtesy of the John Carter Brown Library.

the 1780s there was an increased desire among some colonists and colonial officials to fix a highly detailed and precise racial nomenclature. Moreau de Saint-Méry's racial taxonomy and nomenclature in *Description of the French Part of Island of Saint-Domingue* was the most detailed, methodical, and revealing example of this new effort. For the first time in the French colonial context, and perhaps for the first time in history, someone attempted to identify all possible combinations of racial mixture between the poles of black and white, even those that went far beyond any possibility of visual perceptibility. Moreau attempted to identify and classify racial mixtures that were many generations removed from an original mixture of "black" and "white." For these reasons, Moreau's endeavor went beyond the visual classifications that were created by the Spanish artists. *Casta* paintings documented the appearance of only the first generations of the offspring of various racial combinations.[107] Moreau also went further than the racial classifications of naturalists and the images of *casta* painters through his use of quantification and his attempt to give each combination a name that corresponded to a precise calculation of racial descent. After several pages of tables illustrating the problems of the nomenclature of racial classification and the inadequacies of the common uses of the terms, Moreau presented several more pages of illustrative tables based on the idea that human beings could be divided into 128 constituent parts so that "the White and the Black each formed a whole composed of 128 parts that are white in the one and black in the other."[108] By dividing people up into 128 parts, he created a sense of race that was both fractional and fine grained.[109]

In these tables, anyone who was fewer than eight parts white was deemed black, while anyone with more than eight parts white would fall into one of nine categories between blacks and those who are deemed to be completely white.[110] A *mulâtre* (mulatto), for instance, was meant to refer only to someone who was between forty-nine and seventy parts white: one part less and the person was a *marabou*; one part more and the person was a *quarteron*.[111] Moreau made it clear that this quantified approached was necessary because skin color was not reliable as an ultimate criterion of differentiation. It did not perfectly match the supposed realities of lineage, since surely there were quarterons whose skin was "two times whiter than a Spaniard or an Italian."[112]

Moreau's efforts were an attempt to track racial difference beyond the visible appearance to identify minute invisible traces of descent, even recognizing the nonwhiteness of someone who was said to be 177 parts white and one part black.[113] In fact, if this person with a single black part had a child with someone who was completely of European descent, and that person also had children with a white partner, and this line of descent continued on for generations, Moreau imagined that a trace of blackness would remain, even if it was only a single part black and 8,191 parts white.[114] While the trace of blackness at this extreme might have been invisible, it was nonetheless calculable. Like an asymptotic curve approaching a fixed limit, the lineage could infinitely approach whiteness without ever reaching it. It was this sort of "line stretched almost to infinity" that Moreau was attempting to draw attention to, so as to create a tool of racial differentiation that appeared real and efficacious, even if it existed only in the ether of the calculations and the rhetoric of the text.[115] Through this new process of quantification, Moreau tried to convert the smallest traces of blackness into discreet, recognizable entities that would be difficult, if not impossible, to eliminate from a line of descent. Moreau, therefore, used the arbitrary division of people into 128 parts to reify racial difference. He attempted to make racial difference less abstract by creating a tool through which small traces of blackness could be turned into epistemic objects, and, perhaps, made into the means for extending social and legal inequalities to people who would have otherwise been able to enjoy the full social and legal privileges of whiteness. "If racial mixing threatened to contaminate, the masters had to conjure purity out of phantasmal impurity," Joan Dayan observed about Saint-Domingue in this period; "this sanitizing ritual engendered remarkable racial fictions."[116] Moreau's endeavor can be read as one of these remarkable racial fictions that attempted to conjure purity through a delineation of phantasmal impurity.

In unpublished reflections from around 1780, not long before Moreau claimed to have finished his *Description of the French Part of the Island of Saint-Domingue*, he suggested a way to maintain the colonial social order in the Indian Ocean colonies through the biopolitical maintenance of racial differences. Responding to news that a small number of racially mixed people had slipped into the Île de France from Île Bourbon (now La Réunion), Moreau proposed a kind of racial engineering. He argued that it was important that the government acknowledge the distinction between black people and white people and that it would be preferable if they made a "total separation between them."[117] He began by laying out the justification for preventing this mixing, arguing that mulattoes were inferior because they united the worst of "both whites and blacks."[118] After asserting that white people had a natural "contempt of all mixed blood, of whatever degree," Moreau reasserted the importance of distinguishing between skin colors, and he suggested government action.[119] "It is therefore important that the Government always acknowledge a distinction between the two colors, and even their nuances, and it would be better still to make a total separation between them," Moreau wrote.[120] He then clarified that this separation would be both spatial and genealogical, that it would put an end to all contact and any possibility of reproduction. "Île de France for a long time preserved its purity and was without mélange," Moreau wrote, "and the little mixed blood which has slipped in there is not numerous and without any [inconvenience?] could, I believe, be sent back to Île Bourbon, from which the majority have come, and where circumstances forced a blind eye to mixed alliances."[121] This reflection is only a passing reference to a segregationist biopolitics of racial differentiation, but it gives his published writing about race and racial classification a new edge. It reveals how his epistemic interventions in colonial questions of race were not disconnected from a sense that racial engineering of a sort could be practiced. It is not simply that he published such fevered and fearful calculations of descent and racial mixing, but that he wanted the government to create policies to enforce the separation of black and white, ensuring that mélange did not occur.

"Surely no one will make us desire the incorporation and the [reproductive] mixing of the Races?" asked Pierre-Victor Malouet, a one-time junior administrator in Saint-Domingue who became a plantation owner and one of the most prominent French authorities on colonial affairs in the late eighteenth century.[122] His rhetorical question, with its overstated certainty and reactionary ring, provided its own answer. Writing in 1775, Malouet argued that the stigmatization of slavery must be increased so as to counter the desire for mixing, and therefore, as he put it, to avoid the alteration, debasement, and dissolution of individuals, families, and nations.[123] Although it is still a little-known dimension of the eighteenth century, a number of people did desire an "incorporation and . . . mixing of the Races" that went beyond the individual desire for sexual relationships. In fact, this included Jean-Samuel Guisan, whom Malouet would later be responsible for bringing to Guiana to work in royal service in the French colony. It also included Bory and Hilliard d'Auberteuil, who wrote their plans at the same time as Malouet posed his question.

Bory's and Hilliard d'Auberteuil's plans for human breeding were important examples of a nascent discourse that argued for the desirability of large-scale projects to control the reproduction of populations, but they were also useful models for understanding how a constellation of related ideas about human difference became modern ideas of race. There is no single moment or place from which a modern "scientific" idea of race arose, but it appears that the period from the 1750s to the 1780s in France and the French Atlantic colonies was crucial in bringing about significant conceptual transformation. The new understanding of the radical malleability of human bodies, as well as the ideas about human breeding that were made possible by this understanding, seems to have played a significant role in the development of modern ideas of race. The Buffonian revolution raised questions about human variation and "race" that were both exciting and troubling, particularly for people who lived in the Atlantic world or had an administrative or scientific interest there. Bory's and Hilliard d'Auberteuil's incorporation and transformation of metropolitan ideas about race and breeding is further evidence of the importance of including the Atlantic world and the colonial context in the history of biopolitics and the development of ideas of race.[124]

Although these proposals for selectively breeding humans to racially engineer Saint-Domingue were not enacted, their conception demonstrates the extent to which idea ideas about selective breeding had developed in the late eighteenth century. They draw our attention to the manner in which ideas of human breeding were already tied up with ideas of race and the realities of slavery in the colonies. Biopolitical proposals based on similar ideas of race and reproduction continued into the nineteenth century and took on a new urgency for colonial officials and governments that were interested in using the reproduction of enslaved people as a means of mitigating the economic effects of the end of the trade in enslaved people. Some of these proposals aimed to increase populations of enslaved people in light of a possible reduction or end of the trade, while others were intent on improving the quality of specific racial groups or limiting the reproduction of those seen as problematic or inferior.[125] Some of these plans, in a manner not unlike Bory's and Hilliard d'Auberteuil's proposals, also drew on metropolitan scientific ideas and reified race conceptions and categories, helping to make "races" by transforming them into more homogenous groups while at the same time addressing those groups who were not easily fit into the nascent racial categories, such as the *mulâtres* of Bory and Hilliard d'Auberteuil.

The fact that Bory and Hilliard d'Auberteuil published their proposals almost simultaneously in the 1770s shows that even as modern ideas of race were coming into being, both sides of the dialectic of race were already present. There was already a fundamental tension between those who wanted to increase human variation and "improve" the races through mixing and those who wanted to erect new boundaries of reproductive segregation and create new categories of differentiation.[126] People of mixed descent— mestizo, mulatto, *métis*, and hybrid—were the clearest embodiment of this tension, and their very existence repeatedly confounded attempts to create a science of race in the nineteenth century.[127] The management, if not the production or elimination, of people who seemed to fall between racial categories was, of course, a major force in the development of European colonial policies, discursive formations, and their entanglement with ideas of race.[128] The figure of the métis was a nexus in the nineteenth-century imperial biopolitical complex. "In linking domestic arrangements to the public order, family to the state, sex to subversion, and psychological essence to racial type," Ann Laura Stoler has written, "*métissage* might be read as a metonym for the biopolitics of empire at large."[129] Something similar could be said about the centrality of métissage and the métis in nineteenth- and twentieth-century biopolitical projects such as the eugenics movement.

The treatment of people that were thought to be racial hybrids continued to demonstrate the fundamental paradox of the Enlightenment, sometimes in a single proposal or body of ideas. Even the discourse of racial improvement could become an eliminationist discourse of exclusion. Building on the Buffonian foundation of secular monogenesis that included all peoples in the same species, some thinkers argued that some races should, in effect, be bred out of existence. This resulted in a paternalist discourse of improvement that relied on hybridization to gradually eliminate races. Writing from within the Buffonian paradigm in the middle of the nineteenth century, for example, Michel-Hyacinthe Deschamps was one of the thinkers who believed that monogenesis implied an equality of malleability between races, but he wanted to see some races improved through hybridization in a way that would have eliminated their (supposedly) racial characteristics. For Deschamps and others, it was the very idea of physical equality (the equality of malleability) that made it possible to eliminate race, or at least the racial characteristics of large populations of people who were deemed to have degenerated from primordial whiteness. Deschamps argued that populations could be brought back to whiteness through a sustained biopolitical project of selective crossbreeding. "The *regeneration* of the *human species,* or the return of all the colored races to the white type," Deschamps explained, "is possible by suppressing the odious prejudice, by means of perpetual crossbreeding of the métis with the primordial, now European, white race. The natives of an island, a country, of a vast colony would be whitened." For Deschamps, the promise of biological regeneration and the cultural salvation of nonwhite populations lay in making them white. In other words, it lay in making them no longer what they were, no longer different from Europeans, at least in terms of their appearance. In a sense, it was a program of breeding them out of existence, transforming them beyond recognition. "Negroes would not have to be *born slaves,* our *inferior brothers,*" Deschamps continued; "they are our equals in the order of creation; they have a right—as we do—to the sun, to liberty, and to the banquet of life."[130] That is, in the logic of Deschamps's argument, they had a right not to be "negroes" any longer, but instead to become white and to enjoy freedom and civilization.

The question of the métis and the ambivalent relationship between improvement and exclusion (or elimination) continued as a scientific and administrative problem well into the twentieth century.[131] It became even more intense after the renewed imperial expansion of the late nineteenth century and the resurgence of a scientific position that was characterized as "neo-Lamarckean," though it remained within the general parameters established by the Buffonian paradigm.[132] Though the full range and depth of connections between the eighteenth-century visions of racial engineering and subsequent ideas and practices is only beginning to be established, it appears that this dialectic between the belief in human mutability and the reactive assertion of immutability played an important role in establishing the contours and the tensions at the heart of the development of ideas of race and racial policies in the nineteenth and twentieth centuries.

[CHAPTER FOUR]

In Society, but Not of It

In the most famous and important piece of writing published on the eve of the French Revolution, Abbé Sieyès claimed that vast majority of the population that constituted the Third Estate of France "encompasses everything that belongs to the nation, while everything that is not the Third Estate cannot be regarded as being of the nation."[1] In *What Is the Third Estate?* (*Qu'est-ce que le Tiers État?*), Sieyès identified the nation in a way that excluded "the privileged," a characterization that most importantly excluded the nobility from the nation, but could more generally have been taken to exclude anyone with special privileges enshrined in law, which included the clergy.[2] These people were deemed to be outside of the nation, even though they lived within its territory.[3] They were characterized by Sieyès as "those for whom the Nation is foreign," and he deemed even actual nonnaturalized foreigners residing in France to be more worthy of political participation.[4] It was as if, for Sieyès, the privileged suddenly existed in the state of nature outside of the nation, or between nations, even while they lived inside the nation's territorial boundaries among its members. The nobles in particular were singled out as "a people apart within the great nation" (*un peuple à part dans la grande nation*).[5] The logic of being both "apart" and "within" the nation came to play an important role in the French Revolution and the fashioning of a new nation and body politic.[6] In addition to underlying important developments in the formation of the new political structures related to citizenship, it developed into a number of legal mechanisms employing unusual legal fictions.[7] For example, it produced the strange situation where people suspected of being counterrevolutionary could be treated as if they had illegally left the country, as if they were émigrés, even if they had never departed. They could also be treated as if they were without a legal domicile, even as they continued to live in their own home that they had never left.[8]

These types of internal exclusion, whereby groups of people were included in a community or a society as an excluded group—simultaneously apart and within, inside and outside—were, of course, not new to the French Revolution. In some sense, the traditional subjects of these exclusions—such as outcasts, criminals, and enslaved people—have played fundamental social roles in many societies throughout world history. A number of classic works of social science, therefore, focus on forms of internal exclusion, even if they do not employ this terminology.[9] The conceptual and legal formulation of the social forms of these internal exclusions reach far back into the past. It involved ancient ideas about enslaved people, foreigners, and citizens, as well as the intermediary categories of people between free men and chattel slaves, such as helots. It also included a number of forms of restricted citizenship and partial civil incapacity, including *atimia* in ancient Athens (a form of limited disenfranchisement in which particular rights were taken from a citizen who was deemed to have lost honor) and a number of significant formulations of internal exclusion in ancient Roman law, such as *infamia* (a public mark of infamy, which was a legal form of disgrace and partial disenfranchisement).[10] Furthermore, and perhaps most fundamentally, women in many times and places were included in communities while at the same time being denied participation in political or public life.[11]

Nonetheless, the last decades of the Old Regime saw something new in the conceptual history of these forms. In a new way, biological and physiological logics were joined to the legal and social logics of internal exclusion, forming novel biopolitical arguments. People began to give a new biological grounding to arguments about the differences between individuals of various groups. At the same time, new ideas about collective bodies as forms of organized bodies led to novel justifications and a new sense of urgency for excluding groups of people (or for altering their preexisting forms of exclusion). Furthermore, these new ideas began to be put into practice in biopolitical projects.

This chapter focusses on the ways that three groups of people in Old Regime society were conceptually and legally refashioned so as to be excluded. The ways that they were refashioned differed significantly, and the three groups varied in size from the largest group making up half the population to the smallest one of a few thousand people. However, all the cases were similar in that they exemplified new biological facets of exclusionary biopolitical arguments; all three groups were refashioned in biopolitical terms, as older forms of social exclusion were given biological justifications, which then were used in administrative measures to refashion the exclusions in law. The biological existence of the people making up these groups also became newly important, and their possible impact on the large collective body of the population became a more pressing concern. Individuals from these groups were treated as if they were in society, although they were not full members of society. In the first part of the chapter, I focus on the group making up a significant portion of the poor population of France, the mobile poor, who were included in the newly expanded and redefined category of vagabond. In the second part of the chapter, I continue my analysis by focusing on the several thousand people of African descent living in France between the commencement of the Seven Years' War in 1756 and the French Revolution in 1789. The third part of the chapter focusses on what was by far the largest of the three groups: the women of France. Women were seen as being obviously central the biopolitical reproduction of the collective body, yet they faced new arguments for the continuation and the entrenchment of the wide variety of legal and social exclusions to which they were subject. The reformulation of these subjectivities—women, blacks, and vagabonds—played a role in establishing the internally exclusive logic of "in but not of" that can be seen so clearly in Sieyès's political thought and that manifests with such ramifications in French Revolution. These Old Regime developments laid the foundation for some of the most important arguments and assumptions about civic equality and political participation: who should be excluded from citizenship and why.

All three of these cases of the refashioning of exclusion took place on the foundation of biopolitical understandings of individual bodies and collective bodies. They help reveal more about the process through which the citizen was fashioned in the Old Regime, through the construction of what they were not. Even though royal subjects were not legally citizens in Old Regime France, Peter Sahlins has shown that there was an "absolutist model of the citizen that took shape in the collusion and slippage between French jurists and the crown."[12] In this long process over the sixteenth and seventeenth centuries, and in the breakdown of the absolutist model in the last decades of eighteenth century, the citizen was defined in law not through positive statements about what a citizen was. Following the early modern logic of contradistinction (*à contrario*), Old Regime jurists defined "the quality of being French" (*qualité de francaise*) primarily by establishing what it was not. Sahlins, Jean-François Dubost, and Charlotte Catherine Wells have demonstrated how this process relied primarily on the foreigner or alien (*étranger, aubain*) as an oppositional figure against which the quality of being French was fashioned.[13] Central to this process was the *droit d'aubaine*, the right of the king to seize the property of nonnaturalized foreigners who died in the kingdom.[14] Through this right of seizure, the arguments of jurists, and the ruling of judges, in effect, the legal quality of being French was defined and articulated through a process of double negation in which the opposite of French was established and the quality of being French implicitly became what the opposite was not.

One important sign of the unraveling of the absolutist model of citizenship in the last decades of the Old Regime was the way that foreigners began to be treated with increased suspicion and policing at the same time as there was an increase in naturalizations.[15] I argue that there were other developments, and other figures of nonbelonging, that played a role in undermining the Old Regime model of citizenship and establishing the conceptual and legal space in which the citizen of the Revolution was to be created. The refashioning of the vagabond as a new extreme form of incapacity, in which a person was reduced to the functional status of the living dead, was another important part of this process of reconstructing the citizen through constructing what citizens were not.[16] The free person of color in France—no longer an enslaved person (legally) but now seen by some as a dangerous foreign interloper in the collective body—and women—so obviously necessary to the reproduction of the collective body that new justifications for exclusion had to be formulated—were two additional figures that became important in the development of ideas of citizenship and the collective body in the decades preceding the Revolution.

In a direct fashion, the exclusion of women, vagabonds, and people of African descent in the Old Regime played a role in the forming the logic and the arguments for the exclusion of women, the enslaved, the indigent during the Revolution. In an indirect manner, these refashioned categories helped establish what the citizen of the Revolution would be in the sense that their exclusion erected boundaries of belonging and helped clear the conceptual and legal space in which the citizen was fashioned. Also, in an indirect manner, these Old Regime exclusions played a role in the process through which other excluded figures of French Revolutionary law such as the émigré and the "enemy of the people" were made into legal "nonsubjects." These nonsubjects were people who were included in the juridical system as those to whom rights and legal protections were denied (or denied partially or temporarily) because of some sort of absence or externality.[17]

In addition to their significance in revealing the development of the conceptual foundations of some aspects of political thought in the French Revolution, particularly the forms of inclusion and exclusion that revolved around a new conception of the citizen and the form of internal exclusion that was articulated clearly and consequentially by the Abbé Sieyès in *What Is the Third Estate?*, these three cases were significant for three other primary reasons. First, they represent important stages in the development of the exclusionary strain of Enlightenment biopolitics. Second, they were cases in which biopolitical ideas were implemented in actual changes to government policies, practices, and laws. Finally, these cases suggest new genealogical connections between Enlightenment biopolitics and contemporary biopolitical theory. For example, the characterization of vagabonds as existing in a state of living death—in which they were beastly habitual criminals to be put into a form of unfreedom and reduced to what Enlightenment jurists called "natural life"—has a number of striking similarities to Giorgio Agamben's conceptions of *homo sacer* and "bare life" (*la nuda vita*), which built in turn on Walter Benjamin's concept of "bare life" (*das bloße Leben*) and Hannah Arendt's characterizations of the abject condition of stateless refugees and concentration camp inmates in twentieth-century Europe.

All three cases that I analyze in this chapter also give a new weight to Foucault's suggestion that the birth of biopolitics saw new forms of biologically dividing up populations. Foucault made this observation in relation to the ways that states incorporate racism into their practices and techniques of government. Acknowledging that racism existed before biopower, Foucault argued that "it is indeed the emergence of this biopower that inscribes it [racism] in the mechanisms of the State."[18] The legal and administrative regime of regulating the lives of the "black" (following a new legal designation) residents of metropolitan France that I analyze in this chapter exemplifies this process, revealing the ways that, already in the eighteenth century, the state incorporated racism in its mechanisms of power in a quite advanced form in the metropole as well as the colonies. Foucault argued that racism "is primarily a way of introducing a break into the domain of life that is under power's control"; it "is a way of fragmenting the field of the biological that power controls. . . . It is, in short, a way of establishing a biological-type caesura within a population that appears to be a biological domain."[19] While this is a characterization of state racism and biopower, it can also be applied to the other two cases that I analyze in this chapter. The reconfiguration of vagabonds and women, I argue, were also attempts to create biological-types caesuras within the population. Rather than something that was specific to state racism, these processes of fragmentation and differentiation were characteristic of biopolitics more generally. While there were specific historical contexts and circumstances for all three of these cases of biopolitical differentiation, they were also part of the more general dialectic in which new forms of group belonging and collective being were imagined at the same time as collectivities were divided up into biologically differentiated groups. Much as species and individual were conceived in relation to one another, so to the population, political body, social body, and nation were imagined and reimagined along with newly differentiated and excluded groups of people like vagabonds, "blacks," and women.

During the 1760s and 1770s, traditional definitions of the category of vagabonds were revised, and the government aimed to contain and neutralize the large numbers of mobile people who had no fixed abode, work, or property.[20] Responding to the confluence of economic and demographic factors that created large numbers of mobile workers who were not always able to find steady work in the 1750s and 1760s, and anticipating the return of large numbers of sailors and soldiers at the close of the Seven Years' War, the administration solicited proposals for ways to deal with vagabonds and beggars. The most important of these works, *Memoir on Vagabonds and Beggars* (*Mémoire sur les vagabonds et les mendiants*), focused on vagabonds, portraying them not just as an impoverished portion of the population that was undeserving of charity, but as a group of savage natural criminals that posed an existential threat to society and the nation. The work was published anonymously in 1764, but not for the common reason that the author feared retribution from the state or condemnation by the church for unorthodox opinions. In fact, the work was published at the behest of Comptroller-General Henri-Léonard-Jean-Baptiste Bertin with royal approval.[21] The work may have been published anonymously because the author knew it to be provocative and extreme and he feared retribution from the many people that he included and vilified in his characterization of vagabonds. From the very opening of the *Mémoire*, the author established a tone of hostility and heightened rhetoric, identifying "the infinite evil" of vagabonds.[22] In his general hostility for the mobile and "undeserving" poor, this author was not alone in his denunciation. The state's solicitation of proposals for remedies from the newly formed royal agricultural societies resulted in a number of harsh and sweeping proposals containing echoes of previous police crackdowns on vagrancy and begging, such as the Great Confinement, which began in 1719 and carried on into the 1720s.[23] The *Mémoire*'s characterizations of vagabonds and the proposed actions against them were, however, the harshest and most sweeping of this new wave of proposals, while also being the most influential among administrators forming government policy.

The anonymous author of the *Mémoire* was a magistrate from Orléans, Guillaume-François Le Trosne, who wrote the work around the same time as he became a member of the physiocratic school of political economy.[24] Among the most extreme of his recommendations was perpetual confinement in harsh labor camps, a condition that Le Trosne himself compared to enslavement and recommended even for a first offense.[25] Le Trosne also transformed the notion of the offence, arguing that rather than a specific crime against a person or property, these vagabonds were guilty of crimes against society simply by the fact that they had no work, property, or fixed home. They were guilty for their state of being, rather than for any specific act. Le Trosne argued that their status as vagabonds would inevitably lead them to violent criminal acts that would become habitual, permanently transforming them into a beastly "race." While the crown did not enact all of Le Trosne's suggestions, it did enact a number of measures in line with his proposal. Furthermore, Le Trosne's characterization of vagabonds as being in society, but not of it, and his development of this logic of internal exclusion in his later political economic treatises were echoed in the works of people writing about vagabonds and beggars, as well as in the political ideas of Abbé Sieyès that helped give shape to the early stages of the French Revolution, particularly in terms of the conceptualization of the nation and citizenship.

Le Trosne's work appeared at a time when several social and economic pressures converged with immediate historical circumstances in a way that increased the numbers of mobile poor who had long existed in early modern France, particularly in relation to seasonal agricultural work.[26] Many of the people who found themselves wandering the countryside in the 1760s, liable to be labeled as vagabonds, were forced into mobility through the effects of large-scale demographic and economic transformations in the preceding decades. Rural population growth and rising prices had led to a greater number of people in the countryside who were completely dependent on wage labor.[27] The combination of population growth and rising prices had depleted savings and led to an increase in the sale of family farms. The result was a population of rural poor people who were more vulnerable to the fluctuations in prices, wages, and the demand for labor. The changes contributed to an out-migration from villages as people went in search of opportunities. The growth of the mobile poor became a particular concern of the administration as the Seven Years' War was winding down and administrators anticipated an influx of deserters and demobilized soldiers and sailors, who were long associated with unruly behavior and social disorder because of their worrying unrootedness and their capacity for violence. Criminal bands of vagrants had also formed in some regions of the country in the 1740 and 1750s, complicating the issue and creating real cause for concern among the victimized population and the administration.[28]

Le Trosne's characterization of vagabonds as savage-like enemies within, who needed to be enslaved and isolated in harsh work camps, built on these concerns while also responding to, and building on, new Enlightenment theories of stadial progress in which groups of people were thought to move through stages characterized by interconnected forms of economic, social, and political development. Le Trosne adapted this theory to his vision of the racialized enemies that were in, but not of, society. In Le Trosne's account of the savage vagabonds, one did not have to travel to the South Pacific, the Americas, or any other distant location to find large numbers of people living supposedly as if in earlier stages of historical development. Eliminating distance and collapsing space, Le Trosne presented a version of the simultaneity of the nonsimultaneous in which people living contemporaneously within the same territorial boundaries lived as if in different historical eras.[29] In articulating this, Le Trosne gave a new theoretical inflection to long-standing general prejudices about peasants and other provincials. Yet his idea about the existence of savages within civilization was something more than one finds in the old tropes about unrefined peasants existing alongside their more civilized compatriots.[30] In the example of vagabonds in France, he saw the spatial intermingling of extremely different stages of development. This was not merely a case of something like the different stages of historical development existing around the world, as Turgot claimed.[31] It was an example of the simultaneity of the nonsimultaneous within a single territory. In Le Trosne's account, France was not simply an advanced civilization defined by its highly developed agriculture, commerce, and arts. It was also an advanced civilization riddled with people who embodied a primitive form of presocial development, effectively living in, and embodying, the state of nature.

Le Trosne articulated this quite explicitly in an extraordinary sentence of the memoir that situated the vagabonds in light of the work of previous theorists of the state of nature and stadial progress. "They live amid society without being members of it," he wrote, explaining that vagabonds "live in that state where men would be if they had no law, no police [in the broad eighteenth-century sense], no authority." Le Trosne finished the sentence by clarifying that vagabonds were "in that state that is supposed to have existed before the establishment of civil society, but that, without ever having existed for a whole people, finds itself, by a singular contradiction, realized in a civilized society."[32] In Le Trosne's characterization, vagabonds were nothing less than walking avatars of the state of nature, primitive beings from an earlier stage of development living among the members of a civilized society without belonging to society. Whereas some philosophes complained that the "natural man" of social contract theorists, like the "savage" of many naturalists and protoethnographers, was merely "a metaphysical being," a fictional figure used for the purposes of argument, Le Trosne argued that there were true savages living in the heart of civilization.[33] In fact, these savages in France lived at the very time and place that the term and concept of "civilization" began to be used by one of Le Trosne's fellow physiocrats, the marquis de Mirabeau.[34]

The spatial and temporal intermingling of the savage and the civilized, in Le Trosne's characterization, results in a state of perpetual warfare, but not one of "all against all" as in Hobbes's characterization of the state of nature. Instead, the war is between vagabonds and everyone else, as vagabonds daily wage war against the members of society through their acts of theft and violence that imperil the personal security and property of all. The fact that "they live in a veritable state of war with all citizens" makes them nothing less than an "enemy of society."[35] Vagabonds, Le Trosne argued, therefore, should be condemned to the galleys in perpetuity.[36] The king had disbanded the galley corps in 1748, and the sentence of rowing in the galley ships was replaced by hard labor in newly created camps, the *bagnes*, located in the naval ports of Brest, Toulon, and Rochefort.[37] Following the Enlightenment concern with proportional punishment, articulated famously by Cesare Beccaria in the same year as Le Trosne's *Memoir on Vagabonds* was published, Le Trosne made it clear that perpetual harsh punishment in the galleys, that is, the new labor camps, would be "in exact proportion to the crime."[38]

For Le Trosne, vagabondage is a "habitual crime."[39] It becomes a state of being, and a chosen one at that. The vagabond is not like some misbehaving youth who has made a bad decision or gotten carried away by enthusiasm or events. Vagabondage is "the effect of idleness chosen upon reflection by a man with only his work for subsistence."[40] Also, unlike the unpremeditated crime of passion, "the crime of a vagabond . . . is not the crime of a moment [but] an offence of reflection, continual and habitual."[41] Entering into this state of criminality creates "a habitual disposition to theft, to murder, and to all crimes" and makes the vagabond inhuman.[42] "It extinguishes all vestiges of reason and humanity in him," literally dehumanizing him until he crosses over a categorical threshold and becomes nothing more than a "ferocious beast."[43] Although vagabonds may be enemies of society because of specific acts of aggression against people, they also seem to occupy a status that is fundamentally opposed to humanity and natural law. They were, therefore, not unlike the figure of the "enemy of humanity" (*hostis humani generis*), a characterization that had conceptual and legal roots in antiquity, but was refashioned in various early modern discourses, particularly natural law, as Dan Edelstein has argued.[44] At several points in the text, Le Trosne asserts the oppositional character of vagabonds through a variety of dehumanizing analogies, calling them "voracious insects" and comparing them to wolves, one of the natural scourges of the French countryside.[45] While the state gave a reward of ten livres for each head of a wolf, Le Trosne claimed that vagabonds "are infinitely more dangerous to society."[46] This last comparison also resonated with tales of one of the classic liminal characters of early modern folklore, the half-human and half-wolf beast, the *loup-garou* (the werewolf) and similar monstrous beasts that were still said to stalk parts of the country in the late eighteenth century.[47]

Le Trosne also reduced the humanity of vagabonds by arguing that even before the state could condemn them to the galleys, they were already dead in social and civil terms. He did this through an invocation of the legal concept of "civil death." The concept has obscure origins in late medieval and early modern law, although the jurists who fashioned it often claimed to find its origins in the ancient Roman law of Justinian's *Digest*.[48] As a working magistrate and the mentee of the famous jurist Robert-Joseph Pothier, who wrote about civil death and was one of the great authorities and compilers of Justinian's *Digest*, Le Trosne must have been well acquainted with the concept.[49] He discusses it explicitly in the *Memoir*, using it as a concept by which to frame the vagabond and to demonstrate how the vagabond was a type of person reduced to natural life.[50]

The term "civil death" is slightly misleading because, in practice, this type of death was meant to reach beyond the civil realm. As the most prominent eighteenth-century French analyst of the concept, François Richer, explained, civil death was meant to be, in effect, a complete extraction from civil society, formally dispossessing such condemned persons of their homeland and family, and barring them from all forms of social interaction and contractual agreement.[51] Effectively, they were meant to have no civil existence. Yet, while the law could formally strip them only of civil existence, the civilly dead were also supposed to be treated as if they were also deprived of social and natural life. In this sense, at least in the minds of some jurists in eighteenth-century France, civil death was meant to be as complete as real, physical death. As Le Trosne's teacher Pothier put it, "civil death is an image of natural death."[52] Although the civilly dead man was still alive, possessing "natural life," Richer wrote that he was "considered by society as if he were naturally dead."[53] Montigny, commenting on civil death in a prominent eighteenth-century work of jurisprudence, wrote that civil death was a "true imitation of natural death," and the condemned were considered by society as if they were "not living beings."[54] In effect, the concept of civil death fashioned a category of the living dead: people for whom all social and civil life had been stripped and only natural life remained. In the harsh paradox of the concept, even natural life was not supposed to qualify the civilly dead person for any form of recognition or social existence. If they were treated as anything more than "naturally dead," it was, according to Montigny, only because of a "sort of commiseration absolutely indepen-dent of the law."[55]

The existence of individuals reduced to bare biological life is reminiscent of the figure of *homo sacer*, the obscure figure of archaic Roman law that Giorgio Agamben brought to the fore of scholarship on biopolitics.[56] The *homo sacer* was a person who could be killed with impunity, but could not be killed in a sacrificial ritual. Agamben's analysis of this figure—and his adaptation of Walter Benjamin's concept of "bare life" (*das bloße Leben, la nuda vita*) and Hannah Arendt's analysis on stateless people and concentra-tion camp inmates who experienced "a modern expulsion from humanity" that placed them outside of the realms of law and politics and left them with "the abstract nakedness of being nothing but human"—introduced an important focus on the role of internal exclusion (or "inclusive exclusion") in biopolitics.[57] The concepts of *homo sacer* and bare life have been taken up widely and now are as central to contemporary biopolitical theory as any of Foucault's concepts. As theoretically productive as it has been, however, Agamben's choice of a figure as obscure as *homo sacer* itself obscures the nu-merous traditional figures of internal exclusion that have played much more prominent roles in the history of political and legal thought. This includes the figures of the enslaved, barbarians, and outlaws that have been import-ant figures through which internal exclusion was thought since Greek and Roman antiquity, at least.[58] While these figures remained important in the early modern era, the legal concept of "civil death" came to play a central role in modes of inclusive-exclusive thinking. It was the concept through which there was the most extensive, explicit, and precise rethinking of forms of internal exclusion in which people were reduced to bare life. Le Trosne contributed to this discourse in a manner that presented the vaga-bond as an even more extreme form of the living dead.

In the *Mémoire*, Le Trosne invokes the concept of civil death to argue that vagabonds were already reduced to this type of bare life, even before they could be recognized by the state and condemned to the galleys. "He knows only natural life," Le Trosne wrote about the vagabond; "for him, it is all that he possesses."[59] In a sense, the vagabond was always already in a state of living death even before a legal judgment could be pronounced by the state. Becoming one of the living dead was, therefore, not the product of the legal procedure itself, but rather of the choice of vagabonds to enter into their rootless and adversarial state of existence. Le Trosne believed that legal procedures should then be revised so that the status of vagabonds as a type of living dead could be quickly and decisively recognized.[60] The state needed to catch up. Since vagabonds were, in a sense, already guilty, all that was needed was the most minimal formal procedure to establish this. The state needed a way to quickly confirm the status of the living-dead vaga-bond. Le Trosne wanted the investigation to be short and simple, removing the requirement for a formal deposition *par récolement et confrontation* and replacing it with a simple cross-examination.[61] Once these ferocious and beastly vagabonds were taken into custody and quickly found guilty, their formal extraction from civil life was complete: "they are no longer in the order of Citizens; they no longer have a civil existence."[62]

Given that vagabonds had already lived like the civilly dead, that is, like the living dead, before being condemned, they needed to receive a punish-ment that was worse than civil death. Going beyond the existing notions of civil death, Le Trosne argued that once condemned, vagabonds must also be seen as having been "acquired by the State."[63] Their bare life must be harnessed so that they can be made to labor, contributing to the wealth and vitality of the nation. Seemingly untroubled by the long-standing French legal principle that "there are no slaves in France," Le Trosne states that the vagabonds would belong to the state "as slaves do to a Master."[64] The vagabond, like a ferocious wild animal, could be subdued and tamed only by being put "in chains."[65] The dehumanizing connection to beasts and the enslaved suggests the ways that various figures of internal exclusion were conceptually connected. The vagabond and the slave, like animals, were denied full humanity. Interestingly, Le Trosne even goes on to characterize vagabonds as a "race," in a way that appears to imply the biological con-cept of race, as opposed to the common eighteenth-century meaning of the French term *race* as "kind" or "type."[66] This appears to be an example of how biopolitical thinkers in the eighteenth century were forming ideas of race and biopolitics together.

Although he does not directly distinguish vagabonds as a biologically distinct variety of human being that possesses its own unalterable persistent essence, as in the modern sense of race, he does biologically differentiate them in several ways. First, as I have already shown, he characterized them as beast-like figures of living death devoid of reason and humanity whose very existence as vagabonds created a "continual and habitual" way of be-ing.[67] This is a form of biological difference that seems to be distinguished from a modern sense of race in that Le Trosne did not argue that vagabonds inherited their unalterable way of being; in fact they entered into it by choice. He did not explicitly argue that vagabonds were members of a bio-logically distinct variety of human being that was genealogically linked to similar individuals through reproduction and that their essential difference could be transmitted across generations, though he did imply that it was important to stop them from biologically reproducing. It is telling that he refers to them as a race precisely in the context of the biological issues of reproduction and extinction. He argues that the perpetual isolation of vagabonds in harsh labor camps will be salutary, not only for the present state of society but also "for the future."[68] The isolation in camps is important because it means that vagabonds cannot reproduce. The social "contagion of example" will be contained, as will the possibility for biological reproduction.[69] "He will not form more vagabonds," Le Trosne writes; "the race will be removed forever."[70] Le Trosne presents this project of negative eugenics aimed at exterminating a class of habitual criminal as an important step in defending the health and vitality of the social body. I do not think that we can conclude from this that he thought that vagabonds were a "race" in the fully modern biological sense utilized in the nineteenth century, but he did present them as a group that was biologically differentiated in that its members were not fully human and they could not be rehabilitated or transformed (back) into reasoning members of society and humanity.

Le Trosne made vagabonds appear similar to enslaved people of African descent in a number of other ways. He did this through a number of rhetorical moves and explicit comparisons, highlighting what he saw as shared characteristics and presenting vagabonds as carrying out a similar function in terms of forced labor, though the labor was to be for the benefit of all rather than the pecuniary benefit of owners. In addition to strengthening and vivifying the social body by isolating vagabonds and keeping them from reproducing, Le Trosne also presented the contribution of enslaved vagabonds to economic productivity as one of vivification. This type of vitalist political economic logic was on display in his discussion of what the vagabonds would do once they became slaves of the state. Since there would be so many of them, the galleys (or the bagnes) would presumably fill up. After that occurred, they could be sent to the mines and other ports to work. They could also be used to complete massive public works projects like the building of canals. While the existing bagnes were located in a few limited locations within the kingdom, the widespread distribution of these new slaves of the state across the kingdom would bring, as Le Trosne put it, "circulation and life to certain provinces."[71] Circulating these slaves of the state through the kingdom was presented a salutary, vivifying measure. It seemed to hold the possibility of contributing vital energy to stagnant or decrepit provinces. Le Trosne envisioned so many people being found guilty of being vagabonds that he mentioned that when all the possible metropolitan sites are filled with labor camps, the vagabonds could be shipped to the colonies. When those in turn fill up, the vagabonds could be traded with North Africans for enslaved Christians.

Another means by which Le Trosne differentiated vagabonds and created an association with chattel slavery was by arguing that they should be made to be more physically different through new practices of branding that differed from the traditional practices of branding criminals. Le Trosne's suggestions for new practices of branding would have brought the vagabonds closer to the condition of a racialized other, who could not change or conceal their status as enslaved and abject. Visibility and irreversibility here are key. While most categories of criminals sent to the galleys were traditionally branded with "GAL" on their shoulder, Le Trosne wanted the vagabonds sent to the galleys to be more easily identified. He wanted them to be always and unavoidably identified as the enemies of society that they were. The traditional shoulder brand was a means that officials could use to determine the identity of someone as being a *galérien* (someone convicted of a crime and sent to the galleys as punishment) if they ever escaped or if they were released but apprehended again for suspicion of wrongdoing. Importantly, Le Trosne wanted to change the location and the function of the brand. He wanted to make it a visible marker of difference, calling for a "G" to be branded on the cheek or brow of all vagabonds sent to the galleys. This would also presumably differentiate them from other galériens, who would still be branded on the shoulder, since not everyone sent to the galleys was guilty of being such a dangerous enemy. This external and readily apparent mark of differentiation would bring the outward appearance of the vagabonds in line with their status, as Le Trosne understood it. Not unlike the newly racialized "blacks" and people of color in France, or the enslaved and free people of color in the colonial biopolitical plans, such as those of Bory and Hilliard d'Auberteuil, the branding would create a more rigorous correspondence between the outward appearance, the civil status, and the supposedly essential character of the vagabonds. It would mark them as a race apart, "domestic enemies" who could be killed by anyone if they were found to have escaped the labor camps.[72] As articulated in Le Trosne's vision, the condition of these branded slave-like convicts, condemned to perpetual hard labor, was brought closer, at least in the basic outlines of their condition, to the circumstances of the enslaved people in the colonies and those brought to France, though of course the circumstances of vagabonds were supposedly the result of their own choice and it was not a condition passed on through reproduction.

Some of Le Trosne's successors would continue this racialized understanding of the abject and mobile poor. The most prominent commentator on vagabonds in the period between the publication of Le Trosne's text in 1764 and the Napoleonic era was Abbé Charles-Antoine-Joseph Leclerc de Montlinot. He came to prominence writing essays on the vagabonds and beggars, as well as operating some of the *dépôts de mendicité*, the workshops of compulsory labor where some of the mobile poor were confined after their creation in the 1764 by royal declaration.[73] Montlinot continued Le Trosne's harsh characterization of the "undeserving" poor, identifying a "race of beggars" (*mendiants de race*), many of whom were vagabonds.[74] While the term "race" in eighteenth-century French did not refer only to a tightly defined and specific sense of "race" in the modern sense, it was already being used in association with the modern sense of biological race. Reading Montlinot as implying the relationship of biological race and vagabonds (beggars) is supported by the fact that he explicitly characterized "beggars" as a fundamental and essential group whose character could not be changed. Like Le Trosne, Montlinot utilized this racial characterization to cast people within this group as evil and immoral in their essence.[75] More than just lazy or victims of circumstance, this "species of men" had no principles or morality and could not be reformed.[76] They were the "scum of the nation," waging an unending war against society.[77] Montlinot envisioned deporting them to colonies, suggesting that the government could send them, along with women who were "debauched" yet fertile (that is, prostitutes who could have children), to populate an unnamed distant territory where they could roam freely as savage vagabonds and eventually "civilize themselves."[78] Although it involved sending them to a colony instead of internal labor camps, and displacing their reproduction abroad rather than snuffing it out at home, this is another biopolitical proposal of exclusion based on the desire to segregate a population and control its ability to reproduce. Le Trosne and Montlinot followed the same biopolitical logic to different ends. Montlinot took up an important position on the Committee on Beggars during the French Revolution, and he continued to propose biopolitically oriented deportation programs aimed at the undeserving poor, particularly vagabonds and the "race of beggars."[79] Le Trosne's racializing logic and Montlinot's terminology also reached beyond government bodies, as the "race of beggars" became a subject of the novelist and popular author of utopian schemes Restif de la Bretonne, and the popular writer Louis-Sébastien Mercier.[80]

In addition to the influence of Le Trosne's reconceptualization of vagabonds, there were a series of other practical and immediate effects of Le Trosne's argument, as provincial administrators endorsed his vision and police officials greatly expanded the category of vagabond in practice in a similar way to Le Trosne's expansion in theory.[81] This resulted in a significant increase in the number of vagabonds and beggars apprehended by the police.[82] One of the royal declarations of 1764 that began the process of establishing a new variety of prison-like workshops where some vagabonds and beggars were confined (called *dépôts de mendicité*), "unmistakably echoes the words of the semi-official propagandist Le Trosne," as Thomas

Adams wrote.[83] In the preamble, the declaration echoed Le Trosne's in-clusive exclusive logic when it claimed that banishment would not suffice as a punishment because vagabonds already lived among people as if in a state of banishment. Their life was "a type of voluntary and perpetual ban-ishment."[84] The state, in a sense, accepted Le Trosne's characterization of vagabonds as a class of the living dead. Also, following Le Trosne's recom-mendation, the declaration made time in the galleys the punishment for vagabondage, although it did not endorse the idea of making this confine-ment perpetual. Even in the light of the conceptual recasting of the figure of the vagabond and the practical policy implications of his work, perhaps the most significant effect of Le Trosne's work on vagabonds was the general contribution it made to the development of the biopolitical logic of inter-nal exclusion.

In his arguments about vagabonds, Le Trosne employed the logic of in-ternal exclusion in a way that created two categories of people that had an unusual social position in which they were not completely in or out of so-ciety, arguing that the existence of one form of internal exclusion justified, and in fact, necessitated, the formation of another form. One category was composed of the vagabonds before they were apprehended by the state, and the other category was composed of those vagabonds that had been apprehended. He argued that vagabonds had already entered into a form of liminal incorporation in the social body by choosing to exist among the members of society while not being members themselves. This existing in society, but not belonging to the collective or making an economic contri-bution, would necessarily lead to a relationship of parasitic opposition in which vagabonds, because they had no property and supposedly refused to work, would be forced to steal from those people who remained within society and labored to support themselves and contribute to the common good. For this crime of seemingly exiting society while remaining among its members, Le Trosne argued that vagabonds should be forced into another form of internal exclusion in which they would be made to contribute to the productivity that they had chosen to undermine. Using the criterion of productive labor to characterize the social status of vagabonds, Le Trosne argued that the state had the right and the responsibility to transform vaga-bonds from a form of unproductive internal exclusion to a productive form. This logic of internal exclusion and the criterion of economic productivity came to play a central role in the longer works of social and political theory that he wrote following his brief but influential work on vagabonds.

The *Mémoire* seems to have been the occasion for Le Trosne's radical-ization in terms of his ideas about fashioning the collective body. As his political economic thinking developed in the years following the almost simultaneous publication of the *Mémoire* and his conversion to physiocracy, Le Trosne expanded his arguments about internal exclusion, moving from the question of the vagabond's position in society to issues of citizenship and active political participation. He moved from considerations of protecting the social body to the issue of how to construct the body politic and "the nation." As discussed in chapter 1, Le Trosne was one of the Enlightenment political theorists reconceptualizing the body politic, seeing it as a body that could be organized into a truly animated and living form, like an organism. Le Trosne believed that new provincial assemblies would be an essential tool in bringing about this organismic state. In the decade following the publication of his work on vagabonds, his ideas about collective bodies developed in other ways as well.

In several works in the 1770s, Le Trosne's idea about the collective body and his exclusionary arguments became more specifically political as he replaced "society" with the "nation" as the body from which people were to be excluded. He also provided a new argument of exclusion based on the criterion of land ownership, in accordance with the importance given to agricultural production by the physiocrats. In *Of the Social Order* (*De l'ordre social*) of 1777, Le Trosne identified the productive class (of agriculturalists primarily) and the class of landowners as the two classes that "principally" made up the nation.[85] Emphasizing the role of landowners and farmers in holding together society and producing true wealth for the nation, Le Trosne echoed his language of vagabonds being in, but not of, society, claiming that in relation to landowners and farmers "other citizens are in the nation, but they are not, properly speaking, of the nation."[86] Those who were not fixed to the land through agricultural investment or production could take their wealth and their work beyond the territorial limits of the kingdom; they were not, therefore, worthy of active political participation in the form of the new provincial assemblies that Le Trosne proposed.[87] Le Trosne developed this "in but not of" logic and applied it to a wide variety of groups, excluding merchants, artisans, traders, and the clergy from the nation.[88]

Although Le Trosne's books on political economy did not rise to the level of prominence of works by other political theorists who attempted to reimagine the body politic as an organized body, such as Rousseau and Le Trosne's fellow physiocrat Mercier de la Rivière, his works did receive broad notice, and they played a role in the formation of the ideas of the most important political theorist of the early stages of the French Revolution, Abbé Sieyès. This is evident, in general terms, in the manner in which Sieyès employed the logic of internal exclusion in his influential arguments that the Third Estate was the entire nation and the other orders of society were in, but not of, the nation. An extensive analysis of Sieyès as a biopolitical thinker who created his own important arguments about the organization of collective bodies is the subject of the next chapter. At this point, however, it is worth pointing out that the work of Le Trosne seems to have been an important intellectual resource for Sieyès in his formation of a political philosophy. One reason for this is that Le Trosne did not merely divide the nation into the productive and the unproductive, as Abbé Gabriel-François Coyer, for instance, had done in his well-known arguments for the transformation of nobility in the 1750s. Le Trosne also used this distinction as the criterion in deciding who would be included or excluded from active political participation in the nation.[89] It is telling that in 1788, in his first published work, *Essay on Privileges* (*Essai sur les privilèges*), Sieyès denounced the privileged orders by comparing them to beggars and pointing out that the privileged really believed that they were another species. Drawing attention to their special variety of "privileged begging" (*la mendicité privilégiée*), Sieyès presented them as another race of beggars.[90] Signs of Le Trosne's ideas are also evident in Sieyès's formation of the distinction between active and passive citizenship.[91] One of Sieyès's most characteristic suggestions, which was in fact adopted in a modified form by the National Assembly in December 1789, was the formation of two types of citizenship. The passive form of citizenship, which applied to the vast majority of the male population of the Third Estate, hence the vast majority of the male population, ensured social inclusion and the protection of rights while enshrining political exclusion. Those with passive citizenship could not vote or stand for office. The active form of citizenship, reserved for those who "contributed" to the public establishment in the form of a significant monetary payment, ensured full social and political inclusion for the group that Sieyès at times estimated to be only around one tenth of the nation, while "nine tenths of the nation" would be passive citizens.[92] In Sieyès's articulation of it, and the legislative creation of it, the category of the "passive citizen" was a primary example of the ways that the logic of internal exclusion came to play a role in the Revolution. Passive citizens were included in the social body and granted civil rights, while simultaneously being excluded from the political body of those actively involved in voting and standing for office.

There are several reasons to believe that Sieyès may have drawn on Le Trosne in the formation of the logic of internal exclusion that characterized his defining ideas about the treatment of the privileged, the formation of the nation, and distinctions of citizenship. In his writing, Sieyès demonstrates ideas about the law and the relationship between the natural order and the social order that indicate a knowledge and appreciation of Le Trosne's writing, particularly *Of the Social Order*.[93] By 1777, when this work was published, Sieyès had already carried out a deep study of the physiocratic school of political economy, and he had even prepared a substantial analytical essay that he intended to be his first publication, though for unknown reasons he withdrew the work as it was about to go print.[94] Furthermore, there are several elements of Sieyès's political proposals during the Revolution that are similar to ideas suggested by Le Trosne, suggesting that Sieyès may have drawn on Le Trosne's ideas, even if they were not absolutely essential to his political thought in the way that Rousseau's work was. For example, it is possible that Sieyès's suggestion for the spatial reorganization of France into new administrative units (what would become the *départements*), drew on Le Trosne's discussion of ideas on this topic in *On Provincial Administration*.[95] In 1787 and 1788, Sieyès was a representative to one of the provincial assemblies established by Comptroller-General Calonne. As a representative in Orléans, the very province where Le Trosne lived and worked, Sieyès may have come across Le Trosne's ideas in conversation with his fellow representatives as well as in the reading he carried out to prepare for his position.[96]

Out of his somewhat specific arguments about vagabonds, through the development of his political economy, Le Trosne helped establish social and political arguments that provided one of the intellectual resources for revolutionaries to rethink "the frontier" between the privileged and the unprivileged. This conceptual and political frontier was, as Keith Baker has argued, "the issue upon which the very constitution of social and political order was seen to hinge."[97] It was through analyzing the character of this frontier, and accentuating the political and social stakes involved in distinguishing it, that Sieyès established himself as "the first and most profound theorist of the French Revolution."[98]

Another consequential form of internal exclusion that took shape in the 1770s was the refashioning of the enslaved people brought to metropolitan France. They became targets of new administrative procedures that transformed their legal subjectivity from "slaves" to "blacks" while implementing a new regime of surveillance and control that aimed to remove all "blacks, mulattoes, and free people of color" from the metropole.[99] This regime was justified with biological arguments about race, and it aimed to stop reproduction between people of color and the white residents of France. At numerous times and places in the empires of the early modern Atlantic world, colonial administrators wanted to reduce or eliminate marriage and concubinage between white colonists and free people of color, the enslaved, and indigenous peoples. But in the French context, around the period of

FIGURE 5. Portrait of a young man of African descent made by Marie-Victoire Lemoine in France in 1785. The young man's identity and status are unknown, though his fine clothing implies a connection to a wealthy family.

the Seven Years' War, there was a noticeable and significant shift in the reasons that administrators gave for wanting to limit intermarriage and concubinage. A new concern with the biological effects of reproductive mixing joined the traditional concerns with the social disorder that administrators believed could result from "misalliances." One of the best examples of this shift was the creation of a set of laws known as the Police des Noirs. Though slavery was banned in metropolitan France by long-standing legal convention, the government had created formal exceptions that allowed colonists to bring enslaved people with them while visiting France. While, in theory, these exceptions allowed for only a limited residence in France for religious education or apprenticeship in a trade, in practice, enslavers kept enslaved people in France for extended periods (see figure 5).[100] While a small portion of the people of color registered by authorities in the 1770s came from the greater Indian Ocean (primarily India and the Mascarene Islands), in the most precise accounting, 93.5 percent of people of color registered by the authorities were of African descent.[101] The total number of enslaved and free people of color in the metropole was relatively low: probably fewer than ten thousand people at any given time, and more likely only half that number, or less, in a metropolitan population of over twenty million.[102] Yet over the course of a few years in the late 1770s, the Police des Noirs created a set of regulations, institutional arrangements, and bureaucratic tools to identify, track, detain, displace, and eliminate a specific population (all the people of color in France) as a way of reinforcing the institution of slavery in the colonies and in the name of biologically safeguarding the strength and vitality of the larger population of white French subjects.

The first set of laws began to be formed in 1776 and became law in 1777 after having been royally decreed and registered (formally acknowledged and endorsed) by all the Parlements (appeals courts that were consulted on laws) of France. These laws were created within the Colonial Office (Bureau des colonies) of the Ministry of the Marine. The minister Antoine de Sartine, who formed a special committee to draft the legislation, personally oversaw them. Sartine solicited opinions from a variety of people involved in the judiciary, the police, and colonial administration. Because of a number of subsequent legal questions and practical difficulties in successfully implementing the laws, the Police des Noirs continued to be officially augmented and debated into the 1780s. Creating the basic structure of the Police des Noirs regime, the first declaration prohibited anyone from bringing a black, mulatto, or other person of color into France; levied a fine if this occurred; ordered that depots be constructed in port cities where arriving enslaved people would be housed before being returned to the colonies; required registration of all "domestics" by enslavers and the possibility of loss of the "domestic" if registration was not completed; required all free people of color in France to register themselves; required local authorities to send copies of the registration to the ministry; and ensured that all people of color brought to France would remain the same legal status (free or enslaved) during their time in the country while they waited to be sent back to the colonies (i.e., the enslaved could not be freed or sue for their freedom). Following the Declaration of 1777, the administration issued several *arrêt* that were meant to clarify some legal issues, but they also extended the range of measures to include mandatory identification papers (*cartouches*) to be issued annually to all the people of color in France. An arrêt issued on April 5, 1778, went as far as banning "blacks, mulattos, and other people of color" from marrying whites.

Colonial administrators at this time were also quite concerned with the surveillance and policing of the free people of color in the colonies. An illuminating example of this administrative concern, and how it might have influenced the creation of the metropolitan regulations, can be seen in the proposal of Jean-Baptiste Estève, discussed earlier in chapter 3 in relation to his disgust with intermarriage and his desire for free people of color to wear an identifying mark. As the seneschal and lieutenant of the admiralty of Cap Français in Saint-Domingue, Estève submitted a proposal to the minister of the marine in 1774 that included a plan for a new regime of policing the free people of color of Saint-Domingue. As one of the chief officials in charge of maintaining public order on the island, Estève was particularly concerned with the population of free people of color because "the policing of slaves," he wrote, "depends heavily on the policing of free people of color."[103] He wanted to create a centralized system of surveillance that would allow the government to know "the number and the strength" of the free people of color of Saint-Domingue, and he proposed a comprehensive project for identifying, enumerating, and immobilizing this segment of the population. Estève's proposal was motivated by a fear of the disorder and insubordination that could be created by the free people of color and a sense that the administration needed to better harness them as a buffer between enslaved people and white people. It was impossible to completely stop the mixing of enslaved people and free people of color, but he wanted to limit the opportunity for free people of color to aid enslaved people who had fled enslavement. He worried that the administration would not have any chance of achieving this goal unless it knew the exact size of this part of the population, its distribution across the colony, and the exact location of each domicile in which free people of color lived.

In certain respects, Estève wanted to impose (or reimpose) some of the conditions of slavery on free people of color by limiting their movement and requiring them to have a fixed domicile. He wanted to put an end to the "continual vagabondage" of some free people of color. He also wanted to force them to register once a year with a special office that would create an alphabetical list of all legitimate free people of color so as to limit the ability of enslaved people who had escaped to illegitimately claim to be free. In addition to echoing the severe restrictions on mobility and the compilation of exhaustive inventories of the enslaved, Estève proposed some measures that would have gone beyond the traditional practices of surveillance and policing of the enslaved. For example, he wanted the nominative census of free people of color to be distributed to various administrative offices and police forces across the colony as an aid to policing, whereas nominative

censuses of enslaved people were carried out only for the purposes of taxation and in relation to mandatory militia service. He also wanted to require
free people of color to bear an external mark to publicly signify their status
as legitimately free. In addition to enabling administrators to better police
free people of color, Estève intended that his system would aid administrators in making informed decisions about whether to "encourage" or "hold
back" this part of the population based on the needs of the colony. The various tools would also make it easier to achieve this management of the population. There is no evidence that the local administrators of Saint-Domingue
or the Ministry of the Marine acted on this proposal, but within three years,
the ministry created a similar system of surveillance and control that aimed
to identify and eventually eliminate all blacks, mulattoes, and free people
of color in France.

In general terms, the creation of the Police des Noirs was a sign of colonial concerns affecting metropolitan France. It was an attempt to refashion
the French body politic in response to the arrival of enslaved people from
the colonies. But as Estève's proposal suggests, the Police des Noirs were
also an example of particular administrative tools and practices being imported from the colonies. The Polices des Noirs represent a coalescing of
various police measures developed over the previous century. What was
new about the regulations was the way these measures were brought together, the presence of some of them for the first time in the metropole, the
identification of those who were subject to the regulations as "blacks" rather
than "slaves," the new role that fears of biological degeneration played in
motivating and justifying the regulations, and the heightening of language
in unpublished ministerial documents calling for the elimination of a racially defined group. The attempt to implement the laws brought about the
first racial census of France, while the consideration of further laws such
as the banning of *all* marriages for people of color in France established a
new precedent of the government considering the racial engineering of the
population. Sue Peabody and Pierre Boulle have insightfully analyzed the
legal and political dimensions of the creation of the Police des Noirs, but
this unprecedented set of racial laws has yet to be fully situated within the
larger context of scientific theories of race, ideas about the mélange of races,
and attempts to racially engineer populations.[104] In short, it has yet to be
shown that the Police des Noirs were fundamentally biopolitical.

There were some eighteenth-century precedents for the regulation of
enslaved people in France, such as the royal declaration of 1738 that attempted to limit or eliminate intermarriage between whites and the enslaved in France. This declaration seems to have been motivated primarily
by a desire to limit the general social interaction between the enslaved and

whites, and more particularly to limit the social and familial integration of the enslaved so as not to create additional impediments to enslaved people being returned to the colonies within the three years prescribed by law.[105] The first regulations that mixed these social concerns with a biological sense of racial contagion came in 1763 at the close of the Seven Years' War, when the minister Choiseul ordered the "total expulsion" of enslaved people from France because he thought colonial cultivation suffered in their absence and that the mixing of whites and enslaved blacks in the metropole caused "disorder" and "mixed blood." He also asked the metropolitan intendants in charge of administering the provinces to send him lists of all the enslaved people and enslavers that resided in their generality.[106] Building on these racial concerns expressed in 1763, the ministerial documents relating to the creation of the Police des Noirs laws in 1777 and 1778 demonstrate a pronounced concern with the biological effects of the mixing of people of African and European descent. There were many references in these documents to the dangers of marriage between blacks and whites, to the ways that it could "taint the blood" and "disfigure" the population. There were also repeated denunciations of the "monstrous" children that resulted from intermixture.

The shift toward extreme statements of the dangers of biological contagion was particularly pronounced in the documents submitted to the ministry by Guillaume Poncet de la Grave. This powerful royal official was a *procureur du roi*, the king's legal representative at the Table de marbre, an appeals court in the Admiralty court system that had jurisdiction over all matters dealing with the seas, including enslaved people brought overseas to France. Poncet de la Grave was one of the leading forces demanding that the Ministry of the Marine create the Police des Noirs. He also became one of the members of the committee drafting the laws. He had sent requests for these types of measures to the ministry beginning in the 1760s, but his reasoning took on a more biological character in the documents he sent to the ministry in the second half of the 1770s. For instance, in one statement disparaging intermarriage between blacks and whites, Poncet de la Grave directly subsumes reproduction under the authority of the state and talks about offspring as "children of the state." He worried about the effects of "monstrous assemblages" of black and white, slave and free, producing "creatures that are neither one species nor the other, forming an oddity that will soon disfigure the children of the state."[107]

Poncet de la Grave articulated the biological threat in two ways, arguing that black people harmed the population in general through racial degeneration resulting from intermarriage, and that they were a "plague on society" because they introduced a dangerous and undefined illness into the population that had been particularly harmful because it seemed to combine with syphilis, causing this traditional scourge to spread more widely in a more virulent form. This was harmful to individual bodies, "destructive of citizens" as well as the collective body of the population, weakening "population in its very principle."[108] Poncet de la Grave presented black reproduction itself as diseased and vitiating. His shifting discourse from the 1760s to the 1770s helps reveal the way that the creation of the Police des Noirs seems to have resulted in part from the proliferation of new understanding of human malleability and racial degeneration. It was only after the idea that individual human bodies, as well as large human groups, could be easily and quickly modified over a brief number of generations that a large-scale plan of negative eugenics would appear to become not merely possible, but necessary. The stakes of intermarriage were no longer only vague worries about "tainted blood," but instead the concerns were about the wholesale and precipitous degeneration of the entire population of France, and therefore the state itself. It was only after the emergence of a belief in extreme human malleability that one could claim, as Poncet de la Grave did in 1777, that a few thousand people of color in France were "the greatest danger to the white nation."[109] Tellingly, Poncet de la Grave's biopolitical concerns continued to develop over the years, and in the quite different context of the Napoleonic era, he wrote two works expressing support for new pronatalist measures that rewarded large families, and he called for further efforts of the government to create biopolitical policies to ensure the healthy reproduction of the population.[110]

Poncet de la Grave and the other men who created and deliberated about the Police des Noirs did not explicitly refer to the names or ideas of naturalists, yet the laws they formed demonstrate a concern with race and racial purity that reflected the new understanding of human malleability. They repeatedly invoke this biological concern to justify their extreme calls for the elimination of people of African descent in France. The ministerial documents discuss the need to "purge the Kingdom of a black population," to "wipe out [anéantir] the race in the Kingdom," to "accelerat[e] . . . the extinction of the blacks in France."[111] The commission and its outside commentators considered the possibility of "the total extinction of this species [of blacks]" and envisioned an "era in which it [the black race] will cease to exist" in France.[112] Some of the men who encouraged, created, and reappraised the Police des Noirs hoped to achieve this by combining purges of individuals with the creation of the means to "absolutely prevent" the "monstrous" marriages of blacks and whites—the mixing that "infects" the kingdom.[113] In this vision, the combination of purging some people from the territory and preventing those who remained from reproducing would eventually lead to all the people of color in France dying out.

The ministerial documents reveal a number of motivations for the creation and proposed augmentation of the laws: the sense that black people in France were socially disruptive; the fear that the enslaved who were brought to France and then returned to the colonies would take with them a newfound independent spirit that would undermine colonial order and slavery; and the perceived need for greater enslaved labor in the colonies, particularly when the slave trade was interrupted by warfare (as during the Seven Years' War and the American War of Independence). But it was only after the new sense of the radical malleability of human bodies and belief in the rapid transformations that could occur within a few generations of intermarriage was combined with the great concern with the physical quality of the population that a few thousand people of African descent in France could be considered a great threat to the health of the whole population.

These types of sentiments were not restricted to the individuals involved in the Police des Noirs. They can be seen in a variety of sources, particularly those written by people who worked in the colonial administration. Writing in the year before the Police des Noirs began to be created, the colonial administrator and plantation owner Malouet expressed a similar sentiment about the extreme threat that people of color posed to the vitality and even the existence of the French nation. Malouet warned that "if the black man is assimilated to the whites among us" through reproductive mixing, there would be a proliferation of mulattoes among "all Orders within the State." This kind of mixing and assimilation would have wide-reaching and dire consequences, since individual racially mixed bodies were a part of the collective body and able to bring about significant transformations in collective forms of existence. "It is in this way," wrote Malouet, expressing the interconnection and the stakes, "that individuals, families, [and] Nations alter, degrade, and dissolve."[114] The motivations behind statements such as this were often multiple, and they sometimes included a personal financial interest in maintaining slavery, as was the case with Malouet.[115] This type of statement, however, could not have functioned as a compelling assertion of imminent and dire threat without the new understanding of the radical malleability of human bodies. Even someone, such as Malouet, who did not explicitly invoke Buffon or related naturalists, still built on this midcentury shift in ideas of human variation, reproduction, and breeding. He worked within the conceptual and rhetorical sphere of possibilities that had been created only in the preceding decades.

Created in this context, the Police des Noirs had ramifications for later biopolitical laws and practices in a number of ways, both direct and indirect, general and particular. The most immediate and direct impact on later biopolitical laws came in 1803 when Napoleon revived the 1778 ban on intermarriage in France as a part his effort to reestablish the French colonial empire by retaking Saint-Domingue and reestablishing slavery.[116] It appears that some of Police des Noirs regulations, in fact, remained in effect into the 1820s.[117] Regardless of how long they stayed in effect, even before the Revolution they were never well enforced, and they failed to transform the population because of a lack of legal clarity, the impracticality of the intensive policing and bureaucratic effort necessary, and disagreements between different institutions of the royal government over authority and jurisdiction.[118] Their greater significance in the history of biopolitics is in the establishment of a number of conceptual, legal, and practical precedents. The first was in relation to means of the surveillance of populations. The second was in terms of the transformation of populations through interventions in reproduction. And finally, the manner in which the regulations and decrees refashioned people of African descent in the law and created the legal figure of "the black" as a new form of incapacity and dispossession, neither an enslaved person nor a free person with full civil capacity.

In terms of surveillance, the Police des Noirs instituted a surveillance regime that created three important precedents for the surveillance of populations in the metropole. First, it identified categories of the population through skin color and racialized notions of descent, invoking the new biological sense of racial difference that was developing in this period. Second, it carried out a racial census of this group of "blacks, mulattoes, and people of color." The census was the first nominative census in metropolitan France that aimed at comprehensiveness. It was also unprecedented in the amount of information it recorded about each individual and the identification of individuals by racial category. Third, the Police des Noirs established the first system of identity papers in metropolitan France that both intended that identity papers be issued to all the members of a population and also would require that such papers be carried by all the members of the population at all times. The second arrêt was to clarify that these Police des Noirs identification papers (*cartouches*) were to be issued annually (see figure 6).

Identification papers were not in themselves new.[119] The paperwork of identification came to Europe from Arab sources in the thirteenth century, and mobile papers of identification such as letters of introduction and letters of safe passage became common in the Middle Ages in Europe. By the second half of the fifteenth century, some European states began to make passports obligatory to all travelers, transforming identification papers

FIGURE 6. One of the identity papers (*cartouches*) issued by the royal administration
for the administrative jurisdiction of Nantes, to be filled out annually by local
administrators and carried at all times by "blacks and people of color" in France,
as decreed by the Police des Noirs legislation (ca. 1777–78). The cartouche reads:
"Of ____, seventeen hundred ____, named ____, native of ____, age __ years,
baptized, [and] arrived in France in the month of ____, seventeen hundred ___, on the
vessel ____, landed at the port of ____, currently in the service of _____,
living in Nantes, on the street ____, declared to the registry, in execution of the
Declaration of the King, the ____ seventeen hundred sixty-____." Archives nationales
d'outre mer, Aix-en-Provence, France, F[1B]4, dossier 2, folio 226.

from an expensive means of securing safe passage or an official verification
of diplomatic authority to a means of state policing and surveillance.[120] The
cartouches of the Police des Noirs were different from these earlier forms
of identity papers and passports, even after these earlier forms came to include physical descriptions of the person being identified.[121] The cartouches
were necessary not merely for traveling, but for living in France. They had
more in common with the passports envisioned for free people of color in
Saint-Domingue by Estève and the manumission papers that some colonial

administrators wanted to require free people of color in Saint-Domingue to carry at all times. Historians of passports and the development of modern forms of identity argue for the importance of the innovations made during the Revolutionary era.[122] While the types of passports and identity papers that were utilized during the Revolution were certainly important, creating new connections between forms of identity and nationality, they were prefigured as tools of surveillance and state control by the racial identity papers of the Police des Noirs.

While the Police des Noirs regime ushered in unprecedented forms of surveillance in metropolitan Europe, the most historically significant—and certainly more shocking than these measures to identify and track a racially differentiated group—was the creation of measures to eliminate the population of African descent from France. In addition to the surveillance regime, the Police des Noirs included policies that would later become known as "negative eugenics," that is, the attempt to discourage or prevent the reproduction of a segment of the population deemed undesirable. This biopolitical means of exclusion and elimination emerged from the back-and-forth between colonial and metropolitan spheres. It is one of the most intriguing pieces of evidence of the manner in which the metropole and the colonies were deeply intertwined in the eighteenth century. In a sense, the creation of the Police des Noirs was a formal recognition of this intertwining while also being an attempt to limit and reverse the ways that the colonial population of enslaved people was intertwined with the collective body of the population in metropolitan France. It was an attempt to reassert the exclusion of enslaved people from the population of metropolitan France, taken as a social, political, and biological collective body. It was an effort to return people of African descent back to a colonial form of inclusive exclusion in which they would be fully banished from the metropole and included in the French Empire only as the excluded enslaved of the colonies.

One of the other conceptual acts that contributed most to the formation of new ideas of citizenship and the fashioning of a body politic in the late eighteenth century was the creation of new scientific theories arguing that there were considerable differences between the sexes. The construction of these theories of sexual dimorphism was an important step in the formalization of women's limited role in the public sphere and the establishment of the scientific justification for excluding women from being counted among those who would constitute the body politic after 1789. Scholars have shown that the eighteenth century saw the gradual erosion and displacement of the ancient model of sexual difference that assumed a single model of the human body and explained the differences between men and women as differences of degree based on differing quantities of life force (heat) and (gestational) development. In this traditional model, women were, in a sense, inferior and underdeveloped men.[123]

This hierarchical model of a one-sex body differentiated by degrees of development (or perfection) was replaced with a dimorphic model based on a notion of fundamental and irreducible difference. The two-body model, with its implication of greater bodily differences and the elimination of the continuum connecting the bodies of men and women, made possible new hierarchical arguments that were often articulated through the idea of complementarity, a seemingly more benign, or "enlightened," form of sexual difference that nonetheless reinforced the sense of irreconcilable difference.[124] The development of scientific ideas of sexual difference reached its height in Europe in the second half of the eighteenth century, with German, French, and British theorists playing central roles. One of the major contributions of French theorists in the second half of the eighteenth century followed from the prominence of organization theory in France and the manner in which it was readily adapted to explain differences between men and women, reaching far beyond the merely physical.

These developments across the eighteenth century were part of a larger and longer process whereby ideas of equality and inequality gradually developed in relation to one another, sometimes in a direct fashion and sometimes in a less direct and more general process of mutual formation. In short, it was not a coincidence that the dimorphic model and new arguments for sexual inequality began to be fashioned in the wake of a variety of radically egalitarian philosophical systems that appeared in the late seventeenth century, building on Cartesianism and establishing strains of Radical Enlightenment thought.[125] While philosophers like Spinoza and his teacher Franciscus van den Enden created radical egalitarian systems that were important models in some ways for later eighteenth-century thinkers, it was the work of a French Cartesian cleric, François Poulain de la Barre, that established the first comprehensive European philosophical system arguing for a fully universalist concept of equality that did not make any exceptions or equivocations on the question of women's equality.[126] While his were by no means the first philosophical arguments for "natural equality" between the sexes, they established a new level of comprehensiveness and philosophical rigor that played a role in eliciting intellectual arguments against equality.[127] Poulain de la Barre's arguments also continued to be rearticulated and expanded on in later works throughout the century, appearing in new forms in Montesquieu's *Persian Letters* (*Les lettres persanes*, 1721), as well as in the anonymously published *Woman Not Inferior to Man* (1739) and *Female Rights Vindicated* (1758), among others.[128] Along with prominent arguments for natural equality that focused on the social and educational causes of the perceived unequal abilities of men and women, the Enlightenment saw lively and persistent discussion of equality and inequality in the light of ideas of sex and gender difference.[129]

By the second half of the century, arguments for radical equality as well as arguments for essential and deep sexual difference had become more extreme. I want to look at two specific cases that represent important steps in the mutual formation of radical equality and inequality. The first case demonstrates the coupling of extreme ideas of equality with a deep assumption of difference. Even in the most utopian of philosophical work, heightened arguments for equality and social transformation could exist alongside assumptions about intractable sexual difference. In fact, they could even throw this assumption of difference into relief and make it appear all the more natural, significant, and unavoidable. The second example demonstrates how the assumptions and arguments for sexual difference and inequality were consolidated in France into a single model of sexual difference that became the most compelling and comprehensive theoretical assertion of inequality. This model, published in 1775 by the physician Pierre Roussel, established a new level of scientific authority for an understanding of deep and holistic sexual difference that argued for physical, intellectual, emotional, moral, and social inequality. It built directly on the theory of organization that developed midcentury.

The mutual development of ideas of equality and difference was expressed in a striking manner in the metaphysical system of a heterodox Benedictine abbé who briefly caught the interest of Diderot and corresponded with philosophes such as Robinet and Rousseau in a failed attempt to spread his "true system" beyond the confines of the disciples who gathered around him in his benefactor's chateau in the 1760s. Abbé Léger-Marie Deschamps was one of a number of authors who contributed to a new flowering of utopian literature in the second half of the eighteenth century in France. Much of this literature was built around the spirit of egalitarianism and the ideas of eliminating private property and instituting forms of communal living.[130] Deschamps's contribution to this body of work was the creation of a complete system of metaphysics that grounded his vision of radical social and economic transformation. Deschamps was concerned with the "half light" of the philosophes, and he criticized them for being "metaphysicians without metaphysics."[131] His creation of a complete and idiosyncratic philosophical system was highly abstract and, at times, extremely abstruse, building on difficult concepts and distinctions such as the whole, the All, and the nothing. Although his system had some genealogical relation to ideas of organization, and he attempted to engage theorists of organization such as Diderot, Rousseau, and Robinet, his philosophical system transcended obvious and direct connection to philosophical precursors.[132]

As comprehensive and absolute as his metaphysics was, so too was his vision of transformation. Deschamps wanted nothing less than to bring about a complete transformation of the world based on the underlying wholeness and unity of the universe that his system supposedly revealed. He wanted a radical ontological transcendence. Evil and unhappiness had to be overcome. This could be brought about only through an absolute clearing that created a new and pure space for the ideal state of being to emerge, which Deschamps called "the state of morals." As Deschamps told Rousseau, it was necessary to "clean the place out completely."[133] This involved the elimination of all existing social, political, legal, and economic arrangements including private property, marriage, monogamy, the division of labor, sexual mœurs, most elements of the built environment, almost all technology, and all books.[134] The problem with the reformism of the philosophes was that it was not total. "It is in destroying by half, as the philosophes do, that trouble is created in the present state," Deschamps claimed, "but the same would not be true of total destruction, seeing that its effects would be the union of men."[135]

The revealing element of Deschamps's system for my purposes was his ideas about how humans would be transformed by changes to their environment and the existing structures of their everyday lives. The change would be both moral and physical. The state of morals would bring about changes in ways of being, while also transforming the physical being of human bodies. People would become good, happy, stronger, and more robust. But the changes would go beyond this. In fact, they would go so far that it was impossible to fully envision them. "Both physically and morally," Deschamps wrote, "they would be what it is beyond me to render as it should be, because of the extreme difference there would be in all regards between what they would be and what we are."[136] Deschamps believed that as the differences of experience were removed from people's lives, external differences of appearance would eventually disappear until people came to resemble one another. The physical manifestation of this transformation would be so complete that even people's faces "would have almost the same form."[137] In the long run, humans would come to resemble one another more than "the most similar animals of the same species."[138] In effect, the homogenizing effects of the state of morals would produce only two basic types of people. All men would transform into one more or less identical man and all women would transform into one more or less identical woman.[139] After this homogenizing and unifying of people, this final state of historical development would be the fulfillment of "the state of union without disunion."[140]

Yet, for all these changes, foreseeable and unforeseeable, one significant difference would remain among people: sexual difference. Even in a utopian vision that radically reenvisioned human existence based on a metaphysical system so complete that it encompassed every element of the universe and prescribed new egalitarian forms of human existence of such an extreme difference that they were unable to be represented—even then, a fundamental difference between the sexes remained. This was because the universe as a whole, in addition to being composed of males and females, could be thought of as being metaphysically male and female.[141]

The development of this Enlightenment metaphysics of deep sexual difference was accompanied by a parallel development of scientific theories of deeper and more holistic physical differences between the sexes. As Londa Schiebinger has demonstrated, it was in this period that scientists constructed theories of bodily sexual difference that went all the way down to the bone, literally.[142] "Discovering, describing, and defining sexual differences in every bone, muscle, nerve, and vein of the human body became a research priority in anatomical science," in France and in German lands beginning in the 1750s.[143] Anatomical arguments about things like pelvic size and the proportion of body size and head size were used to argue for natural bodily differences that corresponded to different social and familial roles of men and women. Women's role as mothers was emphasized from the different perspectives of these anatomical observations. In addition to arguments for sexual difference reaching down into the deep interior of bodies, in the second half of the eighteenth century difference was also newly distributed throughout the body, reaching beyond the localized differences of organs and body parts to embrace the whole, as Ludmilla Jordanova has argued.[144] This latter theory of distributed difference drew on the theory of organized bodies and made organization central to arguments of sexual difference. Building on the holism and specific physiological arguments of organization theory, femaleness and sexual difference were distributed throughout the entirety of the organized being. In the most extreme form of this line of thought, factors like education and environmental influence were eliminated, and sexual difference became a result only of organization. In other words, in this most extreme form of the argument, sexual difference was fully biologized and essentialized.

The most important theorist of deep and distributed sexual difference during the Enlightenment was the Montpellier-trained vitalist physician

Pierre Roussel, who presented his arguments at length in 1775 in a book on the physical and moral dimensions of women, *Système physique et moral de la femme*. The book became the central work of its sort because Roussel stated the distributed sense of sexual difference in an explicit and programmatic fashion and because he supported his argument with extensive discussions of the mechanisms of physical difference and the manner in which this led to sexual differences in the realm of the moral.[145] He argued that men and women appear somewhat similar in childhood, but by puberty the bodies of men begin to change in a way that announces their "destination," and women stay closer to their "primitive constitution."[146] Compared to the bodies of men, the bodies of women stay rounder, softer, and weaker, and their temperament stays closer to that of a child.[147] In adult bodies, sexual difference, "whose essence is not limited to a single organ," Roussel wrote, "instead extends, by more or less sensible nuances, to all the parts" of the body. This meant that "the woman is not a woman only in one place, but also from every perspective from which she may be viewed."[148]

In Roussel's system, sexual difference permeated the body and could be found even in tiny blood vessels, nerves, ligaments, and tendons. Most importantly, it also existed in the mucus or "cellular tissue" that was said to envelope the organs and fibers of the body, enabling sensibility and its communication between the parts of the body. This difference of organization resulted in a difference of female sensibility that could not be explained as, in the words of Roussel, "an effect of their education or their way of life."[149] Removing the environment as a causal role, Roussel claimed that in the difference of cellular tissue and sensibility "there is an innate radical difference that exists in all countries and among all peoples."[150] Based on this purported physiological difference, Roussel created a new and highly detailed version of the much older argument that women were more susceptible to the passions and less capable of using reason to restrain them. Building an elaborate theory explaining how women's organization made them more susceptible to sensory arousal, Roussel argued that they were nevertheless incapable of having this sensory arousal leave a lasting impression, which supposedly created severe limits on their intellectual development. Women were subject to the "tyranny of sensations," incapable of abstraction, and mired in "immediate causes."[151] This prevented them from raising themselves "up to the heights from which to embrace a view of the whole."[152] In this way, Roussel constructed a vision of sexual difference that reached deep from within the mucous of the body up to an elevated intellectual and spiritual plane where one could have "elevated conceptions" regarding the "levels of nature" and "the source of beings."[153]

The vitalist physician Bordeu, whom Roussel greatly admired and who he knew as both a mentor and a friend, first claimed the importance of cellular tissue in the functioning of sensibility.[154] Roussel also demonstrated a vitalist emphasis on the principle of life and its perpetuation, placing an enormous emphasis on women's role in reproduction. In so doing, Roussel constricted what he saw as the natural purpose of women's lives, eliding anything to do with their own happiness or fulfillment, or even their multidimensional domestic role as mothers and wives. At times, he even limited women's purpose solely to the act of giving life itself. This supposed difference in natural purpose between the sexes also accounted for the difference in organization, particularly the formation of the body to accomplish gestation, birth, and nursing. "After having given life to a new being," Roussel wrote, "her task is done" and "the plan of nature fulfilled."[155] This was not just a general emphasis on motherhood or domesticity. Women's purpose was reduced to the biological act of reproduction and the immediate support of life after birth, separate from the long-term nurturing of child rearing. In Roussel's logic, their centrality to the reproduction of the population is precisely what necessitated their constriction to the social and biological role of mother. One form of biopolitical importance (as reproducers) was used to justify their biopolitical exclusion. Because they were the ones that gave "life to a new being," their lives had to be reduced to little else than biological reproduction and its correlated social roles of wife and mother. The near absolute difference in the social, political, and biological roles of women was presented merely as the necessary consequence of their absolute bodily difference from men. Roussel's argument for women's sexual difference was, therefore, strikingly absolute. It presented women's bodily difference as permeating every part of the body, inside and out, and as it relates to form and function, passion and intellect, the social and the biological. It reached from women's individual bodies to the collective body, through their sole allowable social function as those who reproduce. As Roussel put it, in terms that were unusual in the eighteenth-century arguments of bodily difference, it was "an innate radical difference" (*une difference radicale, innée*).

As extreme as it appears, Roussel's work was widely appreciated in its day, and it established a form of argument based in organization theory that consolidated many preexisting cultural and scientific prejudices and rearticulated them in terms that became dominant among those attempting to provide scientific explanations of sexual difference and scientific justifications for the exclusion of women from the public sphere, particularly following the significant advances of women in political clubs and in popular events of the French Revolution.[156] As Geneviève Fraisse has observed about the scientific discourse on women's sexual difference that Roussel inaugurated, it repeated and built on his arguments without much disagreement or controversy.[157] In fact, arguments and examples began to be stated with even more certainty and the presumption of self-evidence. Referring to the *querelle des femmes*, the debates about the nature and status of women that occurred in early modern Europe, Fraisse observes, "there was no *querelle* in these discourses."[158] In fact there was little critique of the biological arguments of this literature. After the French Revolution began, a significant number of women, and a few men, wrote works contesting the inequality of women, but they focused their critiques on the supposed links between physical difference and the moral, intellectual, social, and political inequality of women and men. Rather than targeting and attempting to undermine the arguments of biological difference and physical inequality, they focused on the supposed moral, intellectual, social, and political ramifications of this difference. As Carla Hesse has argued, they "responded to the reduction of their personhood to their bodies by stressing the contingent relationship of their moral being to the biological."[159] This played a role in establishing "a distinctive poetics of self-making" and a robust literature arguing for women's moral, intellectual, social and political equality, without displacing or discrediting the scientific arguments of difference. In fact, these arguments would only become further entrenched, providing much of the scientific foundations for theories of sexual and gender difference in the nineteenth and twentieth centuries.[160]

During the Revolution, arguments to exclude women from the rights enumerated in the Declaration of the Rights of Man and Citizen and deny them political participation were often consonant with Roussel's arguments, sometimes even sounding like simple rearticulations.[161] During the Revolution women who were accused of transgressing their "natural" role were repeatedly denounced, not only for specific acts of disruption of the social and political order, but for embodying a monstrous aberration of dimorphic sexuality and, therefore, embodying an affront to the entire natural order.[162] Whether applied to intellectual women who asserted equality and declared the rights of women (such as Olympes de Gouges and Madame Roland), to organizers who helped establish political clubs (such as Etta Palm d'Aelders and Théroigne de Méricourt), or to the many women who participated in direct political actions such as the October Days, labels like "mixed beings" and "men-women" were used to denounce their supposedly monstrous and unnatural organization.[163] Extending this language of the monstrous transgression of the natural order and building on Roussel's ideas of strict dimorphic organization, by 1802, perhaps the leading figure in the human sciences, Pierre-Jean-Georges Cabanis, declared that all female savants were "uncertain beings, who are, properly speaking, of neither sex."[164]

Roussel's work had already been through five editions by 1809, and some of the most prominent savants of the late eighteenth century and the early nineteenth century, such as Cabanis and Julien-Joseph Virey, developed and entrenched this line of argument. A whole scientific discourse developed out of it, emphasizing the role of organization in sexual difference, arguing for a strict and holistic sexual dimorphism, and expounding on the intellectual and social ramifications of biological sexual difference.[165] The basic argument became deeply institutionalized within the field of medicine and in the rapidly expanding field of lycée and university education, as a host of physicians and educators established "the natural history of women" and propagated the theories of sexual difference and inferiority.[166] This theoretical perspective also became institutionally entrenched, when, for example, Roussel, Cabanis, and another important theorists of sexual difference, Paul-Victor de Sèze, became members of the section on moral and political sciences within the National Institute of the Sciences and Arts, when it was established in 1795 to replace various royal academies of the Old Regime, including the Academy of Science.[167] Women's exclusion from the public sphere was also formalized in new ways in these years, as they were barred access to all public institutions of higher learning, for example.[168] Arguments for exclusion also found confluence with Napoleon's reassertion of social and legal patriarchy, crystallizing in the Code Civil of 1804 that saw many of the legal gains achieved by women during the Revolution undermined or reversed.[169]

In France, as Lynn Hunt has argued, women came to constitute "a clearly separate and distinguishable *political* category" only in the French Revolution.[170] But before this could happen, the scientific theories that came to justify the exclusion of women from politics were thoroughly articulated, and they had gained wide intellectual acceptance. In a sense, women's exclusion was being refashioned even before their inclusion could be practically realized in the Revolution. The prerevolutionary establishment of the idea of absolute and holistic sexual difference between men and women constrained the revolutionary advocates of the rights of women, leaving them fewer practical options and encouraging them to advocate in the name of women as a separate and distinct group, thereby recognizing and entrenching the very difference that they were attempting to overcome.[171] Even in arguments for political or social equality, therefore, difference was usually assumed. Many women disputed the claims of moral, intellectual, social, and political inequality between men and women, but the argument for the physical difference and inequality between sexes was largely un-contested. In fact, during the Revolutionary and Napoleonic eras, it was articulated in a greater number of works, becoming widespread and insti-tutionally entrenched. In a bitter irony that has not been fully appreciated, ideas derived from the theory of organization played an important role in rethinking the democratic body politic in new inclusionary terms and also in excluding women from that body. Put another way, the organization of women's bodies was made relevant for the organization of the body politic, as the political and the physiological senses of "organization" intersected in the exclusion of women from the body politic. The idea that sexual differ-ence was rooted in bodily organization created the theoretical foundation for what Fraisse has called "exclusive democracy."[172] Organization theory, therefore, played an important role in the formation of the constitutive par-adox of modern feminism, the practice of democracy, and the historical struggle for women's rights and true equality.[173]

The conceptual refashioning of women, vagabonds, and black people in France at the end of the Old Regime are significant episodes in the his-torical of biopolitics for several reasons. First, they were biopolitical re-conceptions that led to, enabled, or justified the implementation of laws, governmental policies, and procedures. In other words, these were exclu-sions that were enacted, not just imagined. New laws and regulations per-taining to vagabonds in the Old Regime built on Le Trosne's arguments, as did the legal and administrative approach to vagabonds in the French Revolution and the early nineteenth century.[174] The refashioning of black people and the category of "blacks" can be seen within the ordinances and regulations of the Police des Noirs. And the scientific arguments about the sexual difference of women played a role in justifying various forms of le-gal, social, and political exclusion of women during the Revolution. These biopolitical acts of refashioning also played a relatively direct role in new arguments about citizenship during the Revolution by providing new bio-political justifications for the exclusion of enslaved people, vagabonds, and women. But in addition to this direct role, they also played a somewhat in-direct, but conceptually important, role in establishing the contours of the citizenship debate and the terms by which citizens and noncitizens came to be defined. They were figures through which the logic of "in but not of" was formed.

Finally, the refashioning of these three subjectivities—the three cate-gories of exclusion—also have a significance in the longer term and larger historical dialectic of inclusion and exclusion. Acknowledging that there was no one historical moment when the dynamic relationship between inclusion and exclusion began (as I implied in the introduction to this chapter, it stretched back at least to antiquity, in both its conceptual and practical dimensions), while also recognizing that the events of the French Revolution were extremely consequential for the modern history of this dynamic (reestablishing many of the terms through which this dynamic evolved over the nineteenth century and into the twentieth century), the second half of the eighteenth century was important in introducing biopolitical terms and concepts that had not existed in the earlier history and that played an important role in conceptually making possible the reconfiguration of the dynamic of inclusion and exclusion that took place during the Revolution.

CHAPTER FIVE

New Citizens, New Slaves

In 1778, in the last of his major works included within the thirty-six volumes of *Natural History*, Buffon pondered the ability of the human species to improve itself in an intentional and controlled fashion. Reflecting on the Enlightenment science of self-improvement, which he had done so much to help create, he probed the realms of the possible and wondered if there was any limit to what humans could achieve. Fifteen years before Condorcet went into hiding during the Terror and wrote his celebrated essay that similarly probed the limits of progress and the human ability to bring it about, Buffon asked of man: "And what could he not do to himself, that is to say his own species, if the will were always directed by intelligence? Who knows to what point man could improve either his moral or his physical nature?"[1] Although not a direct response to these questions, the proposal by Abbé Emmanuel-Joseph Sieyès to breed "a species between men and animals" for the purpose of enslavement can be seen as both the apotheosis of Buffon's line of thought and a grotesque subversion of it.[2] The proposal to breed anthropomorphic slaves for the French colonies built directly on possibilities opened up by the revolution in the life sciences and the sciences of man brought about by Buffon and his colleagues, yet it developed them in a paradoxical and horrific fashion. It envisioned humans transforming themselves into new beings that were less than human and, therefore, supposedly less worthy of moral consideration and compassion.

In the introduction to this work, I suggested that the brief and bizarre manuscript proposal about the monkey-human hybrids was a radical biopolitical work that nonetheless represented many of the primary characteristics of eighteenth-century biopolitics. In this chapter, I analyze this proposal further, demonstrating how it fit within the intellectual and political context of the era. I also show that the proposal was not an aberration in the corpus of Sieyès. Although the creation of half-human slaves was his most radical and unsettling idea, his body of work is full of radical biopolitical ideas. In fact, Sieyès was a thoroughly biopolitical thinker who built on Enlightenment ideas and practices, including the theory of organization, bringing them into the French Revolution and playing a significant role in realizing, and at times radicalizing, the biopolitical ideas of the previous decades.

Sieyès has been called "*the* man of 1789" and the "key" to the French Revolution (see figure 7).[3] "In the field of theory," Hannah Arendt argued, he "had no peer among the men of the French Revolution."[4] Keith Baker confirmed that he was "the first and most profound theorist of the French Revolution," while Murray Forsyth argued that he "articulates the political theory of the French Revolution" and that his "system of political ideas is superior in originality, breadth and depth to that of any of his contemporaries."[5] Yet for someone recognized as a profound political thinker, universally acknowledged as a central figure in setting the tone and framing the political problems on the eve of the French Revolution, Sieyès has an unusually small presence in the scholarship on the French Revolution and the history of political thought.[6] As the author of the canonical pamphlet *What Is the Third Estate?*, and as an ideologist of the nation, Sieyès is a standard element of narratives of the Revolution and the development of nationalism, but the breadth and intricacies of his political philosophy have still have not received enough analysis. Compared to the many on major political thinkers of the era, such as Rousseau or Kant, few books have been dedicated to analyzing Sieyès's political ideas. This is all the more surprising if we consider that in addition to his authorship of *What Is the Third Estate?*, Sieyes held political office in almost all stages of the Revolution. He played an important role in the establishment of the National Assembly and in the articulation of the rights of man, was a singular force in the establishment of new territorial and administrative divisions in France, had a role in forming the constitution of the Year III, held several senior positions in the Directory government, played a central role in organizing the coup of Napoleon Bonaparte in 1799 and in drafting the constitution of the Year VIII, hence playing an important role in both opening and closing the French Revolution.

While there are a number of reasons for the state of historical interest in Sieyès, three peculiar features of his corpus contribute to the state of the scholarship on his ideas. The first is that every one of his publications was a political work, usually focused on immediate questions or practical concerns, such as whether the king should have veto power, how the country should be divided up into administrative departments, or the best structure for the judiciary. Sometimes these issues provided Sieyès with ample opportunity to invoke philosophical principles and articulate grand visions of social and political transformation in light of questions of great

FIGURE 7. Portrait of Emmanuel-Joseph Sieyès painted by Jacques-Louis David, made in 1817 while the two were in exile in Brussels. Used by permission of Harvard Art Museums / Fogg Museum, Bequest of Grenville L. Winthrop.

significance, such as the specifics of a new constitution or the elimination of the Old Regime social order of enshrined privileges. The full range of Sieyès's intellectual engagements, however, particularly in the two decades before the Revolution, was not available to scholars before his last archival manuscripts were rediscovered and consolidated in the collections of the

French National Archives in the 1960s. His extensive notes on philosophy, the drafts of his early political economic writing, extensive bibliographies of books he wanted to acquire, voluminous drafts and notes exploring political theory, and his early nineteenth-century notes exploring issue at the intersection of science and philosophy are vital sources in enabling a full analysis of the development and the character of his thought.[7] In addition to the analysis of this published and unpublished writing, Sieyès political philosophy must be evaluated and analyzed within the context of the theory of organization that developed in the second half of the eighteenth century. When seen from this light, it is clear not only that Sieyès was a major figure in the tradition of organic social and political thought, but also that his work and its intellectual and political ramifications help us better appreciate the connections between the ideas of the Enlightenment, the Revolution, and the nineteenth century. While the Revolution was, in many ways, a major historical break, the continuities of intellectual development were, from certain perspectives, more significant than is often portrayed. In direct opposition to Foucault's classic account of the rupture of the classical episteme around 1800, the development of biopolitical ideas and the concept of organization helps reveal important ways that, during the Revolution and the early nineteenth century, scientific and intellectual figures, such as Sieyès and the group of Idéologues with which he was associated, built on intellectual and scientific foundations laid by Enlightenment thinkers.[8]

Sieyès's endorsement of vitalist and organizational principles largely has been absent from the analysis of his political ideas, even though Sieyès's political writing from the eve of the Revolution through his draft of a constitution in Year VIII (1799) demonstrates a highly developed and specific conception of organized bodies and their properties. The organic aspect of Sieyès thought has been recognized in limited ways, but it has not been shown to play a constitutive role in his political theories. In his excellent analysis of Sieyès's organic metaphors, Antoine de Baecque came closest to this, but he treated Sieyès's organicism as remaining in the domain of metaphor and not playing a constitutive role in the theoretical foundation of his political thought. Paul Bastid discussed the organicism of Sieyès's later philosophical manuscripts, though he did not integrate this into the analysis of his political thought, nor did he connect this to the earlier writing of Sieyès.[9]

I argue that Sieyès did not merely employ organic metaphors throughout his work; he constructed his "social art" and many of his political ideas on the principle of "organization" (in the specific sense that it acquired in the

Enlightenment). Organization played an important role in his innovative ideas about the nation, administrative structures, constitutions, and the desirable form of the body politic. This fact provides a new perspective from which to situate Sieyès within the history of ideas and to evaluate his larger importance as a political thinker. Instead of being analyzed exclusively from within the history of political thought, Sieyès needs also to be placed within the philosophical and scientific context of late eighteenth-century vitalism and theories of organization. In fact, placing his work in this context results in a new understanding of the idea of representation that was his primary contribution to the history of political thought.[10] Sieyès built on previous ideas about organized bodies and developed a new idea of how an organized political body could be created in a virtual form through the mechanism of representation. This virtual body politic was unlike anything that came before, even as Sieyès selectively drew on ideas from earlier political theorists such as Rousseau and Hobbes.

As he formulated a politics of organization, Sieyès developed ideas about how the collective body of what he called the "public establishment" should be refashioned through different types of exclusions. His call in *What Is the Third Estate?* to exclude "the privileged" was his most well received, and it has become his most famous, but he formulated a number of other forms of internal exclusion that were equally radical. The first, and largest, group to be inclusively excluded were those who might be included in the nation while not being granted any form of active participation in politics. This group included women, children, vagabonds, beggars, servants, and anyone else in a position of subservience to a master (broadly conceived).[11] The second group was composed of people that were also deemed ineligible for active political participation; they would also be granted a lesser form of citizenship that recognized their natural and civil rights, while not granting them an active role in politics. This latter group of laborers made up a significant percentage of the male population. Sieyes saw the creation of the new group of monkey-human slaves as a means of transforming the political economic circumstances in France so as to improve the passive citizens with the hopes of making them active citizens. While an investigation of the context within which Sieyès created his proposal can do nothing to change the moral grotesqueness of the ideas expressed, it can help reveal how it was scientifically conceivable and, in the opinion of Sieyès, politically and socially necessary. It can also help demonstrate how the proposal fit into a radical biopolitical project to bring about a transformed world that would see greater social and political inclusion, as well as the exclusion and immiseration of large groups of people and the new hybrid beings. It will also show that for Sieyès, the creation of new citizens was dependent on the creation of new slaves.

Sieyès was something of an enigma to his contemporaries, even those who knew him personally.[12] Many of his arguments and positions on issues had the appearance of contradiction, even if he had complex explanations for why they were not. For example, he had a career in the church for decades, rising to the position of the canon of the cathedral of Chartres, yet he detested organized religion, privately calling it the "first enemy of man."[13] He argued that in the Old Regime the Third Estate was nothing, but that it must become everything. His argument for the Third Estate's claim to be the entire nation was grounded in its productive contributions to the nation, yet he argued full citizenship should be extended only to the portion of the population who had the means to be free of labor. He argued that productive labor should be one of the primary criteria for inclusion in the nation, yet he denigrated workers as "human beasts."[14] On the eve of the Revolution, he joined the abolitionist Society of Friends of the Blacks (Société des amis des noirs), while in private, probably around the same time, he argued for the breeding of new slaves and the creation of indentured servitude that he called a temporary "slavery of need."[15] He advocated a "political metaphysics" yet did not publish philosophical works.[16] One of the better representations of how other people found him opaque was the response he was said to have given when asked what he had done during the Terror. His response, which was likely an apocryphal saying projected onto his enigmatic figure, was simply: "I survived." Some people detected a fundamental misanthropy in his character, as when Germaine de Staël observed that "the human race displeased him, and he did not knew how to treat it."[17] In light of his biopolitical ideas, particularly the breeding of less-than-human slaves, she seems to have seen something essential about him: "One would say that he wanted to deal with something other than men, and that he would renounce it all, if only he could find a species more to his taste somewhere on earth."[18]

In the most general terms, the political theory of Sieyès can be understood as a combination of some of Hobbes's ideas of representation, Rousseau's approach to generality and the creation of an organized political body demonstrating true unity, and physiocratic ideas (from Le Trosne particularly) of internal exclusion (who, how, and why to include and exclude groups from the social, political, and national body). Sieyès combined and developed all of these in his own idiosyncratic style, drawing out the organization theories underlying some of the ideas of Rousseau and the physiocrats. He made these ideas of organization more prominent and more central to his theories of how to turn collective bodies into organized and animated forms. Given the available evidence, it is clear that by the time of Napoleon's Consulate and Empire, Sieyès explicitly agreed with the core ideas of organization theory, particularly as articulated by the Montpellier school of vitalism. His philosophical manuscripts from the time period leave little doubt that he agreed with much in the physiological theories of his friends Pierre-Jean-Georges Cabanis and Anthelme-Balthasar Richerand, as well as Richerand's intellectual hero Théophile Bordeu, though of course, as a creative and cantankerous thinker, Sieyès had his own interpretations, rearticulations, adaptations, and philosophical preoccupations.[19] While it is difficult to know when or why Sieyès first engaged with these ideas, manuscripts indicate that Sieyès was already engaged with these theories and endorsing some of the basic principles of organization by the 1770s. In his metaphysical notebook of 1773, commenting on Quensay's *Encyclopédie* article "Evidence," Sieyès wrote that "everything is relative," that a person is a "multitude of bodies," and that "I am at the same time cause and effect."[20] His reading notes and his bibliographies from the early 1770s include many relevant scientific theorists of organization such as Buffon, Vandermonde, Diderot, La Mettrie, Robinet, Bonnet, John Gregory, and Jean-Baptiste-Claude Delisle de Sales.[21] It is also clear that in these years he studied political theorists of organization, such as Rousseau and the physiocrats.

A number of philosophical manuscripts written by Sieyès during the Consulate and the Napoleonic Empire, while Sieyès was no longer directly involved in politics, reveal his clearest and most explicit connections to the development of vitalism and organicism in the second half of the eighteenth century.[22] They are working notes that record Sieyès's engagement with questions of vitalism, organization, cognition, and the relationship between the physical and the moral. They have titles such as "On Life," "On Relations," "Central Point of the Human System," and "Questions and Research on Simple Forces." Repeatedly, they engage with the fundamental questions of vital materialism and organization, asking, "what is vital force?"[23] They are searching, sometimes rambling, notes that cross back and forth, circle around, and veer between topics, positing answers, revising them, and raising new questions.[24] They are very much a record of thought in motion. Their value is not just that they reveal Sieyès engaging extensively in a natural philosophical inquiry into these topics, but also that they provide many instances of his endorsement of key propositions of vitalism and organization theory. An analysis of these manuscripts, in particular, helps reveal how Sieyès's language of political organization was more than simply the use of organic metaphors. While his political writing during the Revolution already demonstrated all the hallmarks of organization theory, these late manuscripts make his dedication to the terms, concepts, and principles of organization even clearer.

Reflecting on the properties of interconnection and interdependence of parts within organized bodies, for example, Sieyès wrote about the circular causation among parts, recognizing this "circle of life" within a body and writing about the ways that "action and reaction" characterize physical, moral, and political order.[25] He differentiated between mechanical, chemical, and vital forces and argued that "when organic and vital forces arise in a series of combinations, their products are very different from what they would be if left to mechanical and chemical forces alone."[26] In line with the vital materialists, Sieyès thought that "life is only a phenomenon resulting from a particular combination." Life then was an emergent property, and it did not have a separate existence like some kind of external thing that could be added to dead matter so as to give it vital properties.[27]

He also explicitly engaged in questions of levels of life and the nesting of beings at different scales of existence. He says that if we look at an object like a garden from too high a vantage point, we may not see the living beings in it. Taken collectively, "as a single individual," it may appear not to be alive. If we inspect it more closely, however, we may be able to see the millions of tiny living beings in it. He says that if there were enormously large and intelligent beings inspecting earth from outer space, they may have the same difficulties finding life on the planet. He then is led to ask about life on these different scales of being: "Who knows if a grain of sand is not, in truth, like my garden or like the terrestrial globe, a world peopled by the particular life of beings many billions of times smaller."[28] In addition to William Blake's musings about the world in a grain of sand, and the cosmic views of a tiny earth seen by large creatures in the fiction of Bernard Le Bouvier de Fontenelle and Voltaire, this image of three levels of being brings to mind the image of a garden that Leibniz used, along with the related image of a fish pond, to express his ideas about the nesting of beings within beings.[29] "Each portion of matter can be conceived of as a garden full of plants, and a pond full of fish," Leibniz wrote in the *Monadology* about the relationship between monads and corporal substances, "but each branch of the plant, each limb of an animal, each drop of its humors, is still another such garden or pond."[30] Even if he had this Leibnizian image in mind while composing this reflection on the levels of being, it is also significant that Sieyès employed that key term of Montpellier vitalism, "particular life."[31] Like many of the late eighteenth-century organization theorists, including a number of the Montpellier vitalists themselves, Sieyès seems happy to have drawn on a Lebnizian sense of nesting, taking monads as a means of thinking about the relation of parts and wholes, even while leaving aside much of the metaphysics of Leibniz.

In a passage attempting to refute Marie-François-Xavier Bichat's search for a central point in the organized body of humans (a self or *moi*), Sieyès very clearly articulated the characteristic ideas of organization theory that Bordeu was so important in helping establish: the distributed nature of organic unity and the existence of levels of life within the organized body. "What are you trying to say with your *point* coupled with the epithet *central*," Sieyès asked rhetorically.[32] "The whole of man is a harmonic combination composed of several distinct systems, which are in turn composed of several organs concurring in the same goal in each system," he wrote.[33] "To seek for the central point," he continued "whether of the whole, or of each part of this very complicated organization, is an expression devoid of sense."[34] For Sieyès, as for the Enlightenment theorists of organization, organic unity was thoroughly distributed throughout the body and its systems. It could not be located as having a central point either in the whole or in one of the constituent parts. Sieyès directly connected these vitalist organizational ideas about the human body to the body politic. He made this connection explicit, writing that in the human being "there is here concurrence of powers, admirable equilibrium[;] it is a federated republic, not a monarchy."[35] As in the image of the bees that Enlightenment organization theorists employed, the body was a swarm of bees settled into a cluster, with order, structure, and integration, but without a queen (or king).

Although this passage by Sieyès is from the early nineteenth century, responding to the work of Bichat, Sieyès argued for a model of humans as organized beings that was consistent with the articulation of these ideas in the Enlightenment and the rearticulation in the physiological works of his friends Cabanis and Richerand. We know that in the face of Bichat's alterations to some of the central theories of medical vitalism, Sieyès held to the more orthodox understanding that was typical of the Montpellier school, which both Cabanis and Richerand built on.[36] Following the 1802 publication of his *Relations of the Physical and the Moral in Man*, Cabanis was the most distinguished theorist of organization and the most prominent and well-respected practitioner of the science of man. Richerand was a close associate of Cabanis and Sieyès, and more generally a fellow traveler of the Idéologues. He became one of the most prominent physiologists in France and one of the most important torchbearers of the Montpellier tradition, having authored one of the most popular physiological texts of the period, *New Elements of Physiology* (*Nouveaux éléments de physiologie*) in 1801.[37] Richerand was also a champion of Théophile Bordeu, editing a volume of his complete works that appeared in 1818, with an introduction by Richerand that was the longest account of the life and thought of Bordeu then available.[38] Even though Sieyès maintained that he was no specialist in physiology, when Cabanis and Richerand prepared revised editions of their major books, both of them solicited, and received, feedback from Sieyès.[39]

Even if we do not know precisely when Sieyès turned to organization theory, it is evident that he agreed with its basic propositions and that he utilized its key terms and shared its key concerns from his first published works, the three political pamphlets that he published between November 1788 and May 1789. In fact, from the first paragraphs of the first of these pamphlets that he wrote, Sieyès distinguished between the true unity of the organized political body and a mere sum of disunited individuals spread across a territory. In his *Views of the Executive Means Available to the Representatives of France in 1789* (*Vues sur les moyens d'exécution dont les Représentans de la France pourront disposer en 1789*), circulated in manuscript in 1788 and published in 1789, in response to the call for the convocation of the Estates-General, Sieyes observed that a part of the public was just beginning to be able to distinguish "a nation organized as a political body from an immense flock of men spread over a surface of twenty-five thousand square leagues."[40] Sieyès, like many early modern political thinkers, believed that in a large and populous nation, the multitude of individuals could become a truly united and singular collective being only through representation.[41] Even if a large number of people were excluded from political participation, with only "active citizens" remaining, this group would still be far too numerous to meet in person to deliberate. Sieyès believed that citizens could be assembled only virtually, through representatives. With "five to six million active citizens, spread over more than twenty-five thousand square leagues," Sieyès said, driving the point home clearly, "it is certain that they can aspire to a legislature only by *representation*."[42]

There are also signs in *What Is the Third-Estate?* That Sieyès's approach to politics was informed by the relational and holistic epistemology of organization theory. From his early political interventions in the public debates that occurred between the calling of the Estates-General in 1788 and the beginning of the Revolution in the middle of 1789, Sieyès made it clear that this epistemology informed his political prescriptions and his approach to the social art more generally. As he described in *What Is the Third-Estate?*, the recognition of any type of truth is a holistic phenomenon. People best perceive truth all at once and as a whole, not in pieces or parts. Toward the end of the pamphlet he wrote critically of those who argued the truth could be presented in pieces.[43] Opposing the advocates of "moderation" in early 1789, Sieyès declared that "it is false to imagine that the truth can be divided and isolated so that it enters the mind more easily in small *portions*."[44] Instead, it was better for people to be able to perceive truth in a holistic manner, recognizing the totality of parts in a single simultaneous experience, an idea that was not unlike the one behind Quesnay's *tableau œconomique*, which Sieyès studied closely and which may have influenced his many extraordinary attempts to graphically represent the administrative structure of the nation.[45] Minds "often need a sharp shock," and "truth can never have too much light to make the kind of strong impressions that engrave it forever deep in the soul."[46]

Continuing with the analogy of illumination, and invoking the distinction between the physical and the moral, Sieyès made explicit his dedication to an epistemology of relational holism, arguing that light "in the moral world . . . consists of the relations between and the totality of all the truths pertaining to a subject."[47] Sieyès also connected the perception of truth as an act of an individual to the perception of truth at the scale of the nation. Acknowledging that "in so enormous a mass as a nation" it is not possible for everyone to perceive the truth simultaneously, it is nonetheless necessary to strive toward a situation in which everyone is capable of perceiving the truth. This is the work of reason, which succeeds "only when it is spread widely."[48] Only when it enables people to understand and appreciate the true social principles laid out by philosophers can reason bring about the beneficial transformation of collective life.[49] The light of reason must be disseminated, because "only in striking everywhere is it able to strike true, because it is then that public opinion is formed."[50] Social truths have the potential to be put into practice and transform the social world only when the individuals making up the nation holistically perceive them.

In the holistic model of organization theory—and in Rousseau's adaptation of it in political theory—Sieyès found a way of approaching the challenge of balancing holism and individualism. Throughout his political writing, Sieyès was concerned with finding a way to form a political association while retaining, and even fostering, the individual liberty of those entering into the association. While this was a classic problem of political theory, Sieyès, like Rousseau, drew on the new ideas of organic unity and the properties of organized bodies to create a new solution. Sieyès was trying to find a form of government that acknowledged, and allowed for, the fact that while an organism is a single unified whole, it is still composed of parts that must be left to function with some considerable degree of autonomy or freedom. While an organized body was united and coordinated through its organization, with its integrated and interconnected parts working in harmony, the parts were not commanded by some central point or single authority. The parts had to be coordinated, but not dominated. Sieyès believed that the parts (individuals) must be allowed to function as they should, that is, in conformity with natural order and the properties of an organized body. But in their private affairs, people must be left to be as free as possible.

The necessity of both collective unity and a high degree of personal freedom required a new type of body politic that Sieyès called an "organized body politic."[51] This form of body politic was based on a new idea of representation. "Men have bodies that are already organized," and families are organized by nature, Sieyès claimed, but large collective bodies like the social body or the body politic are not naturally organized.[52] They must be organized. "The organization of society takes art," which Sieyès, following the physiocrats, called "the social art."[53] Sieyès distinguished between the organization of a multitude of individuals in a social body and the political organization of a body politic. While a social body could be formed without "degrading" people, in politics, the organization had to occur virtually, in order to protect individual liberty. For Sieyès, therefore, the only way that the multitude of individual bodies could become a desirable form of organized political body was in the virtual realm of representation. Only representation was able to organize the body politic in a way that gave it form, life, and unity, while retaining the liberty and rights of individuals. It was only through representation that the body politic could become an organized body while individuals retained their semiautonomy. Sieyès believed that politically organizing individuals or the sum total of individuals (an aggregate that he referred to as "the people") degrades them.[54] The people as an actual group of dispersed individuals should remain only an aggregation. They should be transformed from an aggregation to an association only in a virtual form when they are given a true unity through representation. "In the representative system there are not two organized bodies: the people and its representation."[55] Rather, only the representation is organized. This way of coming together in representation is the only way that the people can reunite and become a political whole. As Sieyès wrote, "it alone is the people reunited."[56] Strictly speaking, representatives are not named by the people (the whole), but by groups of people who meet to choose their individual representative. The only way that these groups of people, or *the* people, could become united was through the coming together of their elected representatives. In other words, Sieyès was not simply pointing to the virtuality of representation. He was arguing that through representation a virtual organized body politic could be formed, and that, in fact, it should be. It was the virtuality of the organized body politic that set Sieyès's idea apart from other eighteenth-century articulations of virtual representation.[57]

For Sieyès the nation always exists—it "exists before everything"—but national unity does not necessarily always exist.[58] A primitive form of the nation existed as soon as people had the desire to unite.[59] But a nation becomes truly united only through the reuniting of the people, which, in a populous nation, can happen only virtually, through political representation. For Sieyès, instead of the social contract, it was the mechanism of representation that created national unity and gave birth to the organized body politic. "The unity of the nation, the national integrity is not anterior to the will of the reunited people, which is only in its representation. Unity begins there."[60] Since a dispersed group of individuals is not in itself "an organized body," it is the reuniting of the people in representation that forms what he called "the first organized body."[61] The body politic, therefore, is not merely a metaphorical organism. One of the innovations of these ideas about representation is that the mechanism of representation makes the body politic a virtual organism. It is an actual organized body in a virtual state.

In Rousseau's system of political organization, individuals were transformed through the formation of a collective. They give themselves over to it and get back a new "partial existence" in return. They must abandon themselves to the whole to be transformed.[62] Sieyès did not agree with this. He wanted the individual to remain relatively free from the transforming power of the whole. In order to do this, he had to envision the collective body as a virtual body, one that could be organized (given form and life), but that would not subsume or sacrifice the individual.

Sieyès found numerous ways to translate these theoretical considerations in the practical political prescriptions. In September 1789, on the occasion of debate about creating a veto power for the king, Sieyès articulated several of his core ideas about the best structure of the government. Opposing a specific version of federation, as well as the political principle of structured counterforces balancing one another within the structure of the government and the idea that through a veto power the king should be able to bypass the representative legislature and appeal to the will of the people, Sieyès made the case for representation and unity. He opposed the principles that would "cut, split, and tear France into an infinity of small democracies."[63] Instead of transforming France into a confederation of municipalities, districts, or provinces bristling with internal barriers and heterogeneous customs, Sieyès wanted to see "a general administration that, starting from a common center, will fall uniformly on the most distant parts of the empire."[64] Employing the language and logic of organization, and stressing the relation between the particular life of the parts and the life of the whole, Sieyès argued that France "is a unique *whole*, composed of integral parts; these parts must not have separately a complete existence, because they are not merely united wholes, but parts forming only one whole."[65] In short, a form of government was needed that would ensure the organic unity of the nation. A monarchical veto power, the balance of powers, and a federative structure all had to be opposed for this reason.

When Sieyès used organic metaphors and the language of organized bodies he was not simply perpetuating theological ideas that had been intentionally or unintentionally transformed to obscure the theological origins.[66] His organic terms and metaphors were not simply concealed versions of theological concepts such as the mystical body. The evidence reveals that Sieyès was a thoroughly organizational thinker who explicitly jettisoned older theological concepts that had played such an important role in absolutist political theory. For example, when he characterized the type of existence of an entity like the nation, he rejected the unifying function of the mystical body and instead explained that the nation was ontologically like a species of animal, in Buffon's sense. He claimed that, like "a species in natural history," the nation had two aspects of its existence, one that was perpetual and one that was unfolding in time through the succession of individuals.[67] The nation was both something that had always existed (it "exists prior to everything") and something that persisted over time, maintaining its identity through reproduction and the gradual replacement of the individuals constituting the whole.[68]

Sieyès also believed this type of gradual replacement should characterize the turnover in the legislative assemblies of the nation. His proposal for renewal by thirds—whereby only one-third of the representatives would be replaced on a rotating basis so that the terms of office would be overlapping in a regular fashion, constantly renewing the vitality of the assembly— shared the same naturalistic ontology as species and the nation.[69] Sieyès, in fact, employed this idea of gradual renewal in a number of his political proposals. One of the most revealing organismic concepts of gradual renewal and revitalization came in his proposals for the Constitution of Year III (1795), when he made it clear that the constitution should be "like any organized being," containing within itself a "principle of conservation and of life."[70] A constitution should not be suspended, nor should it be completely replaced all at once. Just as the organic body of an animal must be able to assimilate organic molecules to grow and reproduce, the constitution also must be able "to assimilate the materials necessary for its proper development."[71] Sieyès complicated his analogy by saying that although the constitution was like an organized body, it was not precisely like either a species or the body of an individual. While it is not clear precisely what type of organized body Sieyès thought would have been the best analogy, it was very clear, as he reiterated, that constitutions should be like "every organized body," demonstrating all the appropriate properties of these bodies.[72] Since the constitution was not quite like either a species or an individual in Sieyès's articulation, it may have been partaking, in fact, in the ontology of organization and demonstrating some of the features of both species and individuals, while not being reducible to either. This antireductive approach to organized bodies that mediated harmonically between parts and whole is reminiscent of Buffon's treatment of species as both an unchanging and eternal whole and a constantly changing succession of linked individuals. Interestingly, in another manuscript reflecting on the formation of the body politic, Sieyès also discussed the animating properties of constitutions, observing that the only law to properly be called constitutional was that which "gives existence and life to political bodies."[73]

In his early discussions about the relationship between the territorial redivision of France and the reorganization of the administrative order, Sieyès again resorted to the organized body's distinctive relationship between parts and wholes to characterize the existence of scales of organization, and hence levels of life, within the organized body of the nation. One of the reasons new divisions were needed was because there were several existing divisions that were not integrated. They overlapped, and they did not share common boundaries. "Which of the four or five divisions that exist currently ought to be adopted?" Sieyès asked. "The governments, dioceses, bailiwicks, and generalities, etc., are all of different sizes and have different borders."[74] He argued that the parts, the administrative units, had to be reconstructed so that they were nonoverlapping entities with clear and distinct boundaries that could be rationally integrated at different scales. Once these new units existed, a new relationship could be established between them, and between them and the whole. Concerning Paris and its existence within the new spatial and administrative order that he proposed, Sieyès wrote about how the city would exist as a semiautonomous whole as well as a part in the great organic whole of the nation. From an administrative perspective, the city would be a *commune*, and it would have a double existence as both a whole in itself and a part of a greater whole. It would be "in some ways independent," administering its own local affairs, while also being a part of the great whole of France.[75] "In this new relation," communes were meant to be more than confederated states; they were also "true parts, integral and essential to one and the same whole."[76] In this way, Sieyès felt it necessary to underline, the administrative relation between units would be different from the one between the states and the federal government in the United States. Recognizing the double relation is "important so that one never compares us to the United States of America."[77] Sieyès's dislike of federations was similar to his dislike of governments modeled on a balance of powers. He opposed these systems in favor of his own system of unity that he came to characterize as "organized unity."[78] There could not be fully separate lives of states within the state, as with federalism, nor could there be distinct and opposing parties or factions within the state. Sieyès's vision of a type of "division with unity," as he also called it, was characterized by distinctive (but not opposed or complete) parts integrated harmoniously, producing a "unity of action."[79]

In his first published work, *Essay on Privileges*, Sieyès wrote that "the privileged truly have come to see themselves as another species of men."[80] The tone of outrage should not mislead us to believe that Sieyès was against the division of people into different species, races, or types. He simply believed that the correct criteria needed to be used when making the distinction. Throughout his published and unpublished writing, Sieyès created many types of divisions, mostly related to political economy and the great importance that he gave to the criteria of labor.[81] Many of his divisions of people related to the ability to work, whether in the sense of manual labor or intellectual labor. For example, in just two pages of his early political economic notes, Sieyès extended the classifying work of the physiocrats and Turgot, creating over fifty names for divisions and subdivisions of classes of people. He identified the substantive class, the industrious class, the auxiliary class, the reproductive class, the coproductive class, the reverent class, and the dispositive class, along with many others.[82]

Sieyès also used political economic criteria as the basis for more substantive divisions between groups of people, often combining the fundamental criteria of labor with what he believed to be inequalities of intellectual ability that were the result of some combination of natural and social differences. Education came up often, though he did not dwell on the causes of the differences as much as he did on the effects that they produced in the population. In fact, a major theme running throughout Sieyès's social and political writing was the resulting differences between what he thought of as the well-educated and intelligent men (who were capable of understanding society) and the workers, whose lives were so consumed with labor that they were not able to develop whatever intellectual abilities and social understanding with which they were naturally endowed. The distinction between these groups played a major role in his political theory, and, in fact, the distinction between "active citizens" and "passive citizens" became enshrined in law for a period during the Revolution.[83] For men to qualify as active citizens, Sieyès argued that they needed to know something of the social bond. It was, therefore, the role for people who were capable of reflecting on social existence in a systematic and circumspect manner. Men who had some wealth, were not consumed by excessive labor, and, therefore, had the opportunity "to receive a liberal education, to cultivate their reason, and to take an interest in public affairs" formed the class of the Third Estate available to be active citizens, the "available classes" (*les classes disponibles*).[84] Their education, intellect, and their possession of the ability and opportunity to reflect on the nature of social and political order differentiated them from laborers and made them "much more capable of knowing the general interest and of interpreting, in this regard, their own will."[85] Both active and passive citizens would have their civil and natural rights recognized and protected, while only active citizens would be able to participate in the political process.

Sieyès's characterization of the large number of people that fell into the class of laboring "passive citizens" was often quite elitist and paternalistic, describing them in various terms, some of which were extremely denigrating. He wrote of them as a different "species of men" that were "auxiliaries" to the citizens. "This uneducated multitude that compulsory labor absorbs in its entirety" was composed of people that he alternately referred to as "working machines," "working companions," "instruments of labor," and "human instruments of production."[86] With the category of passive citizens, Sieyès made a significant percentage of the population part of the collective body only through an extreme and legally recognized form of internal exclusion. Certainly the inclusion of passive citizens was more humane than the kind of internal exclusion of the vagabonds in Le Trosne's vision; the passive citizen had rights whose protection was enshrined in law, and they were not reduced to the social and legal status of the living dead. However, passive citizens were kept from playing any active role in the fashioning of either the body politic or the social body. In fact, in Sieyès's writing about them, they emerge as more of a means than an end. Their productive labor is of great use, but they may have to be transformed by the government if they are ever to become something more than this.

In his private writing, Sieyès sometime wrote in even harsher terms about the character and abilities of passive citizens, calling into question the humanity of these "biped instruments, without liberty, without morality, without intellectuality."[87] He asked directly: "are these what we call men?"[88] In some of his writing, he seemed to answer this question with ambivalence, presenting workers as liminal beings that were neither fully human nor fully animal. Metaphorically, at least, they existed as "human beasts" living on the frontier between lifeforms. Even in relation to his peers and the previous generation of philosophes, Sieyès's descriptions of laboring people were harsh and dismissive. For example, at the time that he wrote of the majority of the population as "human beasts" (*les bêtes humaines*), the phrase was not widely used by his contemporaries, and, in fact, it would not appear in written works with any frequency until the second half of the nineteenth century.[89]

Beyond the exceptionality of the characterization of "human beasts," the passage where Sieyès used this phrase is one that best reveals his biopolitical orientation. Capturing ideas of paternalism and elitism, as well as the idea that governments should intervene to transform this group into a politically capable and fully human group, Sieyès wrote that "we must invite governments to metamorphose human beasts into citizens."[90] The choice of the verb "metamorphose" (*métamorphoser*) implied a transformation of kind, not just quality, seemingly indicating the distance that Sieyès believed to exist between fully human active citizens and these animal-like workers. The regenerative projects that may have succeeded in this metamorphosis were not a great subject of Sieyès's concern. He gave much more attention to the formation of the political principles and administrative structures than he did to either the general question of regeneration or the specific question of how to transform the workers of France. Yet his most radical and revealing biopolitical proposal envisioned an inversion of the metamorphosis of human beasts into people.

In some sense, the idea of breeding human-monkey slaves was a desperate and radical attempt to change the circumstances in metropolitan France so that the so-called working machines that composed the vast majority of the male population could be educated and improved. If these metropolitan workers were freed from labor (or at least excessive labor), they might be able to be educated about the principles of social life, hence becoming capable of fulfilling the duties of active citizenship. In several places in his writing, Sieyès also seemed to indicate that women might one day be able to become active citizens, though some of them, if not all, would also need improvement through education.[91] The possibility of this vast expansion in social and political inclusion, attempting to draw in somewhere between ten to twenty million people in the realm of active citizenship (depending on whether women were to be included), was predicated on the creation of new hybrid beings who were to exist solely so that they could remove the burden of labor from metropolitan French workers. Surprisingly, the proposal for anthropomorphic slaves is largely absent from the scholarship on Sieyès. If it is mentioned at all, it may be only parenthetically acknowledged or explained away as "mordant and maladroit irony" in the vein of Voltaire and Jonathan Swift.[92] The exceptions are few, with William Sewell's excellent analysis being the only case of an author analyzing the proposal at length.[93] It is as if Sieyès's anthropomorphic slaves were so extraordinary that they could not be sensibly related to the corpus of his political thought or to the seriousness and hopefulness of the Revolution. Yet the context surrounding Sieyès's proposal deserves more analysis because the proposal is a striking example of the links of inclusion and exclusion in Enlightenment biopolitical thought. It also represents something more general about the development of political thought in the Age of Revolutions, as people grappled with questions of popular sovereignty and experimented with practical and institutional means of including larger numbers of people in political processes.

One of the other striking features of these breeding ideas is that they were not as isolated as they might first appear. Significantly, Sieyès made a separate reference to the crossbreeding of humans and monkeys in another strange passage in an unpublished manuscript that is collected with his notes on the Constitution of the Year III. He speculated that if most of humanity perished in some global catastrophe, then perhaps the few remaining survivors could reproduce with "the race of orangutan monkeys," repopulating the earth with hybrid beings, who would be of lesser ability than humans, but would have the distinct advantage of existing.[94] More significant than this passage, however, is the fact that his proposal for breeding anthropomorphic slaves was conceptually linked to various forms of biopolitical internal exclusion envisioned by him and his Enlightenment predecessors. His proposal can also be situated within various books that he read, or expressed an interest in reading, in the decades before the Revolution. Related ideas about human-animal interfertility and the possibility of fertile breeding between humans and other apes were expressed in the writing of people that he knew during the Revolution, including some of his closest associates and intellectual interlocutors, such as Condorcet. By the time of the manuscripts that he wrote in the first decades of the nineteenth century, Sieyès explicitly articulated a belief in the inheritance of acquired character and in the connection between the physical and the moral. In agreement with his friends Condorcet and Cabanis, as well as the naturalist Lamarck, whom he read, Sieyès wrote that "organs do improve, and improvements are transmitted to the races by propagation."[95] During the Revolution, in 1793, Sieyès wrote that the improvement of the breeds of domestic animals was "one of the activities most worthy of the attention of a true legislator."[96]

It is difficult to know exactly how well Sieyès was acquainted with the contemporary works in the life sciences before he wrote his early nineteenth-century manuscripts, but there is evidence to suggest that he paid attention to fields like natural history, physiology, anatomy, and medicine throughout his adult life. He included a large number of books from these fields in bibliographies that he drew up in the 1770s as a young man thinking about the books he wanted to acquire. He listed scientific works that included sections on animal and human breeding, such as Buffon's *Natural History* and Robinet's translation of John Gregory's *A Comparative View*.[97] Later manuscript notes make clear that Sieyès did at some point read Buffon, as well as another naturalist who wrote about animal and human breeding, Delisle de Sales.[98] Sieyès also expressed interest in one of the most developed biopolitical texts of the century, Vandermonde's two-volume *Essay on the Manner of Perfecting the Human Species*. In the section of Sieyès's bibliography dedicated to natural history and anatomy, Vandermonde's *Essay* is the first entry, accompanied by sentence length paraphrases from two reviews of the book that characterize Vandermonde as an "able doctor" and make reference to the chapter in the *Essay* on the crossing of the races.[99] Even if Sieyès did not read Vandermonde's book, he would have had access to extensive quotations and summaries in these lengthy digest-style reviews. While Vandermonde died young in the 1760s, Sieyès had another opportunity to encounter his ideas around the time of the Revolution when he made the acquaintance of Vandermonde's younger brother, the mathematician and political economist Alexandre-Théophile Vandermonde.[100]

The relationship between humans and apes had fascinated early modern Europeans as they began to read reports from travelers to Africa and Asia. By the middle of the eighteenth century, natural historians gave significant attention to apes and monkeys because of their resemblances to humans, but also because of theoretical questions about the continuity of the great chain of being as well as philosophical questions about whether humans were distinct from apes. These questions also played a central role in the development of the science of man. Great naturalists like Buffon and Linnaeus wrote extensively about apes and monkeys, but so too did Rousseau and De Pauw.[101] One of the more disturbing features of this body of work was the report of sexual intercourse between African people and various apes. Sometimes these reports were endorsed, or at least acknowledged by leading naturalists as possibly being true. Buffon, for example, took an ambivalent position on the relationship between people and monkeys and the reported sexual intercourse. In an entry on monkeys, he stated that there is not a genealogical link between men and monkeys. Yet, later in the article, he mentioned reports of sex between African women and apes, without rejecting the accounts.[102] Others, such as Delisle de Sales, thought that humans could be bred with orangutans to create new hybrid beings.[103] Creating these beings was considered a real enough possibility that it also elicited considerations in the realm of jurisprudence. In his *Theory of Criminal Law* (1781), the future revolutionary leader Jacques-Pierre Brissot acknowledged the mixing of species and the possibility of creating anthropomorphic hybrids. He mentioned an orangutan and human coupling, claiming that "everyone has heard of . . . the love of monkeys for our women," but he argued that mixing should be considered a crime since it would never be advantageous to humans and could ultimately make the species "entirely disfigured and unrecognizable."[104]

In the second half of the eighteenth century in Paris, monkeys joined canaries and parrots as the most popular exotic pets.[105] They could be found in homes of the wealthy, and occasionally they could be seen for sale on the streets and at fairs. They could also be found described in printed advertisements and occasional articles in periodicals where their characteristics and behavior were compared to humans and they were reported to be able to carry out human tasks that might be of use in domestic service.[106] Buffon reported seeing a chimpanzee (referred to as an orangutan) at a fair greeting people and strolling with them before seating itself at a table and carrying out a polite tea service.[107] In addition to monkeys being associated with small domestic duties, when human-animal hybrids were invoked in eighteenth-century French writing, it was not uncommon to relate them to domestic service or forced servitude. This association clearly related to the use of domesticated animals as beasts of burden, but it also often evoked the dehumanization of enslaved people. In his *Philosophical Dictionary* (*Dictionnaire philosophique*), for example, when Voltaire inquired into what he took to be a gap in the chain of being, dividing humans and apes, he asked how hard it was to imagine an intelligent "two-legged animal without feathers" that could not use language, but could nonetheless "respond to our signs and serve us."[108] In *D'Alembert's Dream*, Diderot also connected slavery to the breeding of hybrids. "We should no longer reduce men in our colonies to the condition of beasts of burden," the character of Dr. Bordeu tells Mademoiselle de Lespinasse, with her replying, "quick, quick, doctor, get to work and make us some goat-men."[109]

The presence of actual monkeys and apes, combined with the popular work of the naturalists and philosophes, spawned interest that was met by authors of fictional works about anthropomorphic monkeys as well as animal-human hybrids, often of a monkey-human mixture. Sieyès was an acquaintance of one of the most successful of these authors, Restif de la Bretonne, who wrote popular works in each of these subgenres, following his 1781 novel of human-animal hybrids in the Southern Hemisphere with *Letter from a Monkey* (*Lettre d'un singe*), in which a human-baboon hybrid writes to his the community of baboons warning them not to become too much like humans.[110] While imprisoned in Vincennes from 1777 to 1780, Honoré-Gabriel de Riqueti, comte de Mirabeau, prodigal son of the physiocrat Mirabeau, claimed to pass much of his time reading Buffon.[111] The future revolutionary leader and political ally of Sieyès (for a time) also wrote a number of erotic works that drew on the life sciences and contemporary natural history. For example, writing on the topic of bestiality in one of these pieces of imaginative erotica, *Erotika Biblion*, Mirabeau brought together Buffon's animal-breeding experiments, ideas of human and animal copulation, notions of racial difference, and the discourse on physical improvement. Claiming that monstrous coupling between humans and animals occurred more often in Africa, Mirabeau wondered if this would be "the true school of alterations, degradations, and perhaps of the physical perfection of the human species."[112]

It must be stressed that a belief in the ability of humans and apes to produce fertile hybrids was a feature of imaginative literature not only in the late eighteenth century. Since it related to fundamental scientific and philosophical questions about the definition of species and the distinctness of humans, the possibilities of human hybridity and the social, political, and moral implications continued to be topics of serious inquiry at the end of the century, and in fact, through much of the nineteenth century, and even in a few shocking cases, into the twentieth century.[113] In the middle of the eighteenth century, serious naturalists kept an open mind about a number of reported beings that might strike us as fantastical, such as Patagonian giants. They were also open to the possibilities of undiscovered hybrids. "Nothing should be seen as impossible," Buffon wrote in 1755; "expect anything and suppose that all that can be is. Ambiguous species, irregular productions, anomalous beings will then cease to astonish us."[114]

One of the late eighteenth-century savants to publish ideas about the possibility of human hybrids was Condorcet, one of the most important savants of the time and one of Sieyès's closest collaborators.[115] Having commented on Daubenton's sheep-breeding experiments and the possible implications for human improvement in 1777, Condorcet returned to the issue of breeding several years later in his capacity as an editor of the complete works of Voltaire.[116] Condorcet discussed the unity of the human species and the possibilities of creating "intermediary species" between humans and animals in an editorial footnote that he added to a volume of Voltaire's *Essay on Manners* (*Essai sur les mœurs*) published in 1784.[117] While Voltaire was a notorious polygenist, arguing against the common origins of the races of human beings, Condorcet followed Buffon's monogenetic approach to human origins and his use of the fertility of offspring as the criteria to determine species boundaries. Commenting on a passage in Voltaire's text about

African albinos being below black Africans and above apes in the great chain of being, Condorcet speculated that the difference between humans and apes was greater than that between horses and donkeys. But since the difference was not as great as that between horses and bulls, Condorcet believed a hybrid being could be produced from the mixing of humans and apes. While this crossing might usually result in infertile hybrids, Condorcet believed that chance would occasionally produce hybrids that were able to reproduce, allowing for the propagation of an "intermediary species." A human-ape hybrid, therefore, was a theoretical possibility, though it would "probably always remain at the level of the possible" since the crossing of species was so rare in nature and this type of crossing would be "so odious" in the civilized state. For Condorcet, the barriers to the creation of human-ape hybrids were primarily ones of social and moral acceptability and presumed disgust, rather than scientific possibility.[118] Sieyès has a similar position on the question of the scientific possibility, though in his archival manuscript the selective breeding of hybrid anthropomorphic beings was presented as not only theoretically possible, but politically necessary, and, in that sense, perhaps desirable.

In the late summer of 1789, as news of the unfolding French Revolution arrived regularly in Königsberg, Immanuel Kant began the last stage of revising the third of his major philosophical critiques, *Critique of the Power of Judgment*.[119] The work appeared quickly after Kant finished writing in March of 1790. Although he did not identify the French Revolution by name, he did include one reference to it, which was, in fact, the only published evidence of Kant's early reaction to the Revolution.[120] In the second half of the work, writing about organized beings and the organization of nature, Kant included a footnote referring to the idea of organization in politics. "In the case of a recently undertaken fundamental transformation of a great people into a state," Kant wrote, "the word *organization* has frequently been quite appropriately used for this institution of the magistracies, etc., and even of the entire body politic."[121] In the same work, Kant made a conceptual connection between individual organized bodies, large organized political bodies, civil society as a form of organization, and even a worldwide form of political organization. In his reflections on the aptness of term *organization*, and his reference to the French Revolution, Kant likely had Sieyès in mind, as he was the primary political commentator employing the concept.[122] In their similar applications of ideas of organization to politics, both Sieyès and Kant drew on Rousseau as well as Enlightenment theorists of organization working in the sciences.[123]

During the Directory government that followed the Terror, because of the appearance of political and philosophical similarities, a number of intermediaries attempted to arrange a meeting between Kant and Sieyès. These came to nothing, and intermediaries like Wilhelm von Humboldt and Konrad Engelbert Oelsner were left to compare and contrast the two men's abilities and the character of their ideas.[124] One similarity that persisted was the reliance on ideas of organization. Among Sieyès, the Idéologues, and their associates, organization became a central concept in understanding and intervening in the natural and the social world. As this group of savants steadily consolidated institutional power and intellectual influence, it was not uncommon for them to lecture about "the physiological science of governments," as Constantin-François Chassebœuf, comte de Volney, did; or to draft a proposal on the "organic law of political order in France," as Sieyès did; or to teach a "course on social organization," as did Pierre-Louis Roederer.[125] It was only after the commencement of the French Revolution, and the writing of Sieyès and Kant on political organization, that the political sense of the term "organization" became popular enough to be included in dictionaries.[126] Sieyès developed his theories of political organization along with his plans for biopolitical transformation. Like the authors of eighteenth-century biopolitical plans more generally, Sieyès assumed that large-scale social, economic, and political problems could be solved by intervening in the processes of life at the micro level of the generation of individual beings. His ideas about organization on the large scale and his ideas about the breeding of individual organized beings were not disconnected. They were united by their conceptual foundation in scientific ideas about organized bodies, and they both envisioned transforming and reorganizing the body politic through unique visions of internal exclusion.

CHAPTER SIX

Making the New Man

Writing in 1791 about the sudden transformations brought about by the French Revolution, Condorcet wrote that the events of the Revolution "*put a century of distance* between the man of one day and that of the next."[1] This change, this progress that seemed to catapult the French forward in time, shifting the whole landscape of possibilities and separating people from their own past selves, occurred with great suddenness. In fact, Condorcet claimed, it occurred in "*a single instant*."[2] Scholars rightly remember Condorcet as an enthusiastic advocate for the inevitable progress of humanity, though his rhetoric of swift and extreme advancement was by no means unusual after the outbreak of the French Revolution. Time and again, in speeches, pamphlets, and periodicals, people living through the French Revolution claimed that events had already, or soon would, open up a great historical chasm as France and the French people were so quickly and dramatically improved that they would appear to have somehow jumped into the future, leaving behind the rest of humanity and becoming something so different that it was perhaps justified to think of them as a new race or a new species.[3] Quotations of this sort abound, as many people with very different intellectual dispositions and political interests from those of Condorcet made these kinds of statements throughout the various stages of the Revolution, from the early days in 1789 to the Republic, into the Terror and through the Thermidorean Reaction into the Directory.[4] "Everything will change: mœurs, opinions, laws, customs, usages, administration," the Parisian observer Nicolas Ruault enthusiastically wrote to his brother in late July 1789; "soon we will be new men."[5] At the height of the Terror, shortly after Condorcet was arrested and found dead in prison, Robespierre observed that it was tempting to see the French as "a different species" because they "seem to have advanced two thousand years beyond the rest of the human species."[6] After Robespierre fell and the Thermidorean Reaction commenced, former president of the National Convention Jean-Antoine-

Joseph Debry found new reason to believe that although the great transformation had not yet occurred "the moment is propitious: change habits, found a race of new men."[7]

These types of statements, with their radical hopefulness, at times lapsing into hyperbole, were one of the defining features of the French Revolution. They represented the experiential awareness of historical actors as they lived through momentous change and faced enormous social, political, and military challenges. They also indicate the manner in which these experiences encouraged revolutionary leaders to imagine surpassing "the limits of the possible and the impossible," as Robespierre memorably put it.[8] The rhetorical nature of this hope of rapid transformation should not obscure the fact that a number of people attempted to imagine, and to implement, practical means of regeneration that would in fact transform people to such an extent that they might begin to actually resemble another species, or at least that they would have such a new physical, moral, and political constitution that they would be like the "new man" envisioned and invoked repeatedly as a powerful trope from the early days of the Revolution (see figure 8).

Pierre-Jean-Georges Cabanis, the most influential and representative savant of the Directory period, was one of these people.[9] He was also probably the most enthusiastic and explicit inquirer into the potential for social and biological improvement through the study of organization, particularly the bodily organization of humans. Organization appeared, in Cabanis's estimation, to reveal the very principles of human perfectibility. His writing makes clear that for some participants in the French Revolution the biopolitical vision of an improved people, a nation composed of "new men," was not some vague hope for improvement or some metaphorical sense of transformation (see figure 9). It was not merely an envisioned change of ideas, spirit, or mœurs (customs and disposition). Cabanis believed that the physical and moral improvement of the human species was not only possible, but attainable. In fact, the transformations could be so great as to qualify as a true creation of a new race. Like a number of prominent biopolitical thinkers, such as Buffon in the middle of the eighteenth century and Condorcet in the early years of the Revolution, Cabanis claimed that transformations to an individual's organization, that is, organic changes in *le physique* and *le morale* (the physical dimensions of the body as well as thought and feeling), could be passed on from parents to offspring. This meant that physical education and a new regime of habits could affect bodily organs and, as he put it, "create faculties, and even, in some fashion, new senses."[10] Looking into the future, Cabanis saw that "when these means have acted on

FIGURE 8. *Man, Finally Satisfied in Having Recovered His Rights, Gives Thanks to the Supreme Being* by Jacques-Louis Pérée (Year III [1794–95]). This somewhat ambiguous image of the "new man" shows him near nude with a muscular, idealized physique. He stands on the symbols of the Old Regime, looking up toward the Supreme Being with some trepidation as he gives thanks. He holds a pickax in his right hand and a scroll with the "rights of man" in the other. Used by permission of the Bibliothèque nationale de France.

Le Francois d'autrefois. Le Francois d'aujourd'hui.

FIGURE 9. *The French of Yesteryear. The French of Today* (*Le Francois d'autrefois. Le Francois d'aujourd'hui*, 1790). This image contrasts the small and effete Frenchman of the past with the large and strong Frenchman of the present, clad in the uniform of the National Guard and with a liberty cap on his bayonet. Used by permission of the Bibliothèque nationale de France.

several successive generations, all the rest being equal, men are no longer the same, no longer of the same race."[11] Literally, these would be "new men."

Throughout the stages of the Revolution, the projects of making the new man and remaking the body politic were linked. In this chapter, I will focus on the primary means by which revolutionary leaders attempted to remake human beings in the first stages of the Revolution, the intensification of regenerative projects during the Terror, and the various ways that savants envisioned the realization of further transformations in the wake of the Terror and in the beginning of the Napoleonic era. The first part focuses on the role of habit in revolutionary regeneration as habit came to appear to legislators as if it were a means to affect people in both body and mind, gently yet firmly breaking them away from old ways of being and thinking. Because of the ability of habits to transform body and mind, habit appeared to be a means of biologically transforming people. This made habit a target of biopolitical intervention as a way of transforming individuals and the population as a whole. The focus of many of these early regenerative projects was on the manipulation of the environment so as to bring about new habits, and hence, new ideas and ways of being. After the intensification of these type of regenerative projects during the Terror, savants gave new theoretical attention to the nature of habit and the ways that it might be used so as to bring about the transformation of subjects without those subjects being aware of the changes.

During the Directory, *médecin-philosophes* such as Cabanis and Jean-Louis Alibert, as well as philosophes such as Antoine-Louis-Claude Destutt de Tracy and François-Pierre Gontier Maine de Biran, formulated a new concept of habit that I characterize as "existential." This concept of habit emphasized habits as "ways of being" created through interaction with the environment (the *milieu*) and capable of affecting the internal organization of the body. Some *médecin-philosophes*, such as Cabanis, also believed that these physical changes within the body could affect mental faculties and therefore result in changes in intellectual ability. Given this powerful concept of habit as both an interface between body and society and as a means of manipulating the body through social changes, habit became even more important as a tool of regeneration that could bring about the improvement of the species as well as some of the social, political, and even economic goals of the French Revolution that had still not been realized after the end of the Terror. In the Directory, therefore, habit became the tool (the mechanism that could be manipulated) to affect a change of bodily organization so as to improve the species and consolidate and realize some of the hopes of the Revolution. If done properly, it was believed, this could lead to im-

provements in individual bodies that could be inherited in future generations, gradually spreading through the entire population and perhaps the
species. Savants who articulated habits in these broad philosophical and
biological terms grounded their arguments in the theories of organization
that were formulated by Enlightenment naturalists and physiologists. They
also built on Condorcet's belief that both physical and moral improvements
to organization could be passed on through reproduction, thus making it
possible for individuals and the species to be improved physically and mentally. In this biopolitical discourse, therefore, habit became much more than
the relatively unreflective repetition of actions or patterns of thought; it
became a means of physically and mentally transforming people. In short,
it became a novel target for biopolitical projects of regeneration.

At the outbreak of the Revolution, France was a country of profound differences in language, law, custom, and belief. As Pierre Rosanvallon has
put it, the bond that was necessary to unite the French people and provide
the foundation for the nation was "a political proposition before it [was] a
sociological fact."[12] Revolutionary leaders needed to find ways to fashion
the "new men" of the Revolution and to transform the disparate peoples
and practices of metropolitan France into a more homogenous and unified
nation. How could the miraculous regeneration that was envisioned in the
first years of the Revolution possibly be realized? While a number of scholars have written excellent work analyzing ideas of regeneration, the role of
habit has not yet been appreciated.[13] From the earliest days of the Revolution, however, the manipulation of habit emerged as a prime candidate
since many revolutionary leaders shared Mirabeau's and Cabanis's belief
that "habits govern the human species."[14] Later during the Terror, the central importance of habit was still being proclaimed. For example, one member of the Committee of Public Safety, Jacques-Nicolas Billaud-Varenne,
identified "the empire of habit" as both the primary impediment to bringing
about revolutionary change and the most influential factor in the long-term
formation of "national character."[15] Habit was something to be overcome,
but also something to be utilized. It both threatened and made possible a
successful revolution. In the words of Destutt de Tracy, one of the leading
savants of the Directory, habit was "that general cause of all our progress on
the one hand and our blindness on the other."[16]

During the various phases of the Revolution there was widespread agreement among political leaders and intellectuals that the best way to influence
habits was to do so when they were being acquired. For this reason, there
was a great focus among revolutionary leaders on the education of young
people. Accordingly, there were extensive debates and many publications

written about how to create a new system of education.[17] Some leaders even suggested that the state create a system of communal education where children would be taken away from their parents in order to completely separate the young from the prejudices and malformed habits of their elders. In these types of schools, control could be exerted over every dimension of a child's life, or as one revolutionary leader put it, "the totality of the existence of the child belongs to us."[18]

One of the primary reasons that habit was an appealing tool to be used in revolutionary projects of regeneration was that habit offered a means of transforming people's mœurs and their beliefs without those people being fully aware of the transformation. It could bring people to a certain way of being without having to convince people through arguments and appeals to reason. More than a century before the Revolution, this point was made particularly clear by Pascal, one of the many predecessors that the revolutionaries invoked in their arguments about the importance and efficacy of transforming people through the means of habit.[19] "With no violence, art or argument," Pascal wrote, "it makes us believe things, and so inclines all our faculties to this belief that our soul falls naturally into it."[20] Writing in a theological context, Pascal emphasized that beliefs can slip into our way of being through habit because habit assures that the beliefs stay with us, close to us—steeping and staining us—even if our attention is not kept on them. "How few things can be demonstrated! Proofs only convince the mind; habit proves the strongest proofs and those that are most believed," Pascal wrote.[21] "Once the mind has seen where the truth lies," he believed, "we must resort to habit in order to steep and stain ourselves in that belief which constantly eludes us, for it is too much trouble to have the proofs always present before us."[22]

Although they referred to Pascal and other moralist philosophers of the seventeenth century, the French revolutionary savants primarily grounded their approach to habit (both the explicitly theoretical articulations and the practical applications) in the sensationist philosophy the Enlightenment figures developed on the foundations provided by John Locke in his *Essay concerning Human Understanding* (1689). The key expositors of French Enlightenment sensationism—Condillac, Bonnet, and Helvétius—were the primary intellectual resources that the revolutionaries drew on.[23] Rousseau, who wrote a considerable amount about habit, particularly in relation to questions of education in his pedagogic novel *Émile*, also figured prominently. But while Rousseau provided a theoretical justification of the importance of habit—he claimed, for instance, that "education is certainly only habit"—Rousseau's approach to the manipulation of habits differed quite sharply from the predominant approaches of the revolutionaries.[24] While the revolutionaries were trying to mold new citizens, Rousseau argued in *Émile* that the role of educators was to keep their students from developing habits (at least in childhood): "The only habit that one should allow a child is to contract none."[25] David Hume, the author of the most philosophically profound analysis of custom and habit in the eighteenth century, does not appear to have been an intellectual resource for the revolutionaries, and he remained better known in France for his historical and political economic writing than for his philosophical works.[26]

Condillac was the most important Enlightenment philosophical source referred to by the revolutionaries writing about habit. This is not surprising given that Condillac was the primary French Enlightenment theorist of sensationism and that he himself claimed that the idea behind all his books was that "one must, so to speak, relearn [how] to touch, to see, to judge; a new system of all the habits must be constructed."[27] Condillac placed habit at the core of what made humans distinct from animals. Unlike animals, every person had two selves, "the self of habit and the self of reflection."[28] Although these two dimensions of human beings could be distinguished as separate selves, they were harmoniously integrated, Condillac argued, as when a mathematician walked down a street with his body carried by habit and his reflection fixed on a mathematical problem.[29] Condillac believed that habit played such an important role for humans that it could bring about changes in reflective reasoning to the degree that people could come to sense the truth even in the absence of demonstrative proof. It was possible to "contract so great a habit of understanding" that concerning "the relations of things . . . we sometimes have a premonition of the truth before having grasped its demonstration."[30]

Of all the revolutionary tools that might have encouraged the development of dramatic new abilities, such as the intuition written about by Condillac, the metric system was a prime candidate. While habit could transform people by affecting their everyday practices, it could also make them more rational through accustoming people to well-ordered, rational thinking. One of the leaders of the temporary agency created to oversee the implementation of the metric system made this point, arguing that "if we want the people to put some order in their acts and subsequently their ideas, it is necessary that the custom of that order be traced for them by all that surrounds them." He then emphasized the educational dimension of the metric system, arguing that it was "an excellent means of education to be introduced into those social institutions which conjure up the most disorder and confusion. Even the least practiced *esprits* will acquire a taste for this order once they know it." This is the case because the order "will be retraced by the objects which all citizens have constantly before their eyes and in their hands."[31] Although this claim may seem extravagant to contemporary readers, it conforms perfectly to the sensationist epistemology that dominated the Enlightenment and had only grown stronger during the early stages of the Revolution. In this model, sense information—and to a degree, people's reflections on it and memories of it—were the source of not only what people thought, but also how people thought. Greater rationality could, therefore, be achieved through receiving sensations that shared the characteristics of rational thought, such as proportion and regularity (e.g., between cause and effect). Simply seeing and handling things in the world could shape processes of thought. Therefore, if there were metric "order" (i.e., proportion, regularity, etc.) in the things that people saw and handled, they would almost automatically begin to think in a more orderly fashion.

Many members of the representative assemblies in the first stages of the Revolution recognized both the necessity of affecting people through everyday sensory impressions and the plethora of opportunities to do so. The metric system was far from the only tool of regeneration that was thoroughly banal and seen as a powerful tool precisely because of its ordinariness and ever presence. Many argued that legislators needed to utilize every resource available to them to help transform people into new citizens. It was in this vein, in a report on the seemingly minor issue of the official seal of the Republic, that Abbé Grégoire made the oft-quoted point that "when reconstructing a government anew, everything must be republicanized."[32] Even the seal was important because legislators "must not miss any occasion to impress the senses, to awaken republican ideas."[33] If all elements of the government, even its stationery and emblems, were to be recreated, it was, as Grégoire wrote, because then "the soul is penetrated by objects constantly reproduced in front of its eyes; and this composition, this set of principles, facts, and emblems that ceaselessly retraces before the citizen his rights and duties, shapes, so to speak, the republican mold that gives him a national character and the attitude of a free man."[34]

The sensationist epistemology behind the creation of the seal of the Republic and the metric system was on display in the naming of metric units. New words were created to indicate relationships between measurements. For instance, in measurements of distance, there was a regularity of suffixes based on "-meter" that indicated that they were a family of the same type of measurement. Old Regime measurements of distance like the *aune*, *pied*, and *pouce* were replaced by measurements whose names indicated an obvious relationship: the kilometer, the meter, the centimeter, and so on. Prefixes were also standardized so that one could easily know that a kilogram was a thousand grams just as a kilometer was a thousand meters. This regularity within families of measurements, as well as between them, was supposed to transmit a sense of order to users of the system, even if those users were not fully aware of the order. The architects of the metric system believed that even if the sense of order was not fully recognized, the thought processes of users would be positively affected. One advocate of the metric system, beginning with a paraphrase of Condillac, asserted that "a well-made language is essential for proper reasoning; the former nomenclature [of weights and measures] had none of these properties."[35] By adopting the properties of a well-made language, the metric system was supposed to be a pedagogical tool that could affect all people through their daily use.[36]

At the end of Year II, only weeks after the fall of Robespierre and the end of the Terror on 9 thermidor (July 27, 1794), Robert Lindet presented a report to the Committee of Public Safety that attempted to provide a plan for overcoming the effects of the Terror. It was a characteristic document of the Thermidorean Reaction in its scope and clarity, as well as its emphasis on unity (national, political, and social), economic recovery, educational reform, and historical forgetting.[37] Lindet's vision of how to bring an end to the chaos and divisions brought about during the Terror began with the familiar revolutionary invocation of reason. But Lindet's report was also characteristic of the new attention given to practical means of bringing about regeneration during the Thermidorean Reaction. While Lindet's report emphasized the spread of reason and enlightened principles through formal instruction (whether in schools or festivals), it was joined by an even greater interest in transforming people through their everyday practices, that is, through informal or indirect means of instruction.

Although many revolutionary leaders remained interested in social engineering through the manipulation of the environment and daily institutions and structures, they also realized that other means had to be developed in order to regenerate the entrenched habits and prejudices of older people. This, in fact, was the great challenge of revolutionary regeneration, which only became more pressing after the Terror, as the revolutionary leaders acknowledged that regeneration would not be miraculous, nor could it be successfully forced on people. As the important political economist Jean-Baptiste Say wrote in an essay on the means of reforming the mœurs and habits of the nation, "we made bad republicans each time that we tried to make men such while holding a gun to their head. We gained nothing more than appearances."[38] After the Terror, revolutionaries took stock of the failures of the early years of the Revolution and the violence of the Terror and recognized that they needed to try a different approach to regeneration that did a better job of influencing people in a more indirect and effective manner. To constitute real and lasting changes in people, the changes had to be made at a more fundamental level of human being, and without the appearance of coercion. "If one wants to establish some way of being or some habit of life," Say wrote, "the last thing to do is to order people to conform to it."[39]

The new attention to transforming people's habits through everyday practices was joined by a new interest in the actual mechanisms through which practices could transform habits, which would in turn change bodily organization in a way that could be passed on. In this period, therefore, habit came to receive an unprecedented amount of analytical attention, largely through the work of the group of loosely affiliated intellectuals known as the Idéologues (led by Cabanis and Destutt de Tracy) and their influence in the section on moral and political sciences at the National Institute of the Sciences and Arts.[40] One of the most apparent signs of this new theoretical interest in habit was the essay contest sponsored by the Class of Moral and Political Sciences on the subject of moral habits and happiness in 1798 and the two subsequent contests on the influence of habit on thought, one in 1799 and another in 1802.[41] This last contest elicited Maine de Biran's submission *The Influence of Habit on the Faculty of Thought* (*Influence de l'habitude sur la faculté de penser*), which won first prize, was published by the institute, and established a new standard in French philosophy for rigor and insight in the analysis of the relationship of thought, habit, and the body.[42] With good reason, when the twentieth-century phenomenologist Maurice Merleau-Ponty gave a series of lectures tracing the history of the philosophy of embodiment, he chose Maine de Biran as one of the three most important French philosophers in this tradition.[43] In his treatise on habit, Maine de Biran emphasized the way that habits can affect our thinking below the level of awareness: "the most general effect of habit is to remove all resistance, to destroy all friction; it is like a slope that one slides down without perceiving it, without thinking of it."[44] The leading savants of the Directory and Consulate were keenly aware of the importance of habit not only because it was fundamental to human nature and progress, but also because it appeared to be an effective and peaceful way to transform people even if they were somewhat resistant—as many were, especially in the provinces. It made it possible, as Roederer claimed, to "conduct men without bayonets, create agreement between them without tribunals, [and] make them happy without disappointment."[45]

In this vision, habit was so powerful because to have a new habit was not only to do things differently, or to think about things differently; it was to inhabit a new way of being. Human organization was such that even a fleeting impression could create "a lasting disposition" in the organs, as Destutt de Tracy wrote.[46] A series of impressions then, could do even more. Destutt de Tracy argued that habit did not merely create "a disposition in our organs";

it could do more than this, bringing about "a permanent way of being."[47] A habit had the potential to change one's very being because it could change one's organization, that is, the very structure and function of one's body and mind. This potential could be used to bring about rapid increases in intelligence, and, in fact, Destutt de Tracy argued it had allowed humans to make enormous advances from their primitive state. He believed that humans had improved themselves so much that by the end of the eighteenth century they resembled "the man of nature" as little as a chicken resembles and egg or an oak resembles an acorn. Even if the ultimate reasons for this remained mysterious, Destutt de Tracy argued, it was organization that made this improvement possible.[48]

Habit developed from our existence in the world, yet in turn, it played a role in determining how we existed in the world. It was both effect and cause. As the young *médecin-philosophe* Jean-Louis Alibert wrote in 1798, habit was "a type of education that we are given by time, the places, and the objects that surround us," while at the same time it must also "be regarded as an essential and fundamental base on which the edifice of our entire existence rests." This was due to the "absolute influence that habit exercises at all times on the moral and physical system of man."[49] Habit, therefore, was not merely an epiphenomenal effect of deeper essences, structures, faculties, dispositions, or passions in human beings, nor was it merely a tendency to unthinkingly repeat certain actions. As Cabanis wrote, habits were "particular ways of being" that were perpetuated even in the absence of the causes that brought them about.[50] Habit was the existential internalization of the external world, a way in which the outside affected the internal organization. This internal transformation of bodily organization played a role in determining who people were and how they existed in the world. Once habit was constituted in a human being, it became partially constitutive of that human being.

The development of ideas about habit during the Revolution by people such as Cabanis, Destutt de Tracy, Alibert, and Maine de Biran resulted in a novel concept of habit that I call existential because it was about ways of being rather than about repetition of actions, and it focused on how people's interactions with the external world affected them internally. While this existential concept of habit built on the work of Enlightenment philosophies of sensationism, it harnessed its insights about sense impressions and the influence of the environment and combined them with an understanding of the organized body. The concept of organization allowed sensationist philosophy to be radicalized in the form of the existential concept of habit. The concept of organization made this radicalization possible in two ways. It provided a means of conceiving of external stimuli as creating lasting changes in the structures and the functions of the body (since already in the eighteenth century the concept of organization related to both the structures and the functions of the bodies). It also provided a framework for thinking about these changes to the body being passed on through reproduction, since as Buffon and many other theorists of organization believed, biological reproduction was merely the reproduction of the organization of parents in the form of a new being.

Following from this existential concept of habit, to recreate habits was to recreate people. Therefore, to transform the basic structures of the social and economic world—such as weights and measures—in a way that forced people to develop new habits was a way of transforming people's very being, affecting both who they were and how they were (their ways of being as well as the structures and functions of their bodies and minds). But because the 1795 implementation of the metric system, and other regenerative projects with similar goals, had not succeeded in achieving an adequate transformation of either individuals or the collective body, members of the Class of Moral and Political Sciences argued that the government needed to work to reform these regenerative practices and find new means of effectively bringing about broad, deep, and lasting transformations. Savants like Cabanis rearticulated the theory of organization, its centrality to the science of man, and the way that it could potentially be better exploited by legislators. One of the primary inspirations for his work, and one of the reasons that transforming people through habit came to seem like such a promising means of bringing about significant changes in the population, and the species more generally, was the belief expressed by some savants, the most important being Condorcet, that improvements to physical organization could affect the mental abilities and be passed on through reproduction. The inheritance of mental improvements was one of the primary reasons that Condorcet was so optimistic about the potential progress of the human mind. Before turning to the further analysis of Cabanis's ideas and proposals about improvement, I want to look further into Condorcet's ideas, to give a better sense of the work on which Cabanis built and also to demonstrate some of the continuities and connections with earlier biopolitical ideas about human and animal breeding.

Condorcet was the most illustrious of the Enlightenment philosophes to live to see the Revolution.[51] By the time of the Revolution he was the long-serving permanent secretary of the Royal Academy of Science, and during the Revolution he became an elected deputy of the Legislative Assembly and a founding member of the Society of 1789, a short-lived but influential group of political moderates that included many of the leading philosophes and savants of the day as well as a number of prominent political leaders and wealthy men.[52] Condorcet also participated in the explosion of print during the Revolution, editing several newly founded journals and contributing a number of articles to other journals. Before proposing an ambitious system of public education in 1792, Condorcet published a series of five articles on public instruction in the *Public Man's Library* (*Bibliothèque de l'homme public*). In one of the articles published in 1791, he sought to establish that "culture" and "instruction" can improve people's faculties and that these improvements can be transmitted from parents to children. "It is . . . not as chimerical as it might seem at first glance to believe that culture can improve whole generations and that the improvement of individual faculties can be transmitted to their descendants," Condorcet wrote; "indeed, experience seems to prove this."[53] Condorcet went on to clarify that this transmission of improvement was not simply a matter of improved parents being better able to teach children. He pointed to the inheritance of modifications to the organization of living beings through reproduction. A great variety of physical features of bodies as well as intellectual faculties could be improved through reproduction. "Observation of domestic animals seems to offer an analogy consonant with this opinion," he wrote; "the way these breeds have been raised not only changes their size, shape, and purely physical characteristics; it also seems to affect their natural traits and their character."[54] He then argued that it was not only perfectly reasonable but also "simple" to believe that these observations of animals' improvement were a solid empirical basis for his conclusion: "It is therefore simple enough to believe that if several generations of men receive an education directed toward a constant goal, if each of the individuals comprising them cultivates his mind by study, succeeding generations will be born with a greater propensity for acquiring knowledge and a greater aptitude to profit from it."[55] Condorcet went on to underline the genealogical link between the intellectual capacities of children and their parents: "the intensity of our faculties is associated, at least in part, with the perfection of the intellectual organs; and it is natural to believe that this perfection is not independent of the state in which they are found in the person from whom we inherit our existence."[56] Although he attempted to soften the radicality of his arguments with the assertion that this was a "simple" and "natural" belief, following from the observation of animals and reasoned extrapolation—and he further softened the connection between intelligence and inheritance with the double negation, claiming that the perfection of the intellectual faculties of a child and the perfection of the same faculties in the parent were "not independent"—Condorcet formulated a radical idea that even many of the leading philosophes of the Enlightenment had found difficult to endorse. Within Enlightenment biopolitics, Le Camus had suggested in the 1769 revised edition of *Medicine of the Mind* (*Médicine de l'esprit*) that improvements to physical organization could be passed on and *might* be manipulated so as to improve the mind.[57] Charles-Georges Le Roy, the lieutenant of the hunt at Versailles, contributor to the *Encyclopédie*, and friend of Buffon, Diderot, Helvetius, Quesnay, and Daubenton, wrote in his *Letters on Animals* (*Lettres sur les animaux*) that improvements in the senses of animals and acquired dispositions of humans could be passed on to successive generations.[58] Nevertheless, even Enlightenment philosophes who accepted the concept of organization and the heritability of changes to bodily organization doubted whether these changes could bring about the improvement in mental faculties, a skepticism that Diderot expressed in his refutation of Helvétius.[59]

Condorcet refined his own argument about the inheritance of mental improvements and articulated it in an even more direct and forceful way in the last paragraphs of his famous work *Sketch for a Historical Picture of the Progress of the Human Mind* (*Esquisse d'un tableau historique des progrès de l'esprit humain*), written while he was in hiding during the Terror, which famously probed the limits of progress and the human ability to bring it about.[60] The *Sketch* was merely a preliminary study for a longer and more comprehensive work that Condorcet planned but was unable to complete. He had taken extensive notes, some of which also discussed the improvability and inheritability of bodily organization and the relationship between this and the example of domestic animals.[61] There are many possible sources for Condorcet's knowledge of improvement of domestic animals, but we know for certain that Daubenton's sheep-breeding experiments were one of the examples that he was acquainted with. In his capacity as the secretary of the Royal Academy, he wrote a commentary on one of Daubenton's reports on sheep breeding given to the Academy. In "On Wool" ("Sur les laines"), a short piece published in 1780, Condorcet observed that Daubenton had found the means to improve sheep and produce higher-quality wool through selective and systematic crossbreeding.[62] He commented that Daubenton's work helped to identify laws of inheritance for sheep, and he wondered if these results could be found to be more general, whether they would hold true for other domestic animals, or whether there would be different laws that would require different breeding practices to bring about improvement. In the last paragraph, Condorcet wondered about the relationship between these observations on animals and what it might mean for understanding the improvement of the human species. He concluded that Daubenton's observations about the importance of the mother's traits in sheep breeding did not seem applicable: "in the human species, the observations of M. Daubenton do not seem general."[63] Condorcet was not yet ready to come to any conclusions, since he did not think that there was enough knowledge to differentiate the role of influences on the human improvement, but he was already wondering about the applicability of animal breeding for understanding human improvement.

By the time he wrote his works on public education in 1791 and the *Sketch* in 1793, though he did not claim to have found laws of inheritance and improvement for the human species, he strongly believed that this improvement could occur, that it could be physical as well as mental, that it could be fostered through education, and that this was at the root of his radical hopefulness in the continued and possibly unbounded improvement of the species. "But are not our physical faculties and the strength, dexterity, and acuteness of our sense, to be numbered among the qualities whose perfection in the individual may be transmitted?" Condorcet wrote. "Observation of various breeds of domestic animals inclines us to believe that they are, and we can confirm this by direct observation of the human race."[64] Moving on to questions of mental faculties, he asked, "Finally may we not extend such hopes to the intellectual and moral faculties? May not our parents, who transmit to us the benefits or disadvantages of their constitution, and from whom we receive our shape and features, as well as our tendencies to certain physical affections, hand on to us also that part of the physical organization which determines intellect, the power of the brain, the ardor of the soul or the moral sensibility? Is it not probable that education, in perfecting these qualities, will at the same time influence, modify, and perfect the organization itself? Analogy, investigation of the human faculties, and the study of certain facts, all seem to give substance to such conjectures which would further push back the boundaries of our hopes?"[65] Condorcet's writing demonstrates the manner in which animal breeding continued to act as a viable model of, and argument for, the controlled improvement of human beings. Although he did not advocate the breeding of humans, Condorcet argued that people could be improved like animals had been, and that this improvement could be mental as well as physical. Condorcet reaffirmed the ideas that changes to the "organization" of bodies could be passed on from one generation to the next, and, moreover, that this provided an opportunity to systematically and intentionally improve the species. Cabanis was a friend of Condorcet and a member of the same intellectual and social circles during the Revolution.[66] Cabanis admired the elder Condorcet and was inspired by his vision of progress and improvement laid out in the *Sketch*, a work that the Directory government ordered be printed in a run of two thousand copies after the end of the Terror in 1795. Cabanis was personally involved in the reprinting the *Sketch* in a new edition of 1804.

Cabanis laid out his vision of a regime of species improvement in a series of speeches in 1796 at the newly inaugurated National Institute of the Sciences and Arts. He conceived of this regime in explicitly biopolitical terms, believing that the biological improvement of the species had the potential for tremendous social and political ramifications. It could be a decisive tool in consolidating the gains of the Revolution and establishing a stable and prosperous polity. The title of the first of these addresses captures the broad scope of his project and its relation to organization theory: "General Considerations on the Study of Man, and on the Relations of His Physical Organization with His Intellectual and Moral Faculties" ("Considérations générales sur l'étude de l'Homme, et sur les rapports de son organisation physique avec ses facultés intellectuelles et morales").[67] As he repeated in 1802, in his most famous work, *Relations of the Physical and the Moral in Man*, a collection and expansion of these speeches, he called for nothing less than the perfection of the human species, since—as he wrote elsewhere— "the hope of improving man, of making him more sensible, better, and happier, is no longer chimerical."[68] Cabanis believed that this could be achieved if the savants of the institute, along with like-minded colleagues, redoubled their efforts to develop the science of man in a manner in which it could aid legislators and realize the regenerative hopes of the Revolution. In the speeches and in *Relations*, Cabanis foreground the breadth of his vision and his aspirations. While it was "possible to improve the particular nature of each individual," Cabanis claimed, the effect that a consistent program of improvement could have on the species as a whole over several generations is "even more profound."[69]

The regime of improvement that Cabanis envisioned drew on Buffon's approach to species as a collective being. One "must consider the human species like an individual," Cabanis wrote, echoing Buffon's "Second View."[70] The indefinite duration of the existence of this species-individual makes it possible to bring it closer and closer to "a perfect type" for which there was no indication in its primitive state.[71] Given this possibility, a regime of species improvement must "aspire to perfect human nature in general."[72] Cabanis chided those in a position to contribute to this regime of species improvement for "totally neglecting the race of man," even while they had given so much time and attention to improving animals and making plants more useful and agreeable.[73] Invoking the trope of animal improvement, as did so many Enlightenment biopolitical theorists, Cabanis then connected the new regime of improving the human species to the still relevant imperative of revolutionary regeneration. As Cabanis presented it, this was not merely a question for naturalists, philosophical physicians, or other practitioners of public hygiene; it was a political question that had not abated as the Revolution had taken its course. Species improvement and regeneration of the collective body was still necessary. It was not acceptable to act as if it were "more essential to have large and strong oxen than vigorous and healthy men, fragrant peaches or nicely speckled tulips rather than wise and good citizens!"[74] Writing about the dangers of legislators who have not studied humans and human nature in their general movements, rather than simply from the perspective of individuals, Cabanis argued that a circumspect appraisal of the species and collective action was necessary in order to assure that legislators were not led astray, creating a malfunctioning and flawed polity. The kind of anthropological bird's-eye view afforded by the science of man was necessary in order to ensure that the legislators "organize" a nation and a body politic that was "a machine animated and living in all its parts," rather than some decorative machine that could be admired, but that could not function.[75]

Cabanis was probably the most enthusiastic and explicit inquirer into the potential for social and biological improvement through the study of organization, particularly the organization of humans. He believed that "the very organization of the human race" held "the principle of its perfection."[76] As he repeatedly and clearly stated, it is "by virtue of his organization, [that] man is endowed with a perfectibility for which it is impossible to assign a limit."[77] Though he thought it surely had a limit, as with everything in nature, it was still unknown and to be determined. Cabanis was one of the era's great proponents of scientific improvement of human beings. He believed that a more fully developed knowledge of the relationship between *le physique* and *le moral* would identify the "invisible reins of human nature" that would facilitate savants "to transform—without pain—good sense into habit," and "to extend all the faculties of man, to refine and multiply all his pleasures."[78] It was through man's grand project of self-improvement, with its "idea and certainty of perfection, always progressive, always unlimited, that he may in some way embrace the infinite."[79]

Cabanis's work helped reorient approaches to improvement and revive interest in the possibilities of selectively breeding human beings. His writing not only consolidated ideas about organization and organized bodies that savants developed over the previous half century; it also provided one of the most popular and accessible accounts of a biopolitics built on these ideas of organization. Cabanis played an important role in rearticulating and popularizing the idea that projects combining breeding with the transformation of organization through education and good habits could produce greater results, more quickly, than would education and habit alone. While it was true that education and new habits could bring about improvements on their own, Cabanis emphasized that the resulting changes to the organization of individuals could be brought together in a manner that concentrated improvements and accelerated their perpetuation throughout the species. Cabanis's powerful summation of Enlightenment organization theory, his harnessing it for the political project of improvement, and his unrivalled position in the intellectual field during the Directory contributed to a revival of eugenic projects in the years after the coup of 1799 that brought Napoleon to power. As I touch on in the next chapter, the Consulate and the Empire saw a variety of approaches to eugenics, drawing on ancient and Enlightenment precedents to create a new syncretism that extended the breeding strain of Enlightenment biopolitics into the nineteenth century while beginning the series of adjustments and reformulations that would continue through the development of the eugenics movement and the implementation of large-scale eugenic policies in the twentieth century.

Analyzing Cabanis's writing in the light of the formation of biopolitical concepts of habit and organization also provides a new perspective from which to assess the intellectual context of the close of the eighteenth century and the dawning of the nineteenth century. There are a few consequences of this identification of an existential concept of habit that emphasized ways of being and built on the concept of organization and the vital materialist model of the organized body. First, identifying this existential concept of habit contributes a new episode to the burgeoning scholarship on the history of the philosophy of habit, indicating a wider context in which to understand the important contributions of Maine de Biran and another way to account for the shift in ideas of habit from the eighteenth century to the nineteenth century.[80] More importantly, the existential concept of habit also provides a new perspective for those inquiring into "the role that habit has played in conceptions of the relations between body and society, and the respects in which such conceptions have been implicated in processes of governance," as a team of scholars have written in a programmatic statement attempting to establish a new scholarly framework for the study of habit and its history.[81] The development of the concept of habit in the projects of regeneration during the French Revolution powerfully demonstrates the relations between body, society, and governance and their importance in the philosophical formation of a concept of habit at the close of the eighteenth century. This case also reveals how the existential concept of habit built on Enlightenment biopolitics and was refashioned in a way to play a role in the biology and biopolitics of the nineteenth century.

Second, recognizing this concept of habit necessitates a new appreciation of the character of the philosophy of the so-called Idéologues, who have been presented as being disciples of Condillac who reproduce his philosophy of sensationism.[82] Certainly Condillac and sensationism were important to them, but the role of organization adds additional dimensions to their thought. This is particularly true of Cabanis, who most extensively and most clearly articulated the concept of habit and rearticulated the Enlightenment concept of organization. Third, this gives a new perspective from which to appreciate the manner in which organization, habit, and environment (*milieu*) developed in the years of the French Revolution as truly biopolitical concepts. They were not simply biological or political. This point, then, opens up a new perspective from which to interpret the work of the naturalist Jean-Baptiste Lamarck, most famous for his scientific development in the early nineteenth century of the concept of organization, his emphasis on the importance of interactions between organized body and milieu, and his account of the role of habit as the mechanism to explain how an organized body is transformed through its interaction with a milieu.

Rather than argue that Lamarck's "scientific" ideas were "influenced" by the political and philosophical ideas of habit, organization, and environment, I suggest that the development of the existential concept of habit in the context of the French Revolution can help us appreciate that this body of related ideas and concepts developed in a manner that was biopolitical. That is to say that in the second half of the eighteenth century, as they developed, these ideas were not simply biological or political. They were not of two separate realms. They were not moved back and forth, nor were they "imported" from one to the other nor "translated" from one realm to the other. Although they were sometimes employed as metaphors or analogies linking distinct and separate conceptual realms, often this was not the case. They developed in the conceptual realm in which biological and political perspectives were intertwined and in which there was a common language and there were common foundations for understanding. By the end of the century, "habit," just as much as "organization," was a biopolitical concept that could be used in a hybrid manner, while still remaining useful in ways that placed more emphasis on either the biological or the political dimensions.

In this light, Lamarck's contributions to ideas of organization, habit, and the transformation of species appear differently. This is not to take away from Lamarck's originality or to ignore the ways that he developed these concepts and drew on chemistry to formulate novel biological mechanisms to account for bodily changes.[83] Instead, it can be a perspective from which to more fully appreciated these developments in what he called "biology" while better understanding how they related to the context of eighteenth-century biopolitics. As Kyla Schuller has recently argued, Lamarck was an important figure in providing the conceptual foundations for a number of developments in the nineteenth-century biopolitics of "impressibility."[84] He was important and consequential not only because of the formulation of a "neo-Lamarckianism" late in the nineteenth century, but also because people earlier in the century built on his ideas in their original Lamarckian form. His writing, particularly his landmark *Zoological Philosophy* (*Philosophie zoologique*) of 1809, was important in establishing the idea that the body and the mind could be transformed through interaction with the external environment (in the form of "impressions," "sensations," and "feeling" that affected the structures and functions of the body) and that the resulting changes could be passed on through sexual reproduction.[85] But as I have demonstrated in discussions of organization, habit, and heritability in this chapter, and earlier in the book, these ideas were not new when Lamarck published them in the nineteenth century. Lamarck drew on common biopolitical resources—including the work of Enlightenment naturalists, such as his patron Buffon, and revolutionary theorists of the science of man, such as his friend Cabanis—to reimagine habit, milieu, organization, and inheritance through a variety of new biological mechanisms. In rearticulating these ideas and emphasizing their biological aspects, Lamarck not only helped found the new discipline of "biology"; he also helped reestablish the biological dimension of biopolitics in the nineteenth century.

CHAPTER SEVEN

An Evolving Constellation

The ideas and practices of Enlightenment biopolitics did not end with the French Revolution or with an epistemic shift around 1800. They persisted and were reconfigured into new concepts, theories, practices, and policies, while being brought into relation to new conceptual configurations, economic challenges, and political and social problems. This is true of strains of Enlightenment biopolitics—breeding and exclusion—as well as quickly developing approaches related to hygiene, statistics, and public health. Some of the continuities were direct and self-conscious on the part of the nineteenth-century historical actors, but often Enlightenment biopolitical ideas remained as a loose grouping of intellectual resources that could be drawn on and transformed to fit with changing circumstances. Enlightenment biopolitics provided the foundation for modern biopolitics more generally, but the structures built on this foundation, not to mention the edifices and internal ornaments, continued to be transformed as they were reconceived and reappropriated, interpreted anew and misunderstood, mobilized and disconnected from their original contexts. Throughout the book I have noted ways in which Enlightenment biopolitics was connected to later permutations—in more direct ways through people, policies, and sometimes ideas, and also in a less direct fashion through shifts in conditions of possibility and conceptual genealogies. I want to turn to an analysis of several of the ways that practical and conceptual elements of Enlightenment biopolitics actively played a role in nineteenth-century and twentieth-century developments, and the way that these ideas and practices were kept alive and modified even as major conceptual, scientific, and historical transformations increasingly demanded the reconfiguration of the biopolitical constellation as a whole, while they also obscured the relationship between these developments and those in the eighteenth century.

First, analyzing a phrase used by a deputy of the National Convention in 1793, I will explore the manner in which Enlightenment biopolitics played a role in establishing some key concepts and intellectual dispositions that

French Revolutionary leaders built on, bringing out their implications, contesting their ambiguities, and developing them in a way that helped establish some of the political concepts that remained at the center of politics across the nineteenth century. The analysis, transformation, and disagreement about conceptions of sovereignty, citizenship, rights, and the nation emerged from the French Revolution to play a central role in nineteenth-century political discourse, as well as in the actual push and pull of politics in practice.

Second, I will turn to look at how a number of the biopolitical interconnections of colonial and metropolitan ideas, practices, and problematics in the eighteenth century established an intellectual and practical legacy that continued to play a role in the imperially interconnected development of biopolitics as new disciplinary formations took shape in the nineteenth century. Eighteenth-century natural history, the science of man, and colonial biopolitics contributed to the reformation and redirected of some biopolitical problematics in the French Revolution. The roughly ten years between the outbreak of the Revolution and 1800 saw a redirection of some biopolitical concerns from colonial populations to the population within France, as the imperative of revolutionary regeneration led to the development of a grand statistical project aimed at knowing the quality and quantity of the metropolitan population. This project built on colonial precedents, and it was directed by a former colonial administrator, Nicolas-Louis François de Neufchâteau. The formation of this massive project, the development of an internal travel literature that explored the people and places within France, and a renewed interest in overseas expeditions and imperialist expansion led to a new formation of anthropology that fully and explicitly intertwined the study of physical and cultural variations of the human species within France and without.

Next, I demonstrate how Enlightenment ideas about selectively breeding human beings reemerged in the Napoleonic era as several people in France developed new projects to improve the population in the wake of the perceived failure of the regenerative projects of the French Revolution. I then look at the ideas of Auguste Comte and his formulation of a "biocracy" as well as his continuation of organismic forms of social thought. I use Comte's work as a way of reflecting on how the Enlightenment origins of organicism have been largely obscured by the rise of Romanticism. But as attested to by Comte himself, the Buffonian naturalism of the Enlightenment created the foundations for nineteenth-century biopolitics as well as organicist social and political thought. The organicist thought of the nineteenth century continued to develop ideas about collective beings such as society, the body politic, the economy, and the state. Models, metaphors, and analogies of

organic collective bodies developed and became so widespread and so conceptually fundamental to ways of conceiving of collective entities that the
directionality of comparison was inverted, and some people began to write
about organisms as if they were societies. Finally, I return to the question
of how the history of Enlightenment biopolitics affects how we understand
the Enlightenment and its legacy. But first, I want to begin by analyzing
a little-known phrase used during the French Revolution, demonstrating
that it can reveal much about not only the development of biopolitics in the
eighteenth century, but also its legacy, showing the conceptual connections
that can be made between this phrase and the theorizing about biopolitics
that has occurred from the end of the Second World War to today.

"For am I badly mistaken," Pierre-Marie-Augustin Guyomar asked in 1793,
"or does a white or black skin no more characterize the exclusion from sovereignty in the human species than a male or feminine sex [*un sexe mâle,
féminin*]?"[1] This expression of universalist egalitarianism, with its unusual
phrase "sovereignty in the human species" (*la souveraineté dans l'espèce humaine*), appeared in a short written work that Guyomar submitted to his
fellow members of the National Convention as they debated the formation
of a new French constitution in April 1793. Guyomar fashioned himself
"the partisan of political equality between individuals," and in this disser-
tation, also published as a pamphlet, he was one of only two deputies to
express his support for the inclusion of women as citizens.[2] Arguing that
great strides had recently been made against prejudice toward people of
African descent, Guyomar developed the analogy with women, demanding
that people liberate themselves "from the prejudice of sex."[3] Guyomar was
somewhat marginal in terms of political power in the National Convention
before the Terror, and he was exceptional in the sense of being one of the
very few deputies to speak out for the extension of citizenship and political
rights to women. Nonetheless, his expression of a biological conception of
sovereignty and his equation of it with the new collectivized sense of political sovereignty was not only an expression of a thorough egalitarianism;
it was also a striking example of the biopolitical terms through which fundamental concepts such as sovereignty, rights, the citizen, and the nation
came to be thought of during the French Revolution.[4]

To unpack the significance of the unusual phrase "sovereignty in the human species" and to begin to reveal its biopolitical importance, it is illuminating to turn to Hannah Arendt's inquiry into the "perplexities of the rights
of man" and the manner in which Giorgio Agamben built on this inquiry in
his biopolitical analysis of the Declaration of the Rights of Man and Citizen.
Arendt drew attention to the challenge of rights being attributed to both

"man and citizen," arguing that the paradox of grounding of rights in the abstract figure of "man" and also in the "citizen" of the modern nation-state was revealed most acutely by the experiences of two categories of people in the period between the world wars and in the Holocaust. Stateless people who had lost their citizenship (and recourse to the rights guaranteed by a nation) and the inmates of Nazi camps were two forms of people "forced to live outside the scope of all tangible law," and, in fact, "forced to live outside the common world."[5] They were reduced to the "abstract naked-ness of being human," and they became instances of "the human being who has lost his place in the community, his political status in the struggle of his time, and the legal personality which makes his actions and part of his des-tiny a consistent whole."[6] This "modern expulsion from humanity," Arendt argued, reduced such people to "mere existence" and left them only "that which is mysteriously given us by birth and which includes the shape of our bodies and the talents of our minds."[7] It also revealed that human rights relied completely on nation-states to guarantee those rights through the form of "national rights." "The conception of human rights, based on the assumed existence of a human being as such," Arendt argued, "broke down at the very moment when those who professed to believe in it were for the first time confronted with people who had indeed lost all other qualities and specific relations—except that they were still human."[8] While one may question Arendt's grouping of stateless people and camp inmates, as well as the claim that there is a place outside of (tangible) law, her drawing at-tention to the paradox of "man and citizen" combined with her ideas about people being reduced to mere existence and bare natural life, as well as her emphasis on birth and "natality," raised important questions about the coherence of the principles of the rights of man and the practical limits of ideas of human rights. They also instigated a philosophical discourse on "human rights," an inquiry into the "right to have rights," and Agamben's biopolitical reflections on rights, sovereignty, and bare life.[9] Arendt's de-scription of people who had lost "lost all other qualities and specific rela-tions" echoed her friend Walter Benjamin's definition of people reduced to "bare life" (*das bloße Leben*).[10]

Agamben built on Benjamin's concept of bare life and Arendt's connec-tion of it to the rights of man and citizen in his book *Homo Sacer*, arguing that "declarations of rights represent the originary figure of the inscription of natural life in the juridico-political order of the nation-state."[11] Agamben pointed to the significance of the Declaration of the Rights of Man and Citi-zen arguing that the mention of birth in the first article indicated something fundamental and previously passed over. As Agamben read it, the claim that "men are born free and equal in rights" was not a trivial invocation of birth, but a sign of the grounding of rights in "bare natural life as such."[12] He argued that "the principle of nativity" and "the principle of sovereignty" were "irrevocably united in the body of the 'sovereign subject' so that the new nation-state may be constituted."[13] Agamben argued that "citizenship names the new status of life as origin and ground of sovereignty."[14] Invoking Sieyès distinction between active citizens and passive citizens, and quoting Jean-Denis Lanjuinais's articulation of the common list of people to be excluded from the rights of active citizenship (minors, women, criminals, and the mentally ill), Agamben helped bring into focus that these exclusions were more than just limitations of universalist principles or exceptions to the hyperbolic statement of a democratic ideal; they were also biopolitical statements about the new concatenation of sovereignty and species, the biological and the political, inclusion and exclusion, citizen and nation. "Instead of viewing these distinctions as a simple restriction of the democratic and egalitarian principle, in flagrant contradiction to the spirit and letter of the declarations," Agamben wrote, "we ought to first grasp their coherent biopolitical meaning."[15] He clarified this biopolitical meaning by drawing attention, not just to inclusion and exclusion, but to the way that the drawing of a biopolitical boundary between inside and outside is a redrawing of the threshold of life. "One of the essential characteristics of modern biopolitics (which will continue to increase in our century) is its constant need to redefine the threshold of life that distinguishes and separates what is inside from what is outside. Once it crosses over the walls of the *oikos* [the private, domestic sphere] and penetrates more and more deeply into the city [as in *cité* or *civitas*, the public, political sphere of common life], the foundation of sovereignty—nonpolitical life—is immediately transformed into a line that must be constantly redrawn."[16] One does not have to follow Agamben to the ends of his argument—agreeing with his conclusions about how this relates to the existence of "a new living dead man, a new sacred man" (that is, *homo sacer*), nor his controversial assertion that concentration camps are "the hidden matrix and *nomos* of the political space in which we are still living"—in order to appreciate how his analysis of bare life and rights allow a fuller appreciation of the biopolitical nature of the rights discourse of the French Revolution.[17] His arguments are stimulating, but as much as anything, they serve to raise the question about how developed biopolitical thinking was during the Revolution and how it got to be advanced enough so that rights, sovereignty, the citizen, and the nation could all be conceptually grounded and intertwined with birth in a new way that relied on bare biological life.

In order to see statements about rights, sovereignty, the citizen, and the nation, not just as products of the extraordinary circumstances of the

Revolution, but also as the outcomes of long-developing conceptual and practical approaches to the biopolitical, it is useful to return to Guyomar's "sovereignty in the human species" by way of Agamben, who quoted the deputy of the Legislative Assembly, Lanjuinais, discussing "the members of the sovereign."[18] In fact, Guyomar and Lanjuinais both used the phrase *les membres du souverain* in their interventions in the debates about citizenship and the constitution on April 29, 1793.[19] Agamben is correct that "members of the sovereign" was an important phrase, but it did not originate in the French Revolution. If we trace it back to its first usage, we find that it demonstrates the formation of biopolitics in the Enlightenment. It also reveals how Enlightenment biopolitics helped establish some of the fundamental concepts and understandings that were available to French revolutionaries as they reimagined the polity, forged a new politics, and tried to find novel ways to bring about the radical regeneration of the population. The first use of the phrase "members of the sovereign" that I have found is by Rousseau in *The Social Contract* roughly thirty years before Lanjuinais, Guyomar, and other French Revolutionary leaders employed the phrase. It is a powerful and condensed expression of Rousseau's concept of sovereignty, in which he introduced the idea that the sovereign could be a single "person" in the form of a collective being, a single body composed of individual citizens.[20] This was a new concept of sovereignty and citizenship, while also being a new account of the process by which citizens became members of a unified body politic.

Rousseau's innovation can be seen clearly when contrasted with Hobbes's notion of how a people is unified and made into a single political body. Hobbes, like early modern theorists of sovereignty from Bodin to Bossuet, gave a great importance to the unifying power of the single person who would represent the multitude. In fact, Hobbes argued that the body politic could be unified (becoming a single body politic) only by being represented by a single person. Representation here is key. "A Multitude of men, are made *One* Person, when they are by one man, or one Person, Represented," Hobbes wrote in *Leviathan*, "for it is the *Unity* of the Representer, not the *Unity* of the Represented, that maketh the Person *One*. And it is the Representer that beareth the Person, and but one Person: And *Unity*, cannot otherwise be understood in Multitude."[21] Distinguishing between Rousseau and Hobbes, and summarizing Rousseau's decomposition of the corporate society of orders and estates "into a multiplicity of individuals, to be reconstituted analytically as a political community of citizens equal before the law," Keith Baker has written, "for Rousseau, as for Hobbes, this transformation of multiplicity into unity could be achieved only by the absolute and irrevocable submission of every individual to a single, unitary person. But Rousseau . . . located that person not in the natural person of a monarch but in the collective person of the body of citizens as a whole."[22] As I argued in chapter 1, Rousseau understood this collective person of the body of citizens—this collective body—as an organized body. This model of the body politic allowed Rousseau to reconceive the political relation between part and whole, citizen and sovereign. In other words, the relational holism of the organized body allowed Rosseau to develop a biopolitical concept of sovereignty in which the body politic was made up of citizens who remained individual passive subjects of the state while also being, in his words, active "members of the sovereign." Each citizen had his own individual life and was a part of the life of the collective being. Or to put it in the terms of vital materialists like Bordeu and some of the other philosophes who developed the Enlightenment concept of organization, citizens had both their "particular life" and their "collective life"; each of them was both a relatively autonomous individual and an integrated part of a singular whole; they retained the individuality of their existence and the distinctness of their will while their existence grounded and contributed to the collective life and the general will.

The work of Rousseau and Enlightenment biopolitics helps make intelligible, and meaningful, Guyomar's use of the term "sovereignty" in the phrase "sovereignty in the human species." In a certain sense, Guyomar simply uses the term "sovereignty" in this phrase to mean membership. But he does not seem to have meant merely generic membership. If he meant merely membership in a generic sense, he could have written of "membership" in the human species rather than employ a political term that, as far as I can determine, had never been used in this biological manner to refer to membership in a species. It seems that he employed this novel usage, risking misunderstanding, because he wanted to create the conceptual homology between being a member of the species and being a member of the sovereign. Guyomar was clearly building on Rousseau, and he made a point of invoking Rousseau and *The Social Contract* twice in his pamphlet, ending his argument with a quotation from the book.[23] Because of the way that membership in sovereignty had been reimagined by Rousseau and enacted in the Revolution, Guyomar's novel usage implied a connection between being a member of a biological species and being a member of a political body. Guyomar's use of "sovereignty," therefore, relates the political meaning to the issue of biological species, articulating an explicitly biopolitical meaning of "sovereignty" and revealing the connections between sovereignty and the species, political life and biological life, being a citizen and being a human. In his usage, Guyomar conflated membership in the species and membership in the sovereign, implying that to be an individual of the human species was to have a legitimate claim to be a member of the sovereign, that is to say, to be an active citizen participating in politics. Neither women nor people of color should be excluded from either sovereignty in the species or collective political sovereignty. All members of the species should be members of the sovereign. In other words, all members of the human species are entitled to the rights of full citizenship, without exclusion or qualification, though presumably individuals could disqualify themselves through various forms of being counterrevolutionary.[24] Inclusion was the assumption, and exclusions were secondary occurrences.

This interpretation of the sovereignty as a biopolitical concept that is neither simply biological nor simply political is supported by the rest of Guyomar's argument in his pamphlet and his careful attention to issues of terminology. The pamphlet begins, for example, with an etymological discussion of the Latin term *homo* and comparison of it with the general meaning of the French term *l'homme* (man in general, encompassing everyone) in contrast to the use of *l'homme* to distinguish from *la femme* (that is, an individual man as opposed to an individual woman).[25] Guyomar stated that he preferred the term *l'individu* (individual) over *l'homme* since he felt that it was "more appropriate to indicate people of every sex [*les hommes de tout sexe*], of every age, all members, in my view, of the great family that inhabits the world."[26] Guyomar's use of the phrase "the human species" (*l'espèce humaine*) in his phrase "sovereignty in the human species" appears to employ the naturalistic understanding of human beings as composing a biological species, a meaning that was distinguished from other terms, such as "mankind" or "the human race" (*la genre humaine*) and "humanity" (*l'humanité*), that were used at the time to refer to humans as a whole. Guyomar, in fact, used *la genre humaine* in a passage in the text when he was not referring to biological differences of sex or race, and he used other nonnaturalistic phrases to refer to all humans collectively, writing of the "peoples of the universe" and the "inhabitants of the globe."[27]

At various points in the pamphlet, Guyomar explicitly related biological species and political belonging. He recognized the existence of biological sexual difference, for example, but he did not believe that this should result in a difference in citizenship or rights. "I do not understand how a sexual difference makes for one in the equality of rights," he protested.[28] He did not believe in the existence of a "line of demarcation drawn by nature between the sovereign part and the subject part of the human species."[29] The problem with the exclusion of women, therefore, was that it would establish a division that would be literally unnatural. Although men and women differ, according to Guyomar, it did not make the human species into a subject part and a sovereign part. That was the work of deputies who were unwilling to grant women citizenship. They were the ones creating a situation in which "women are born and remain slaves, unequal in rights."[30]

To write about "sovereignty in the human species" and to make it the ground of citizenship and rights was to fully and reciprocally incorporate the biological and the political.[31] In this articulation, these realms were not just related, added, or made available to one another; they were intertwined, enfolded, and implicated in one another; they existed together in a way that represented a new entity that was both conceptual and practical: biopolitics. It was, in fact, to argue that this was self-evident. It was an attempt to represent the political as already biological. Entering the contest over what was "self-evident" about "the rights of man and citizen"—and "natural rights" more generally—Guyomar formulated his inclusive and egalitarian arguments about rights and citizenship on the assumption that questions of belonging were already addressed by our species-being, even before they could be formulated in political terms.[32] Guyomar presented this as a given, underlining this claim to self-evidence by presenting his biopolitical concept of sovereignty in the form of a rhetorical question.[33] "For am I mistaken . . . ?" he asked.

Two centuries before scholars of biopolitics were writing of "biological citizenship," there was already a profound and explicit connection being made between biological life and citizenship.[34] Also, 150 years before Arendt articulated the idea that there exists a "right to have rights" that stems from belonging to the human species, Guyomar explicitly connected the rights of citizenship to nothing other than belonging to the human species.[35] This full and reciprocal conceptual incorporation of the biological and the political long preceded biopolitical concerns of political thinkers such as Arendt, Foucault, and Agamben, while also revealing how far biopolitical thought had developed by the late eighteenth century.

The French Revolution saw the creation of an internal ethnographic project to study provincial French people as if they were colonial subjects or the so-called savages of the New World in order to facilitate their transformation into a more "civilized" and homogenous population. This project drew on ideas, practices, and dispositions developed in Enlightenment biopolitics and inaugurated the nineteenth-century nation-building project of turning "peasants into Frenchmen."[36] A striking example of the ways that the colonial and metropolitan worlds were already intertwined by the Revolution can be seen in the ways that peasants and "savages" of the New World came to be thought about together. For example, in 1791, François de Chateaubriand, the iconic counterrevolutionary chronicler of revolutionary displacement and loss, fled the tumultuous circumstances of France in search of safety in the United States. He hoped to find the vitality of a new nation and unspoiled wilderness. While he found some of this, he also found that his expectations were repeatedly frustrated. In several of his written works, he returned to one of the events from this trip that seemed to capture his misguided preconceptions and his disappointment with the New World. As a self-professed "disciple of Rousseau," Chateaubriand was dismayed that on his first encounter with Amerindians, instead of simple and pure "noble savages," he found them dancing a French country dance led by "a little Frenchman" in a powdered wig.[37] Three years before Chateaubriand met these Frenchified Native Americans, the English traveler Arthur Young had an almost inverse experience when he traveled through the French town of Combourg, where the brother of Chateaubriand lived and where François himself spent some of his childhood on an estate purchased by his father with money earned, in part, through the transatlantic slave trade.[38] Young found the nearby countryside to have a "savage aspect." It was inhabited by "people almost as wild" as their countryside, and "husbandry [was] not much further advanced . . . than among the Hurons."[39] Chateaubriand's anecdote of Frenchified Amerindians and the mirror representation of Indian-like peasants in Chateaubriand's France point toward the way that, by the era of the Revolution, France and the Americas were deeply and surprisingly intertwined through the movement of people, the ties of colonial commerce, the proliferation of written works about distant lands and peoples, and the formation of intellectual and cultural dispositions built from the collision of worlds that were both far apart and strangely close.

The use of Native Americans as a reference point in discussing French peasants was not merely a practice of foreign travelers like Young. There had long been comparisons made between French peasants and the "savage" native peoples of the New World, from the writing of the early Jesuit missionaries in New France to Voltaire's observation that there were still savages in Europe.[40] During the French Revolution, urban travelers in the countryside and local elites often referred to peasants as "savages" and occasionally compared them to Amerindians. One French nobleman, for example, complained of local peasants dancing "like Hurons and Iroquois," while a provincial informant wrote to Paris about the local "savages" and "men of nature" whose language he compared to that of the Iroquois.[41] Another revolutionary, the radical and hyperbolic Sylvain Maréchal, complained in 1793 that half of the French population was composed of the sort of savages that "so astonish us when encountered in accounts of voyages."[42] The perception of Indian-like peasants is a striking example of the way that even metropolitan people, places, and events deep in rural France and seemingly unrelated to the colonies of the eighteenth-century French Empire could be affected by the history of colonialism.

The connections between the eighteenth-century approach to colonial population and the approach to the population of metropolitan France during and following the French Revolution was more than merely conceptual or rhetorical. It was a question of not just the similarity between peasants and "savages," or the rhetorical uses of comparing them, but a similarity in the approaches to developing knowledge about these populations. During the Revolution, new epistemic tools were developed in order to better know the metropolitan population so that they might be regenerated and improved. Some of the practical and intellectual precedents and the dispositions embodied in this new approach to regeneration were first developed in biopolitical approaches to colonial populations, including colonial censuses and projects aimed at knowing and regulating the enslaved population. This connection is best exemplified by the development of an internal travel literature that turned the gaze of philosophical travelers onto the people and places of metropolitan France; the development of a grand statistical project to gather quantitative and qualitative information about France and its population, undertaken during the Directory by the former colonial administrator François de Neufchâteau; and last, the explicit connection in the work of the Society of the Observers of Man between an external anthropology directed at knowing distant cultures and races and an internal anthropology directed at knowing the population of France.

In *Voyage dans le Jura*, a piece of internal travel literature published in Year IX (1800), Joseph-Marie Lequinio, a former deputy to the Legislative Assembly and fervent "representative on-mission" during the Terror, chose to start his long narrative with a detour. On route from Paris to the mountainous Jura region of eastern France, Lequinio took the reader to Buffon's estate at Montbard. Lequinio lingered in the great man's workroom hoping to draw inspiration and maybe some authority from an association, however distant and contrived, with the deceased master whose very name stood for natural history well into the nineteenth century.[43] This symbolic invocation is a good representation of how the literary form of voyages through the provinces took shape in the last decades of the Old Regime, transformed during the Revolution, and became a new literary form by the beginning of the nineteenth century.[44] The voyages in the provinces became voyages in the *départements*. In addition to using the newly formed administrative units to define their purview, the authors of this subgenre also responded to the political imperatives of the era by exhibiting a new interest in culture of the local inhabitants and the triangular relationship between this culture, the physical characteristics of the inhabitants, and their environment. The gathering of knowledge of local particularities had two primary purposes: to discover what was already common and shared, so as to foster the political and social unity; and to find the true extent and nature of local differences, so as to lessen them. The "universality" of France could be discovered in the particularities, but so too could the targets of regenerative projects intended to homogenize the people and make them into a unified nation.

This was a relatively new endeavor because while there were Old Regime traditions of gathering knowledge of the kingdom for the king, it was only in the last years of the regime that authors showed an interest in detailed information focusing on the local inhabitants. Works of internal travel literature began to appear in these years as so-called philosophical travelers began moving beyond the vague and often-repeated clichés of regional character that had dominated literary accounts of the provinces for centuries.[45] This process of transformation was not complete until the political imperatives of the Revolution created a corresponding epistemological imperative. The two editions of *Voyage d'Auvergne* published by Pierre-Jean-Baptiste Legrand d'Aussy in 1788 and 1794 captured the transformation of this literature during the Revolution. After being criticized for caring more about rocks than people, Legrand d'Aussy expanded his second edition with a significant amount of information on the local inhabitants, discussing their mœurs and customs as well as the physical characteristics of the "races" in the region.[46]

The changes brought about by the political imperatives of the Revolution and the desire to grasp the whole of France in its particularities and commonalities can also be seen in the heightened interest in statistics by bureaucrats and savants in this era. Like internal travel literature, this revitalized field grew in popularity and became increasingly institutionalized. The numerous projects to gather statistics on the departments and their inhabitants also reflect an anthropological shift. For example, in 1790s when a minor forestry official won a major prize for the creation of set of guidelines and questions that travelers could utilize in gathering statistics about the departments, he included the customs and mœurs of local inhabitants as well as physical (or "racial") characteristics such as the color of their hair and skin.[47] This is the same type of detailed anthropological information found in the works of Enlightenment naturalists, as well as in the questionnaires and instructions written for foreign travelers embarking on scientific expeditions in the era.[48]

The development of statistics as a part of a biopolitical project of regeneration, and its connection to earlier modes of gathering biopolitical knowledge in the colonies, can be seen in the striking case of François de

Neufchâteau's formation of the grand statistical project under the Directory. Even though he rarely made explicit references to the colonies after 1789, his formative experience as a magistrate in Saint-Domingue at the end of the Old Regime can be found in his belief in the state's need to have detailed and reliable knowledge of the natural variation of its territory and the cultural variation of its people. As he made clear during the Revolution, this kind of knowledge was crucial to the state's ability to effect true regeneration and to consolidate and stabilize the Republic. Although greater uniformity and national unity were the goal, he recognized that laws, agricultural production, economic reforms, and tactics of cultural regeneration and education had to be adjusted to fit local circumstances. The massive statistical project that he undertook as the minister of the interior in the Directory was meant to represent these circumstances in unprecedented detail and thoroughness.

During the first years of the Revolution, he played a role in organizing the department of the Vosges. Later, he was a deputy to the Legislative Assembly, and he was elected to the National Convention, although he never sat. During the Directory, he became a *commissaire*, the minister of the interior (twice), and a director. Before this revolutionary career, he had been a precocious poet and a teacher, then turned to the practice of law. After five years as a magistrate in Lorraine, François de Neufchâteau sought and received a position as a magistrate in Saint-Domingue. His time in the colony proved to be formative, and in fact, he was politically radicalized during his four years in Saint-Domingue. It was there that he developed ideas on popular sovereignty, the links between public credit and political representation, and the disassociation of rights and privileges that would play an important role in his political career, as well as in the Revolution more generally.[49]

His experiences in the colony were also formative in the development of his legal philosophy and his ideas on the relationship between law and politics. After initial frustrations, he abandoned the traditional role of the magistrate and adopted a voluntaristic approach to positive law that focused on the ability of the law to be quickly and appropriately created for specific circumstances, or adapted to them. In Saint-Domingue, he became more of an active creator of the law than a passive representative of the monarch's authority and its expression through the law. As the intendant of Saint-Domingue wrote in a letter to François de Neufchâteau, this approach "would seem to have arrogated some of the power reserved to the sovereign."[50]

In addition to developing a more radical relationship between royal sovereignty and the role of positive law through his experience in the colonies, François de Neufchâteau also developed several administrative dispositions that would play a role in the project for which he is best know: the attempt to create a comprehensive statistical survey of France during the Directory. This massive project to create a broad and detailed representation of the nation enlisted officials from all over France to gather information about an extremely wide variety of commercial, political, religious, agricultural, natural, and cultural topics. Although statistical projects in the service of centralized power had been slowly growing in importance since the late seventeenth century, François de Neufchâteau's grand project was the first to attempt to integrate both qualitative and quantitative information from all regions of France. Many subjects of the survey, such as the cultural beliefs and customs of the peasantry, had never before been included in a large centralized statistical project. This grand statistical project of the minister of the interior reflects the interest in statistics that François de Neufchâteau developed while a magistrate in the colonies. Additionally, it bears the stamp of the much longer history of statistics in the colonial management of people.

Although it is often overlooked in the scholarship on the development of the state and its tools of knowing and managing the population, since the seventeenth century the colonies played a crucial role in the development of comprehensive surveys of populations and commerce. The first complete nominative census in French history was taken in the colonies, and scholars have identified a total of 286 censuses taken in the French colonies from the beginning of the eighteenth century to 1790.[51] The colonies were sites for the development of these biopolitical tools for several reasons: the populations were small enough to make comprehensive surveys appear practical; enslavers were required for the purpose of taxation to provide inventories of the enslaved people they owned; the health and size of the free and enslaved populations were always precarious and in need of attention; commerce and productivity were of a heightened importance in the colonies; and people saw statistical knowledge as instrumental in creating and maintaining order in slave societies where the enslaved often outnumbered free people by significant numbers. The difference between the colonies and the metropole with respect to administrative innovations was something recognized by François de Neufchâteau. "It is a great advantage of the state of our colonies," he wrote "that they lend themselves to the introduction of useful reforms more easily than the kingdom."[52]

It is not coincidental, therefore, that it was in the colony that François de Neufchâteau developed his concern with statistics as an administrative tool of knowledge and improvement. As an enslaver who had several enslaved people in his household, he was obligated to complete administrative forms identifying and enumerating the enslaved people, both for the purposes of tax assessment and in relation to the mandatory militia service, as is evidenced by archival documents.[53] In his administrative position, he also concerned himself with the policing of the enslaved population and the free people of color. For example, he endorsed the idea of producing medals that would replace the more easily forged manumission papers issued to free people of color. With information inscribed on the medals, it was argued, law enforcement officers tasked with policing people fleeing enslavement, the *maréchaussée*, would have an easier time determining a person's identity on the spot, and they would have a more certain means of judging the legitimacy of claims to freedom.[54]

François de Neufchâteau's new interest in biopolitical surveillance, particularly of a statistical variety, was evidenced in his books on Saint-Domingue, which included numerous discussions of the population, as well as tables that enumerated the population and detailed the varieties of agriculture in Saint-Domingue.[55] In these writings, he also demonstrated a new attentiveness to the particularity of regional variations based on differences of climate and location. He discussed natural differences between the colony and the metropole that would necessitate differences in government, law, agriculture, and commerce, and he also divided Saint-Domingue into its regions and analyzed the internal differences of each with greater detail.[56]

Building on this new interest in statistics and local variation, the grand statistical project of the Directory brought together descriptive and quantitative traditions in the service of a comprehensive survey of France. This effort presented a new attempt to relate the variety of particular differences to the newly conceived whole of France.[57] The new administrative importance of the relations between the departments and the nation—the parts and the whole—resulted in a new epistemological importance that was reflected in the statistical project. As François de Neufchâteau explained in his instructions to the officials gathering the information, "the grandest knowledge of localities" was necessary in order to "embrace the universality of France."[58] A more detailed and comprehensive knowledge of the parts was necessary to truly know France as a whole.

In 1800, as a major state-sponsored expedition prepared to set out for Australia, the government called on the newly formed Society of the Observers of Man to advise the expedition's scientists on the study of the cultural and racial characteristics of the native inhabitants that they would encounter.[59] The author of the resulting "Consideration on the Various Methods to Follow in the Observation of Savage Peoples" attempted "to present a complete framework that might bring together all the points of view from which these [savage] nations might be envisioned by the philosopher."[60] Joseph-Marie Degérando was the author of this document, noted in the history of anthropology for its adherence to comprehensiveness and to many of the methodological principles that came to define the modern discipline. Degérando was also an official in the Ministry of the Interior who took part in the massive statistical survey of France.[61] He was not, therefore, merely an important historical figure in the formalization of the anthropological study of exotic others in far-off lands. He was also an associate of Grégoire and François de Neufchâteau, both of whom were at the forefront of the creation of the anthropology of the internal other and the institutionalization of statistics as a major tool of the state.[62] As in the case of Le Trosne's Enlightenment vision of the simultaneity of the nonsimultaneous, in which vagabonds were avatars of a "savage" presocial past living among the "civilized" people of metropolitan France, figures of the Revolution like Degérando, Grégoire, and François de Neufchâteau conceived of the simultaneity of the nonsimultaneous existing in a way that intertwined the local and the global. Much as Degérando believed that the *voyageur-philosophe* traveled in time as he sailed across the seas separating Europe from far-off places in the Pacific, participants in the regenerative projects of the French Revolution, such as Grégoire, believed living vestiges of the past existed within the territory of France so that something like regional dialects and peasant "patois" became privileged sites of intervention for the regenerative projects.[63] Linguistic difference became a target; it was a means to minimize the cultural, intellectual, and maybe even racial differences between the "savage" and the "civilized" within France.

In the biopolitical vision of these revolutionaries, "primitive" forms of otherness that called out for "improvement" and "regeneration" could be found in the provinces as well as colonies and little-known distant lands.[64] In fact, the connections between the global and the local, internal anthropology and its external variation, was one of the fundamental issues addressed by the Society of the Observers of Man. It was something of and about which they were aware and explicit. As Louis-François Jauffret, the perpetual secretary of the society, announced in one of its founding documents, the members intended to study people that originated in different continents and countries, but also people from different cities and villages within the same country.[65] They would try to find objective racial differences between people of African and European descent, but they would also create what he called an "anthropological topography of France" based in an "anthropology of the different regions."[66] In fact, as implied by the Society of the Observers of Man's adopting the ancient motto "know thyself," knowing thyself and knowing the human species were inseparable and mutually reinforcing. True knowledge of humans would emerge from the relation of the near and the far, the local and the global, self and other (both internal and external forms).

Through the anthropological orientation developed in the Enlightenment and refashioned during the Revolution, the Society of the Observers of Man oriented themselves toward the new imperial ventures of the nineteenth century as well as the process of "internal colonization" that aimed to complete the construction of the nation by making "peasants into Frenchmen."[67] In the nineteenth century, this tradition of developing physiological and anthropological knowledge of the inhabitants of France so as to racially classify and possibly transform them developed though twists and turns into a fully developed approach to the internal "anthropology of France."[68] By the late nineteenth century, on the eve of the founding of the eugenics movement and during the imperial "scramble for Africa," the study of the "races of France" and the application of quantitative measures of racial differentiation such as the cephalic index resulted in evidence that was taken by some to be proof of racial variation and degeneration in the heart of the country (see figure 10).[69]

The tradition of analytically separating these internal and external strains of anthropology and biopolitics misrepresents their emergence and development, as well as the contexts in which they were understood. In the period between the French Revolution and the late nineteenth-century convergence of racial science, eugenics, and imperialism, there were many conceptual, practical, and personal connections.[70] For example, conceptually, much as it was not unusual for the surgeon and journalist Jacques-Louis Moreau de la Sarthe in the early nineteenth century to have observed that "a peasant from Lower Brittany, thrown suddenly into the middle of one of the big cities in France, would be just as astonished and perplexed as a Huron or an Iroquois," it was not unusual by the 1840s to find the colonial métis discussed alongside examples of the supposedly savage French provincial types such as the Breton.[71] Sometimes the conceptual, practical, and personal connections were found in a single person, such as Alexandre Moreau de Jonnès, the founder and director of the French Bureau of Statistic from 1833 until 1852, who spent a formative period in the Caribbean colonies during the Revolutionary era making extensive ethnographic and statistical observations and working under Victor Hugues when he carried out a new type of racial census in the colonies.[72] Furthermore, Moreau de Jonnès—who wrote the first scholarly statistical study of slavery, published on the "ethnogenesis" of "Caucasians," wrote numerous taxonomic studies of New World animal and reptile species, and wrote extensively on the Caribbean climate and tropical disease—was also the cousin of Moreau de

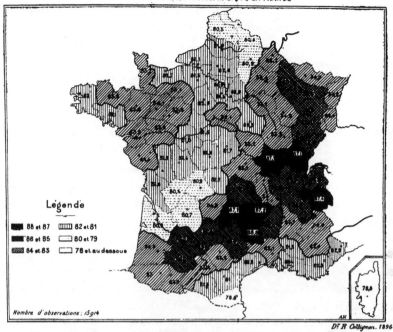

RÉPARTITION DE L'INDICE CÉPHALIQUE EN FRANCE

FIGURE 10. A map of numerical scores of the cephalic index, based on head measurements, provided as proof of racial differentiation within France. Originally in René Collignon, *Anthropologie de la France: Dordogne, Charente, Corrèze, Creuse, Haute-Vienne* (Paris: Société d'anthropologie de Paris, 1894); reprinted in *Annales de Géographie*, no. 20 (January 15, 1896): 159.

Saint-Méry, one of the most thorough and extreme of Enlightenment racial taxonomists.[73]

Another figure who reveals the historical and intellectual interconnections between internal and external anthropology, as well as between biological and political thought in the Third Republic, was the biologist and politician Jean-Marie-Antoine de Lanessan. He was the great advocate of Buffon's ideas in late nineteenth-century France, leading a Buffon revival. He was also a formulator of neo-Lamarckianism and the first governor-general of Indochina. As a biologist, he conducted experiments with colleagues that played an important role in providing an empirical basis for some of the theories of neo-Lamarckian eugenics, and he wrote numerous books, including the large synthesis *Transformism* (*Le Transformisme*), published in 1883, and *Transformism and Creationism* (*Le Transformisme et*

Créationisme), published in 1914. As an advocate of Buffon's ideas and his legacy, he published a fourteen-volume edition of the complete works of Buffon; a revised critical edition of Buffon's correspondence; and articles, such as "Buffon and Darwin," in which he vigorously argued that Buffon's ideas about the transformation of species constituted a theory of transformism that was superior to Darwin's theory of evolution.[74] As a politician, he held numerous ministerial posts, including minister of the navy from 1899 to 1902, and was a part of the radical and radical socialist coalitions between 1881 and 1914, also for a time serving as the political editor of the radical republican daily *Le Siècle*. He had visited Indochina as a young man, and he was a member of the Société d'anthropologie and later the Société d'ethnographie.[75] He wrote large reports on the state of the colonies, and he was the governor-general of Indochina from 1891 to 1894. In short, his involvement in biopolitics through the conjuncture of colonialism, biology, and politics was intellectual, administrative, and anthropological. The traditional separation between the historiographies of France and its colonies, particularly the first colonial empire, has obscured the fact that the development of ideas and practices in the two spaces were never truly separate, even while the places themselves were. The two have always been connected in a circular fashion with neither the metropole nor the colony exclusively influencing or being influenced by the other. The history of biopolitics, from the eighteenth century to the twentieth century, helps reveal this interconnected history.

Before turning to the revival of proposals for human breeding in the later Revolution, I want to analyze the ideas of Abbé Grégoire, one of the most important revolutionary leaders advocating for projects of regeneration. Grégoire was a major figure of the Revolution who brought biopolitical ideas developed in the late Enlightenment and radicalized in the Revolution into the nineteenth century. Grégoire's work demonstrates the manner in which Buffonian ideas of animal crossbreeding and Vandermonde's ideas of selectively breeding humans were models of biopolitical thought and intellectual resources that were available to theorists of regeneration during the French Revolution and to the formulators of eugenic plans during the Napoleonic era. It also helps us understand how the Buffonian paradigm of understanding species, race, breeding, degeneration, and regeneration carried on as the dominant frame of analysis of these issues in France until the middle of the nineteenth century, as Claude Blanckaert has demonstrated.[76] Even after a number of political and scientific shifts in the mid-nineteenth century, Buffon was revived again by people like Lanessan and repurposed in the Third Republic as neo-Lamarckianism was formed and questions of colonial governance revived issues of race and assimilation related to "the métis question."

Grégoire is a fascinating case because he was a prominent leader in many phases of the Revolution and one of the leading theorists of regeneration, for which he drew on an eclectic combination of intellectual and religious beliefs.[77] The philosophical abbé from the eastern region of France was directly involved in many of the most important and representative projects of regeneration: he undertook a project to gather information on the many languages and dialects spoken in France with the goal of "annihilating the patois"; he presented ideas for the education of children and was a member of the Committee on Public Instruction; he advocated for the political rights and cultural assimilation of Jews and people of color; he was a representative on-mission to the countryside during the Terror; and he was involved in numerous attempts to improve French agriculture. Through the vicissitudes of the Revolution, Grégoire remained one of the most articulate and strenuous advocates for the creation of the "new man" and the large-scale improvement of the people. While he claimed that revolutionary "France is truly a new world," the government still needed to be extremely active in order to achieve a complete regeneration.[78] He wanted nothing less than, in his own words, to "reconstruct human nature."[79] To achieve this, he tirelessly worked to bridge "the enormous distance between what we are and what we could be."[80] Like most of the revolutionary leaders calling for this type of dramatic transformation, Grégoire drew on numerous models of improvement and discourses of regeneration that came from religious, classical, and various Enlightenment philosophical and biopolitical traditions. Throughout his work, as in the synthetic discourse of revolutionary regeneration more generally, we find evidence of a strong natural historical and anthropological perspective informing a biopolitical vision, even before the Revolution.

In his written work considering the regeneration of populations, Grégoire revealed that the Enlightenment natural history of Buffon and his associates, as well as the biopolitical works and the science of man that emerged from this work, were an important source of his outlook. Before the Revolution, as a member of the educated elite of Alsace and Lorraine, Grégoire was a cofounder of a philanthropic society in Nancy that was associated with the quasi-masonic Société des philantropes of Strasbourg.[81] As the members of the Nancy society announced in their programmatic founding document, they aimed to be "practical-philosophes" working for the "moral, political, and physical perfection" of humanity, with a special focus on enlightening local farmers and the "simple inhabitant of the countryside."[82] One of their central goals was to encourage members to take ethnographic journeys within France and the surrounding territories to study local inhabitants. In the 1780s and the 1790s, Grégoire fulfilled the ethnographic goal of the philanthropists with journeys through the Vosges, Alsace, and Switzerland, writing several published and unpublished reports on his travels in the Vosges. One of his accounts of a trip in the late 1790s is full of ethnographic observations and references to naturalists and internal travel literature from the last years of the Old Regime.[83]

Grégoire also demonstrated his acquaintance with Enlightenment biopolitics, and the natural history and the works from the science of man that biopolitical ideas built on, in his writing on the "physical, moral, and political regeneration" of the Jewish people, which earned him a prestigious essay prize from the Metz Academy in 1788 and his first high-profile contribution to the republic of letters. For Grégoire, the regenerative powers of systematic crossbreeding that were discussed in Buffon's early works were striking examples of the human ability to restore nature and transform degenerated bodies. The two volumes of Vandermonde's *Essay on the Manner of Perfecting the Human Species* also appear to have been a source for Grégoire in his development of a biopolitics of improvement. Grégoire was a part of the Buffonian tradition of ideas of human breeding before and during the Revolution, and he often used the naturalistic and racialized sense of regeneration, as can be seen clearly in his writing about the physical improvement of people through reproductive mixing. He first used this concept in his 1788 prize-winning essay on the regeneration of the Jewish people, in which he directly named Buffon and Vandermonde as authoritative sources.[84] Grégoire believed that the Jewish people had physically and morally degenerated, but that they could be saved (physiologically, morally, and perhaps spiritually) by being brought into a more intimate relationship with Christians. One of the important steps in the process of regeneration, Grégoire argued, should be the "crossing of the races" in order to counter the degeneration that Grégoire, following Vandermonde, believed resulted from Jewish people marrying only other Jewish people.[85] As Alyssa Goldstein Sepinwall has shown, he went on to develop this point about crossing in his famous writing about people of African descent, eventually calling for the intermarriage of blacks and whites, Greeks and Turks, Catholics and Protestants, and Europeans and South Asians.[86] While the systematic crossbreeding of "races" was not a major focus of Grégoire's work, it is noteworthy that in addition to drawing on Buffon and Vandermonde, he drew on colonial resources in order to claim that there were benefits to crossing. In his *Letter to Philanthropists* (*Lettre aux philantropes*) of 1790, written in support of the extension of rights to free people of color, Grégoire claimed that the "mixed blood" people of the Caribbean colonies

were more robust because they were the products of racial mixing, supporting his argument about "this crossed, and thus robust, race" with citations
of an article on "mulattoes" written by Guillaume-Leonard de Bellecombe,
a former governor-general of Saint-Domingue, and Hilliard d'Auberteuil's
Considerations on the Present State of the French Colony of Saint-Domingue.[87]
Grégoire's ideas of biological mixing fit within his vision of the creation of
a universal Catholic Church, but they never lost their natural historical and
colonial relevance. Even though some of Grégoire's political and religious
ideas had changed by the time of the Restoration, when he again called for
the intermarriage of blacks and whites in the 1820s, he still echoed Buffon
and Vandermonde and built on the theoretical foundation that had been
laid in the Enlightenment. "All physiologists attest that the crossed races are
generally more robust," Grégoire claimed in his 1823 book about marriage
and divorce in Haiti.[88]

In the years in between Grégoire's suggestions about the physical regeneration of the Jewish people and his suggestion that strategically employed crossing could help address specific politic and social problems,
other people revived Enlightenment ideas on breeding humans. During
the Consulate and the empire, there was a renewed interest in selective
breeding of humans so as to increase the quantity, quality, and rate of "improvement" of people over the course of generations. Eugenic projects of
selective breeding reappeared again as a tool to increase and perpetuate
improvements, carrying them into the future and multiplying the effects
in the collective body of the species (or some subset of the species, such as
a national "population"). This included the suggestion for a government-
administered project of selective breeding of humans, formulated by well-
established naturalists like Julien-Joseph Virey in *The Art of Improving Man,
or Spiritual and Moral Medicine* (*L'art de perfectionner l'homme, ou De la
médicine spritituelle et morale*, 1808); for the use of selective animal breeding
as a model for human breeding in *The Laws Clarified by the Physical Sciences, or Treatise on Legal Medicine and Public Hygiene* (*Les lois éclairées par
les sciences physiques, ou Traité de médecin-légale et d'hygiène publique*, 1799)
by François-Emmanuel Fodéré; and for similar proposals by the surgeon
J.-A. Millot and the physician Paul Mahon.[89] These proposals largely built
on the theoretical foundations of organization theory and the life sciences
as they were refashioned in the Enlightenment science of man and mobilized in the political context of revolutionary projects of regeneration.

One of the most striking attempts to finally realize the new man of the
Revolution was Louis-Joseph-Marie Robert's plan published in 1801 for
creating larger, stronger people through a process he called "meganthropo-
genesis" (*mégalantropogénésie*).[90] In a sense, Robert proposed a practically

oriented project to fulfill the somewhat miraculous and vague hopes for regeneration that characterized the early years of the Revolution. Assuring his readers that his proposal for the breeding of *grands hommes* was not chimerical or magical, but based on "cold and reasoned meditation," Robert called on the state to create a three-stage eugenic system.[91] Fashioning his own unique approach to breeding bigger, better, stronger, and more beautiful people, Robert started with physiognomy as a tool to aid administrators in assessing and selecting the best young boys and girls. Robert believed that physiognomy, as it was developed in popular works by the Swiss pastor Johann Kaspar Lavater and the Dutch naturalist Petrus Camper, provided the means for aesthetics judgments to guide physiological improvement. In a simple sense, physiognomy provided administrators of the eugenic project the ability to judge the internal quality of individual bodies through outward bodily signs. Robert wanted all young people selected for inclusion in his proposed program to receive a rigorous neoclassical education that would not only raise the abilities of all involved but would also act to differentiate the students within a hierarchy of merit. Throughout the work, Robert was most concerned with the improvement of boys, using Buffon to argue that women were, in fact, always the cause of the degeneration of races. Furthermore, women's political and social exclusion was to be reinforced with a gender-specific course of education that prepared them for their supposedly natural role as mothers, while boys were prepared for public life and heroic pursuits.[92] Robert thus created a masculinist and militarized vision of eugenic improvement fit for the Napoleonic era.[93]

Once the true abilities of the separately educated male and female students became clear, marriages would be arranged between the deserving youths. While physiognomy aided in the selection of the most promising young people and education improved and differentiated them by ability, the selective marriage matches would maximize the greatness of the offspring. In a final step, the nation would then celebrate the marriages in a new version of the Revolution's national festivals, returning the project of selectively breeding individuals to the collective realm of improving the nation as a whole, and perhaps the species as well.

Although Robert drew on an eclectic variety of medical and natural historical sources, Buffon was invoked from the very first paragraph of the introduction, and Buffon's concern about degeneration caused by marriages of poorly matched couples was given a central role in the theoretical justification of the project.[94] When the discussion turned to countering degeneration in the ninth chapter, Buffon's discussion of horse breeding was the first to be discussed.[95] Robert's large-scale project, combining both social and biological engineering, received a great amount of attention, although its prescriptions were never acted on. The reception of Robert's proposal brought into relief the normative limits of plausibility and acceptability; even though Robert's plan was thought by some to be scientifically possible, it still received a fair amount of ridicule for its social, political, and moral naïveté and for the grandiose style of its presentation.[96] It is worth noting that in addition to publishing a second edition of his work and vociferously contesting his critics, Robert also published another work related to biopolitics and the Revolution, *On the Influence of the French Revolution on the Population* (*De l'influence de la Révolution française sur la population*, 1802).[97]

Robert was not the only writer at this time that doggedly, and sometimes quixotically, pursued the revival of Enlightenment eugenic ideas. In fact, eugenic ideas that built on the theory of organization and suggested selective breeding were also articulated by several physiologists and physicians who were important transition figures transmitting Enlightenment approaches to biopolitics and organization to nineteenth century social thinkers. In 1803, Jean Burdin published *A Course of Medical Studies, or Exposition on the Study of Man Compared to That of Animals* (*Cours d'études médicales, ou Exposition de la structure de l'homme*).[98] In volume 3, on the vital functions, Burdin wrote about crossbreeding and perfectibility in the case of animals and humans. He thought that properly directed breeding held out the possibility of producing "a new species."[99] Writing about human racial variation, he identified three races (white, Mongol, and black) that have well-defined characteristics and "a remarkable organic disposition." He claimed some types are found to have a "very marked superiority of organization" and demonstrate a "more rapid perfectibility."[100] The act of reproduction held out the possibility of improvement because people could make the most of this superior organization, particularly if care were taken in attending to the fact that, Burdin thought, the influence of the mother was more manifest in the essential and internal organs of the child, while the father had a greater influence on the exterior and accessory organs.[101] Furthermore, people could change their likelihood of developing certain illnesses if they attended more to the most remarkable fact about reproduction: that individuals can "transmit, not only the particularities of their organization, but also the disposition to certain illnesses to which they were subject."[102] An attentiveness to organization and reproduction could, therefore, play a role in improving public health.

As the description on the title page of the work explained, Burdin intended the work for young physicians and veterinarians, but also for "all people who want to acquire notions of the physical science of man well enough to usefully apply them." Even though Burdin's book was a relatively minor work, it came to fulfill this latter intention in ways that likely exceeded the author's expectations. Burdin and his book came to came to play a central role in the development of Henri Saint-Simon's influential utopian vision of a world transformed through a new type of "social organization." When he met Saint-Simon and began to frequent his salon, Burdin was a young physician and a member of the Société médicale d'émulation, the most important and intellectually serious medical society in Paris. The society included a number of young physicians, some of them mentored by Cabanis, who were important in the theoretical articulation of habit and organization.[103] Burdin came to act as an intermediary and an informant for Saint-Simon, appearing as an authority in Saint-Simon's most important early work that placed physiology at the foundation of social theory, "Memoir on the Science of Man" ("Mémoire sur la science de l'homme") of 1813.[104] Burdin came to function as Saint-Simon's primary source for the physiological theories that provided the naturalistic foundation for his hugely influential project for social, political, and economic transformation.[105] Coming out of the French Revolution, Saint-Simon reimagined political and social organicism for a new generation, drawing directly on Enlightenment physiology and the life sciences to create his own eclectic social philosophy, which was as daring—and at times outlandish—as it was consequential for the development of French political thought and social reorganization in the wake of the Revolution and as the country began or renewed its engagement with questions of industrial development, global trade, technological transformation, and continued political instability.

In the middle of the nineteenth century, several decades after breaking with Saint-Simon and developing his own expansive philosophical system encompassing the social and natural world, detailed in the six volumes of his *Course on Positive Philosophy* (*Cours de philosophie positive*), Auguste Comte embarked on a grand new work that would more directly enfold politics within his system of positivism.[106] In the four volumes of the *System of Positive Politics* (*Système de politique positive*), which commenced publication in 1851, Comte's vision expanded well beyond the limits of the natural sciences and "sociology," a term that he helped establish in its modern sense.[107] Like many of the disciples and former disciples of Saint-Simon, Comte grounded his work in a biological perspective and developed theories about the character and function of society as an organism.[108] In *System of Positive Politics*, he moved beyond the social organism and the idea of humanity as an organism to imagine an even grander "Great-Being" encompassing all humans past, present, and future. This ultimate "collective being" was, Comte claimed, somehow even more lively and "real" than individual people.[109] It would be at the center of a new natural polity that would eventually also include the plants and animals that were useful to humans. Together, incorporated into a "vast biocracy," humans, plants, and animals would work together to modify the earth and bring about the improvement of the Great-Being.[110] Humans would be at the privileged pinnacle of this hierarchically organized biocracy, administering and overseeing an all-encompassing biopolitics.

While scholars have pointed to Comte's biocracy as a conceptual precursor to Foucault's twentieth-century articulation of biopolitics, they seem to have overlooked the fact that Comte himself traced the development of the biocratic approach back to the Enlightenment.[111] In *System of Positive Politics*, after the description of biocracy, Comte acknowledged that, "given the nature of his genius and the general course of his meditations, the great Buffon was surely moving in the direction that led to such an appreciation."[112] Writing with the self-importance of a system-building founder of a secular religion, which he was, Comte continued by excusing Buffon for not going all the way and explicitly articulating a transhistorical, whole-earth, multi-species biocracy. In addition to being trapped in the Old Regime system of thinking and being, which Comte characterized as "the old human regime," Buffon's problem was that Comte had not yet expressed his sociological ideas. Given these circumstances, Comte concluded, "he got as close as permitted."[113]

Recognizing and contextualizing Comte's ideas about biocracy helps highlight the genealogical connections between Enlightenment biopolitics and the biopolitics of the twentieth century. Comte's biocracy, for example, not only was broadly Buffonian; it also carried vitalist ideas of organization from the Montpellier school into the nineteenth century.[114] For example, the articulations of *biocratie* made by followers of Comte, such as Pierre Lafitte, also built on Buffon, explicitly acknowledging his importance and bringing biocracy even closer to what was called "biopolitics" by the twentieth century. "The general theory of biocracy," wrote Lafitte in 1883, is "the conception of man's systematic organization of vital modifiability."[115] In 1929, Édouard Toulouse, the most prominent psychiatrist in France between the world wars and a leading advocate of eugenics and "mental prophylaxis," called for the radicalization of the positivist concept and the realization of a "biocracy."[116] As Richard C. Keller has written about Toulouse, "he dreamed of remaking France into what he called a 'biocracy,' or a 'state in which the rules of evolution would be directed by the life sciences.'"[117]

While the work of Comte and the positivist conception of biocracy are among the historical stepping-stones that help reveal the long-term connections between phases of the development of biopolitics, there were others. Comte was grand and explicit in his articulation of an encompassing politics of life, but he was by no means unique among nineteenth-century social, political, biological, and medical thinkers in envisioning a system to bring about the physical, moral, and social improvement of humanity. Like a number of these theorists, Comte saw a place for selective breeding and negative eugenic practices as a part of this work of improvement.[118] Like Comte's "biocracy," new terms built from Greek and Latin words and prefixes were coined by others theorists to characterize these visions. Some of these terms referred to the processes of tending plants, others to animal breeding. People wrote of human culture, *hominiculture*, stirpiculture, human husbandry, and tending the human stable. A host of others combined biology with sociology or anthropology, resulting in biosociology, sociobiology, anthroposociology, anthropotechniques, human zootechniques, and eubiotechniques.[119] A significant new vocabulary of human improvement, therefore, took shape in the nineteenth century and found its way into the twentieth century. Most of it built on the biopolitical tradition established during the eighteenth century, and much of it was created well before 1883, when Francis Galton made his own innovative linguistic combination to coin the term "eugenics." It was also well before the first use of the term "biopolitics" by the Swedish political scientist Rudolph Kjellén in his 1916 book *The State as a Form of Life* (*Staten som Lifsform*). Kjellén worked within the tradition of understanding the state as a living organism, and he employed a conception of biopolitics that already had some of the elementary features of what Foucault articulated in the 1970s.[120]

Conclusion

A historical account of the Enlightenment birth of biopolitics, with its reformulation of social and political exclusions and its formation of eugenic ideas and policies, affords a new perspective from which to view the era in which it emerged. The existence of biopolitical ideas and plans in the eighteenth century raises the question of how the Enlightenment produced such powerful discourses of inclusion based on ideas of toleration, equality, liberty, cosmopolitanism, and natural rights at the same time that it produced powerful and lasting discourses of exclusion based on the perception, and the conceptual creation, of differences of race, sex, and gender. This is one of the unresolved and central questions (perhaps the question) of the Enlightenment, one that sits at the historical foundation of modern democratic thought, and continues to elicit troubling questions about the legacy of the Enlightenment. One reason that this is an unresolved question is that scholars have often presented the Enlightenment as being fundamentally either emancipatory or repressive, as if it were a project of liberation or one of quasi-totalitarian domination based in a hypocritical application of a professed universalism. Both of these strains of interpretation have their roots in narratives that took shape in the era surrounding the Second World War, when fierce ideological conflicts between liberalism, communism, and fascism accompanied the rise of fascist states and unprecedented warfare, leading to catastrophic devastation and displacement, and, finally, the Holocaust. The emancipatory narrative emerged from a series of major synthetic interpretations trying to redeem or defend the Enlightenment, all of which were written by scholars whose lives were significantly impacted by the rise of fascism and the outbreak of the Second World War, including Ernst Cassirer, Paul Hazard, Franco Venturi, and Peter Gay.[1] In the summary judgment of the last of these major synthetic interpreters, the philosophes "undertook to devise forms—a social, ethical, political, and aesthetic program—for the sake of freedom."[2] A more pessimistic narrative of the Enlightenment as an origin of fascism and totalitarianism emerged from various works, most of which did not claim to present synthetic interpretations of the Enlightenment, but nonetheless identified a problematic core of Enlightenment thought. Many of these works were also written by scholars who had been directly impacted by the rise of fascism and the outbreak of war. Scholars such as Carl Becker, Isaiah Berlin, and the German émigrés George Mosse, Max Horkheimer, and Theodor Adorno provided a foundation for many of the postmodern, postcolonial, and feminist critiques of the Enlightenment that came to prominence in the late twentieth century.[3] Although some, like Horkheimer and Adorno, retained hope for the redemption and development of some aspects of the thought of the historical Enlightenment, some critiques presented the Enlightenment as absolutely irredeemable. "The Enlightenment leads to Auschwitz," wrote one scholarly critic; "after Auschwitz, the Enlightenment is a bankrupt, discredited, blighted dialectic."[4]

This dichotomous approach to the Enlightenment can still be seen in some of the most prominent works that attempt to celebrate or denounce the Enlightenment and its legacy. While this book focuses on a topic that has a dark and troubling history, particularly as biopolitical ideas were increasingly put into practice in the nineteenth and twentieth centuries, I hope to have shown that the historical Enlightenment of the eighteenth century is nonetheless best understood when the false binaries and questionable genealogies that are often used in moralistic denunciations or celebrations of the Enlightenment as a whole are jettisoned. At the most basic level, Manichean narratives positing a black-and-white story of good and evil, whether arguing for the positive or negative view of the Enlightenment, misrepresent the historical past by arguing for one side of a binary at the expense of the other.[5] More than this, however, such narratives obscure the constitutive and intimate connections that existed between the ideas and practices at either pole of the binaries they assume, whether these binaries are moral or conceptual. An analysis of the Enlightenment birth of biopolitics provides, I hope, a perspective from which to demonstrate the inadequacy of Manichean narratives and to identify the ways that the development of modern forms of inclusion and exclusion, emancipation and domination, were not only linked, but mutually constitutive.

Historical attention to these ideas and practices of political and social exclusion is particularly important in light of the defenses and reclamations of the Enlightenment, both within the academy and in the popular media.[6] As various postmodern and postcolonial critiques of the Enlightenment mounted at the end of the twentieth century, a wave of defenses of the historical Enlightenment took shape in the early twenty-first century. This resulted in the heightening of binaristic representations of the Enlightenment as either emancipatory or totalitarian, worthy of celebrating and perpetuating or having created a legacy to be overcome and relegated to the past. Defenders of the Enlightenment have articulated equally extreme and misrepresentative statements. One advocate of Radical Enlightenment ideas has even defended this tradition by asserting that the "package" of values that supposedly follow from its philosophical foundations are inherently and absolutely superior to all possible alternatives. "For anyone who believes human societies are best ruled by reason as defined by the Radical Enlightenment," he wrote, "ordering modern societies on the basis of individual liberty, democracy, equality, equity, sexual freedom, and freedom of expression and publication clearly constitutes a package of rationally validated values which not only were, but remain today, inherently superior morally, politically, and intellectually not only to Postmodernist claims but to *all* actual or possible alternatives, no matter how *different*, national, and Postcolonial and no matter how illiberal, non-western, and traditional."[7] Driving home the absolutism and comprehensiveness of his position, this advocate concluded that "the social values of the Radical Enlightenment, in short, have an absolute quality in terms of reason which places them above any possible alternative."[8] In the stark choice presented, there are no possible modifications and no viable alternatives, only a radical faithfulness to select Enlightenment philosophical principles and values. This choice, however, is sustained only by a representation that unduly ignores or downplays the contradictions, qualifications, and practical dilemmas posed by even the most radical Enlightenment ideas.

While reevaluating the Enlightenment can be productive, the new defenses and celebrations threaten to create an imbalanced representation, overemphasizing radical emancipatory ideas in a way that obscures the complexity and ambiguity of Enlightenment thought, reinforcing a false narrative of a "clash of civilizations" between "the West and the rest," and in fact attenuating the emancipatory potential of the radical ideas of the Enlightenment.[9] This has led to perplexing attempts to connect contemporary events to Enlightenment origins, as when Jonathan Israel, one of the leading scholarly figures in this defense of the Enlightenment, characterized the provocative onetime Dutch politician and leading figure of the European right-wing critique of Islam, Ayaan Hirsi Ali, as "an heir to Spinoza," the seventeenth-century philosopher who was supposedly the godfather of Radical Enlightenment thought.[10] While Enlightenment biopolitical proposals are not simply vindications of Max Horkheimer and Theodor Adorno's sweeping and influential generalization that "Enlightenment is totalitarian," they nonetheless complicate and undermine a number of the new defenses and reclamations of the Enlightenment and its legacy.[11]

To best understand the Enlightenment and how we still grapple with its legacy, we should approach the extremes of emancipation and domination and search for the many links that connect them, rather than allowing our analytical perspective to become skewed toward one extreme or the other, presenting the Enlightenment as simply emancipatory or totalitarian. These two extremes developed in relation to one another, and our understanding of discourses of inclusion is historically incomplete and morally, politically, and intellectually impoverished if we do not understand them in relation to the ideas and practices of exclusion with which they developed. The Enlightenment remains "good to think with" because many of our modern notions of equality, toleration, liberty, democracy, sovereignty, and natural rights emerged or were reconfigured in the Enlightenment, but also because they developed in relation to troubling and persistent ideas and practices—such as exclusion based on differences (preexisting or constructed) of race, sex, and gender—that played a role in attenuating or undermining the emancipatory potential.[12] Even for the idea of universal equality—a cornerstone of the radical strain of Enlightenment thought—a rigorous and accurate, not to mention politically meaningful, history must remain attuned to the complex manner in which ideas of equality were always created in relation to ideas and practices of inequality.[13]

Although we should correct the more extreme, reductive, and anachronistic statements or innuendos equating the Enlightenment with totalitarianism—whether made by Horkheimer and Adorno, Foucault, or some of their less sophisticated successors—we should not jettison Horkheimer and Adorno's awareness of the dialectical character of the Enlightenment, with its vital focus on unintended consequences and dialectical reversals, or Foucault's awareness of the inseparable relation between power and knowledge, freedom and domination. We can continue to combat uninformed and ahistorical arguments while acknowledging that there were those figures of the Enlightenment who created dehumanizing plans to engineer human populations. Furthermore, these men and their ideas were not as exceptional as they first appear, and they were not alone among figures of the Enlightenment in formulating biopolitical plans to exclude groups of people and transform populations. Acknowledging this conflicted reality of the Enlightenment is necessary if we are to have an understanding of its ideas that is nuanced and robust enough to inform present and future debates about the role of equality and inequality, inclusion and exclusion, rights and race. Whether we want to oppose, radicalize, draw on, or overcome the Enlightenment, a recognition of its complexity is fundamental and necessary.

Acknowledgments

For comments on parts of this work, I'd like to thank David Armitage, Bernard Bailyn, David A. Bell, Jorge Cañizares-Esguerra, Paul Cohen, Suzanne Desan, Claude-Olivier Doron, Ari Finnsson, Élie Haddad, Julie Hardwick, István Hont, Lynn Hunt, Andrew Jainchill, Michael Kwass, Antoine Lilti, Mary Lindemann, Laura Mason, Ted McCormick, Darrin McMahon, William O'Reilly, Bhavani Raman, Pernille Røge, E. Nathalie Rothman, Emma Rothschild, Stephen Sawyer, John Shovlin, Anne Simonin, David Todd, Lilia Topouzova, Eliot Tretter, Cécile Vidal, Ben Vinson III, Tamara Walker, Charles Walton, and Rebecca Woods.

Additionally, for support and conversations along the way, I want to thank Josh Arthurs, Ben Brower, Francis Cody, Judy Coffin, Paul Cohen, Eric Jennings, Mary Lindemann, Sean Mills, Mary Nyquist, Boris Pantev, Nathan Perl-Rosenthal, Bhavani Ramen, Dominque Reill, Peter Reill, Amanda Ricci, Ken Rogers, Josh Rosenblatt, E. Nathalie Rothman, Jim Sidbury, Mary Terrall, Eliot Tretter, Tamara Walker, and Ashli White.

I would like to thank the organizers, audiences, and commentators at seminars and workshops where I presented parts of this book: Harvard University, the University of Cambridge, Sciences Po, the University of Miami, the University of Texas at Austin, the University of Toronto, Concordia University, École des Hautes Études en Sciences Sociales, and Utrecht University, as well as a number of conferences of professional associations.

Research for this book has been supported by the Mellon Foundation, the Connaught Fund at the University of Toronto, the University of Toronto Scarborough, and fellowships at the Centre for History and Economics at the University of Cambridge and the Institute for Historical Studies at the University of Texas at Austin.

For research assistance, I thank Henry Coomes and Ari Finnsson.

Part of chapter 3 appeared in a different version in the *American Historical Review* 115, no. 5 (December 2010): 1364–94. I'd like to thank editors Robert A. Schneider and Sarah Knott, as well as the six anonymous reviewers. Part of chapter 7 appeared in a different form as "Colonizing France: Revolutionary Regeneration and the First French Empire," in *The French Revolution in Global Perspective*, edited by Suzanne Desan, Lynn Hunt, and William Max Nelson (Ithaca, NY: Cornell University Press, 2013).

At the University of Chicago Press, I thank Mary Al-Sayed, who acquired the book and saw it through peer review. I'd also like to thank Darrin McMahon, Dylan Montanari, Caterina MacLean, and the reviewers for the press. I thank Kathleen Kageff for her expert copyediting and Derek Gottlieb for his able indexing.

For support that goes so far beyond the book, I'd like to thank my parents, Bill and Joan, and my sister, Anika. I'd also like to thank Lilia and Max, *nous co-naissons au monde*. It is an astonishment to have my life intertwined with yours.

Abbreviations

AN	Archives nationales, Paris, France
ANOM	Archives nationales d'outre mer, Aix-en-Provence, France
Archives parlémentaires	*Archives parlémentaires, de 1787 à 1860: Recueil complet des débats législatifs et politiques des chambres françaises, première série (1787–1799)*
Encyclopédie	Denis Diderot and Jean le Rond d'Alembert, eds., *Encyclopédie, ou Dictionnaire raisonné des sciences, des arts et des métiers, par une Société de gens de lettres*, 1st ed., 17 vols. (1751–65)
HN	Georges-Louis Leclerc, comte de Buffon, *Histoire naturelle, générale et particulière*, 15 vols. (Paris: Imprimerie royale, 1749–67)
HN Supplément	Georges-Louis Leclerc, comte de Buffon, *Histoire naturelle, générale et particulière: Supplément*, 7 vols. (Paris: Imprimerie royale, 1774–89)
MARS	*Mémoires de l'Académie royale des sciences*
OC	*Œuvres complètes* (used for various authors; full bibliographical data is given at first citation of each)
OP	*Œuvres philosophiques* (used for various authors; full bibliographical data is given at first citation of each)
SVEC	*Studies on Voltaire and the Eighteenth Century* (changed formally to *SVEC*, then to *Oxford University Studies in the Enlightenment*)

Notes

1. Abbé Emmanuel-Joseph Sieyès, "Esclaves d'une espèce qui ait moins de besoins et moins propre [à] exciter la compassion humaine," 284 AP 3, dossier 1, cahier 2, Archives nationales, Paris, France, hereafter AN. The document with editorial changes is reprinted in Emmanuel-Joseph Sieyès, *Écrits politiques*, ed. Roberto Zapperi (Paris: Éditions des Archives Contemporaines, 1985), 75. I quote from the original. All translations from French are mine unless otherwise noted. The precise date of this document cannot be established. The only significant analysis of the document is William H. Sewell Jr., *A Rhetoric of Bourgeois Revolution: The Abbé Sieyes and "What Is the Third Estate?"* (Durham, NC: Duke University Press, 1994), 153–58; the entire chapter is essential reading, 145–84.

2. Sieyès, "Esclaves d'une espèce."

3. Sieyès.

4. On Swiftian satire and literary readings of ideas of human breeding, see Jenny Davidson, *Breeding: A Partial History of the Eighteenth Century* (New York: Columbia University Press, 2009).

5. Additional evidence from the oeuvre of Sieyès is discussed in chapter 5, while unearthing the biopolitical context is the topic of this book.

6. Sieyès, "Esclaves d'une espèce."

7. Sieyès.

8. On Aristotle's idea and the early modern theory of natural slavery, see Anthony Pagden, *The Fall of Natural Man: The American Indian and the Origins of Comparative Ethnology* (Cambridge: Cambridge University Press, 1982), 27–56.

9. Michel Foucault, *The History of Sexuality*, vol. 1, *An Introduction*, trans. Robert Hurley (New York: Random House, 1978), 141–42. Also see Michel Foucault, *Security, Territory, Population: Lectures at the Collège de France, 1977–78*, ed. Michel Senellart, trans. Graham Burchell (New York: Palgrave Macmillan, 2007); and Michel Foucault, *"Society Must Be Defended": Lectures at the Collège de France, 1975–76*, ed. Mauro Bertani and Alessandro Fontana, trans. David Macey (New York: Picador, 2003), 242–43. A different meaning of "biopolitics" predated Foucault; see Thomas Lemke, *Biopolitics: An Advanced Introduction* (New York: New York University Press, 2011).

10. On political arithmetic, see Peter Buck, "Seventeenth-Century Political Arithmetic: Civil Strife and Vital Statistics," *Isis* 68 (1977): 67–84; Andrea Rusnock, "Biopolitics: Political Arithmetic in the Enlightenment," in *The Sciences in Enlightened Europe*, ed. William Clark, Jan Golinski, and Simon Schaffer (Chicago: University of Chicago Press, 1999), 49–68; Thierry Martin, ed., *Arithmétique politique dans la France du XVIIIe siècle* (Paris: INED, 2003); Ted McCormick, *William Petty and the Ambitions of Political Arithmetic* (Oxford: Oxford University Press, 2009); and Ted McCormick, "Political Arithmetic's 18th Century Histories: Quantification in Politics, Religion, and the Public Sphere," *History Compass* 12, no. 3 (2014): 239–51.

11. The language of "reciprocal incorporation" is used by Timothy Campbell and Adam Sitze, "Introduction," in *Biopolitics: A Reader* (Durham, NC: Duke University Press, 2013), 2.

12. Like many scholars of biopolitics, I use the term in a way that includes some of what Foucault sometimes characterized as biopower, governmentality, and "anatomopolitics"; see Catherine Mills, *Biopolitics* (New York: Routledge, 2018), 5. For more on definitions and their difficulties, see Lemke, *Biopolitics*; Paul Rabinow and Nikolas Rose, "Biopower Today," *BioSocieties* 1 (2006): 195–217; Laura Bazzicalupo, "The Ambiguities of Biopolitics," *Diacrtitics* 36, no. 2 (Summer 2006): 109–16; and Campbell and Sitze, "Introduction," 1–40. Also see Michelle Murphy's attempt at "unfaithfully rethinking Foucault's initial formulation of 'biopolitics'" in *Seizing the Means of Reproduction: Entanglements of Feminism, Health, and Technoscience* (Durham, NC: Duke University Press, 2012), 11. For a self-consciously tendentious historicist reading, see Roger Cooter and Claudia Stein, "Cracking Biopower," in *Writing History in the Age of Biomedicine* (New Haven, CT: Yale University Press, 2013), 183–204.

13. For historical scholarship on eighteenth-century biopolitics, particularly emphasizing statistics and health concerns, see Rusnock, "Biopolitics"; Andrea A. Rusnock, *Vital Accounts: Quantifying Health and Population in Eighteenth-Century England and France* (New York: Cambridge University Press, 2002); and Andrea Rusnock, "Biopolitics and the Invention of Population," in *Reproduction: Antiquity to the Present*, ed. Nick Hopwood, Rebecca Fleming, and Lauren Kassel (Cambridge: Cambridge University Press, 2018), 333–45. Also see Claudia Stein's prospectus for a project, "The Birth of Biopower in Eighteenth-Century Germany," *Medical History* 55 (2011): 331–37; and Claude-Olivier Doron, *L'homme altéré: Races et dégénérescence (XVIIe–XIXe siècles)* (Ceyzérieu: Champ Vallon, 2016). For noteworthy analyses of eighteenth-century biopolitics in other disciplines, see Warren Montag, "Necro-economics: Adam Smith and Death in the Life of the Universal," *Radical Philosophy* 134 (November/December 2005): 7–17; Ed Cohen, *A Body Worth Defending: Immunity, Biopolitics, and the Apotheosis of the Modern Body* (Durham, NC: Duke University Press, 2009); Yves Citton, *Zazirocratie: Très curieuse introduction à la biopolitique et à la critique de la croissance* (Paris: Amsterdam, 2011); Daniel Nemser, *Infrastructures of Race: Concentration and Biopolitics in Colonial Mexico* (Austin: University of Texas Press, 2017); Robert Mitchell, "Enlightenment Biopolitics: Population and the Growth of Genius," *Eighteenth Century* 59, no. 4 (Winter 2018): 405–27; Greta Lafleur, *The Natural History of Sexuality in Early America* (Baltimore: Johns Hopkins University Press, 2018); Richard A. Barney and Warren Montag, eds., *Systems of Life: Biopolitics, Economics, and Literature on the Cusp of Modernity* (New York: Fordham University Press, 2019); and the special issue edited by Greta Lafleur and Kyla Schuller of *American Quarterly* 71, no. 3 (September 2019).

14. The humanity of the Sami people of the Artic (referred to as Lapps, *les Lappons*) and the Khoekhoe people of South Africa (referred to as Hottentots) were most often questioned. Enlightenment articulations of the human are part of a much longer historical process of constituting groups of people that are treated as fully human, not quite human, or subhuman. On the formation of an "ontological lack" and its role in the formation of a regime of universal "Man," see Sylvia Wynter, "Beyond the Word of Man: Glissant and the New Discourse of the Antilles," *World Literature Today* 63, no. 4 (Autumn 1989): 637–48. On Wynter's work and its relation to theories of biopolitics, see Alexander G. Weheliye, *Habeas Viscus: Racializing Assemblages, Biopolitics, and Black Feminist Theories of the Human* (Durham, NC: Duke University Press, 2014).

15. See Emmanuel Chukwudi Eze, ed., *Race and the Enlightenment: A Reader* (Cambridge, MA: Blackwell, 1997).

16. See Karen Offen, *European Feminisms, 1700–1950: A Political History* (Stanford, CA: Stanford University Press, 2000); Siep Stuurman, *François Poulain de la Barre and the Invention of Modern Equality* (Cambridge, MA: Harvard University Press, 2004); and Barbara Taylor and Sarah Knott, eds., *Women, Gender, and Enlightenment* (New York: Palgrave Macmillan, 2005).

17. See, for example, Edmund Morgan, "Slavery and Freedom: The American Paradox," *Journal of American History* 59, no. 1 (June 1972): 5–29; Uday S. Mehta, "Liberal Strategies of Exclusion," *Politics and Society* 18, no. 4 (1990): 427–54; and Étienne Balibar, "The Idea of 'New Enlightenment' (*Nouvelles Lumières*) and the Contradictions of Universalism," in *Political Theology and Early Modernity*, ed. Graham Hammill and Julia Reinhard Lupton (Chicago: University of Chicago Press, 2012). There is an older tradition of black intellectuals such as Baron de Vastey, W. E. B. Du Bois, and C. L. R. James pointing out contradictions between discourses of liberty and the realities of enslavement and racism. For a narrative of noncontradiction arguing that historically "freedom and race are not just enemies but also allies," see Tyler Stovall, *White Freedom: The Racial History of an Idea* (Princeton, NJ: Princeton University Press, 2021), 5. I use lowercase "white" and "black" because I want to register that these terms referred to categories that were fluid, contested, and actively being constructed. They functioned differently from contemporary terms for racial identification. They were not proper nouns or clearly identifiable racial terms utilized extensively for self-identification but biopolitical terms used most commonly and fastidiously by administrators and people involved in the sciences. I want to avoid reifying the historical racial categories while also giving a sense of how French colonial actors were attempting to transform and fix them, particularly in their attempts to precisely identify what they thought to be the many gradations of mixture of "black" and "white," as well as how this correlated with specific gradations of skin color.

18. For example, on European imperial expansion and the universalizing moral core of Christianity and natural rights thought, see Sankar Muthu, *Enlightenment against Empire* (Princeton, NJ: Princeton University Press, 2003), 272.

19. On this "co-occurrence," see Étienne Balibar, *Citizenship*, trans. Thomas Scott-Railton (Cambridge: Polity, 2015), 72, 80; and Étienne Balibar, *Citizen Subject: Foundations for Political Anthropology*, trans. Steven Miller (New York: Fordham University Press, 2017). On the intertwining of ideas of equality and inequality, see Siep Stuurman, "How to Write a History of Equality," *Leidschrift* 19, no. 3 (December 2004): 23–38; and Siep Stuurman, *The Invention of Humanity: Equality and Cultural Difference in World*

History (Cambridge, MA: Harvard University Press, 2017). On inclusion and exclusion in social contract theory, see Carole Pateman, *The Sexual Contract* (Stanford, CA: Stanford University Press, 1988); and Charles W. Mills, *The Racial Contract* (Ithaca, NY: Cornell University Press, 1997); in Lockean liberalism, see Mehta, "Liberal Strategies of Exclusion"; on the "liberal paradox," see David Theo Goldberg, *Racist Culture: Philosophy and the Politics of Meaning* (Cambridge, MA: Blackwell, 1993), 6–7; on "exclusive democracy" and sexual difference, see Geneviève Fraisse, *Reason's Muse: Sexual Difference and the Birth of Democracy*, trans. Jane Marie Todd (Chicago: University of Chicago Press, 1994); and on the language of inclusion and exclusion in encyclopedias, see Devin J. Vartija, *The Color of Equality: Race and Common Humanity in Enlightenment Thought* (Philadelphia: University of Pennsylvania Press, 2021).

20. Jean-Jacques Rousseau, "Economie ou œconomie (morale et politique)," in *Encyclopédie* (1755), 5:337–49; included as *Discours sur l'économie politique*, in Rousseau, *Œuvres complètes*, hereafter *OC*, ed. Bernard Gagnebin and Marcel Raymond (Paris: Éditions Gallimard, 1964), 3:251.

21. On intervention as a defining characteristic of later biopolitics, see Nikolas Rose, *The Politics of Life Itself: Biomedicine, Power, and Subjectivity in the Twenty-First Century* (Princeton, NJ: Princeton University Press, 2007), 83; and Hans-Jörg Rheinberger, "Beyond Nature and Culture: Modes of Reasoning in the Age of Molecular Biology and Medicine," in *Living and Working with the New Medical Technologies*, ed. Margaret Lock, Allan Young, and Alberto Cambrosio (Cambridge: Cambridge University Press, 2000), 19–30.

22. On the development of eugenics and state-sponsored programs of population management and "improvement," see Alison Bashford and Philippa Levine, eds., *The Oxford Handbook of the History of Eugenics* (Oxford: Oxford University Press, 2010); and Amir Weiner, ed., *Landscaping the Human Garden: Twentieth-Century Population Management in a Comparative Perspective* (Stanford, CA: Stanford University Press, 2003). On genetic engineering and interventions in life, see Rose, *Politics of Life Itself*.

23. Sieyès, "Esclaves d'une espèce." Sieyès envisioned these new slaves being directed by black overseers whose status as enslaved or wage laborers was not made clear.

24. Sieyès wrote at the top of the document: "Slaves of a species that would have fewer needs and be less apt to excite human compassion" (Esclaves d'une espèce qui ait moins de besoins et moins propre à exciter la compassion humaine).

25. See Abbé Emmanuel-Joseph Sieyès, "Lettres aux Économistes sur leur système de politique et de morale," 284 AP 2, dossier 10; included in *Des manuscrits de Sieyès*, ed. Christine Fauré, Jacques Guilhaumou, and Jacques Valier (Paris: Honoré Champion, 1999), 1:170–84. On Sieyès and political economy, see Marcel Dorigny, "La formulation de la pensée économique de Sieyès d'aprés ses manuscrits (1770–1789)," *Annales Historiques de la Révolution française* 6 (1988): 17–34; and Sewell, *Rhetoric*.

26. Joachim Faiguet de Villeneuve, *L'économe politique: Projet pour enricher et pour perfectionner l'espèce humaine* (London, 1763).

27. Sieyès, "Esclaves d'une espèce."

28. Although I agree with Sewell that there is some ambiguity and possibly geographical displacement in Sieyès's references in the document to warm and cold "countries" and to "a large nation," there is nothing to indicate that these countries or this nation is necessarily imaginary. In fact, as Sewell also recognizes, Sieyès's words leave

open the possibility that he envisioned this plan as a solution for any number of actual countries, including France. Sieyès, "Esclaves d'une espèce"; Sewell, *Rhetoric*, 155–56.

29. On dangerous experiments, thought experiments, and inhumane proposals, see Julia V. Douthwaite, *The Wild Girl, Natural Man, and the Monster: Dangerous Experiments in the Age of Enlightenment* (Chicago: University of Chicago Press, 2002), particularly 7 and 72–73; and Carolyn Purnell, "Instruments Endowed with Sensibility: Remaking Society through the Body in Eighteenth-Century France" (PhD diss., University of Chicago, 2013). Also see Davidson, *Breeding*, 171–72.

30. On the marginalization of race and the oversight of colonialism in Foucault's work, and in the nineteenth-century history of biopolitics, see Ann Laura Stoler, *Race and the Education of Desire: Foucault's History of Sexuality and the Colonial Order of Things* (Durham, NC: Duke University Press, 1995); and Ann Laura Stoler, *Carnal Knowledge and Imperial Power: Race and the Intimate in Colonial Rule* (Berkeley: University of California Press, 2002). On the "necropolitics" of slavery and how it complicates accounts of biopolitics, see Achille Mbembe, "Necropolitics," *Public Culture* 15, no. 1 (2003): 11–40. On Agamben's oversight of slavery, race, and colonialism, see David Scott, "Preface: Soul Captives Are Free," *Small Axe*, number 23 (vol. 11, no. 2, June 2007): viii–x; Marcelo Svirsky and Simone Bignall, eds., *Agamben and Colonialism* (Edinburgh: Edinburgh University Press, 2012); and Weheliye, *Habeas Viscus*.

31. On Roman pronatalist policies, and the way that Louis XIV and his ministers turned to these precedents in creating policies, see Leslie Tuttle, *Conceiving the Old Regime: Pronatalism and the Politics of Reproduction in Early Modern France* (Oxford: Oxford University Press, 2010), 36, 47, 50–51.

32. On the use and meaning of "biology," see Shirley A. Roe, "The Life Sciences," in *The Cambridge History of Science*, vol. 4, *The Eighteenth Century*, ed. Roy Porter (New York: Cambridge University Press, 2003), 416. Also see Cécilia Bognon-Küss and Charles T. Wolfe, eds., *Philosophy of Biology before Biology* (New York: Routledge 2019).

33. This is one reason that I do not believe biopolitics emerged in antiquity. On the antiquity of biopolitics, see Giorgio Agamben, *Homo Sacer: Sovereign Power and Bare Life*, trans. Daniel Heller-Roazen (Stanford, CA: Stanford University Press, 1998); and Mika Ojakangas, *The Greek Origins of Biopolitics: A Reinterpretation of the History of Biopower* (New York: Routledge, 2016).

34. Saliha Belmessous, "Assimilation and Racialism in Seventeenth- and Eighteenth-Century French Colonial Policy," *American Historical Review* 110, no. 2 (April 2005): 322–49; and Tuttle, *Conceiving*, 80.

35. See McCormick, *William Petty*, 195. Petty's idea of "the transmutation of the Irish" is perhaps the best candidate for "'biopolitics' *avant la lettre*," although I do not believe that it qualifies as biopolitics in the sense that I use the term, since Petty's ideas were not properly biological. McCormick's analysis of Petty is compelling, though I find his characterization of these proposals as "social engineering" more persuasive. See McCormick, particularly 12, 168–208, 303–5.

36. On population and pronatalism, see Joseph J. Spengler, *The French Predecessors of Malthus: A Study in Eighteenth-Century Wage and Population Theory* (Durham, NC: Duke University Press, 1942); Carol Blum, *Strength in Numbers: Population, Reproduction, and Power in Eighteenth-Century France* (Baltimore: Johns Hopkins University

Press, 2002); and Tuttle, *Conceiving*. On the history of statistics in France, see J. Hecht, "L'idée de dénombrement jusqu'à la Révolution," in *Pour une histoire de la statistique*, 2 vols. (Paris: INSEE, 1978), 1:21–81; and J. Dupâquier and E. Vilquin, "Le pouvoir royal et la statistique démographique," in *Pour une histoire de la statistique*, 1:83–101.

37. Francis Galton, *Inquiries into Human Faculty and Its Development* (London: Macmillan, 1883).

38. For qualifications like "proto-eugenic" and "pre-eugenic," see Anne Carol, *Histoire de l'eugénisme en France: Les médecins et la procréation, XIXᵉ–XXᵉ siècle* (Paris: Seuil, 1995), 17–37; Davidson, *Breeding*, 5; Michael E. Winston, *From Perfectibility to Perversion: Meliorism in Eighteenth-Century France* (New York: Peter Lang, 2005); and Richard S. Fogarty and Michael A. Osborne, "Eugenics in France and the Colonies," in Bashford and Levine, *Oxford Handbook of the History of Eugenics*. The term "eugenics" is completely avoided in the characterization of eighteenth-century ideas about breeding in both Victor Hilts, "Enlightenment Views of the Genetic Perfectibility of Man," in *Transformation and Tradition in the Sciences: Essays in Honor of I. Bernard Cohen*, ed. Everett Mendelsohn (Cambridge: Cambridge University Press, 1984), 255–71; and Sean M. Quinlan, *The Great Nation in Decline: Sex, Modernity and Health Crises in Revolutionary France, c. 1750–1850* (Aldershot: Ashgate, 2007). On "eugenic regimens," see Anne C. Vila, *Enlightenment and Pathology: Sensibility in the Literature and Medicine of Eighteenth-Century France* (Baltimore: Johns Hopkins University Press, 1998), 103, as well as 89. Kathleen Wellman writes that Vandermonde raised "the specter of eugenics," in "Physicians and *Philosophes*: Physiology and Sexual Morality in the French Enlightenment," *Eighteenth-Century Studies* 35, no. 2 (Winter 2002): 271.

39. Bashford and Levine, *Oxford Handbook of the History of Eugenics*; and Frank Dikötter, "Race Culture: Recent Perspectives on the History of Eugenics," *American Historical Review* 103, no. 2 (April 1998): 467–78.

40. On race, eugenics, and neo-Lamarckianism in the nineteenth and twentieth centuries, see Bashford and Levine, *Oxford Handbook of the History of Eugenics*; Carol, *Histoire de l'eugénisme*; William H. Schneider, *Quality and Quantity: The Quest for Biological Regeneration in Twentieth-Century France* (New York: Cambridge University Press, 1990); and Emmanuelle Saada, *Empire's Children: Race, Filiation, and Citizenship in the French Colonies* (Chicago: University of Chicago Press, 2012). French eugenics was not exceptional in an adherence to Lamarckianism; see Nancy Leys Stepan, *"The Hour of Eugenics": Race, Gender, and Nation in Latin America* (Ithaca, NY: Cornell University Press, 1991).

41. Specialists of Lamarck have long argued that he was not the first to propose the inheritance of acquired characters, though the idea that he was the first persists. On the history and historiography of this issue, see Richard W. Burkhardt Jr., "Lamarck, Evolution, and the Inheritance of Acquired Characters," *Genetics* 194 (August 2014): 793–805. Lamarck received patronage from Buffon and tutored one of his children. See Jacques Roger, *Buffon: A Life in Natural History*, trans. Sarah Lucille Bonnefoi, ed. L. Pearce Williams (Ithaca, NY: Cornell University Press, 1997), 370.

42. On heredity in later eugenics, see Bashford and Levine, "Introduction," in *Oxford Handbook of the History of Eugenics*, 3–5.

43. On hereditary transmission and a basic concept of heredity, see Staffan Müller-Wille and Hans-Jörg Rheinberger, *A Cultural History of Heredity* (Chicago: University of

Chicago Press, 2012), 71; and see Carlos López-Beltrán, "Human Heredity, 1750–1870: The Construction of a Scientific Domain" (PhD diss., King's College London, 1992). For the claim that Buffon's ideas qualified as a "conception of heredity," see Roger, *Buffon*, 127–31.

44. Carlos López-Beltrán, "Perfectionner le corps: Des défauts héréditaires à l'hérédité fatale (1750–1870)," in *L'éternal retour de l'eugenisme*, ed. Jean Gayon and Daniel Jacobi (Paris: Presses Universitaires de France, 2006), 151.

45. On Buffon on generation, reproduction, and heredity, see Roger, *Buffon*, 127–31. On Maupertuis, see Mary Terrall, *The Man Who Flattened the Earth: Maupertuis and the Sciences in the Enlightenment* (Chicago: University of Chicago Press, 2002).

46. Daniel Kevles, *In the Name of Eugenics: Genetics and the Uses of Human Heredity* (New York: Alfred A. Knopf, 1985), 3.

47. Carol, *Histoire de l'eugénisme*, 69–70; John C. Waller, "Ideas of Heredity, Reproduction and Eugenics in Britain, 1800–1875," *Studies in History and Philosophy of Biological and Biomedical Sciences* 32, no. 3 (2001): 473–75; and Bashford and Levine, "Introduction."

48. See Margaret C. Jacob, *Radical Enlightenment: Pantheists, Freemasons, and Republicans* (London: Allen and Unwin, 1981); Margaret C. Jacob, *The Secular Enlightenment* (Princeton, NJ: Princeton University Press, 2019); Ann Thomson, *Bodies of Thought: Science, Religion, and the Soul in the Early Enlightenment* (Oxford: Oxford University Press, 2008); and, with reservations about its methodology, Jonathan Israel, *Radical Enlightenment: Philosophy and the Making of Modernity, 1650–1750* (Oxford: Oxford University Press, 2001).

49. I discuss the openness to metropolitan and colonial reform in later chapters. On this issue, also see Jean Tarrade, "L'administration coloniale en France à la fin de l'ancien régime: Projets de réforme," *Revue Historique* 229, no. 1 (1963): 103–22; Jean Tarrade, *Le commerce colonial de la France à la fin de l'ancien régime: L'évolution du régime de "l'Exclusif" de 1763 à 1789*, 2 vols. (Paris: Pressees universitaires de France, 1972); Michèle Duchet, *Diderot et l'histoire des Deux Indes: ou L'ecriture fragmentaire* (Paris: A. G. Nizet, 1978); and the chapters by Emma Rothschild, John Shovlin, and Pernille Røge in *Enlightened Reform in Southern Europe and Its Atlantic Colonies, c. 1750–1830*, ed. Gabriel Paquette (New York: Routledge, 2009), 37–40, 47–62, and 167–82.

50. Georges-Louis Leclerc, comte de Buffon, *Histoire naturelle, générale et particulière*, hereafter *HN*, 15 vols. (Paris: Imprimerie royale, 1749–67).

51. Phillip R. Sloan, "Natural History," in Knud Haakonssen, ed., *The Cambridge History of Eighteenth-Century Philosophy* (New York: Cambridge University Press, 2005), 2:911–24; Phillip R. Sloan, "The Gaze of Natural History," in Christopher Fox, Roy Porter, and Robert Wokler, eds., *Inventing Human Science: Eighteenth-Century Domains* (Berkeley: University of California Press, 1995), 126–41. On this transformation in natural history, also see Michel Delsol, ed., *Buffon 88: Actes du colloque international pour le bicentenaire de la mort de Buffon* (Paris: J. Vrin, 1992); Roger, *Buffon*; and Peter Hanns Reill, *Vitalizing Nature in the Enlightenment* (Berkeley: University of California Press, 2005), 1–70.

52. On "man-as-species" and "the human species" underwriting the concept of population, see Foucault, *"Society Must Be Defended,"* 242–43, 247; and Foucault, *Security, Territory, Population*, 75.

53. For the best historical accounts of the emergence of new ideas about collective forms of existence in the eighteenth century, see Keith Michael Baker, "Enlightenment and the Institution of Society: Notes for a Conceptual History," *Main Trends in Cultural History*, ed. Willem Melching and Wyger Velema (Amsterdam: Rodopi, 1994), 95–120; and David A. Bell, *The Cult of the Nation in France: Inventing Nationalism, 1680–1800* (Cambridge, MA: Harvard University Press, 2003). Both of these works respond to, and reconfigure, a French line of thought, represented well in Marcel Gauchet, "De l'avènement de l'individu à la découverte de la société," *Annales: Histoire, Sciences Sociales* 34, no. 3 (1979): 451–63; and Brian C. Singer, *Society, Theory, and the French Revolution: Studies in the Revolutionary Imaginary* (New York: St. Martin's, 1986).

54. On the coming into being of scientific objects, see Lorraine Daston, ed., *Biographies of Scientific Objects* (Chicago: University of Chicago Press, 2000).

55. Buffon, "Variétés dans l'espèce humaine," in Georges-Louis Leclerc, comte de Buffon, *Histoire naturelle, particulière*, 15 vols. (Paris: Imprimerie royale, 1749–67), vol. 3 (1749): 370–530. See Sloan, "Gaze." On Linnaeus, see Gunnar Broberg, "*Homo sapiens*: Linnaeus' Classification of Man," in *Linnaeus: The Man and His Work*, ed. Tore Frangsmyr (Berkeley: University of California Press, 1983), 156–94.

56. See Roger, *Buffon*; Sloan, "Gaze"; Michèle Duchet, *Anthropologie et histoire au siècle des Lumières* (Paris: Albin Michel, 1995); and Andrew Curran, *Anatomy of Blackness: Science and Slavery in the Age of Enlightenment* (Baltimore: Johns Hopkins University Press, 2011).

57. Buffon, "Variétés dans l'espèce humaine," 3:530.

58. Most notably, Charles-Augustin Vandermonde, *Essai sur la manière de perfectionner l'espèce humaine*, 2 vols. (Paris: Vincent, 1756).

59. This physical and transmissible type of malleability was not identical to the malleability that some believed resulted from the sensationalism emerging with Locke and developing through the eighteenth century. On this sensationalist malleability, see John Passmore, *The Perfectibility of Man* (New York: Scribner's, 1970).

60. On monsters and the anomalous, see Lorraine Daston and Katharine Park, *Wonders and the Order of Nature, 1150–1750* (New York: Zone Books, 1998); and Michael Hagner "Enlightened Monsters," in Clark et al., *Sciences in Enlightened Europe*, 175–217.

61. On perfectibility, see Bertrand Binoche, ed., *L'homme perfectible* (Seyssel: Champ Vallon, 2004). For a rare example of someone rejecting the idea that all people were perfectible, see the discussion of Abbé Galiani in Curran, *Anatomy of Blackness*, 169.

62. For arguments about inclusion and exclusion, equality and inequality, treating them as contradictory, rather than paradoxical, in my sense, see Mehta, "Liberal Strategies of Exclusion"; Balibar, "Idea of 'New Enlightenment'"; Muthu, *Enlightenment against Empire*; and Stuurman, "How to Write a History of Equality." On "Republican racism" and the treatment of those emancipated from slavery, see Laurent Dubois, *A Colony of Citizens: Revolution and Slave Emancipation in the French Caribbean, 1787–1804* (Chapel Hill: University of North Carolina Press, 2004).

63. The most important exception was Vandermonde, *Essai sur la manière de perfectionner l'espèce humaine*.

64. [Guillaume-François Le Trosne], *Mémoire sur les vagabonds et les mendiants* (Soissons: P. G. Simon, 1764), 8.

CHAPTER ONE

1. Denis Diderot, *Le rêve de d'Alembert*, in *Œuvres philosophiques de Diderot*, ed. Paul Vernière (Paris: Garnier, 1998), hereafter *OP*, 312.

2. Diderot, 288.

3. Diderot, 289–95. Also see Timo Kaitaro, *Diderot's Holism: Philosophical Anti-reductionism and Its Medical Background* (New York: Peter Lang, 1997), 98–101, 110–12.

4. Diderot, *Rêve*, 291.

5. On scientific ideas of organization, see Peter Hanns Reill, *Vitalizing Nature in the Enlightenment* (Berkeley: University of California Press, 2005), 119–58; Roselyne Rey, *Naissance et développement du vitalisme en France de la deuxième moitié du 18ᵉ siècle à la fin du Premier Empire* (Oxford: Voltaire Foundation, 2000), 157–77; and Jessica Riskin, *The Restless Clock: A History of the Centuries-Long Argument over What Makes Living Things Tick* (Chicago: University of Chicago Press, 2016), 110–12, 180–88. Also see the work of John H. Zammito, particularly *The Gestation of German Biology: Philosophy and Physiology from Stahl to Schelling* (Chicago: University of Chicago Press, 2018). On self-organization, see Jonathan Sheehan and Dror Wahrman, *Invisible Hands: Self-Organization and the Eighteenth Century* (Chicago: University of Chicago Press, 2015), 143–82. On the importance of organization around 1800, see Michel Foucault, *The Order of Things: An Archeology of the Human Sciences* (New York: Vintage, 1994), 226–32, 263–79; François Jacob, *Logic of Life: A History of Heredity*, trans. Betty E. Spillman (Princeton, NJ: Princeton University Press, 1973), 74–129; and Joseph Schiller, *La notion d'organisation dans l'histoire de la biologie* (Paris: Maloine, 1978).

6. Théophile de Bordeu, *Recherches anatomiques sur la position des glandes et sur leur action* (Paris: G. F. Quillau, 1751), 452–53.

7. Bordeu, 355, 451, 453. On Bordeu, see Rey, *Naissance*; Elizabeth L. Haigh, "Vitalism, the Soul, and Sensibility: The Physiology of Théophile Bordeu," *Journal of the History of Medicine and Allied Sciences* 31, no. 1 (January 1976): 30–41; and Dominique Boury, *La philosophie médicale de Théophile Bordeu (1722–1776)* (Paris: Honoré Champion, 2004). On Bordeu in the "science of man," see Sergio Moravia, "From *Homme Machine* to *Homme Sensible*: Changing Eighteenth-Century Models of Man's Image," *Journal of the History of Ideas* 39, no. 1 (January–March 1978): 45–60.

8. On Diderot and Maupertuis, see Mary Terrall, *The Man Who Flattened the Earth: Maupertuis and the Sciences in the Enlightenment* (Chicago: University of Chicago Press, 2002), 340–48; and Charles T. Wolfe, "Endowed Molecules and Emergent Organization: The Maupertuis-Diderot Debate," in *Transitions and Borders between Animals, Humans and Machines, 1600–1800*, ed. Tobias Cheung (Leiden: Brill, 2010), 38–65.

9. Jean-Jacques [Jean-Joseph] Ménuret de Chambaud, "Observation," in *Encyclopédie* (1765), 11:318.

10. See Jeffrey Merrick, "Royal Bees: The Gender Politics of the Beehive in Early Modern Europe," in *Order and Disorder under the Ancien Régime* (Newcastle: Cambridge Scholars, 2007), 1–20.

11. Merrick, 4.

12. On the *départements* of glandes, see Bordeu, *Recherches anatomiques*, 422–24, 440–53. On Bordeu and the metaphor of a federation, see Paul Delauney, "L'évolution philosophique et médicale du biomécanisme," *Le progrès médical* 35 (August 27, 1927): 1338;̂ and Moravia, "From *Homme Machine* to *Homme Sensible*," 56.

13. On early modern physiology and the sciences of life, see Jacques Roger, *The Life Sciences in Eighteenth-Century French Thought*, ed. Keith R. Benson, trans. Robert Ellrich (Stanford, CA: Stanford University Press, 1997); and François Duchesneau, *La physiologie des lumières: Empirisme, modèles et theories* (The Hague: M. Nijhoff, 1982).

14. See Kaitaro, *Diderot's Holism*; Colas Duflo, *Diderot philosophe* (Paris: Honoré Champion, 2003); Andrew H. Clark, *Diderot's Part* (Burlington, VT: Ashgate, 2008); and Colas Duflo, *Diderot: Du matérialisme à la politique* (Paris: CNRS, 2013).

15. On emergence and relational holism in quantum mechanics, see Evan Thompson, *Mind in Life: Biology, Phenomenology, and the Science of Life* (Cambridge, MA: Harvard University Press, 2007), 417–41. On the conceptual importance of functions around 1800, see Jacob, *Logic of Life*. For an account of "the animal economy" as a hybrid concept that brought together structure and function, see Charles T. Wolfe and Motoichi Terada, "The Animal Economy as Object and Program in Montpellier Vitalism," in *Science in Context* 21, no. 4 (December 2008): 537–79.

16. Buffon, "Sur la nature des animaux," in *HN* (1753), 4:3; Buffon, "Premier discours," in *HN* (1749), 1:3–62; and Denis Diderot, "Relation," in *Encyclopédie* (1765), 14:62. On comparison and relations in sensationism, see John C. O'Neal, *The Authority of Experience: Sensationist Theory in the French Enlightenment* (University Park: Pennsylvania University Press, 1996); and David W. Bates, *Enlightenment Aberrations: Error and Revolution in France* (Ithaca, NY: Cornell University Press, 2002), 56–72.

17. For an early analysis of Enlightenment relational thinking, though giving too much causal importance to Leibniz, see Ernst Cassirer, *The Philosophy of the Enlightenment*, trans. Fritz C. A. Koelln and James P. Pettegrove (Princeton, NJ: Princeton University Press, 1951), 28–33.

18. See La Mettrie's text and the analysis in Aram Vartanian, *La Mettrie's L'Homme Machine: A Study in the Origins of an Idea* (Princeton, NJ: Princeton University Press, 1960). Also see Ann Thomson, "L'homme machine: Mythe ou métaphore?," *Dix-huitième siècle* 20 (1988): 367–76.

19. See Aram Vartanian "La Mettrie and Diderot Revisited: An Intertextual Encounter," *Diderot Studies* 21 (1983): 155–97.

20. On these topics, see Roger, *Sciences of Life*. On the Hydra polyp, see Aram Vartanian, "Trembley's Polyp, La Mettrie, and Eighteenth-Century French Materialism," *Journal of the History of Ideas* 11 (1950): 259–86; and Virginia P. Dawson, *Nature's Enigma: The Problem of the Polyp in Letters of Bonnet, Trembley, and Réaumur* (Philadelphia: American Philosophical Society, 1987). On Haller and the debates on irritability and sensibility, see Duchesneau, *La physiologie des lumières*; and Hubert Steinke, *Irritating Experiments: Haller's Concept and the European Controversy on Irritability and Sensibility, 1750–1790* (Amsterdam: Rodopi, 2005). On Needham, see Shirley Roe, *Matter, Life, and Generation: Eighteenth-Century Embryology and the Haller-Wolff Debate* (Cambridge: Cambridge University Press, 1981).

21. Charles Bonnet, *Considérations sur les corps organisés* (Amsterdam: Rey, 1762); Jean-Paul Marat, *A Philosophical Essay on Man, Being an Attempt to Investigate the Principles and Laws of the Reciprocal Influence of the Soul on the Body*, 2 vols. (London: Ridley and Payne, 1773).

22. On the spiritual vitalists and Mesmerism, see Michael Sonenscher, *Sans-Culottes: An Eighteenth-Century Emblem in the French Revolution* (Princeton, NJ: Princeton University Press, 2008), particularly, 34–36, 119–28.

23. See Johann Gottfried Herder, "On the Cognition and the Sensation of the Human Soul" (1778), in Herder, *Philosophical Writings*, trans. and ed. Michael M. Forster (Cambridge: Cambridge University Press, 2002), 187–243. Sonenscher cites Herder and discusses the role of this spiritualized vitalism in attempts to revise Rousseau; see Sonenscher, *Sans-Culottes*. On Mesmerism and political theory, also see Robert Darnton, *Mesmerism and the End of the Enlightenment in France* (Cambridge, MA: Harvard University Press, 1968), 106–25.

24. La Mettrie, *L'homme machine*, in Vartanian, *La Mettrie's L'Homme Machine*, 149.

25. See Roselyne Rey, "Psyche, Soma, and the Vitalist Philosophy of Medicine," in *Psyche and Soma: Physicians and Metaphysicians on the Mind-Body Problem from Antiquity to the Enlightenment*, ed. John P. Wright and Paul Potter (Oxford: Oxford University Press, 2000), 257.

26. On vital materialism, see Timothy Lenoir, "Kant, Blumenbach, and Vital Materialism in German Biology," *Isis* 71, no. 1 (March 1980): 77–108; Aram Vartanian, "La Mettrie and Diderot Revisited: An Intertextual Encounter," *Diderot Studies* 21 (1983): 155–97; Peter Hanns Reill, "Between Mechanism and Hermeticism: Nature and Science in the Late Enlightenment," in *Frühe Neuzeit—Frühe Moderne?*, ed. Rudolf Vuerhaus (Göttingen: Vandenhoeck and Ruprecht, 1992), 393–421; Kaitaro, *Diderot's Holism*; Charles T. Wolfe, "Epigensis as Spinozism in Diderot's Biological Project," in *The Life Sciences in Early Modern Philosophy*, ed. Ohad Nachtomy and Justin E. H. Smith (Oxford: Oxford University Press, 2014), 181–201.

27. Buffon, in *HN* (1749), 2:17. Diderot drew on Buffon's text and repeated the claim in "Animal," in *Encyclopédie* (1751), 1:474.

28. On the long history of theories of body and soul, see Wright and Potter, *Psyche and Soma*. On the physical and the moral in the development of Enlightenment human sciences, see Elizabeth A. Williams, *The Physical and the Moral: Anthropology, Physiology, and Philosophical Medicine in France, 1750–1850* (Cambridge: Cambridge University Press, 1994).

29. Louis de La Caze, *Idée de l'homme physique et moral, pour servir d'introduction à un traité de médecine* (Paris: Guerin and Delatour, 1755); Pierre-Jean-Georges Cabanis, *Rapports du physique et du moral de l'homme* (1802), vol. 1 of *Œuvres philosophiques de Cabanis*, ed. Claude Lehec and Jean Cazeneuve (Paris: Presses Universitaires de France, 1956), hereafter *OP*.

30. Victor Riqueti, marquis de Mirabeau, "Fragment d'une préface de 'François l'Amiable,'" in *Les manuscrits économiques de François Quesnay et du marquis de Mirabeau aux Archives nationales (M. 778 à M. 785)*, ed. Georges Weulersse (Paris: Paul Geuthner, 1910), 102. For the second quotation, see Buffon, "Le lièvre," in *HN* (1756), 6:248–50. Also see Quesnay in Weulersse, *Les manuscrits économiques*, 122.

31. See Anne C. Vila, *Enlightenment and Pathology: Sensibility in the Literature and Medicine of Eighteenth-Century France* (Baltimore: Johns Hopkins University Press, 1998); and Jessica Riskin, *Science in the Age of Sensibility: The Sentimental Empiricists of the French Enlightenment* (Chicago: University of Chicago Press, 2002).

32. Haigh, "Vitalism, the Soul, and Sensibility," 40. Also see Thomson, "L'homme machine"; Kaitaro, *Diderot's Holism*; and Timo Kaitaro, "Can Matter Mark the Hours? Eighteenth-Century Vital Materialism and Functional Properties," *Science in Context* 12, no. 4 (2008): 581–92.

33. My idea of ontological images of nature is similar to Blumenberg's about metaphors, images, and nonconceptual thought in the development of ideas, Gordon's ideas of a normative image of humanity, and Tresch's idea of cosmograms. Hans Blumenberg, *Shipwreck with Spectator: Paradigm of a Metaphor for Existence*, trans. Steven Rendall (Cambridge, MA: MIT Press, 2009); Peter E. Gordon, *Continental Divide: Heidegger, Cassirer, Davos* (Cambridge, MA: Harvard University Press, 2010); John Tresch, *The Romantic Machines: Utopian Science and Technology after Napoleon* (Chicago: University of Chicago Press, 2012); and John Tresch, "Technological World-Pictures: Cosmic Things and Cosmograms," *ISIS* 98, no. 1 (2007): 84–99.

34. Eduard Jan Dijksterhuis, *The Mechanization of the World Picture*, trans. C. Dikshoorn (Oxford: Clarendon, 1961).

35. For his insightful take on the harmonic view of reality, see Reill, *Vitalizing Nature*.

36. On mediation and Enlightenment vitalism, see Reill.

37. Denis Diderot and Pierre Tarin, "Anatomie," in *Encyclopédie* (1751), 1:410; and Denis Diderot, *Éléments de physiologie* (1778), in *OC*, ed. Herbert Dieckmann and Jean Varloot (Paris: Hermann, 1987), 17:337.

38. The reference is to Boerhaave, who drew on the Hippocratic and Galenic sense of interconnection; see La Caze, *Idée de l'homme physique et moral*, 68.

39. Buffon, "Le buffle, le bonasus, l'aurochs, le bison et le zebu," in *HN* (1764), 11:290. On interconnection, interdependence, and circularity, also see Pierre-Jean-Georges Cabanis, *Coup d'œil sur les révolutions et sur la réforme de la médecine* (Year XII [1804]), in *OP*, 2:209.

40. Immanuel Kant, *Critique of the Power of Judgment* (1790), ed. Paul Guyer, trans. Paul Guyer and Eric Matthews (Cambridge: Cambridge University Press, 2000).

41. Reill, *Vitalizing Nature*, 129–42. Also see Eric Schliesser, ed., *Sympathy: A History* (Oxford: Oxford University Press, 2015).

42. On "quasi-teleology," see Sheehan and Wahrman, *Invisible Hands*, 148. On Kant and the life sciences, see James L. Larson, "Vital Forces: Regulative Principles or Constitutive Agents? A Strategy in German Physiology, 1760–1802," *Isis* 70, no. 2 (June 1979): 235–49; Lenoir, "Kant, Blumenbach, and Vital Materialism"; John Zammito, *The Genesis of Kant's Critique of Judgment* (Chicago: University of Chicago Press, 1992), 189–227; Philippe Huneman, *Métaphysique et biologie: Kant et la constitution du concept d'organisme* (Paris: Éditions Kimé, 2008); and Zammito, *Gestation*.

43. On the microcosm-macrocosm connections, see Foucault, *Order of Things*; on the body's mirroring, see Leonard Barkan, *Nature's Work of Art: The Human Body as Image of the World* (New Haven, CT: Yale University Press, 1975); and Jonathan Sawday,

The Body Emblazoned: Dissection and the Human Body in Renaissance Culture (New York: Routledge, 1995).

44. Justin E. H. Smith, *Divine Machines: Leibniz and the Sciences of Life* (Princeton, NJ: Princeton University Press, 2011), 144. Also see Catherine Wilson, *The Invisible World: Early Modern Philosophy and the Invention of the Microscope* (Princeton, NJ: Princeton University Press, 1995); and François Duchesneau, *Les modèles du vivant de Descartes à Leibniz* (Paris: Vrin, 1998).

45. Ohad Nachtomy, Ayelet Shavit, and Justin Smith, "Leibnizian Organisms, Nested Individuals, and Units of Selection," *Theory in Biosciences* 121, no. 2 (August 2002): 205–30; Pauline Phemister, *Leibniz and the Natural World: Activity, Passivity and Corporeal Substance in Leibniz Philosophy* (Dordrecht: Springer, 2005), 81–103; Smith, *Divine Machines*, 137–61.

46. See Duchesneau, *Les modèles du vivant.*

47. Abbé Étienne Bonnot de Condillac, *Traité des systêmes*, in *Œuvres philosophiques*, ed. Georges Le Roy (Paris: Presses Universitaires de France, 1947), 164.

48. Charles Bonnet, *Contemplation de la nature*, 2nd ed. (Amsterdam: Rey, 1769), 1:235. See also, Diderot, "Imperceptible," in *Encyclopédie* (1765), 8:589; and Diderot, *Éléments de physiologie*, 17:323.

49. Jean-Baptiste-René Robinet, *De la Nature* (1761–68; Paris: Honoré Champion, 2009), 2:892.

50. Needham's appreciation for Lebiniz is often overlooked. See John Turberville Needham, *Nouvelles observations microscopiques* (Paris: L.-E. Ganeau, 1750), 263; and John Turberville Needham, *Nouvelles recherches physiques et métaphysiques sur la nature et la religion, avec une nouvelle théorie de la terre* (London: Lacombe, 1769), 146–48.

51. Thomas Reid, *Thomas Reid on Animate Creation: Papers Relating to the Life Sciences*, ed. Paul Wood (Edinburgh: Edinburgh University Press, 1995), 89.

52. Louis Bourget, correspondent of Leibniz and Buffon (through an intermediary), believed that inanimate matter such as salt crystals also demonstrated organization. See Roger, *Buffon*, 124–25. With some reservations, also see Joseph Schiller, "La notion d'organisation dans l'oeuvre de Louis Bourguet (1678–1742)," *Gesnerus* 32 (1975): 87–97.

53. Diderot, *Rêve*, 298. Also see Jean-Jacques [Jean-Joseph] Ménuret de Chambaud, "Pouls," in *Encyclopédie* (1765), 13:240.

54. Buffon, "Histoire des animaux," in *HN* (1749), 2:19 and 24.

55. Buffon, 2:19.

56. Diderot, *Éléments de physiologie*, 17:310–11.

57. See Rey, *Naissance*; Duchesneau, *La physiologie des lumières*; and Tobias Cheung, "Omnis Fibra ex Fibra: Fibre Œconomies in Bonnet's and Diderot's Models of Organic Order," in Cheung, *Transitions and Borders between Animals, Humans and Machines*, 66–104.

58. For example, in addition to Diderot, the Montpellier physicians Bordeu, La Caze, Ménuret, and Fouquet, all adopted the idea, see Rey, *Naissance*, 158.

59. Mr. D. G. [Jean-Charles-Marguerite Guillaume de Grimaud], *Essai sur l'irritabilité* (Avignon: Bonnet frères, 1776), 12, quoted by Philippe Huneman, "'Animal Economy': Anthropology and the Rise of Psychiatry from the *Encyclopédie* to the Alienists,"

in Larry Wolff and Marco Cipolloni, eds., *The Anthropology of the Enlightenment* (Stanford, CA: Stanford University Press, 2007), 390, note 2. On Grimaud and how his thoughts evolved, see Elizabeth A. Williams, "Of Two Lives or One? Jean-Charles-Marguerite Guillaume Grimaud and the Question of Holism in Medical Vitalism," *Science in Context* 21, no. 4 (2008): 593–613.

60. Diderot, *Éléments de physiologie*, 17:296.

61. A. O. Lovejoy, *The Great Chain of Being: A Study of the History of an Idea* (Cambridge, MA: Harvard University Press, 1936).

62. Jean-Jacques [Jean-Joseph] Ménuret de Chambaud, "Spasme," in *Encyclopédie* (1765), 15:435; and Sieyès, "Analyse des actes," quoted and translated in Murray Forsyth, *Reason and Revolution: The Political Thought of the Abbé Sieyès* (Leicester: Leicester University Press, 1987), 45. For a distinct, yet related, idea of man as a modifiable "composite," see Jean-Jacque Rousseau, *Émile, première version (manuscrit Favre)*, in *OC*, 4:55–60.

63. On the change to this model of the human, see Moravia, "From *Homme Machine* to *Homme Sensible*."

64. Annabel S. Brett, *Changes of State: Nature and the Limits of the City in Early Modern Natural Law* (Princeton, NJ: Princeton University Press, 2011), 142.

65. Ferdinand Brunot, *Histoire de la langue française: Des origins à nos jours*, vol. 9, part 2 (Paris: Armand Colin, 1967), 721–24.

66. For the history and historiography of the corporate structure of old regime society, see Gail Bossenga, "Estates, Orders, Corps," in *The Oxford Handbook of the Ancien Régime*, ed. William Doyle (Oxford: Oxford University Press, 2011), 141–66.

67. Henri de Lubac, *Corpus Mysticum: The Eucharist and the Church in the Middle Ages*, trans. Gemma Simmonds (Notre Dame, IN: University of Notre Dame Press, 2007); Ernst Kantorowicz, *The King's Two Bodies: A Study of Mediaeval Political Theology* (Princeton, NJ: Princeton University Press, 1957); Paul Friedland, *Political Actors: Representative Bodies and Theatricality in the Age of the French Revolution* (Ithaca, NY: Cornell University Press, 2002), 29–51; and Graham Hammill and Julia Reinhard Lupton, eds., *Political Theology and Early Modernity* (Chicago: University of Chicago Press, 2012).

68. On funeral ritual, see Ralph E. Giesey, *The Royal Funeral Ceremony in Renaissance France* (Geneva: Droz, 1960); on eucharistic model of king's image, see Louis Marin, *Portrait of the King* (Minneapolis: University of Minnesota Press, 1988).

69. For important articulations of the theologicopolitical argument, see Claude Lefort, "The Permanence of the Theologico-Political," in *Democracy and Political Theory*, trans. David Macey (Minneapolis: University of Minnesota Press, 1988); and Marcel Gauchet, *Disenchantment of the World: A Political History of Religion*, trans. Oscar Burge (Princeton, NJ: Princeton University Press, 1997). Lefort's argument was assimilated into the "revisionist" interpretation of the Revolution through the work of François Furet, albeit after undergoing its own sublimation, which partially effaced the origins of this argument. On Lefort and Furet, see Samuel Moyn, "On the Intellectual Origins of François Furet's Masterpiece," *Tocqueville Review* 29, no. 2 (2008): 59–78. On the relation of modern and early modern arguments of political theology, see Hammill and Lupton, *Political Theology and Early Modernity*.

70. On the "empty place," see Lefort, *Democracy and Political Theory*; and Eric L. Santner, *The Royal Remains: The People's Two Bodies and the Endgames of Sovereignty* (Chicago: University of Chicago Press, 2011).

71. See Phillip R. Sloan, "From Logical Universals to Historical Individuals: Buffon's Idea of Biological Species," in *Histoire du concept d'espèce dans les sciences de la vie*, ed. Scott Atran et al. (Paris: Foundation Singer-Polignac, 1987), 101–40; Phillip R. Sloan, "Natural History," in Knud Haakonssen, ed., *The Cambridge History of Eighteenth-Century Philosophy* (New York: Cambridge University Press, 2005), 2:911–24; Jacques Roger, *Buffon: A Life in Natural History*, trans. Sarah Lucille Bonnefoi, ed. L. Pearce Williams (Ithaca, NY: Cornell University Press, 1997); and Paul Lawrence Farber, "Buffon and the Concept of Species," *Journal of the History of Biology* 5, no. 2 (1972): 259–84.

72. See Phillip R. Sloan, "The Gaze of Natural History," in Christopher Fox, Roy Porter, and Robert Wokler, eds., *Inventing Human Science: Eighteenth-Century Domains* (Berkeley: University of California Press, 1995); Sloan, "Natural History"; Roger, *Buffon*; and James Llana, "Natural History and the *Encyclopédie*," in *Journal of the History of Biology* 33 (2000): 1–25.

73. Sloan, "From Logical Universals to Historical Individuals."

74. Buffon, "De la nature: Seconde vue," in *HN* (1764), 13:i–xx.

75. On the Pascalian precedent, see Hans Blumenberg, *Paradigms for a Metaphorology*, trans. Robert Savage (Ithaca, NY: Cornell University Press, 2010), 59–60.

76. Buffon, "Première discours: De la manière d'étudier & de traiter l'histoire naturelle," in *HN* (1749), 1:4.

77. Buffon, 1:4.

78. See Pierre Hadot, *What Is Ancient Philosophy?*, trans. Michael Chase (Cambridge, MA: Harvard University Press, 2002); and Pierre Hadot, *Philosophy as a Way of Life*, trans. Michael Chase (Malden, MA: Blackwell, 1995).

79. Buffon, "De la nature: Seconde vue," 13:iv.

80. Buffon, 13:iv.

81. On the physiocrats, the *tableau*, and eighteenth-century political economy, see Simone Meyssonier, *La balance et l'horloge: La genèse de la pensée libérale en France au XVIIIe siècle* (Montreuil: Editions de la Passion, 1989); Liana Vardi, *The Physiocrats and the World of the Enlightenment* (Cambridge: Cambridge University Press, 2012); and William Max Nelson, *The Time of Enlightenment: Constructing the Future in France, 1750 to Year One* (Toronto: University of Toronto Press, 2021), 60–94.

82. See Vardi, *Physiocrats*, 21, 81–82; and Nelson, *Time of Enlightenment*, 86–92.

83. On the economy not yet being a distinct and autonomous sphere, see Catherine Larrère, *L'invention de l'économie au XVIIIe siècle: Du droit naturel a la physiocratie* (Paris: Presses Universitaires de France, 1992), 6. On the beginning of a holistic reading of the *tableau* and the physiocrats in Marx and Schumpeter, see Louis Dumont, *From Mandeville to Marx: The Genesis and Triumph of Economic Ideology* (Chicago: University of Chicago Press, 1977), 40–46.

84. François Quesnay, "Sur les travaux des artisans: second dialogue," originally in *Journal d'agriculture* (November 1766), reprinted in *François Quesnay et la physiocratie* (Paris: INED, 1958), 2:886.

85. Quesnay, "Sur les travaux," 908–9.

86. Quesnay to Mirabeau, no date, M. 784, no. 70², AN; also included in the original French in Stephen Bauer, "Quesnay's *Tableau Économique*," *Economic Journal* 5, no. 17 (March 1895): 21.

87. Quesnay to Mirabeau, no date, M. 784, no. 70², AN; also included in the original French in Bauer, "Quesnay's *Tableau Économique*," 21.

88. Victor Riqueti, marquis de Mirabeau [and François Quesnay], "Tableau Œconomique avec ses explications," in *L'ami des hommes, ou traité de la population* (1760) 6:1–228 (separate pagination), 21–22.

89. "Avertissement de l'auteur," *Ephémérides du citoyen* 1 (1767): 23–24.

90. See Gustave Schelle, *Le docteur Quesnay* (Paris: Felix Alcan, 1907), 15–17; and Jacqueline Hecht, "La Vie de François Quesnay," in *François Quesnay et la Physiocratie*, 1:215.

91. See, for example, V. Foley, "An Origin of the Tableau Economique," *History of Political Economy* 5, no. 1 (1973): 121–50; Paul P. Christensen, "Fire, Motion, and Productivity: The Proto-energetics of Nature and Economy in François Quesnay," in *Natural Images in Economic Thought: "Markets Read in Tooth and Claw,"* ed. Philip Mirowski (New York: Cambridge University Press, 1994), 249–88; and H. Spencer Banzhaf, "Productive Nature and the Net Product: Quesnay's Economies Animal and Political," *History of Political Economy* 32, no. 3 (2000): 517–51.

92. Christensen, "Fire, Motion"; Banzhaf, "Productive Nature"; and Vardi, *Physiocrats*.

93. Roger, *Life Sciences*; Duchesneau, *La physiologie des lumières*; and Rey, *Naissance*.

94. François Quesnay, *Essai physique sur l'œconomie animale*, 2nd ed. rev. (Paris: Cavelier, 1747). Also see Christensen, "Fire, Motion." On medical ideas of animating fire, see Roger French, "Ether and Physiology," in *Conceptions of Ether: Studies in the History of Ether Theories, 1740–1900*, ed. G. N. Cantor and M. J. S. Hodge (Cambridge: Cambridge University Press, 1981), 111–34.

95. The addressee of the letter is not entirely clear. Importantly, however, Quesnay expressed a shared position on the inadequacy of the mechanical philosophy for physiological understanding. François Quesnay letter, January 16, 1755, in François Quesnay, *Oeuvres économiques complètes et autres textes*, ed. Christine Théré, Loïc Charles, and Jean-Claude Perrot (Paris: INED, 2005) 2:1169–70.

96. On Sauvages, see Roger French, "Sauvages, Whytt, and the Motion of the Heart," in *Clio Medica* 7 (1972): 35–54; Roger French, "Sickness and the Soul: Stahl, Hoffman and Sauvages on Pathology," in *The Medical Enlightenment of the Eighteenth Century*, ed. Andrew Cunningham and Roger French (Cambridge: Cambridge University Press, 1990); Rey, *Naissance*; and Elizabeth A. Williams, *A Cultural History of Medical Vitalism in Enlightenment Montpellier* (Burlington, VT: Ashgate, 2003).

97. Quesnay owned books by many other organization theorists; see "Inventaire et Liquidation après le decés [*sic*] de M. François Quesnay," December 29, 1774, series 3E 45/158, Étude Huber de Versailles, Archives départementales des Yvelines, Yvelines, France.

98. Victor Riqueti, marquis de Mirabeau, *Précis sur l'organisation, ou Mémoire sur les états provinciaux* (1750), vol. 4 of *L'ami des hommes, ou Traité de la population* (Avignon, 1758).

99. Victor Riqueti, marquis de Mirabeau, and François Quesnay, *Traité de la monarchie*, ed. Gino Longhitano (Paris: L'Harmattan, 1999), 40, 74, and 181n409. This work was cowritten between 1757 and 1759 but not published until this edition. See Quesnay's substitution of the technical term "sensible" for "sensitive" and "organized body" for "organized state," 34, 181.

100. Victor Riqueti, marquis de Mirabeau [and Quensay], *Philosophie rurale* (Amsterdam, 1763), 118.

101. Mirabeau [and Quensay], 118.

102. Mirabeau [and Quensay], xviii.

103. Mirabeau [and Quensay], xix.

104. Mirabeau [and Quensay], xviii–xix.

105. Mirabeau [and Quensay], xix.

106. Also see Pierre-Paul Mercier de la Rivière, *Les vœux d'un françois, ou Considérations sur les principaux objets dont le Roi et le Nation vont s'occuper* (n.p., 1788), 26–27.

107. Pierre-Samuel Dupont de Nemours, "Memoires sur les Municipalités" (September 1775), in *Carl Friedrichs von Baden: Brieflicher Verkehr mit Mirabeau und Du Pont*, ed. Carl Knies (Heidelberg: Carl Winter's Universitätsbuchhandlung, 1892), 2:245.

108. Dupont de Nemours, 245.

109. Dupont de Nemours, 246. On theological ideas about the role of the particular will and the "general will" in God's rule, see Patrick Riley, *The General Will before Rousseau: The Transformation of the Divine into the Civic* (Princeton, NJ: Princeton University Press, 1987).

110. Guillaume-François Le Trosne, *De l'administration provinciale, et de la réforme de l'impôt* (1779; Basel, 1780).

111. Le Trosne, *De l'administration provinciale*, 124.

112. Guillaume-François Le Trosne, *De l'ordre social* (Paris: De Bure, 1777), 277.

113. David William Bates, *States of War: Enlightenment Origins of the Political* (New York: Columbia University Press, 2012), 171–214. Bates ultimately sees in Rousseau "a certain *cybernetic* form of order" that underwrites his vision of a "cybernetic political body" (172).

114. Jean-Jacques Rousseau, *Du contrat social, ou Principes du droit politique*, in *OC*, 3:347–470.

115. For a critique of thinking matter (hylozoism) and doubts about the existence of organic molecules, see Rousseau, *Lettre à M. de Franquières* (posthumous, 1782), in *OC*, 4:1140. Also see the thoughts expressed by the character of the Savoyard Vicar in *Émile*, in *OC*, 4:573–86.

116. For earlier organic interpretations, see C. E. Vaughan, "Introduction," in Rousseau, *Du contrat social* (Manchester: Manchester University Press, 1918), xxviii–

xxix; Robert Derathé, *Jean-Jacques Rousseau et la sciences politique de son temps* (Paris: Presses universitaires de France, 1950), 410–13; and Judith Schlanger, *Les métaphores de l'organisme* (Paris: Vrin, 1971), 135–36. Vaughan famously and influentially argued that for Rousseau, contract theory "forms the porch to a collectivism as absolute as the mind of man has ever conceived. . . . In the *Contrat Social* he sets himself to prove it by every argument at his command." C. E. Vaughan, ed., *The Political Writings of Jean Jacques Rousseau* (Cambridge: Cambridge University Press, 1915), 1:39.

117. Rousseau, *Discours sur l'économie politique*, in *OC*, 3:241–78.

118. Rousseau, 3:244.

119. On the medieval uses of the metaphor, particularly the foundational articulation by John of Salisbury, see Tilman Struve, *Die Entwicklung der organologischen Staatsauffassung im Mittealter* (Stuutgart: Hiersemann, 1978). On early modern articulations, see Arlette Jouanna, *Le devoir de revolté: La noblesse française et la gestation de l'État moderne (1559–1661)* (Paris: Fayard, 1989), 281–312; and Jonathan Gil Harris, *Foreign Bodies and the Body Politic: Discourses of Social Pathology in Early Modern England* (Cambridge: Cambridge University Press, 1998).

120. Rousseau, *Discours sur l'économie politique*, 3:245.

121. Rousseau, *Du contrat social*, 3:369–70.

122. See Leo Damrosch, *Jean-Jacques Rousseau: Relentless Genius* (Boston: Houghton Mifflin, 2005); Rousseau to Paul-Claude Moultou (October 10, 1768, and December 12, 1768), *Correspondance complète de Jean Jacques Rousseau*, ed. R. A. Leigh (Oxford: Voltaire Foundation, 1980), 36:143, 202; Henry Cheyron, "Ray and Sauvages annotés par Jean-Jacques Rousseau," *Littératures* 15 (1986): 83–99; and *Dictionaire de Jean-Jacques Rousseau* (Paris: Honoré Champion, 1996), 589.

123. See the entry "Médicine de Montpellier," in *Dictionaire de Jean-Jacques Rousseau*, 589–90. Rousseau was aware of Bordeu, although in one case he was highly critical of Bordeu's prescribed regime for a sick patient. Jean-Jacques Rousseau, *Les confessions de J. J. Rousseau*, in *OC*, 1:550. Also see *Correspondance complète de Jean Jacques Rousseau* (Geneva: Institute et musée Voltaire, 1972), 15:116.

124. Rousseau wrote one of his operas at the same time as he studied chemistry with Rouelle. Rousseau, *Les confessions*, 1:293–95.

125. Jean-Jacques Rousseau, "Unité de mélodie," in *OC*, 5:1143–46.

126. Rousseau, 5:1144.

127. On theological ideas of "general will," see Riley, *General Will before Rousseau*. On Rousseau, and quietist self-abandon more generally, see Charly Coleman, *The Virtues of Abandon: An Anti-individualist History of the French Enlightenment* (Stanford, CA: Stanford University Press, 2014). Curiously, Riley twice acknowledged the similarity between Rousseau's ideas of generality in politics and his writing on organized bodies, yet he left the similarity undeveloped in the first instance, and he completely subsumed it under the intellectual influence of Malebranche in the second. The theological reading must be reassessed in light of the organanismic reading. See Patrick Riley, *Kant's Political Philosophy* (Totowa, NJ: Rowman and Littlefield, 1983), 72–73; and Patrick Riley, "The General Will before Rousseau: The Contributions of Arnauld, Pascal, Malebranche, Bayle, and Bossuet," in *The General Will: The Evolution*

of a Concept, ed. James Farr and David Lay Williams (New York: Cambridge University Press, 2015), 54–56.

128. Jean-Jacques Rousseau, *Institutions chimiques*, ed. Bruno Bernardi and Bernadette Bensaude-Vincent (Paris: Fayard, 1999), 60. For more on Rousseau and chemistry, see Bruno Bernardi and Bernadette Bensaude-Vincent, eds., *Rousseau et le sciences* (Paris: L'Harmattan, 2003); and Bruno Bernarndi, *La fabrique des concepts: Recherches sur l'invention conceptuelle chez Rousseau* (Paris: Honoré Champion, 2006).

129. Rousseau, *Institutions chimiques*, 63, 62, 60.

130. Rousseau, *Lettre à M. de Franquières*, 4:1140.

131. Jean-Jacques Rousseau, *Fragments du Botanique*, in *OC*, 4:1249–50.

132. Rousseau, *Du contrat social*, 3:362.

133. Rousseau, 3:362.

134. Rousseau, 3:360.

135. Rousseau, 3:361.

136. Rousseau, *Émile*, 4:249.

137. Rousseau, 4:249.

138. Rousseau, 4:249. Also see Rousseau, *Discours sur l'économie politique*, 3:259–60.

139. Jean-Jacques Rousseau, *Rousseau Juge de Jean-Jacques: Dialogues*, in *OC*, 1:813.

140. Rousseau, *Du contrat social, ou Essai sur la forme de la république (première version)*, in *OC*, 3:283.

141. Rousseau, 3:284.

142. Rousseau, 3:284. For more on chemistry in Rousseau's writing and political theory, see Bernardi, *La Fabrique des concepts*.

143. Rousseau, *Du contrat social . . . (première version)*, 3:284.

144. On Rousseau and the discourse of abandon, see Coleman, *Virtues of Abandon*, 203–47. On Dumas and the of the term "vitalism," see Rey, *Naissance*.

145. Charles-Louis Dumas, *Principes de physiologie, ou Introduction à la science expérimentale philosophique et médicale de l'homme vivant* (Paris: Deterville, 1800), 1:265. On this point on Dumas and Rousseau, see Reill, *Vitalizing Nature*, 138. For another example of this type of body politic and animal body being analogized by a Montpellier vitalist, see Pierre Roussel, *Éloge historique de M. de Bordeu* (Paris: Ruault, 1778), 4–5. Roussel was a student of Bordeu, and he built on some of Rousseau's ideas of the difference between the sexes in his *Système physique et moral de la femme, ou Tableau philosophique de la constitution, de l'état organique, du tempérament, des mœurs, & des fonctions propres au sexe* (Paris: Vincent, 1775).

146. On organization in political thought after the eighteenth century, see Sheldon Wolin, *Politics and Vision: Continuity and Innovation in Western Political Thought* (Boston: Little, Brown, 1960), chap. 10. On modern organizational thought drawing on "organization" in the sense of an organism, see Jackie Clarke, *France in the Age of Organization: Factory, Home and Nation from 1920s to Vichy* (New York: Berghahn Books, 2011).

147. *Dictionaire de l'Académie française*, 4th ed. (Paris: Bernard Brunet, 1762).

148. "Organisation," in *Encyclopédie* (1765), 11:629.

149. *Dictionaire de l'Académie française*, 5th ed. (Paris: J. J. Smits, 1798).

150. David Williams, *Biographical Anecdotes of the Leaders of the French Republic and of Other Eminent Characters, Who Have Distinguished Themselves in the Progress of the Revolution* (London: R. Phillips, 1798), 2:11.

151. See David Williams, *Egeria, or Elementary Studies on the Progress of Nations in Political Œconomy, Legislation, and Government* (London: Cadell and Davies, 1803); and David Williams, *Preparatory Studies for Political Reformers* (London: Baldwin, 1810). Also see J. Dybikowski, *On Burning Ground: An Examination of the Ideas, Projects and Life of David Williams* (Oxford: Voltaire Foundation, 1993), 190–93; and Sonenscher, *Sans-Culottes*, 42–46, 352.

152. On disease and the *corpus mysticum* in the sixteenth century, see Friedland, *Political Actors*, 45–46.

153. See Johan Heilbron, *The Rise of Social Theory*, trans. Sheila Gogol (Cambridge: Polity, 1995); Dominique Guillo, *Les figures de l'organisation: Sciences de la vie et sciences sociales au XIXe siècle* (Paris: Presses Universitaires de France, 2003); and Claude Blanckaert, *La nature de la société: Organicisme et sciences sociales au XIXe siècle* (Paris: Harmattan, 2004).

154. Foucault, *Order of Things*. On organismic, organic, and vitalist ideas in Romanticism, see Denis Gigante, *Life: Organic Form and Romanticism* (New Haven, CT: Yale University Press, 2009); David Fairer, *Organising Poetry: The Coleridge Circle, 1790–1798* (Oxford: Oxford University Press, 2009); and Robert Mitchell, *Experimental Life: Vitalism in Romantic Science and Literature* (Baltimore: Johns Hopkins University Press, 2013).

CHAPTER TWO

1. Jean-Baptiste-René Robinet, *De la nature*, 5 vols. (Amsterdam, 1761–68); and Jean-Baptiste-René Robinet, *Considérations philosophiques de la gradation naturelle des formes de l'être, ou Les essais de la nature qui apprend à faire l'homme* (Paris, 1768). Also see Terence Murphy, "Jean Baptiste René Robinet: The Career of a Man of Letters," *SVEC* 150 (1976): 183–250; Jacques Roger, *Les sciences de la vie dans la pensée francaise du XVIIe siécle* (Paris: A. Colin, 1963), 642–51; and A. O. Lovejoy, *The Great Chain of Being: A Study of the History of an Idea* (Cambridge, MA: Harvard University Press, 1936), 269–82.

2. "Espèce humaine: Des causes de la dégradation de l'espèce humaine," in Jean-Baptiste-René Robinet, ed., *Dictionnaire universel des sciences morale, économique, politique et diplomatique, ou Bibliothèque de l'Homme-d'Etat et du Citoyen* (1781), 18:343.

3. Plato, *The Republic*, trans. R. E. Allen (New Haven, CT: Yale University Press, 2006), 160–64 (459a–462a); and Tommaso Campanella, *The City of the Sun: A Poetical Dialogue* (1623), trans. Daniel J. Donno (Berkeley: University of California Press, 1981).

4. Anne C. Vila, *Enlightenment and Pathology: Sensibility in the Literature and Medicine of Eighteenth-Century France* (Baltimore: Johns Hopkins University Press, 1998); Michael E. Winston, *From Perfectibility to Perversion: Meliorism in Eighteenth-Century*

France (New York: Peter Lang, 2005); Sean M. Quinlan, *The Great Nation in Decline: Sex, Modernity and Health Crises in Revolutionary France, c. 1750–1850* (Aldershot: Ashgate, 2007); Mark Harrison, "'The Tender Frame of Man': Disease, Climate, and Racial Difference in India and the West Indies, 1760–1860," *Bulletin of the History of Medicine* 70, no. 1 (1996): 68–93; Roxann Wheeler, *The Complexion of Race: Categories of Difference in Eighteenth-Century British Culture* (Philadelphia: University of Pennsylvania Press, 2000); and Katy L. Chiles, *Transformable Race: Surprising Metamorphoses in the Literature of Early America* (Oxford: Oxford University Press, 2014).

5. On climate theory and Buffonian ideas as they relate to human breeding, see Michèle Duchet, "Du noir au blanc, ou La cinquième génération," in Léon Poliakov, ed., *Le couple interdit, entretiens sur le racisme: La dialectique de l'altérité socio-culturelle et la sexualité* (Paris, Mouton, 1980), 177–90; E. C. Spary, *Utopia's Garden: French Natural History from Old Regime to Revolution* (Chicago: University of Chicago Press, 2000), 99–154; Claude-Olivier Doron, *L'homme altéré: Races et dégénérescence (XVIIᵉ–XIXᵉ siècles)* (Ceyzérieu: Champ Vallon, 2016).

6. Charles-Augustin Vandermonde, *Essai sur la manière de perfectionner l'espèce humaine*, 2 vols. (Paris: Vincent, 1756), 1:94.

7. See Nicholas Russell, *Like Engend'ring Like: Heredity and Animal Breeding in Early Modern England* (Cambridge: Cambridge University Press, 1986); Mary Terrall, "Speculation and Experiment in Enlightenment Life Sciences," in Staffan Müller-Wille and Hans-Jörg Rheinberger, *Heredity Produced: At the Crossroads of Biology, Politics, and Culture, 1500–1870* (Cambridge, MA: MIT, 2007), 253–75; Mary Terrall, *The Man Who Flattened the Earth: Maupertuis and the Sciences in the Enlightenment* (Chicago: University of Chicago Press, 2002), 199–230, 310–48. On the royal stud farm in France, see Jacques Mulliez, *Les chevaux du royaume: Histoire de l'élevage du cheval et de la création des haras* (Paris: Montalba, 1983); and Doron, *L'homme altéré*. On Renaissance ideas of breeding, see Mackenzie Cooley, *The Perfection of Nature: Animals, Breeding, and Race in the Renaissance* (Chicago: University of Chicago Press, 2022).

8. On Maupertuis, see Jacques Roger, *The Life Sciences in Eighteenth-Century French Thought*, ed. Keith R. Benson, trans. Robert Ellrich (Stanford, CA: Stanford University Press, 1997), 369–94, 439–41; and Terrall, *Man Who Flattened the Earth*, 199–230, 310–48.

9. By 1780, Buffon's *Natural History* appears to have been the third most owned book in France. See Daniel Mornet, "Les enseignements des bibliothèques privées (1750–1780)," *Revue d'histoire littéraire de la France* 17 (1910): 449–96. Also see Jacques Roger, *Buffon: A Life in Natural History*, trans. Sarah Lucille Bonnefoi, ed. L. Pearce Williams (Ithaca, NY: Cornell University Press, 1997); and Maëlle Levacher, *Buffon et ses lecteurs: Les complicités de l'Histoire naturelle* (Paris: Classiques Garnier, 2011).

10. See Roger, *Buffon*, 116–50; and Peter Hanns Reill, *Vitalizing Nature in the Enlightenment* (Berkeley: University of California Press, 2005), 33–70. On reproduction in the eighteenth century, see Ludmilla Jordanova, "Interrogating the Concept of Reproduction in the Eighteenth Century," in *Conceiving the New World Order: Global Politics of Reproduction*, ed. Faye Ginsburg and Rayna Rapp (Berkeley: University of California Press, 1995), 369–86; and Raymond Stephanson and Darren N. Wagner, eds., *The Secrets of Generation: Reproduction in the Long Eighteenth Century* (Toronto: University of Toronto Press, 2015).

11. Roger, *Buffon*, 130.

12. See William Max Nelson, *The Time of Enlightenment: Constructing the Future in France, 1750 to Year One* (Toronto: University of Toronto Press, 2021), 97–103, 110–16.

13. On horse interbreeding, see Buffon, "Variétés dans l'espèce humaine," in *HN* (1749), 3:529. On the breeding experiments at Montbard, see the notes by Buffon's secretary Trécourt, "Suite des observations faites par Trécourt sur les Loups cines [sic] en 1776," handwritten report, MS 865, fol. 2, Bibliothèque centrale du Muséum national d'histoire naturelle, Paris; and see Trécourt, "Des loups Chiens par Trécourt, Du mûle 1re Génération né le 6 Juin 1778," handwritten report, MS 865, fol. 1, Bibliothèque centrale du Muséum national d'histoire naturelle, Paris.

14. Buffon, "Le chien," in *HN* (1755), 5:195.

15. See, for example, Buffon, "Le cheval," in *HN* (1753), 4:216–17.

16. On regenerating French domestic sheep through breeding, see Buffon, "De la dégénération des animaux," in *HN* (1766), 14:319–20.

17. Buffon, "Le chien," 5:195.

18. Buffon, "De la dégénération des animaux," 14:313.

19. Buffon, 14:314.

20. Buffon, 14:313.

21. See Roger, *Life Sciences*, 466; Claude Blanckaert, "Les conditions d'émergence de la science des races au début du XIXe siècle," in Sarga Moussa, ed., *L'idée de "race" dans les sciences humaines et la littérature (XVIIIe–XIXe siècles)* (Paris: L'Harmattan, 2003), 138; Phillip R. Sloan, "The Idea of Racial Degeneracy in Buffon's *Histoire Naturelle*," *Studies in Eighteenth-Century Culture* 3 (1973): 308–9; John H. Eddy Jr., "Buffon, Organic Alterations, and Man," *Studies in the History of Biology* 7 (1984): 31; and Pierre H. Boulle, "In Defense of Slavery: Eighteenth-Century Opposition to Abolition and the Origins of Racist Ideology in France," in Frederick Krantz, ed., *History from Below: Studies in Popular Protest and Popular Ideology* (Oxford: Oxford University Press, 1988), 225. Duchet's work on Buffon is the notable exception; see Michèle Duchet, *Anthropologie et histoire au siècle des Lumières* (Paris: Albin Michel, 1995), 229–80; and Duchet, "Du noir au blanc."

22. Georges-Louis Leclerc, comte de Buffon, *Correspondance générale*, ed. Henri Nadault de Buffon (Geneva: Slatkine, 1971 [reprint of 1885 ed.]), 173n1.

23. Buffon, "Varitétés des l'espèce humaine," in *HN* (1749) 3:528–29.

24. See Roger, *Buffon*; and Levacher, *Buffon et ses lecteurs*. On new treatises aimed at improving animals through breeding, such as Claude Bourgelat's work on horses and the work on sheep by Claude Carlier and the marquis de Puismarais, see André J. Bourde, *Agronomie et agronomes en France au XVIIe siècle* (Paris: S.E.V.P.E.N., 1967); Mulliez, *Les chevaux du royaume*; and Doron, *L'homme altéré*, 204–18.

25. Spary, *Utopia's Garden*, 110; André J. Bourde, *Agronomie et agronomes en France au XVIIe siècle* (Paris: S.E.V.P.E.N., 1967); Louis Roule, *Daubenton et l'exploitation de la nature* (Paris: Flammarion, 1925), 109–33.

26. Louis-Jean-Marie Daubenton, "Mémoire sur le mécanisme de la rumination, et sur le tempérament des bêtes à laine," *Mémoires de l'Académie royale des sciences,*

hereafter *MARS* (1767; Paris: Imprimerie Royale, 1770 [presented on April 13, 1768]): 389–98; Louis-Jean-Marie Daubenton, "Observations sur des bêtes à laine parquées pendant toute l'année," *MARS* (1772; Paris: Imprimerie Royale, 1775 [presented on November 15, 1769]): 436–44; Louis-Jean-Marie Daubenton, "Mémoire sur l'amélioration des bêtes à laine," *MARS* (1777; Paris: Imprimerie Royale, 1780 [presented on April 9, 1777]): 79–87; Louis-Jean-Marie Daubenton, "Mémoire sur les remèdes les plus nécessaires aux troupeaux," *Histoire de la société royale de médecine* (1776; Paris, 1779 [presented on December 3, 1777]): 312–20; Louis-Jean-Marie Daubenton, "Mémoire sur les régimes le plus nécessaire aux troupeaux, dans lequel l'auteur détermine par des expériences ce qui est relatif à leurs alimens et à leur boisson," *Histoire de la société royale de médecine*, 1777–78 (2) (Paris, 1780 [presented on December 11, 1778]): 570–78. Also see Charles C. Gillispie, *Science and Polity in France at the End of the Old Regime* (Princeton, NJ: Princeton University Press, 1980), 165–68; Bourde, *Agronomie et agronomes*, 2:857–78.

27. Louis-Jean-Marie Daubenton, *Instruction pour les bergers et pour les propriétaires de troupeaux* (Paris: P.-D. Pierres, 1782).

28. Buffon, "Le cheval," 4:216–17. In the species of buffalos and oxen, as with the horse, "the crossed races are always the most beautiful." Buffon, "Le buffle, le bonasus, l'aurochs, le bison et le zebu," in *HN* (1764), 11:295.

29. Spary, "Political, Natural, and Bodily Economies," 188. See Comte d'Angevillier quoted in Richard Drayton, *Nature's Government: Science, Imperial Britain, and "Improvement" of the World* (New Haven, CT: Yale University Press, 2000), 76.

30. Cornelius de Pauw, *Recherches philosophiques sur les Américains, ou Mémoires intéressants pour servir à l'histoire de l'espece humaine* (Berlin: Decker, 1768), 180.

31. On his training at the Jardin de Roi, see April G. Shelford, "Buttons and Blood, or, How to Write an Anti-slavery Treatise in 1770s Paris," *History of European Ideas* 41, no. 6 (2014): 750; and Spary, *Utopia's Garden*, 56.

32. Shelford, "Buttons and Blood," 750.

33. On Armelle, see Shelford, 752.

34. Jean-Baptiste-Christophe Fusée Aublet, "Observations sur les négres esclaves," in *Histoire des plantes de la Guiane françoise* (London, 1775), 2:122.

35. See Julian Swann, *Politics and the Parlement of Paris under Louis XV, 1754–74* (New York: Cambridge University Press, 1995); Dale Van Kley, *The Damiens Affair and the Unraveling of the Ancien Regime, 1750–1770* (Princeton, NJ: Princeton University Press, 1984); and James C. Riley, *The Seven Years' War and the Old Regime in France: The Economic and Financial Toll* (Princeton, NJ: Princeton University Press, 1986).

36. Colin Jones, *The Great Nation: France from Louis XV to Napoleon* (New York: Penguin, 2002), 240.

37. On depopulation concerns, see Carol Blum, *Strength in Numbers: Population, Reproduction, and Power in Eighteenth-Century France* (Baltimore: Johns Hopkins University Press, 2002).

38. See Jean-Jacques Rousseau, "Discours sur les sciences et les arts" and "Discours sur l'origine et les fondemens de l'inégalité parmi les hommes," in *OC*, 3:3–237.

39. See, for example, Buffon, "De la nature: Première vue," in *HN* (1764), 12:xiii.

40. Buffon, 12:xi; and Buffon, "Le buffle, le bonasus, l'aurochs, le bison et le zebu," in *HN* (1764), 11:295.

41. Buffon, "Le chèvre," in *HN* (1755) 5:60. Also see Buffon, "Le cheval," 4:249.

42. Buffon, "De la nature: Première vue," 12:xiii.

43. Buffon, "L'asne," in *HN* (1753), 4:383.

44. Buffon, "Le pigeon," in *HN* (1771), 2:497.

45. Friedrich Melchior, baron de Grimm, *Correspondance littéraire, philosophique et critique par Grimm, Diderot, Raynal, Meister*, ed. Maurice Tourneux (Paris: Garnier, 1877 [September 1, 1753]), 2:279.

46. In addition to his position at the Paris Faculté de Médecine, he was a royal censor, and a member of the Insitut de Bologne. "Eloge de M. Vandermonde," in *Journal de Médecine, Chirurgie, et Pharmacie* 17 (July 1762): 3.

47. Compare Vandermonde, *Essai*, 1:99–104, with Buffon, "Le cheval," 4:215–17. For more on Vandermonde, see Vila, *Enlightenment and Pathology*.

48. Vandermonde's father, Jacques-François, had numerous friends at the Jardin de Roi and presented several memoirs there. A. Birembaut, "Précisions sur la biographie du mathématicien Vandermonde et de sa famille," *Extrait des Actes du Congrès de Luxembourg, 72ᵉ Session de l'Association Française pour l'Avancement des Sciences* (July 1953): 530–33.

49. See "Eloge de M. Vandermonde," 4.

50. Vandermonde, *Essai*, 1:99.

51. Vandermonde, 1:xvi.

52. Anne Carol, *Histoire de l'eugénisme en France: Les médecins et la procréation, XIXᵉ–XXᵉ siècle* (Paris: Seuil, 1995), 19.

53. Vandermonde, *Essai*, 1:100.

54. Vandermonde, 1:100, 103, 107, 106.

55. Vandermonde, 1:vii.

56. Vandermonde, 1:91–92.

57. For Vandermonde's thoughts on improving health, see *Essai*, 1:83–86; for skin color, see 1:92–93. On parentage, see "Eloge de M. Vandermonde," 7. On ideas of hybrids in this era, see Patrick Graille, "Portrait scientifique et littéraire de l'hybride au siècle des Lumières," *Eighteenth Century Life* 21, no. 2 (1997): 70–88.

58. Vandermonde, *Essai*, 1:65.

59. Vandermonde, 1:66.

60. Vandermonde, 1:66, 67, 81 83, 84.

61. Vandermonde, 1:85.

62. Vandermonde, 1:95.

63. Vandermonde, 1:117.

64. Vandermonde, 1:113.

65. Vandermonde, 1:115–16.

66. Vandermonde, 1:116.

67. Vandermonde, 1:116.

68. Pierre Roussel, *Système physique et moral de la femme, ou Tableau philosophique de la constitution, de l'état organique, du tempérament, des mœurs, & des fonctions propres au sexe* (Paris: Vincent, 1775), xxiii–xxv.

69. *Journal encyclopédique*, January 1757, 36.

70. See *Journal des sçavans*, June 1756, 435–42; *Journal de Trévoux* 2, October 1756, 2518–40; *L'année littéraire* 3 (1756): 13–22; and *Journal encyclopédique*, January 1757, 36–49.

71. See *Journal œconomique*, January 1757, 53; *Critical Review, or The Annals of Literature*, December 1756, 464–66; On Formey and Sieyès, see *Des manuscrits de Sieyès*, ed. Christine Fauré, Jacques Guilhaumou, and Jacques Valier (Paris: Honoré Champion, 1999), 2:174–75. Vandermonde's *Essay* is mentioned in a letter from Nicolas-Charles-Joseph Trublet to Jean-Henri-Samuel Formey, August 12, 1756, in *Correspondance littéraire passive de Formey*, ed. Martin Fontius, Rolf Geissler, and Jens Häseler (Paris: Champion, 1996), 196.

72. Joachim Faiguet de Villeneuve, *L'économe politique: Projet pour enricher et pour perfectionner l'espèce humaine* (London, 1763), 132–33.

73. Abbé Henri Grégoire, *Essai sur la régénération physique, morale et politique des Juifs: Ouvrage couronné par la Société Royale des Sciences et des Arts de Metz, le 23 août 1788* (1788; Paris: Flammarion, 1988), 72–78.

74. Johann Peter Frank, *System einer vollständigen medicinischen Polizey* (Mannheim: C. F. Schwan, 1779–1827). On Frank, see Harald Breyer, *Johann Peter Frank* (Leipzig: S. Hirzel Verlag, 1983); and Sara Eigen Figal, *Heredity, Race, and the Birth of the Modern* (New York: Routledge, 2008), 34–35, 98–127. On eighteenth-century German medical police generally, see Caren Möller, *Medizinalpolizei: Die Theorie des staatlichen Gesundheitswesens im 18. und 19. Jahrhundert* (Frankfurt: Klostermann, 2005). On biopower and German medical police, see Claudia Stein, "The Birth of Biopower in Eighteenth-Century Germany," *Medical History* 55 (2011): 331–37.

75. Immanuel Kant, "Of the Different Races of Human Beings" (1775), in Immanuel Kant, *Anthropology, History, and Education*, ed. Robert B. Louden and Günter Zöller, trans. Mary Gregor et al. (Cambridge: Cambridge University Press, 2007), 86–87.

76. Pierre-Louis Moreau de Maupertuis, *Lettre sur les progrès des sciences* (Paris, 1752), 98–108; and Pierre-Louis Moreau de Maupertuis, *Vénus physique* (1745; Paris: Aubier-Montaigne, 1980), 134.

77. On these ideas of Maupertuis and his friendship with Buffon, see Roger, *Life Sciences in Eighteenth-Century French Thought*, 369–94, 439–41; Terrall, *Man Who Flattened the Earth*, 199–230, 310–48; and Michael H. Hoffheimer, "Maupertuis and the Eighteenth-Century Critique of Preexistence," *Journal of the History of Biology* 15, no. 1 (Spring 1982): 119–44; and François Duchesneau, *La physiologie des lumières: Empirisme, modèles et theories* (The Hague: M. Nijhoff, 1982).

78. Terrall, *Man Who Flattened the Earth*, 337.

79. Faiguet de Villeneuve, *L'économe politique*, 119.

80. On Enlightenment populationist thought and pronatalism, see Blum, *Strength in Numbers*; and Leslie Tuttle, *Conceiving the Old Regime: Pronatalism and the Politics of Reproduction in Early Modern France* (Oxford: Oxford University Press, 2010).

81. Faiguet de Villeneuve, *L'économe politique*, 115–16, 122.

82. Faiguet de Villeneuve, 118.

83. Faiguet de Villeneuve, 109–53. Also see Joachim Faiguet de Villeneuve, *Discours d'un bon citoyen sur les moyens de multiplier les forces de l'État & d'augmenter la population* (Brussels, 1760); and the reworking of *L'économe politique* published as Joachim Faiguet de Villeneuve, *L'ami des pauvres, ou L'économe politique* (Paris, 1766).

84. Antoine Le Camus, "Projet pour conserver l'espèce des hommes bien faits, réserver les hommes vigoureux pour la culture des terres, & augmenter le nombre des soldats," in *Memoires sur divers sujets de médecine* (Paris, 1760), 289. This was originally an article in the *Journal œconomique* in February 1757. For more on Le Camus, see Winston, *From Perfectibility to Perversion*; and Quinlan, *Great Nation in Decline*. For Faiguet de Villeneuve's reference to Le Camus, see *L'économe politique*, 113.

85. Le Camus, "Projet pour conserver l'espèce des hommes bien faits," 314. Celibacy was a common target of populationist discourse; see Blum, *Strength in Numbers*, 21–60.

86. Mary Terrall, "Material Impressions: Conception, Sensibility, and Inheritance," in *Vital Matters: Eighteenth-Century Views on Conception, Life, and Death*, ed. Helen Deutsch and Mary Terrall (Toronto: University of Toronto Press, 2012), 121. Referring to the revised second edition of Le Camus, *Médicine de l'esprit* (Paris: Ganeau, 1769).

87. On Diderot's dissent, see Timo Kaitaro, *Diderot's Holism: Philosophical Antireductionism and Its Medical Background* (New York: Peter Lang, 1997), 134–37.

88. Victor Riqueti, marquis de Mirabeau, *L'ami des hommes, ou Traité de la population* (Avignon, 1758), 2:114–15, quoted and translated in Michael Kwass, "Consumption and the World of Ideas: Consumer Revolution and the Moral Economy of the Marquis de Mirabeau," *Eighteenth-Century Studies* 37, no. 2 (2004): 195–96.

89. On these figures, see Quinlan, *Great Nation in Decline*; Winston, *From Perfectibility to Perversion*; and Doron, *L'homme altéré*, 224–25, 228, 248.

90. Louis-René de Caradeuc de la Chalotais, *Essai d'éducation national, ou Plan d'études pour la jeunes* (1763), 9.

91. Denis Diderot, *Supplément au voyage de Bougainville, or Dialogue entre A. et B.*, in *OP*, 500. On Diderot and ideas of breeding, see Pamela Cheek, *Sexual Antipodes: Enlightenment, Globalization, and the Placing of Sex* (Stanford, CA: Stanford University Press, 2003), 164–93; and Sunil Agnani, "'*Doux Commerce, Douce Colonisation*': Diderot and the Two Indies of the French Enlightenment," in Larry Wolff and Marco Cipolloni, eds., *The Anthropology of the Enlightenment* (Stanford, CA: Stanford University Press, 2007), 65–84. For characterization of "Orou's biopolitics" as "tropical eugenics," see Andrew Curran, "Logics of the Human in the *Supplément au Voyage de Bougainville*," in *New Essays on Diderot*, ed. James Fowler (New York: Cambridge University Press, 2011), 165.

92. Kathleen Wellman, "Physicians and *Philosophes*: Physiology and Sexual Morality in the French Enlightenment," *Eighteenth-Century Studies* 35, no. 2 (Winter 2002): 274.

93. Agnani claims that Diderot cited Vandermonde, but this appears to be incorrect. Agnani may have been misled by a footnote created by one of Diderot's modern editors. Contrary to Agnani's claim, Vandermonde's name does not appear in any of the three editions (1770, 1774, or 1780) of Raynal's *Histoire philosophique et politique*. See Agnani, "'*Doux Commerce*"; and Sunil M. Agnani, *Hating Empire Properly: The Two Indies and*

the Limits of Enlightenment Anticolonialism (New York: Fordham University Press, 2013), 32 and 202n47.

94. Diderot knew of, and extensively drew on, the work of Buffon; on the relationship, see Roger, *Buffon*, 339–40; Jacques Roger, "Diderot et Buffon en 1749," *Diderot Studies* 4 (1963): 221–36; Aram Vartanian, "Buffon et Diderot," in Michel Delsol, ed., *Buffon 88: Actes du colloque international pour le bicentenaire de la mort de Buffon* (Paris: Vrin, 1992), 119–33; and Kurt Ballstadt, *Diderot: Natural Philosopher* (New York: Oxford University Press, 2008), 129–73.

95. Denis Diderot, *Le rêve de d'Alembert*, in *OP*, 372–85. For the passage in Guillaume-Thomas Raynal, *Histoire philosophique et politique des éstablissemens et du commerce des Européens dans les deux Indes*, see Denis Diderot, *Œuvres*, vol. 3, *Politique*, ed. Laurent Versini (Paris: R. Laffont, 1995), 705–9, though as noted in note 93 above, the citation of Vandermonde was not made by Diderot.

96. For the identification of Diderot—along with Spinoza and Bayle—as a principal architect of the Radical Enlightenment, see Jonathan Israel, *Enlightenment Contested* (Oxford: Oxford University Press, 2006), 42, 560.

97. See David Coward, *The Philosophy of Restif de la Bretonne* (Oxford: Voltaire Foundation, 1991).

98. Coward, 47n12.

99. Philippe Despoix, "Histoire naturelle et imagination littéraire: *La découverte australe*, ou Rétif lecteur de Buffon," *Études rétiviennes* 32 (2000): 95–111.

100. Nicolas-Edme Restif de la Bretonne, *La découverte australe par un homme-volant, ou Le dédale français* (1781; Geneva: Slatkine, 1979). On reading Buffon and the Bible, see Bronislaw Baczko, *Utopian Lights: The Evolution of the Idea of Social Progress*, trans. Judith L. Greenberg (New York: Paragon House, 1989), 180. Restif de la Bretonne still excoriated Buffon in writing; see Coward, *Philosophy of Restif de la Bretonne*, 120–21.

101. Restif de la Bretonne, *La découverte australe*. On the eugenic ideas in this work, see Laurent Loty, "*La découverte australe* (1781): Une utopie évolutionniste et eugéniste," *Études rétiviennes* vols. 4–5 (1986): 27–35; Cheek, *Sexual Antipodes*; and Amy S. Wyngaard, *Bad Books: Rétif de la Bretonne, Sexuality, and Pornography* (Newark: University of Delaware Press, 2013), 115–25.

102. Nicolas-Edme Restif de la Bretonne, *L'Andrographe, ou Idées d'un honnête-homme sur un projet de règlement, proposé à toutes les nations de l'Europe, pour opérer une réforme générale des mœurs, & par elle, le bonheur du Genre-humain* (1782; Geneva: Slatkine Reprints, 1988), 53, 56.

103. Restif de la Bretonne, 54–55.

104. Mark Harrison, *Climates and Constitutions: Health, Race, Environment and British Imperialism in India, 1600–1850* (Oxford: Oxford University Press, 1999), 104. Also see Wheeler, *Complexion of Race*; Kathleen Wilson, *The Island Race: Englishness, Empire, and Gender in the Eighteenth Century* (New York: Routledge, 2003); Rana Hogarth, *Medicalizing Blackness: Making Racial Difference in the Atlantic World, 1780–1840* (Chapel Hill: University of North Carolina Press, 2017); and Suman Seth, *Difference and Disease: Medicine, Race, and the Eighteenth-Century British Empire* (Cambridge: Cambridge University Press, 2018).

105. [John Gregory], *A Comparative View of the State and Faculties of Man with Those of the Animal World* (London: Dodlsey, 1765). The first edition was published anonymously. On Gregory's ideas about breeding, see Jenny Davidson, *Breeding: A Partial History of the Eighteenth Century* (New York: Columbia University Press, 2009), 92–93; and John C. Waller, "Ideas of Heredity, Reproduction and Eugenics in Britain, 1800–1875," *Studies in History and Philosophy of Biological and Biomedical Sciences* 32, no. 3 (2001): 468.

106. "John Gregory," in *Oxford Dictionary of National Biography* (Oxford: Oxford University Press, 2004); William Smellie, *Literary and Characteristical Lives of John Gregory, M.D. . . .* (Edinburgh, Alex Smellie, 1800), 1–118; and Paul Wood, "The Natural History of Man in the Scottish Enlightenment," *History of Science* 28, no. 1 (March 1990): 91–94.

107. See Wood, "Natural History of Man"; and Paul Wood, "Buffon's Reception in Scotland: The Aberdeen Connection," *Annals of Science* 44, no. 2 (1988): 169–90; Sophia Rosenfeld, *Common Sense: A Political History* (Cambridge, MA: Harvard University Press, 2011), 56–89; and H. Lewis Ulman, ed., *The Minutes of the Aberdeen Philosophical Society, 1758–1773* (Aberdeen: Aberdeen University Press, 1990).

108. See Wood, "Buffon's Reception"; and Wood, "Natural History of Man."

109. On the theory of organized atoms, see Thomas Reid to Lord Kames, November/December 1774, in *The Correspondence of Thomas Reid*, ed. Paul Wood (Edinburgh: Edinburgh University Press, 2002), 78–84. Also see Paul Wood, "Introduction," in Thomas Reid, *Thomas Reid on Animate Creation: Papers Relating to the Life Sciences*, ed. Paul Wood (Edinburgh: Edinburgh University Press, 1995), 3–20.

110. David Skene, handwritten manuscript "Discourses on Natural History," undated (1760s), MS480/1, p. 87, and more generally 83–90, Special Collections, University of Aberdeen, Scotland. On Skene and Buffon, also see Wood, "Buffon's Reception."

111. Skene, "Discourses on Natural History," 85.

112. Gregory, *Comparative View*, 15–16.

113. Gregory, 17.

114. Gregory, 17.

115. John Gregory, *A Comparative View of the State and Faculties of Man with Those of the Animal World*, 4th ed. (Dublin, 1768), 9.

116. Sieyès, *Des manuscrits*, 2:147.

117. On the relationship between Rush and Smith, see Mark A. Noll, *Princeton and the Republic, 1768–1822: The Search for a Christian Enlightenment in the Era of Samuel Stanhope Smith* (Princeton, NJ: Princeton University Press, 1989), 113–15; and Sarah Knott, *Sensibility and the American Revolution* (Chapel Hill: University of North Carolina Press, 2009), 207–17.

118. On Whytt and Cullen from the perspective of vitalism and organization, see Reill, *Vitalizing Nature*, 121–22, 128–31.

119. Samuel Stanhope Smith, *An Essay on the Causes of the Variety of Complexion and Figure in the Human Species* (Philadelphia: Robert Aitken, 1787).

120. See the editorial comments in Samuel Stanhope Smith, *An Essay on the Causes of the Variety of Complexion and Figure in the Human Species*, 2nd ed., ed. Winthrop D. Jordan (Cambridge, MA: Harvard University Press, 1965), xvi–xvii and lviii.

121. For the second edition, see Smith, *Essay on the Causes* (1965). On Blumenbach's relation to vitalism and theorists of organization, see Reill, *Vitalizing Nature*, 143–47. On Kant, Blumenbach, and Buffon on race, see Robert Bernasconi, "Who Invented the Concept of Race? Kant's Role in the Enlightenment Construction of Race," in *Race*, ed. Bernasconi (Oxford: Blackwell, 2001), 11–36.

122. See Noll, *Princeton and the Republic*.

123. Smith, *Essay on the Causes* (1787), 109.

124. Smith, 109.

125. Knott, *Sensibility and the American Revolution*, 207–8. Also see Noll, *Princeton and the Republic*, 112–15.

126. Samuel Stanhope Smith, "Strictures on Lord Kaims's [*sic*] *Discourse: On the Original Diversity of Mankind*," in *Essay on the Causes* (1787), separate pagination, 15.

127. Smith, 19.

128. Smith, 19.

129. Smith, *Essay on the Causes* (1787), 71.

130. See Nicholas Guyatt, *Bind Us Apart: How Enlightened Americans Invented Racial Segregation* (New York: Basic Books, 2016).

131. Guyatt, 220–22.

132. Samuel Stanhope Smith, *The Lectures, Corrected and Improved, Which Have Been Delivered for a Series of Years, in the College of New Jersey: On the Subjects of Moral and Political Philosophy* (Trenton: Daniel Fenton, 1812), 2:176. On this plan, also see Bruce Dain, *A Hideous Monster of the Mind: American Race Theory in the Early Republic* (Cambridge, MA: Harvard University Press, 2002), 69–70.

133. Smith, *Lectures*, 2:177.

134. On the impact of the Haitian Revolution in the United States, see Ashli White, *Encountering Revolution: Haiti and the Making of the Early Republic* (Baltimore: Johns Hopkins University Press, 2010).

135. Georges-Louis Leclerc, comte de Buffon, "*Des époques de la nature*," in Georges-Louis Leclerc, comte de Buffon, *Histoire naturelle, générale et particulière: Supplément*, 7 vols. (Paris: Imprimerie royale, 1774–89), hereafter *HN Supplément*, 5:252.

136. Buffon, 5:253.

137. Buffon, 5:253.

CHAPTER THREE

1. Alexandre-Stanislas, Baron de Wimpffen, *Voyage à Saint-Domingue, pendant les années 1788, 1789 et 1790* (Paris, 1797), 2:87.

2. Wimpffen, 2:87.

3. On the forms of *Exclusif*, see Jean Tarrade, *Le commerce colonial de la France à la fin de l'ancien régime: L'évolution du régime de "l'Exclusif" de 1763 à 1789*, 2 vols. (Paris, Presses universitaires de France, 1972).

4. On "mulatto factories," see H.D. [Michel-René Hilliard d'Auberteuil], *Considérations sur l'état présent de la colonie française de Saint-Domingue*, 2 vols. (Paris, 1776–77), 2:94; and Wimpffen, *Voyage à Saint-Domingue*, 2:87–88. For skepticism about slave stud farms in the early modern French Caribbean colonies, see Arlette Gautier, *Les sœurs de solitude: La condition féminine dans l'esclave aux Antilles du XVIe au XIXe siècle* (Paris: Éditions Caribbéennes, 1985), 71–73. Debate on slave breeding in the United States has focused on the nineteenth century; see Kenneth M. Stampp, *The Peculiar Institution: Slavery in the Ante-bellum South* (New York: Vintage Books, 1956), 245–51; Richard Sutch, "The Breeding of Slaves for Sale and the Westward Expansion of Slavery, 1850–1860," in Stanley L. Engerman and Eugene D. Genovese, eds., *Race and Slavery in the Western Hemisphere: Quantitative Studies* (Princeton, NJ: Princeton University Press, 1975), 173–210; and Paul D. Escott, *Slavery Remembered: A Record of Twentieth-Century Slave Narratives* (Chapel Hill: University of North Carolina Press, 1979), 44–45.

5. Gabriel de Bory, *Essai sur la population des colonies à sucre* (1776), in Bory, *Mémoires sur l'administration de la Marine et des colonies* (Paris, 1789), 50–83; Hilliard d'Auberteuil, *Considérations*.

6. On the development of ideas of race in the seventeenth and eighteenth centuries, see Joyce E. Chaplin, "Race," in David Armitage and Michael J. Braddick, eds., *The British Atlantic World, 1500–1800* (New York: Palgrave Macmillan, 2002), 154–74; "Constructing Race," special issue, *William and Mary Quarterly*, 3rd ser., 54, no. 1 (January 1997); Phillip R. Sloan, "The Idea of Racial Degeneracy in Buffon's *Histoire Naturelle*," *Studies in Eighteenth-Century Culture* 3 (1973): 293–321; Roxann Wheeler, *The Complexion of Race: Categories of Difference in Eighteenth-Century British Culture* (Philadelphia: University of Pennsylvania Press, 2000); Nicholas Hudson, "From 'Nation' to 'Race': The Origin of Racial Classification in Eighteenth-Century Thought," *Eighteenth-Century Studies* 29, no. 3 (1996): 247–64; Winthrop D. Jordan, *White over Black: American Attitudes toward the Negro, 1550–1812* (Chapel Hill: University of North Carolina Press, 1968); Kathleen Wilson, *The Island Race: Englishness, Empire, and Gender in the Eighteenth Century* (New York: Routledge, 2003); and María Elena Martínez, *Genealogical Fictions: Limpieza de Sangre, Religion, and Gender in Colonial Mexico* (Stanford, CA: Stanford University Press, 2008); and Silvia Sebastiani, *The Scottish Enlightenment: Race, Gender, and the Limits of Progress* (New York: Palgrave, 2013).

7. I use "men" to reflect the focus of both Bory and Hilliard d'Auberteuil's on creating a new group of mulatto men and that this focus reflected numerous assumptions about sexual difference and the inheritance of characteristics.

8. On the development of ideas of race in France and its Atlantic colonies in the eighteenth century, see Sue Peabody and Tyler Stovall, eds., *The Color of Liberty: Histories of Race in France* (Durham, NC: Duke University Press, 2003); Guillaume Aubert, "'The Blood of France': Race and Purity of Blood in the French Atlantic World," *William and Mary Quarterly*, 3rd ser., 61, no. 3 (2004): 439–78; Saliha Belmessous, "Assimilation and Racialism in Seventeenth- and Eighteenth-Century French Colonial Policy," *American Historical Review* 110, no. 2 (April 2005): 322–49; Sue Peabody, *"There Are No Slaves in France": The Political Culture of Race and Slavery in the Ancien Régime* (Oxford: Oxford University Press, 1996); Pierre H. Boulle, *Race et esclavage dans la France de ancien régime* (Paris: Perrin, 2007); Yvan Debbasch, *Couleur et liberté: Le jeu du critère ethnique dans un ordre juridique esclavagiste* (Paris: Dalloz, 1967); Elsa Dorlin, *La*

matrice de la race: Généalogie sexuelle et coloniale de la nation française (Paris: Éditions La Découverte, 2006); John D. Garrigus, *Before Haiti: Race and Citizenship in French Saint-Domingue* (New York: Palgrave Macmillan, 2006); Michèle Duchet, *Anthropologie et histoire au siècle des Lumières* (Paris: Albin Michel, 1995); Doris Garraway, *The Libertine Colony: Creolization in the Early French Caribbean* (Durham, NC: Duke University Press, 2005); Andrew S. Curran, *The Anatomy of Blackness: Science and Slavery in the Age of Enlightenment* (Baltimore: Johns Hopkins University Press, 2011); and Claude-Olivier Doron, *L'homme altéré: Races et dégénérescence (XVIIe–XIXe siècles)* (Ceyzérieu: Champ Vallon, 2016); and Henry Louis Gates Jr. and Andrew S. Curran, eds., *Who's Black and Why? A Hidden Chapter from the Eighteenth-Century Invention of Race* (Cambridge, MA: Harvard University Press, 2022).

9. See Claude Quillet, *Callipaedia, seu de pulchrae prolis habendae ratione, poema didacticon* (Leyden, 1655); and Michel Procope-Couteau, *L'Art de faire des garçons* (Montpellier, 1748).

10. On the "indelible mark," see Hilliard d'Auberteuil, *Considérations*, 2:73. On race, marriage, and the regulation of sex, see Jennifer M. Spear, "Colonial Intimacies: Legislating Sex in French Louisiana," *William and Mary Quarterly*, 3rd ser., 60, no. 1 (2003): 75–98; Aubert, "'Blood of France'"; Belmessous, "Assimilation and Racialism"; Peabody, *"There Are No Slaves in France"*; Pierre Boulle, "Racial Purity or Legal Clarity? The Status of Black Residents in Eighteenth-Century France," *Journal of the Historical Society* 6, no. 1 (March 2006): 19–46; Debbasch, *Couleur et liberté*; and Garraway, *Libertine Colony*. On these issues in early America, see Jordan, *White over Black*, 136–78; Martha Hodes, ed., *Sex, Love, Race: Crossing Boundaries in North American History* (New York: New York University Press, 1999); and Merril D. Smith, ed., *Sex and Sexuality in Early America* (New York: New York University Press, 1998). On these issues in early modern Spain and the Spanish Empire, see James Sweet, "The Iberian Roots of American Racist Thought," *William and Mary Quarterly*, 3rd ser., 54, no. 1 (January 1997): 143–66; Martínez, *Genealogical Fictions*; and Patricia Seed, "Social Dimensions of Race: Mexico City, 1753," *Hispanic American Historical Review* 62, no. 4 (November 1982): 569–606.

11. I am not aware of any secondary works that extensively treat Bory. On the Enlightenment and the sciences in Saint-Domingue, see James E. McClellan III, *Colonialism and Science: Saint Domingue in the Old Regime* (Chicago: University of Chicago Press, 2010).

12. Hilliard d'Auberteuil published a variety of works, including histories, political economic polemics, a novel, and a variety of pamphlets; see Gene E. Ogle, "'The Eternal Power of Reason' and 'The Superiority of Whites': Hilliard d'Auberteuil's Colonial Enlightenment," *French Colonial History* 3 (2003): 35–50; Malick Walid Ghachem, "Sovereignty and Slavery in the Age of Revolution: Haitian Variations on a Metropolitan Theme" (PhD diss., Stanford University, 2001); and Malick Walid Ghachem, "Montesquieu in the Caribbean: The Colonial Enlightenment between *Code Noir* and *Code Civil*," in *Postmodernism and the Enlightenment: New Perspectives in Eighteenth-Century French Intellectual History*, ed. Daniel Gordon (New York: Routledge, 2001), 7–30.

13. David P. Geggus, "Slave and Free Colored Women in Saint Domingue," in David Barry Gaspar and Darlene Clark Hine, eds., *More Than Chattel: Black Women and Slavery in the Americas* (Bloomington: Indiana University Press, 1996), 269.

14. On the resistance to mandatory militia service and the revolt of 1769, see Charles Frostin, *Les révoltes blanches à Saint-Domingue aux XVI* et *XVIII* siècles (Haïti avant 1789)* (Paris: l'École, 1975); and Garrigus, *Before Haiti*, 109–39.

15. [Charles-Henri-Hector, comte] d'Estaing, "Mémoire sur les finances et les milices de St. Domingue," undated, F³91, Archives nationales d'outre mer, Aix-en-Provence, France, hereafter ANOM. Many administrators in Saint-Domingue recognized the severity of the problem in their correspondence with the metropolitan officials. For example, Governor-General Gabriel de Bory to Choiseul, June 12, 1762, C⁹ᴬ111, ANOM.

16. Frostin, *Les révoltes blanches*; and Garrigus, *Before Haiti*, 109–39. On the French armies during the Seven Years' War, see Lee Kennett, *The French Armies in the Seven Years War: A Study in Military Organization and Administration* (Durham, NC: Duke University Press, 1967). On Spanish imperial military reforms limiting the role of free people of color, see Ben Vinson III, *Bearing Arms for His Majesty: The Free-Colored Militia in Colonial Mexico* (Stanford, CA: Stanford University Press, 2001).

17. Bory to Choiseul, June 12, 1762, C⁹ᴬ111, ANOM.

18. Bory, *Essai*, 58–59. I have not located a copy of the *Essai* published in 1776, nor have I found evidence of it's existence other than Bory's mention of this year of publication. The passage on breeding people like sheep does appear, in full, in the second edition of *Essai*, published 1781, which Bory refers to as being published in 1780. See the anonymous [Gabriel de Bory], *Essai sur la population des colonies à sucre*, 2nd ed. (La Haye, 1781), 8.

19. Bory, *Essai* (1789), 58–59.

20. Bory, 59.

21. Bory, 59.

22. The only mention of Bory's ideas about breeding that I am aware of is Michèle Duchet, "Du noir au blanc, ou La cinquième génération," in Léon Poliakov, ed., *Le couple interdit, entretiens sur le racisme: La dialectique de l'altérité socio-culturelle et la sexualité* (Paris: De Gruyter, 1980), 187.

23. See Bory's dossier from the Ministry of the Marine, Marine C⁷38, AN.

24. On Mesmerism and the committee, see Robert Darnton, *Mesmerism and the End of the Enlightenment in France* (Cambridge, MA: Harvard University Press, 1968). On Bory's biography, see J. Fr. Michaud, *Biographie universelle, ancienne et moderne*, 45 vols. (1843–65; reprint, new ed., Bad Feilnbach, 1998), 5:404–5; and Étienne Taillemite, ed., *Dictionnaire des marins français*, rev. ed. (Paris, 2002), 59.

25. In addition to Bory, *Mémoires sur l'administration de la Marine et des colonies*, see Gabriel de Bory, *Mémoire dans lequel on prouve la possibilité d'agrandir la ville de Paris sans en reculer les limites* (Paris, 1776); and Bory, "Mémoire sur les moyens de purifier l'air dans les vaisseaux," in *Mémoires de l'Académie Royale des Sciences* (1781; Paris, 1784), 111–19. On Bory's work with the Académie Royale des Sciences and the Institut, see fols. 284–468, Fonds Français 6349, Manuscrits occidentaux, Bibliothèque nationale, Paris.

26. Bory to Choiseul, June 12, 1762, C⁹ᴬ111, ANOM.

27. See the *Ordonnance du Gouverneur Général, portant établissement d'une Compagnie de Chasseurs de gens de couleur*, April 29, 1762, issued by Bory, in Médéric-Louis-Élie Moreau de Saint-Méry, *Loix et constitutions des colonies françoises de l'Amérique sous le Vent*, 6 vols. (Paris, 1784–90), 5:452–53. See also Bory to [Choiseul], June 12, 1762, C⁹ᴬ111, ANOM.

28. Choiseul to Bory, July 31, 1762, C⁹ᴬ111, ANOM.

29. Bory to [Choiseul], July 17, 1762, C⁹ᴬ111, ANOM.

30. Bory to Choiseul, June 22, July 17, and August 22, 1762, C⁹ᴬ111, ANOM; Bory, *Essai* (1789), 55–56.

31. See Bory to Choiseul, June 12, June 22, July 17, August 22, and September 2, 1762, C⁹ᴬ111, ANOM. On enslaved and free people of color in the Saint-Domingue military and police, see Stewart R. King, *Blue Coat and Powdered Wig: Free People of Color in Pre-Revolutionary Saint-Domingue* (Athens: University of Georgia Press, 2001), 52–77, 226–65. On arming enslaved or recently freed people, see Christopher Leslie Brown and Philip D. Morgan, eds., *Arming Slaves: From Classical Times to the Modern Age* (New Haven, CT: Yale University Press, 2006); Ben Vinson III and Stewart R. King, eds., "The New African Diasporic Military History in Latin America," special issue, *Journal of Colonialism and Colonial History* 5, no. 2 (Fall 2004); and Vinson, *Bearing Arms for His Majesty*.

32. King, *Blue Coat and Powdered Wig*, 62.

33. Choiseul to Bory, July 31, 1762, C⁹ᴬ111, ANOM.

34. See Frostin, *Les révoltes blanches*; and Garrigus, *Before Haiti*, 109–39.

35. Bory, *Essai* (1789), 59–60.

36. The sheep-breeding experiments of Jonas Ahlströmer in Sweden beginning in 1723 were an important precedent; however, they were smaller scale and not integrated with theoretical explanation. The extensive experiments of the English breeder Robert Bakewell were very practical in orientation and also not integrated with theories of generation or heredity. Roger J. Wood, "The Sheep Breeders' View of Heredity before and after 1800," in Staffan Müller-Wille and Hans-Jörg Rheinberger, *Heredity Produced: At the Crossroads of Biology, Politics, and Culture, 1500–1870* (Cambridge, MA: MIT, 2007), 229–50. See also Roger J. Wood and Vítěslav Orel, *Genetic Prehistory in Selective Breeding: A Prelude to Mendel* (Oxford: Oxford University Press, 2001). On Bakewell and later breeding, see Rebecca J. H. Woods, *The Herds Shot Round the World: Native Breeds and the British Empire, 1800–1900* (Chapel Hill: University of North Carolina Press, 2017).

37. Marie-Jean-Antoine-Nicolas Caritat, marquis de Condorcet, quoted in Charles C. Gillispie, *Science and Polity in France at the End of the Old Regime* (Princeton, NJ: Princeton University Press, 1980), 166.

38. Louis-Jean-Marie Daubenton, "Mémoire sur l'amélioration des bêtes à laine," in *Mémoires de l'Académie Royale des Sciences* (1777; Paris, 1780), 80.

39. Daubenton, "Mémoire," 81.

40. On the early modern discourse of noble "race," see Arlette Jouanna, *L'idée de race en France au XVIᵉ siècle et au début du XVIIᵉ siècle (1498–1614)*, 2 vols. (Montpel-

lier: Ministère des Universités et de l'Université Paul Valery, 1981); Aubert, "'Blood of France'"; and Doron, *L'homme altéré*, 88–126.

41. Bory, *Essai* (1789), 59. On aesthetics and race, see David Bindman, *Ape to Apollo: Aesthetics and the Idea of Race in the Eighteenth Century* (London: Reaktion Books, 2002).

42. See Ogle, "Eternal Power"; Charles Frostin, "Les colons de Saint-Domingue et la métropole," *Revue Historique* 237 (1967): 381–414; Ghachem, "Sovereignty and Slavery"; Garraway, *Libertine Colony*, 218–26. For additional biographical information (some of it is questionable), see Lewis Leary's introduction to Michel-René Hilliard d'Auberteuil, *Miss McCrea: A Novel of the American Revolution*, trans. Eric La Guardia (1784; Gainesville: University of Florida Press, 1958), 6–11.

43. "Isle de la Grenade," unsigned and undated report on Hilliard d'Auberteuil's arrest, removal from office, and deportation from Grenada, in the personnel dossier, E222, ANOM.

44. "Isle de la Grenade"; and Mercier de la Rivière to Sartine, n.d. [1776], fol. 259, F³91, ANOM.

45. Ogle, "Eternal Power."

46. See the letters in F³91 and E222, ANOM. On the repaying of debts, see Ogle, "Eternal Power," 39. On the fallout from the approbation, publication, and suppression, see fols. 160–67, item 504, Joly de Fleury Collection, Manuscrits occidentaux, Bibliothèque nationale, Paris.

47. Médéric-Louis-Élie Moreau de Saint-Méry, *Description topographique, physique, civile, politique et historique de la partie française de l'isle Saint-Domingue* (Philadelphia, 1797), 1:542.

48. See [Pierre-Ulric Dubuisson,] *Nouvelles considérations sur Saint-Domingue, en réponse à celles de M. H. D^L. par M. D. B.* (Paris: Cellot, 1780); [Descahos,] *Lettre de M. Descahos, habitant riverain du fleuve de l'Artibonite en l'isle de Saint-Domingue* (London, 1781); and Raymond [Julien Raimond], "A Monseigneur Le Maréchal de Castries Ministre et sécrétaire d'Etat au département de la Marine" (September 1786), ANOM, F³91, folio 179 recto to 180 recto.

49. Abbé Henri Grégoire, *Lettre aux philantropes, sur les malheurs, les droits et les reclamations des Gens de couleur de Saint-Domingue, et des aurtres iles françoises de l'Amériques* (Paris: Belin, 1790), 4; and Abbé Henri Grégoire, *De la littérature des Nègres* (Paris: Maradan, 1808), 57, 111.

50. Hilliard d'Auberteuil, *Considérations*, 1:132.

51. Ghachem, "Montesquieu in the Caribbean," 11.

52. Frostin, "Les colons"; and Gordon K. Lewis, *Main Currents in Caribbean Thought: The Historical Evolution of Caribbean Society in Its Ideological Aspects, 1492–1900* (Baltimore: Johns Hopkins University Press, 1983).

53. Ghachem, "Montesquieu in the Caribbean," 15.

54. Hilliard d'Auberteuil, *Considérations*, 2:39.

55. Hilliard d'Auberteuil, 2:72–96.

56. Hilliard d'Auberteuil, 2:88.

57. Hilliard d'Auberteuil, 2:88. In theory, enslaved people were ensured some legal protections under the Code Noir, but the vast chasm between the letter of the law and the actualities of enforcement meant that the enslaved in Saint-Domingue, as in other French colonies of the period, received basically no benefit from these laws. For a detailed analysis of the Code Noir, as well as a critique of the philosophes and the absence of the Code Noir from the French historical record, see Louis Sala-Molins, *Le Code noir, ou, Le calvaire de Canaan* (Paris: Presses universitaires de France, 1987). On the Code Noir and planter violence, see Malick W. Ghachem, *The Old Regime and the Haitian Revolution* (Cambridge: Cambridge University Press, 2012).

58. Hilliard d'Auberteuil did not oppose the segregationist laws of the 1760s and 1770s that aimed at restricting the freedom as well as the social and economic success of the free people of color in Saint-Domingue. On the laws, see Debbasch, *Couleur et liberté*; and John Garrigus, "Race, Gender, and Virtue in Haiti's Failed Foundation Fiction: *La mulâtre comme il y a peu de blanches* (1803)," in Peabody and Stovall, *Color of Liberty*, 78.

59. Hilliard d'Auberteuil, *Considérations*, 2:73.

60. See for example, Hilliard d'Auberteuil, 2:83.

61. Hilliard d'Auberteuil, 2:82–83, 95–96.

62. On Louisiana, see Spear, "Colonial Intimacies."

63. Hilliard d'Auberteuil, *Considérations*, 2:88.

64. Hilliard d'Auberteuil, 2:88.

65. Hilliard d'Auberteuil, 2:83.

66. See Debbasch, *Couleur et liberté*; and Garrigus, *Before Haiti*, 141–70.

67. [Jean-Baptiste] Estève, "Mémoire sur la police des gens de couleur libres, 1774," fols. 127–31, F^{3}91, ANOM.

68. Estève, fol. 128.

69. Estève, fol. 128.

70. Estève, fol. 129.

71. See Laurent Dubois, *A Colony of Citizens: Revolution and Slave Emancipation in the French Caribbean, 1787–1804* (Chapel Hill: University of North Carolina Press, 2004), 262–66; and Dubois, "Inscribing Race in the Revolutionary French Antilles," in Peabody and Stovall, *Color of Liberty*, 102–4.

72. On the earlier European history of externally marking skin for purposes of identification, see Valentin Groebner, *Who Are You? Identification, Deception, and Surveillance in Early Modern Europe*, trans. Mark Kyburz and John Peck (New York: Zone Books, 2007), 95–116. On branding in Saint-Domingue, see Garrigus, *Before Haiti*, 32.

73. On clothing in Old Regime France as both a customary and a legally recognized marker of social distinction (with reference to ancient precedents), see Charles Loyseau, *Traité des ordres et simples dignitez* (1610), in Loyseau, *Les œuvres de maistre Charles Loyseau* (Paris, 1666); and Daniel Roche, *The Culture of Clothing: Dress and Fashion in the "Ancien Régime,"* trans. Jean Birrell (Cambridge: Cambridge University Press, 1994). The preface to Hilliard d'Auberteuil's novel *Mis Mac Rea* (purportedly written by the publisher, but probably by the author) mentions Fénelon's *Télémaque*.

Hilliard d'Auberteuil, *Mis Mac Rea: Roman historique* (Philadelphia, 1784), xi. For a vision of society divided into seven ranks (plus slaves), where each rank wears clothing of a specific color indicating hierarchical position, see François de Salignac de la Mothe-Fénelon, *Les aventures de Télémaque, fils d'Ulysse* (1699), in Fénelon, *Œuvres* (Paris: Gallimard, 1997), 2:160–61.

74. Hilliard d'Auberteuil, *Considérations*, 2:48–49.

75. Hilliard d'Auberteuil, 1:7. See also his similarly worded claim on 2:83.

76. Hilliard d'Auberteuil, 2:94.

77. Hilliard d'Auberteuil, 2:94.

78. Building on Heidegger, Jacques Derrida made the phrase "metaphysics of presence" prominent, particularly through his analysis of Jean-Jacques Rousseau in *Of Grammatology*, trans. Gayatri Chakravorty Spivak (Baltimore: Johns Hopkins University Press, 1976). On Rousseau and transparency, see Jean Starobinski, *Jean-Jacques Rousseau: La transparence et l'obstacle* (Paris: Plon, 1957); and Sophia Rosenfeld, *Revolution in Language: The Problem of Signs in Late Eighteenth-Century France* (Stanford, CA: Stanford University Press, 2001).

79. See Groebner, *Who Are You?*, 95–116. On the ribbons worn by off-duty free colored militiamen in eighteenth-century New Spain, see Ben Vinson III, "Free Colored Voices: Issues of Representation and Racial Identity in the Colonial Mexican Militia," *Journal of Negro History* 80, no. 4 (Autumn 1995): 172.

80. British Jamaica and Portuguese Brazil are the other two societies. See Garrigus, *Before Haiti*, 4–8. On the laws of this campaign, see Debbasch, *Couleur et liberté*. For a comparison of Jamaica and Saint-Domingue, see Trevor Bernard and John Garrigus, *The Plantation Machine: Atlantic Capitalism in French Saint-Domingue and British Jamaica* (Philadelphia: University of Pennsylvania Press, 2016). On the elevated status of some free people of color in Saint-Domingue, and signs of a lack of residential segregation in urban centers, see Dominique Rogers, "Les libres de coloeur dans les capitals de Saint-Dominique: Fortune, mentalités et integration à la fin de l'ancien régime (1776–1789)" (PhD diss., Université de Bourdeaux III, 1999).

81. Garrigus, *Before Haiti*, 165–66.

82. Garrigus, 163; and Laurent Dubois, *Avengers of the New World: The Story of the Haitian Revolution* (Cambridge, MA: Harvard University Press, 2004), 62.

83. Dubois, *Avengers of the New World*, 62.

84. Garrigus, *Before Haiti*, 167.

85. For Raimond's discussion of Hilliard d'Auberteuil, see Raymond [Julien Raimond], "A Monseigneur Le Maréchal de Castries Ministre et sécrétaire d'Etat au département de la Marine" (September 1786), ANOM, $F^3$91, fols. 179 recto to 180 recto.

86. For Maudave's proposal and his correspondence with colonial officials, see $C^{5A}2$ and $C^{5A}3$, ANOM. Selections from Maudave's correspondence can be found in Henri Pouget de Saint-André, *La colonisation de Madagascar sous Louis XV, d'après la correspondance inédite du comte de Maudave* (Paris: Challamel aîné, 1886). On the Kourou expedition, see Emma Rothschild, "A Horrible Tragedy in the French Atlantic," *Past and Present* 192 (August 2006): 67–108.

87. Maudave in Pouget de Saint-André, *La colonisation de Madagascar*, 18–19. On Madagascar and Maudave, also see Duchet, *Anthropologie et histoire*, 53, 131.

88. Belmessous, "Assimilation and Racialism"; and Leslie Tuttle, *Conceiving the Old Regime: Pronatalism and the Politics of Reproduction in Early Modern France* (Oxford: Oxford University Press, 2010), 80.

89. See Jean Samuel Guisan, *Le Vaudois des terres noyées: Ingénieur à la Guiane française, 1777–1791*, ed. Yannick Le Roux, Olivier Pavillon, and Kristen Sarge (Matoury: Ibis Rouge, 2012), 59–60, 169, 320–21, 323.

90. Jean-Samuel Guisan, "Mémoire sur les nègres marrons hollandais qui sont établis sur les terres de la Guyane française au bord du Maroni" (May 1786), C^{14}/60/227–43, ANOM. See Barbara Traver, "A 'New Kourou': Projects to Settle the Maroons of Surinam in French Guiana," *Proceedings of the Western Society for French History* 39 (2011): 107–21.

91. J. M. C. Américain, *Précis des gémissemens des sang-mêlés dans les colonies françoises* (Paris: Baudouin, 1789), 12–13.

92. Américain, 13.

93. Américain, 15.

94. Moreau focusses almost exclusively on mixtures of white and black, though he does mention "Savages, Caribs or West Indians" and "Oriental Indians." Médéric-Louis-Élie Moreau de Saint-Méry, *Description topographique, physique, civile, politique et historique de la partie française de l'isle Saint-Domingue*, ed. Blanche Maurel and Étienne Taillemite, 3 vols. (Philadelphia, 1796; Paris: Société de l'histoire des colonies françaises, 1958), 89, 94.

95. Médéric-Louis-Élie Moreau de Saint-Méry, "Réflexions (vers 1780)," unpublished manuscript, ANOM F3/48, quoted and translated in Megan Vaughn, *Creating the Creole Island: Slavery in Eighteenth-Century Mauritius* (Durham, NC: Duke University Press, 2005), 245 and 302n24.

96. For biographical information on Moreau, see Étienne Taillemite, "Moreau de Saint-Méry," introduction to Moreau de Saint-Méry, *Description* (1796; 1958); and Anthony Louis Elicona, *Un colonial sous la Révolution en France et en Amérique: Moreau de Saint-Méry* (Paris: Jouve, 1934).

97. [Michel-Christian Camus], "Une fille naturelle de Moreau de Saint-Méry à Saint-Domingue," *Société haïtienne d'histoire et de geographie* 46 (March 1989): 51.

98. Dominique Rogers, "Entre Lumières et préjugés: Moreau de Saint-Méry et les libres de couleur de Saint-Domingue," in *Moreau de Saint-Méry, ou Les ambiguïtés d'un créole des Lumières*, ed. Dominique Taffin (Fort-de-France: Société des amis des archives et de la recherche sur le patrimoine culturel des Antilles, 2006), 87; and Marlene L. Daut, *Tropics of Haiti: Race and Literary History of the Haitian Revolution in the Atlantic World, 1789–1865* (Liverpool: Liverpool University Press, 2015), 221–22.

99. Garraway, *Libertine Colony*, 240–92. Also see Daut, *Tropics of Haiti*, 220–52.

100. This work resulted in Moreau de Saint-Méry, *Loix et contitutions des colonies françoises*.

101. Moreau de Saint-Méry, *Description* (1796; 1958).

102. The majority of colonial physicians were trained in Montpellier. Garrigus, *Before Haiti*, 157–58.

103. Médéric-Louis-Élie Moreau de Saint-Méry, *An Essay on the Manner of Improving the Breed of Horses in America* (Philadelphia, 1795), 3.

104. Moreau de Saint-Méry, *Description* (1796; 1958), 59.

105. On the Atlantic Enlightenment and Moreau, see William Max Nelson, "The Atlantic Enlightenment," in *The Atlantic World, 1450–1850*, ed. D'Maris Coffman, Adrian Leonard, and William O'Reilly (New York: Routledge, 2015), 650–66.

106. Moreau de Saint-Méry, *Description* (1796; 1958), 86–100. Also see Joan Dayan, *Haiti, History, and the Gods* (Berkeley: University of California Press, 1995), 228–37; and Garraway, *Libertine Colony*, 260–75.

107. On *casta* painting, see Ilona Katzew, *Casta Painting: Images of Race in Eighteenth-Century Mexico* (New Haven, CT: Yale University Press, 2004); and Tamara J. Walker, *Exquisite Slaves: Race, Clothing, and Status in Colonial Lima* (New York: Cambridge University Press, 2017), 97–127.

108. Moreau de Saint-Méry, *Description* (1796; 1958), 96.

109. He also used actual fractions. Moreau de Saint-Méry, 102.

110. Moreau de Saint-Méry, 99.

111. Moreau de Saint-Méry, 99.

112. Moreau de Saint-Méry, 100.

113. Moreau de Saint-Méry, 99.

114. Moreau de Saint-Méry, 99.

115. Moreau de Saint-Méry, 99.

116. Dayan, *Haiti, History, and the Gods*, 190. On Moreau's taxonomy, 229–37.

117. Moreau de Saint-Méry, "Réflexions," 245 and 302n24.

118. Moreau de Saint-Méry, 245.

119. Moreau de Saint-Méry, 245.

120. Moreau de Saint-Méry.

121. Moreau de Saint-Méry, 245; the brackets and their contents are Vaughn's.

122. Pierre-Victor Malouet, *Mémoire sur l'esclavage des nègres* (Neufchatel, 1788), 40 (some editions of this work with identical publishing information have different pagination). Malouet came to own a plantation in Saint-Domingue through marriage. Jean Tarrade, "L'esclavage est-il réformable? Les projets des administrateurs coloniaux à la fin de l'ancien régime," in Marcel Dorigny, ed., *Les abolitions de l'esclavage: De L. F. Sonthonax à V. Schœlcher* (Paris: Presses Universitaires de Vincennes et Édition UNESCO, 1995), 138.

123. Malouet, *Mémoire*, 40. Although *Mémoire* was published in 1788, the passage appears in a part that Malouet claimed to have written in 1775; see 127.

124. For race as a product of the Atlantic world, see Chaplin, "Race," 154.

125. On issues of population, reproduction, and ideas of race in relation to the possible end to the trade in enslaved people, the actual end, and abolition, see Thomas C. Holt, *The Problem of Freedom: Race, Labor, and Politics in Jamaica and Britain, 1832–*

1938 (Baltimore: Johns Hopkins University Press, 1992); Katherine Paugh, *The Politics of Reproduction: Race, Medicine, and Fertility in the Age of Abolition* (Oxford: Oxford University Press, 2017); Sasha Turner, *Contested Bodies: Pregnancy, Childrearing, and Slavery in Jamaica* (Philadelphia: University of Pennsylvania Press, 2017).

126. On the role of "mixed-race" individuals and families in this history, see Jennifer L. Palmer, *Intimate Bonds: Family and Slavery in the French Atlantic* (Philadelphia: University of Pennsylvania Press, 2016); and Daniel Livesay, *Children of Uncertain Fortune: Mixed-Race Jamaicans in Britain and the Atlantic Family, 1733–1833* (Chapel Hill: University of North Carolina Press, 2018).

127. See Claude Blanckaert, "Of Monstrous Métis? Hybridity, Fear of Miscegenation, and Patriotism from Buffon to Paul Broca," in Peabody and Stovall, *Color of Liberty*, 42–70; Martin S. Staum, *Labeling People: French Scholars on Society, Race, and Empire, 1815–1848* (Montreal: McGill-Queen's University Press, 2003), 122–57; William Stanton, *The Leopard's Spots: Scientific Attitudes toward Race in America, 1815–59* (Chicago: University of Chicago Press, 1960), 66–68, 76–77, 189–91; George W. Stocking Jr., *Race, Culture, and Evolution: Essays in the History of Anthropology* (Chicago: University of Chicago Press, 1982), 42–68; and Nancy Stepan, *The Idea of Race in Science: Great Britain, 1800–1960* (London: Macmillan, 1982).

128. See Ann Laura Stoler, *Race and the Education of Desire: Foucault's History of Sexuality and the Colonial Order of Things* (Durham, NC: Duke University Press, 1995), 52; Ann Laura Stoler, *Carnal Knowledge and Imperial Power: Race and the Intimate in Colonial Rule* (Berkeley: University of California Press, 2002), 79–111; Emmanuelle Saada, *Empire's Children: Race, Filiation, and Citizenship in the French Colonies* (Chicago: University of Chicago Press, 2012); Elisa Camiscioli, *Reproducing the French Race: Immigration, Intimacy, and Embodiment in the Early Twentieth Century* (Durham, NC: Duke University Press, 2009); Damon Ieremia Salesa, *Racial Crossings: Race, Intermarriage, and the Victorian British Empire* (Oxford: Oxford University Press, 2011); Durba Ghosh, *Sex and the Family in Colonial India: The Making of Empire* (Cambridge: Cambridge University Press, 2006); Staum, *Labeling People*, 85–190; Robert J. C. Young, *Colonial Desire: Hybridity in Theory, Culture, and Race* (London: Routledge, 1995); Owen White, *Children of the French Empire: Miscegenation and Colonial Society in French West Africa, 1895–1960* (Oxford: Oxford University Press, 1999); and Patricia M. E. Lorcin, *Imperial Identities: Stereotyping, Prejudice, and Race in Colonial Algeria* (London: I. B. Tauris, 1995).

129. Stoler, *Carnal Knowledge*, 80.

130. Michel-Hyacinthe Deschamps, *Études des races humaines: Méthode naturelle d'ethnologie* (Paris: Leiber et Comelin, 1857–59), 135, quoted in Blanckaert, "Of Monstrous Métis?," 47.

131. In the French imperial context, see Stoler, *Carnal Knowledge*; Saada, *Empire's Children*; White, *Children*; Camiscioli, *Reproducing*; and Christina Elizabeth Firpo, *The Uprooted: Race, Children, and Imperialism in French Indochina, 1890–1980* (Honolulu: University of Hawai'i Press, 2016).

132. On the persistence of the Buffonian paradigm, see Blanckaert, "Of Monstrous Métis?"; and Claude Blanckaert, "Les conditions d'émergence de la science des races au début du XIXe siècle," in Sarga Moussa, ed., *L'idée de "race" dans les sciences humaines et la littérature (XVIIIe–XIXe siècles)* (Paris: L'Harmattan, 2003), 139.

CHAPTER FOUR

1. Abbé Emmanuel-Joseph Sieyès, *Qu'est-ce que le Tiers État?* (1789), ed. Roberto Zapperi (Geneva: Droz, 1970), 126.

2. In his early pamphlets, Sieyès was often inconsistent, or ambiguous, in distinguishing between "the privileged" and "the nobility."

3. Sieyès invoked a territorial sense of the nation in *Qu'est-ce que le Tiers État?*, 187.

4. Sieyès, 211; also see 125.

5. Sieyès, 126.

6. David A. Bell, *The Cult of the Nation in France: Inventing Nationalism, 1680–1800* (Cambridge, MA: Harvard University Press, 2003); Sophie Wahnich, *L'impossible citoyen: L'étranger dans le discours de la Révolution française* (Paris: Albin Michel, 1997); Peter Sahlins, *Unnaturally French: Foreign Citizens in the Old Regime and After* (Ithaca, NY: Cornell University Press, 2004); Jennifer Ngaire Heuer, *The Family and the Nation: Gender and Citizenship in Revolutionary France, 1789–1830* (Ithaca, NY: Cornell University Press, 2005); Anne Simonin, *Le déshonneur dans la République: Une histoire del'indignité, 1791–1958* (Paris: Grasset, 2008); Dan Edelstein, *The Terror of Natural Right: Republicanism, the Cult of Nature, and the French Revolution* (Chicago: University of Chicago Press, 2009); Miranda Francis Spieler, *Empire and Underworld: Captivity in French Guiana* (Cambridge, MA: Harvard University Press, 2012).

7. Anne Simonin, "The Terror as a Legal Fiction," in *Fiction and the Frontiers of Knowledge in Europe, 1500–1800*, ed. Richard Scholar and Alexis Tadié (Burlington, VT: Ashgate, 2010), 123–39.

8. See Spieler, *Empire and Underworld*, 17–37.

9. On "the stranger," see George Simmel, "Exhurs über den Fremde," in *Soziologie* (Leipzig: Duncker und Humblot, 1908), 685–91; on the "liminal phase," see Victor Turner, *The Ritual Process: Structure and Anti-structure* (Chicago: Aldine, 1969); on the social death and "liminal incorporation," see Orlando Patterson, *Slavery and Social Death: A Comparative Study* (Cambridge, MA: Harvard University Press, 1982). On inclusive exclusion, see Giorgio Agamben, *Homo Sacer: Sovereign Power and Bare Life*, trans. Daniel Heller-Roazen (Stanford, CA: Stanford University Press, 1998). On this idea in contemporary political theory, see Sina Kramer, *Excluded Within: The (Un)Intelligibility of Radical Political Actors* (Oxford: Oxford University Press, 2017).

10. On *atimia*, see Mogens Herman Hansen, Apagoge, Endeixis *and* Ephegesis *against* Kakourgoi, Atimoi *and* Pheugontes: *A Study in Athenian Administration of Justice in the Fourth Century B.C.* (Odense: Odense University Press, 1976), 54–98. On *infamia* and other forms of Roman inclusive exclusion, see Paul J. du Plessis, Clifford Ando, and Kaius Tuori, eds., *The Oxford Handbook of Roman Law and Society* (Oxford: Oxford University Press, 2016); and see Robert Knapp, *Invisible Romans* (Cambridge, MA: Harvard University Press, 2011).

11. For a classic account of how social contract theories, for example, were built on patriarchal sexual contracts that inclusively excluded women, see Carole Pateman, *The Sexual Contract* (Stanford, CA: Stanford University Press, 1988).

12. Sahlins, *Unnaturally French*, 215. On the concept of the citizen and the use of the term in the Old Regime, also see Pierre Rétat, "The Evolution of the Citizen from

the Ancien Régime to the Revolution," in *The French Revolution and the Meaning of Citizenship*, ed. Reneé Waldinger, Philip Dawson, and Isser Woloch (Westport, CT: Greenwood, 1993), 3–15.

13. Sahlins, *Unnaturally French*; Charlotte Catherine Wells, *Law and Citizenship in Early Modern France* (Baltimore: Johns Hopkins University Press, 1995); and Jean-François Dubost and Peter Sahlins, *Et si on faisait payer les étrangers? Louis XIV, les immigrés et quelques autres* (Paris: Flammarion, 1999).

14. Dubost and Sahlins, *Et si on faisait payer les étrangers?*; and Sahlins, *Unnaturally French*.

15. Sahlins, *Unnaturally French*; and J.-F. Dubost "Les Étrangers à Paris au siècle des lumières," in *La ville promise: Mobilité et accueil à Paris, fin XVIIe–début XIXe siècle*, ed. Daniel Roche (Paris: Fayard, 2000), 221–88.

16. On the vagabond as a model for "civic degradation" during the Revolution, see Spieler, *Empire and Underworld*, 23.

17. On legal "nonsubjects," see Jean Carbonnier, *Flexible droit: Pour une sociologie du droit sans rigueur* (Paris: Librairie Générle de Droit et de Jurisprudence, 2001), 231–54. On "nonsubjects" during the Revolution, see Simonin, *Le déshonneur dans la République*. On "negative personhood," see Colin Dayan, *The Law Is a White Dog: How Legal Rituals Make and Unmake Persons* (Princeton, NJ: Princeton University Press, 2011).

18. Michel Foucault, *"Society Must Be Defended": Lectures at the Collège de France, 1975–76*, ed. Mauro Bertani and Alessandro Fontana, trans. David Macey (New York: Picador, 2003), 254.

19. Foucault, 254–55.

20. On early modern definitions of vagabonds, see Christian Paultre, *De la répression de la mendicité et du vagabondage en France sous l'ancien régime* (Paris: J. B. Sirey, 1906); and Annabel S. Brett, *Changes of State: Nature and the Limits of the City in Early Modern Natural Law* (Princeton, NJ: Princeton University Press, 2011), 25–31. On approaches to regulating and punishing vagabonds and the "sturdy poor" across early modern Europe, see Robert Jütte, *Poverty and Deviance in Early Modern Europe* (Cambridge: Cambridge University Press, 1994).

21. Thomas McStay Adams, *Bureaucrats and Beggars: French Social Policy in the Age of the Enlightenment* (Oxford: Oxford University Press, 1990), 39.

22. [Guillaume-François Le Trosne], *Mémoire sur les vagabonds et les mendiants* (Soissons: P. G. Simon, 1764), 2.

23. Other examples include Denis-Laurian Turmeau de la Morandière, *Police sur les mendiants, les vagabonds, les joueurs de profession, les intrigants, les filles prostituées, les domestiques hors de maison depuis long-tems, les gens sans aveu* (Paris: Dessain Junior, 1764); and the reprinted manuscript by Fauvelet, "Projet pour purger Paris des mauvais sujet, 22 Mai 1767," in *Les Mémoires policiers, 1750–1850*, ed. Vincent Millot (Rennes: Presses Universitaires de Rennes, 2006), 359–64. For a thorough treatment of the general context, see Thomas McStay Adams, *Bureaucrats and Beggars: French Social Policy in the Age of the Enlightenment* (Oxford: Oxford University Press, 1990); and Robert M. Schwartz, *Policing the Poor in Eighteenth-Century France* (Chapel Hill: University of North Carolina Press, 1988). Also see Paultre, *De la répression*.

24. The only biography of Le Trosne is Jérôme Mille, *Un physiocrate oublié, G.-F. Le Trosne (1728–1780): Étude économique, fiscale, et politique* (Paris: Librairie de la Société du recueil général des lois et des arrêts, 1905).

25. An edict of 1687 made vagabondage punishable by perpetual confinement in the galleys (different from the work camps of Le Trosne's era), but Le Trosne complained that it was never executed, then forgotten. See Le Trosne, *Mémoire sur les vagabonds et les mendiants*, 39; and Guillaume-François Le Trosne, *Discours sur l'état actuel de la magistrature, et sur les causes de sa décadence* (Paris: Panckoucke, 1764), 66. Also see Schwartz, *Policing the Poor*, 19.

26. See Daniel Roche, *Humeurs vagabondes: De la circulation des hommes et de l'utilité des voyages* (Paris: Fayard, 2003); and Olwen Hufton, *The Poor of Eighteenth-Century France, 1750–1789* (Oxford: Clarendon, 1974).

27. For a good summary and analysis of these interlocking economic and demographic factors, see Jack A. Goldstone, "The Social Origins of the French Revolution Revisited," in *From Deficit to Deluge: The Origins of the French Revolution*, ed. Thomas E. Kaiser and Dale K. Van Kley (Stanford, CA: Stanford University Press, 2010), 73–99.

28. Hufton, *Poor*, 266–83.

29. On Le Trosne and the simultaneity of the nonsimultaneous in eighteenth-century ideas of progress, see William Max Nelson, *The Time of Enlightenment: Constructing the Future in France, 1750 to Year One* (Toronto: University of Toronto Press, 2021), 37–48.

30. On representations of peasants, see Amy S. Wyngaard, *From Savage to Citizen: The Invention of the Peasant in the French Enlightenment* (Newark: University of Delaware Press, 2004).

31. Anne-Robert-Jacques Turgot, "Plan du second discours," in *Œuvres de Turgot*, ed. Gustave Schelle (Paris: Félix Alcan, 1913), 1:303–4.

32. Le Trosne, *Mémoire sur les vagabonds*, 8.

33. On Nicole-Antoine Boulanger's discussion of the natural man as a chimera and "metaphysical being," see Anthony Pagden, *The Fall of Natural Man: The American Indian and the Origins of Comparative Ethnology* (Cambridge: Cambridge University Press, 1982), 202.

34. On the history and historiography of the term and concept of civilization, see Michael Sonenscher, "Barbarism and Civilization," in *A Companion to Intellectual History*, ed. Richard Whatmore and Brian Young (Hoboken: Wiley-Blackwell, 2016), 288–302.

35. Le Trosne, *Mémoire sur les vagabonds*, 9, 42. Also see Guillaume-François Le Trosne, *De l'administration provinciale, et de la réforme de l'impôt* (1779; Basel, 1780), 540.

36. Le Trosne, *Mémoire sur les vagabonds*, 39.

37. André Zysberg, "From the Galleys to Hard Labor Camps: Essay on a Long Lasting Penal Institution," in *The Emergence of Carceral Institutions: Prisons, Galleys and Lunatic Asylums, 1550–1900*, ed. Pieter Spierenburg (Rotterdam: Erasmus University, 1984), 110–11. Also see Frédérique Joannic-Seta, *Le bagne de Brest: Naissance d'une institutions carcérale au siècle des Lumières* (Rennes: Presses Universitaires de Rennes, 2000).

38. Le Trosne, *Mémoire sur les vagabonds*, 44. The original Italian edition of Beccaria's famous work *Dei delitti e delle pene* was published in 1764, the same year as Le Trosne's *Memoir*. See Cesare Beccaria, *On Crimes and Punishments, and Other Writings*, ed. Richard Bellamy, trans. Richard Davies (Cambridge: Cambridge University Press, 1995).

39. Le Trosne, *Mémoire sur les vagabonds*, 39.

40. Le Trosne, 41.

41. Le Trosne, 43.

42. Le Trosne, 42.

43. Le Trosne, 42, 46.

44. On the enemy of humanity (*hostis humani generis*), see Edelstein, *Terror of Natural Right*. Edelstein mentions Le Trosne as evidence of how the brigand (and the closely related vagabond) was one of the five main "characters" of the discourse of the enemy of humanity (29–30). Also see Walter Rech, *Enemies of Mankind: Vattel's Theory of Collective Security* (Leiden: Nijhoff, 2013); and Daniel Heller-Roazen, *The Enemy of All: Piracy and the Law of Nations* (New York: Zone Books, 2009).

45. Le Trosne, *Mémoire sur les vagabonds*, 4, 61.

46. Le Trosne, 61.

47. On wolves, werewolves, and the monstrous beasts of the countryside in Old Regime France, see Jay M. Smith, *Monsters of the Gévaudan: The Making of a Beast* (Cambridge, MA: Harvard University Press, 2011). On wolves and werewolves as a medieval and early modern figures that played a role in modern biopolitics, see Agamben, *Homo Sacer*, 104–11.

48. On "civil death," see Spieler, *Empire and Underworld*, particularly 20–21, 84–85; Dayan, *The Law Is a White Dog*, 39–70; Heuer, *Family and the Nation*; and Simonin, *Le déshonneur dans la République*, 318–22.

49. See Robert-Joseph Pothier, *Pandectae justinianeae in novum ordinem digestae, cum legibus codicis, et novellis* (Paris, 1748–52). Pothier reportedly asked Le Trosne to read and revise manuscripts on several occasions. Guillaume-François Le Trosne, *Éloge historique de Pothier* (Orleans: Rouzeau-Montaut, 1773), cxix–cxx.

50. Le Trosne, *Mémoire sur les vagabonds*, 47–48.

51. François Richer, *Traité de la mort civile* (Paris: Durand, 1755), 6, 159.

52. Robert-Joseph Pothier, *Traité des personnes et des choses*, in *Oeuvres posthumes de M. Pothier* (Orléans: De Bure, 1778), 2:596.

53. Richer, *Traité*, 203, 206. Also see Montigny, "Mort civile," in Joseph-Nicolas Guyot et al., *Répertoire universel et raisonné de jurisprudence civile, criminelle, canonique, et benéficiale* (Paris: Panckoucke, 1781), 40:365, 370.

54. Montigny, "Mort civile," 365; and Richer, *Traité*, 6.

55. Montigny, "Mort civile," 370.

56. Agamben, *Homo Sacer*.

57. Hannah Arendt, *The Origins of Totalitarianism* (New York: Harcourt, Brace, 1951), 295, 298. On Agamben's concept of *homo sacer*, the adaptation of "bare life" from Benjamin, and the role of Arendt's thought, see Leland de la Durantaye, *Giorgio Agam-*

ben: A Critical Introduction (Stanford, CA: Stanford University Press, 2009), 202–7. Also see Catherine Mills, *Biopolitics* (New York: Routledge, 2018), 37–80.

58. See Magnus Fiskesjö, "Outlaws, Barbarians, Slaves: Critical Reflections on Agamben's *Homo Sacer*," *HAU: Journal of Ethnographic Theory* 2, no. 1 (2012): 161–80. On the existence of other forms of inclusive exclusion in ancient Rome, see Knapp, *Invisible Romans*.

59. Le Trosne, *Mémoire sur les vagabonds*, 48.

60. Also see Guillaume-François Joly de Fleury's argument for an abbreviated procedure, though without employing the terminology or conception of living death, in Adams, *Bureaucrats and Beggars*, 37.

61. Adams, 41.

62. Le Trosne, *Mémoire sur les vagabonds*, 55.

63. Le Trosne, 54.

64. Le Trosne, 54. On the history of the so-called freedom principle, see Sue Peabody, *"There Are No Slaves in France": The Political Culture of Race and Slavery in the Ancien Régime* (New York: Oxford University Press, 1996). On the geographical discrepancies in the recognition of this principle and the treatment of enslaved people in eighteenth-century France, see Dwain C. Pruitt, "'Opposition of the Law to the Law': Race, Slavery and the Law in Nantes, 1715–1778," *French Historical Studies* 30, no. 2 (Spring 2007): 147–74.

65. Le Trosne, *Mémoire sur les vagabonds*, 47.

66. Le Trosne, 52, 63.

67. Le Trosne, 43.

68. Le Trosne, 52.

69. Le Trosne, 52.

70. Le Trosne, 52.

71. Le Trosne, 56.

72. Le Trosne, 54. For vagabonds as "domestic enemies," see Le Trosne, *Discours sur l'état actuel de la magistrature*, 25.

73. On the formation of the dépôts, their elimination, and their partial return, see Adams, *Bureaucrats and Beggars*.

74. Charles-Antoine-Joseph Leclerc de Montlinot, "Essai sur la mendicité," in *État actuel du dépôt de Soissons, précédé d'un essai sur la mendicité* (Soissons: Ponce Courtois, 1789), 18–25.

75. Montlinot, 23.

76. Montlinot, 24.

77. Montlinot, 24.

78. Montlinot, 25.

79. See Adams, *Beggars and Bureaucrats*; and Kate Hodgson, "French Atlantic Appropriations: Montlinot, Eighteenth-Century Colonial Slavery, and Penal and Forced Labor Schemes between Europe, Africa, and the Americas," *Forum for Modern Language Studies* 51, no. 2 (20015): 1–17.

80. In addition to the work of the *comité de mendicité* during the Revolution, see "Rapport du Bureau du Bien public sur la suppression de la mendicité," *Procès-verbaux des séances de l'Assemblée provinciale du Soissonnois* (Soisson: L. F. Waroquier, 1787), 245. Also see David Coward, *The Philosophy of Restif de la Bretonne* (Oxford: Voltaire Foundation, 1991), 2:176; and Louis-Sébastien Mercier, *Tableau de Paris* (Amsterdam, 1788), 11:117.

81. On the endorsement of intendant Méliand of Soissons, his subdelegate Guise, and the probable early support of Cypierre, the intendant of Orléans, see Adams, *Bureaucrats and Beggars*, 42–43, 272n54. On the practical expansion of the category by the *maréchaussée* and figures like the lieutenant-general of police in Paris, Jean-Charles-Pierre Lenoir, see Hufton, *Poor*, 227–28. It is worth noting that Lenoir was also involved with the Police des Noirs regulations discussed later in this chapter.

82. See the tables in Paultre, *De la répression*, 602–5; two of these tables are also in Hufton, *Poor*, 389–90.

83. Adams, *Bureaucrats and Beggars*, 49.

84. *Déclaration du roi, concernant les vagabonds, et gens sans aveu, donné à Compiègne le 3 Août 1764* (Paris: Simon, 1764), 1.

85. Guillaume-François Le Trosne, *De l'ordre social* (Paris: De Bure, 1777), 405.

86. Le Trosne, 405n2.

87. Also see Le Trosne, *De l'administration provinciale*.

88. See Le Trosne, *De l'ordre social*; and Le Trosne, *De l'administration provinciale*.

89. See Gabriel-François Coyer, *La noblesse commerçante* (London, 1756). Also see Jay Smith, *Nobility Reimagined: The Patriotic Nation in Eighteenth-Century France* (Ithaca, NY: Cornell University Press, 2005), 104–42.

90. Abbé Emmanuel-Joseph Sieyès, *Essai sur les privilèges*, in *Écrits politiques*, ed. Roberto Zapperi (Paris: Éditions des Archives Contemporaines, 1985), 99, 104, 107, and 109.

91. For the distinction between active and passive citizens, see Abbé Emmanuel-Joseph Sieyès, *Préliminaire de la constitution: Reconnaissance et exposition raisonée des droits de l'homme et du citoyen* (Paris, [1789]); Abbé Emmanuel-Joseph Sieyès, *Dire de l'abbé Sieyes sur la question du veto royal à la séance du 7 septembre 1789* (Versailles, [1789]); and Abbé Emmanuel-Joseph Sieyès, "Citoyens, Eligibles, Electeurs," AN, 284 AP 3, dossier 2.3. Also see William H. Sewell Jr., "Le Citoyen / La Citoyenne: Activity, Passivity, and the Revolutionary Concept of Citizenship," in *The French Revolution and the Creation of Modern Political Culture*, ed. Colin Lucas (New York: Pergamon, 1988), 2:105–23; and William H. Sewell Jr., *A Rhetoric of Bourgeois Revolution: The Abbé Sieyes and "What Is the Third Estate?"* (Durham, NC: Duke University Press, 1994), 172–84.

92. Sieyès, "Citoyens, Eligibles, Electeurs." On this document and its context, see Sewell, *Rhetoric*, 164.

93. See Sieyès's writing in *Des manuscrits de Sieyès*, ed. Christine Fauré, Jacques Guilhaumou and Jacques Valier (Paris: Honoré Champion, 1999), vol. 2; and on the relationship between Sieyès and Le Trosne, see Christine Fauré, "Introduction," in *Des manuscrits*, 2:43–50.

94. Abbé Emmanuel-Joseph Sieyès, "Lettres aux Économistes sur leur système de politique et de morale," in *Écrits politiques*, 27–43. On Sieyès and political economy, see Marcel Dorigny, "La formulation de la pensée économique de Sieyès d'aprés ses manuscrits (1770–1789)," *Annales historiques de la Révolution française* 6 (1988): 17–34.

95. See Abbé Emmanuel-Joseph Sieyès, "Views," in Emmanuel-Joseph Sieyès, *Political Writings: Including the Debate between Sieyès and Tom Paine in 1791*, ed. and trans. Michael Sonenscher (Indianapolis: Hackett, 2003), 53–54; Sieyès, *Déliberations à prendre dans les assemblées de bailliages*, included in the anonymous *Instructions envoyées par S.A.S. Monseigneur le duc d'Orléans* (n.p. [February 1789]); and Abbé Emmanuel-Joseph Sieyès, *Observations sur la rapport du comité de Constitution concernant la nouvelle organisation de la France* (Versailles, [October] 1789). On the process of spatial reorganization in general, see Marie-Vic Ozouf-Marignier, *La formation des départements: La représentation du territoire français à la fin du 18ᵉ siècle* (Paris: Éditions de l'Ecole des Hautes Études en Sciences Sociales, 1989).

96. On Sieyès and the provincial assembly of Orléans, see his papers in AN, 284 AP 7, dossiers 3 to 8.

97. Keith Michael Baker, "Sieyès," in *A Critical Dictionary of the French Revolution*, ed. François Furet and Mona Ozouf, trans. Arthur Goldhammer (Cambridge, MA: Harvard University Press, 1989), 313.

98. Baker, "Sieyès," 313.

99. On the shift from the use of "slaves" to "blacks" in this context, see Peabody, *"There Are No Slaves in France,"* 74, 106, and 114.

100. On the Police des Noirs in general, see Peabody, *"There Are No Slaves in France"*; Pierre H. Boulle, *Race et esclavage dans la France de ancien régime* (Paris: Perrin, 2007); and Pierre Boulle, "Racial Purity or Legal Clarity? The Status of Black Residents in Eighteenth-Century France," *Journal of the Historical Society* 6, no. 1 (March 2006): 19–46. See the briefer treatments by Emeka P. Abanime, "The Anti-Negro French Law of 1777," *Journal of Negroe History* 64, no. 1 (Winter 1979): 21–29; and Érick Noël, *Être noir en France au XVIIIᵉ siècle* (Paris: Tallandier, 2006), 79–93.

101. Boulle, *Race et esclavage*, 140–54, 175.

102. No reliable, comprehensive enumerations of people of African descent exist for this time period. Sue Peabody estimates that no more than four to five thousand blacks lived in France at any one time in the eighteenth century. Erick Noël estimates a similar number for the period around the Police des Noirs. Pierre Boulle found relatively certain evidence of at least 2,329 nonwhites resident in France, more or less permanently, in 1777. Peabody, *"There Are No Slaves in France,"* 4; Boulle, *Race et esclavage*, 109; and Noël, *Être noir en France*. Also, see the attempt by scholars to identify and enumerate individual people of color in select locations in France: Erick Noël, ed., *Dictionnaire des gens de couleur dans la France Moderne*, 2 vols. (Geneva: Droz, 2011).

103. [Jean-Baptiste] Estève, "Mémoire sur la police des gens de couleur libres, 1774," fols. 127–31, F³91, ANOM.

104. See Peabody, *"There Are No Slaves in France"*; Boulle, *Race et esclavage*; and Pierre Boulle, "Racial Purity or Legal Clarity."

105. See Boulle, "Racial Purity or Legal Clarity," 22–23. On the Declaration of 1738 and the Edict of 1716, see Peabody, *"There Are No Slaves in France."*

106. "Circulaire aux Intendants de la marine et Commissaires de la ports ou il se fait le la armements pour les Colonies," June 30, 1763, F³90, ANOM; and "Circulaire aux Intendants des Provinces," June 30, 1763, F³90, ANOM.

107. Poncet de la Grave to Chardon, December 19, 1777, no folio number, placed in between fols. 459 and 460. F¹ᴮ4, ANOM.

108. Poncet de la Grave to Chardon, December 19, 1777, fol. 196 recto and verso, F¹ᴮ4, ANOM.

109. Poncet de la Grave to Chardon, December 19, 1777, fol. 195 verso, F¹ᴮ4, ANOM.

110. See Guillaume Poncet de la Grave, *Considérations sur le célibat, relativement a la politique, a la population, et aux bonnes moeurs* (Paris: Moutardier, 1801 / Year IX); and Guillaume Poncet de la Grave, *Défense des considérations sur le célibat, relativement à la population, aux moeurs et à la politique: En réponse à la critique du célibataire anonyme, insérée dans le Journal de Paris du 24 Brumaire, an 10, no. 54, pag. 320 et 321* (Paris: Moutardier, 1802 [Year X]).

111. "Observations: Sur l'avis du comité relativement aux noirs . . . ," March 9, 1782, fol. 51, F¹ᴮ1, ANOM; "Mémoire," unsigned and undated, fol. 96, F¹ᴮ1, ANOM; "Mémoire," written on behalf of "plusieurs Magistrats" advising the minister about the Police de Noirs, undated, fol. 76, F¹ᴮ1, ANOM. For further writing about "purging" the "pernicious germ" infecting the population, also see "Projet d'Arrêt du Conseil: Arrêt du Conseil d'Etat du Roi concernant les Noirs Et Mulatres qui sont actuellement En france," undated, fols. 80–91, F¹ᴮ1, ANOM.

112. "Mémoire," fol. 76, F¹ᴮ1, ANOM; and "Mémoire," unsigned and undated, fol. 96, F¹ᴮ1, ANOM.

113. "Observations: Sur l'avis du comité relativement aux noirs . . . ," March 9, 1782, fol. 51, F¹ᴮ1, ANOM.

114. Pierre-Victor Malouet, *Mémoire sur l'esclavage des nègres* (Neufchatel, 1788), 40.

115. On Malouet as a plantation owner, see Jean Tarrade, "L'esclavage est-il réformable? Les projets des administrateurs coloniaux à la fin de l'ancien régime," in Marcel Dorigny, ed., *Les abolitions de l'esclavage: De L. F. Sonthonax à V. Schœlcher* (Paris: Presses Universitaires de Vincennes et Édition UNESCO, 1995), 138.

116. On the intermarriage ban of 1803, see Jennifer Heuer, "The One-Drop Rule in Reverse? Interracial Marriages in Napoleonic and Restoration France," *Law and History Review* 27, no. 3 (Fall 2007): 515–48; and Marcel Dorigny, *Révoltes et révolutions en Europe et aux Amériques (1773–1802)* (Paris: Belin, 2003), 170. On Napoleon, the colonies, and slavery, see Yves Benot, *La démence colonial sous Napoléon* (Paris: La Découverte, 1992); and Marcel Dorigny and Yves Benot, eds., *1802: Le rétablissement de l'esclavage dans les colonies françaises* (Paris: Maissoneuve et Larose, 2003).

117. Peabody, *"There Are No Slaves in France,"* 138 and 188n5.

118. See Peabody, 121–40; Boulle, "Legal Clarity of Racial Purity," 36–40; and Pruitt, "Opposition of the Law."

119. On the use of *cartouches* and name registers to control the mobility of soldiers following a royal edict of 1716, see Vincent Denis, "Individual Identity and Identification in Eighteenth-Century France," in Ilsen About et al., eds., *Identification and Registration Practices in Transnational Perspective* (New York: Palgrave Macmillan, 2013), 18–19.

120. See Valentin Groebner, *Who Are You? Identification, Deception, and Surveillance in Early Modern Europe*, trans. Mark Kyburz and John Peck (New York: Zone Books, 2007).

121. On physical descriptions and identity documents, see Vincent Denis, *Une histoire de l'identité: France, 1715–1815* (Seyssel: Champ Vallon, 2008), 19–24, 44–58.

122. On the creation of modern identity documents, see John Torpey, *The Invention of the Passport: Surveillance, Citizenship and the State* (Cambridge: Cambridge University Press, 2000); Denis, *Une histoire de l'identité*; and Nathan Perl-Rosenthal, *Citizen Sailors: Becoming American in the Age of Revolution* (Cambridge, MA: Belknap Press of Harvard University Press, 2015).

123. Londa Schiebinger, "Skeletons in The Closet: The First Illustrations of the Female Skeleton in Eighteenth-Century Anatomy," *Representations* 14 (Spring 1986): 42–82; and Thomas Laqueur, *Making Sex: Body and Gender from the Greeks to Freud* (Cambridge, MA: Harvard University Press, 1990).

124. On complementarity, see Londa Schiebinger, *The Mind Has No Sex? Women in the Origins of Modern Science* (Cambridge, MA: Harvard University Press, 1989); also see Stefani Engelstein, "The Allure of Wholeness: The Eighteenth-Century Organism and the Same-Sex Marriage Debate," *Critical Inquiry* 39, no. 4 (Summer 2013): 754–76.

125. See Margaret C. Jacob, *Radical Enlightenment: Pantheists, Freemasons, and Republicans* (London: Allen and Unwin, 1981); Stuurman, *François Poulain de la Barre*; and Jonathan Israel, *Radical Enlightenment: Philosophy and the Making of Modernity, 1650–1750* (New York: Oxford University Press, 2001).

126. Stuurman, *François Poulain de la Barre*. On the comprehensive universalism of Poulain de la Barre and the contrast to Spinoza and van den Enden, see 295–97.

127. On early modern feminism and the *querelle des femmes* from the fifteenth to the eighteenth century, see Joan Kelly, "Early Feminist Theory and the *Querelle des Femmes*, 1400–1789," *Signs* 8, no. 1 (Autumn 1982): 4–28; Constance Jordan, *Renaissance Feminism: Literary Texts and Political Models* (Ithaca, NY: Cornell University Press, 1990); and Stuurman, *Poulain de la Barre* 52–86.

128. Karen Offen, *European Feminisms, 1700–1950: A Political History* (Stanford, CA: Stanford University Press, 2000), 34–35. Charles de Secondat, baron de Montesquieu, *Lettres persanes*, in *Œuvres complètes* (Paris: Gallimard, 1949), vol. 1; Sophia, a Person of Quality, *Woman Not Inferior to Man: or, A Short and Modest Vindication of the Natural Right of the Fair-Sex to a Perfect Equality of Power, Dignity, and Esteem, with the Men* (London: Hawkins, 1739); and the anonymous (by "A Lady") *Female Rights Vindicated: or The Equality of the Sexes Morally and Physically Proved* (London: Burnet, 1758).

129. See Sarah Knott and Barbara Taylor, eds., *Women, Gender, and Enlightenment* (New York: Palgrave Macmillan, 2005); and Offen, *European Feminisms*, 27–76.

130. See Charles Rihs, *Les philosophe utopistes: Le mythe de la cité communitaire en France au XVIIIᵉ siècle* (Paris: M. Rivière, 1970).

131. Deschamps quoted in Annie Ibrahim, "La pensée de Buffon: Système ou anti-système?," in Michel Delsol, ed., *Buffon 88: Actes du colloque international pour le bicentenaire de la mort de Buffon* (Paris: J. Vrin, 1992), 189.

132. For Deschamps's use of the terms and concepts of organization, including its mereology, see Léger-Marie Deschamps, *La vérité, ou Le vrai système* in *Œuvres*

philosophiques, ed. Bernard Delhaume (Paris: Vrin, 1993), 2:404. On Deschamps's relation to ideas of organism, see Bernard Delhaume, "La métaphysique de Dom Deschamps: L'existence, 'Tout' et 'le Tout,'" in *Dom Deschamps et sa métaphysique*, ed. Jacques D'Hondt (Paris: Presses universitaires de France, 1974), 185–206. For Deschamp's relation to various philosophes, as well as the vexed question of intellectual genealogy, see André Robinet, *Dom Deschamps: Le maître des maîtres du soupçon* (Paris: Vrin, 1994).

133. Dom Deschamps, quoted in Bronislaw Baczko, *Utopian Lights: The Evolution of the Idea of Social Progress*, trans. Judith L. Greenberg (New York: Paragon House, 1989), 91.

134. Deschamps, *La vérité*, 297–325.

135. Deschamps, 212, note s.

136. Deschamps, 315.

137. Deschamps, 301, note n.

138. Deschamps, 274.

139. Deschamps, 274.

140. Deschamps, 111, 153.

141. Deschamps, 371, note g.

142. Schiebinger, "Skeletons in the Closet." Also see Schiebinger, *Mind Has No Sex?*; and Londa Schiebinger, *Nature's Body: Gender in the Making of Modern Science* (Boston: Beacon, 1993).

143. Schiebinger, "Skeletons in the Closet," 42.

144. Ludmilla Jordanova, *Nature Displayed: Gender, Science, and Medicine, 1760–1820* (London: Longman, 1996), 175. See also, Ludmilla Jordanova, *Sexual Visions: Images of Gender in Science and Medicine between the Eighteenth and Twentieth Centuries* (Madison: University of Wisconsin Press, 1989).

145. On Roussel, see Anne C. Vila, *Enlightenment and Pathology: Sensibility in the Literature and Medicine of Eighteenth-Century France* (Baltimore: Johns Hopkins University Press, 1998), 225–57; and Yvonne Knibiehler, "Les médecins et la 'nature feminine' au temps du Code Civil," *Annales: Histoire, Sciences Sociales* 31, no. 4 (1976): 824–45.

146. Pierre Roussel, *Système physique et moral de la femme, ou Tableau philosophique de la constitution, de l'état organique, du tempérament, des mœurs, & des fonctions propres au sexe* (Paris: Vincent, 1775), 3, 6.

147. Roussel, 6.

148. Roussel, *Système physique*, 2.

149. Roussel, 16.

150. Roussel, 16.

151. Roussel, 30.

152. Roussel, 30.

153. Roussel, 30.

154. Théophile Bordeu, *Recherches sur le tissu muquex, ou L'organe cellulaire, et sur quelques maladies de la poitrine* (Paris: Didot, 1767). Vila, *Enlightenment and Pathol-*

ogy, 246. For his appreciation of Bordeu, see Pierre Roussel, *Éloge historique de M. de Bordeu* (Paris: Ruault, 1778).

155. Roussel, *Système physique*, xxxv.

156. On women in the Revolution, see Dominique Godineau, *The Women of Paris and Their French Revolution*, trans. Katherine Streip (Berkeley: University of California Press, 1998); and Darline Gay Levy, Harriet Branson Applewhite, Mary Durham Johnson, eds., *Women in Revolutionary Paris, 1789–1795: Selected Documents* (Urbana: University of Illinois Press, 1980).

157. Geneviève Fraisse, *Reason's Muse: Sexual Difference and the Birth of Democracy*, trans. Jane Marie Todd (Chicago: University of Chicago Press, 1994), 72–74, 79.

158. Fraisse, 73.

159. Carla Hesse, *The Other Enlightenment: How French Women Became Modern* (Princeton: Princeton University Press, 2001), 156, and 130–53.

160. Hesse, xiv, 130–53. Fraisse, *Reason's Muse*. Also see Laqueur, *Making Sex*.

161. Joan Wallach Scott, *Only Paradoxes to Offer: French Feminists and the Rights of Man* (Cambridge, MA: Harvard University Press, 1996), 47–49.

162. See Joan B. Landes, *Women and the Public Sphere in the Age of the French Revolution* (Ithaca, NY: Cornell University Press, 1988); and Lynn Hunt, *The Family Romance of the French Revolution* (Berkeley: University of California Press, 1992), 89–123.

163. Godineau, *Women of Paris*, 274–77.

164. Pierre-Jean-Georges Cabanis, *Rapports du physique et du moral de l'homme* (1802), vol. 1 of *OP*, 298. On Cabanis and Roussel, see Martin S. Staum, *Cabanis: Enlightenment and Medical Philosophy in the French Revolution* (Princeton, NJ: Princeton University Press, 1980), 215; and Vila, *Enlightenment and Pathology*, 240–55.

165. See, for example, Julien-Joseph Virey, *Histoire naturelle du genre humain* (Paris: F. Dufart, Year IX [1801]). Also see Knibiehler, "Les médecins"; Fraisse, *Reason's Muse*, 72–102; Martin S. Staum, *Minerva's Message: Stabilizing the French Revolution* (Montreal: McGill-Queen's University Press, 1996), 100; Vila, *Enlightenment and Pathology*, 240–57; and Sean Quinlan, "Writing the Natural History of Women: Medicine, Social Thought, and Genre in Post-Revolutionary France," in *Women, Gender, Disease in Eighteenth-Century England and France*, ed. Anne Kathleen Doig and Felician B. Sturzer (Newcastle: Cambridge Scholars, 2014), 15–44.

166. See Knibiehler, "Les médecins"; Vila, *Enlightenment and Pathology*, 240–55; and Quinlan, "Writing the Natural History of Women."

167. Roussel and de Sèze were technically "associates," while Cabanis was a "member." See Staum, *Minerva's Message*, 232. On de Sèze's views on women, see Vila, *Enlightenment and Pathology*, 246–54.

168. Hesse, *Other Enlightenment*, 110–11. On laws and education debates in these years, see Robert Palmer, *The Improvement of Humanity: Education and the French Revolution* (Princeton, NJ: Princeton University Press, 1985), 221–78.

169. See Staum, *Minerva's Message*; Suzanne Desan, *The Family on Trial in Revolutionary France* (Berkeley: University of California Press, 2004); Knibiehler, "Les médecins"; and Heuer, *Family and the Nation*.

170. Lynn Hunt, *Inventing Human Rights: A History* (New York: W. W. Norton, 2007), 169.

171. Scott, *Only Paradoxes to Offer*.

172. Fraisse, *Reason's Muse*. The original French subtitle of her book (*La démocratie exclusive et la différence des sexes*) drew attention to the idea of "exclusive democracy."

173. This paradox is the focus of Scott, *Only Paradoxes to Offer*.

174. On the legal and administrative approaches to vagabonds in the Revolution and early nineteenth century, see Adams, *Bureaucrats and Beggars*; Isser Woloch, *The New Regime* (New York: W. W. Norton, 1994), 266–96; and Spieler, *Empire and Underworld*.

CHAPTER FIVE

1. Georges-Louis Leclerc, comte de Buffon, "*Des époques de la nature*," in *HN Supplément*, 5:253.

2. Abbé Emmanuel-Joseph Sieyès, "Esclaves d'une espèce qui ait moins de besoins et moins propre [à] exciter la compassion humaine," 284 AP 3, dossier 1, cahier 2, AN. Transcriptions of a number of Sieyès's manuscripts are available in published collections. If a manuscript is available in a published version without significant editorial changes, I cite the published version. If it has been altered significantly, or is unavailable, I cite the unpublished archival version.

3. Murray Forsyth, *Reason and Revolution: The Political Thought of the Abbé Sieyès* (Leicester: Leicester University Press, 1987), 3. Jean-Denis Bredin, *Sieyès: La clé de la Révolution française* (Paris: Éditions de Fallois, 1988).

4. Hannah Arendt, *On Revolution* (New York: Penguin, 2006), 154.

5. Keith Michael Baker, "Sieyès," in *A Critical Dictionary of the French Revolution*, ed. François Furet and Mona Ozouf, trans. Arthur Goldhammer (Cambridge, MA: Harvard University Press, 1989), 313. Forsyth, *Reason and Revolution*, 3.

6. On Sieyès in general, see Paul Bastid, *Sieyès et sa pensée*, new ed. (Paris: Hachette, 1970); Bredin, *Sieyès*; Forsyth, *Reason and Revolution*; William H. Sewell Jr., *A Rhetoric of Bourgeois Revolution: The Abbé Sieyes and "What Is the Third Estate?"* (Durham, NC: Duke University Press, 1994); Jacques Guilhaumou, *Sieyès et l'ordre de la langue: L'invention de la politique moderne* (Paris: Kimé, 2002); and Pierre-Yves Quiviger, Vincent Denis, and Jean Salem, eds., *Figures de Sieyès* (Paris: Publications de la Sorbonne, 2008).

7. Many are available in the two volumes of *Des manuscrits de Sieyès*, ed. Christine Fauré, Jacques Guilhaumou, and Jacques Valier (Paris: Honoré Champion, 1999); and Emmanuel-Joseph Sieyès, *Écrits politiques*, ed. Roberto Zapperi (Paris: Éditions des Archives Contemporaines, 1985). Also see the documents included in Pierre-Yves Quiviger, *Le principe d'immanence: Métaphysique et droit administrative chez Sieyès* (Paris: Honoré Champion, 2008).

8. Michel Foucault, *The Order of Things: An Archeology of the Human Sciences* (New York: Vintage, 1994).

9. See Antoine de Baecque, *The Body Politic: Corporeal Metaphor in Revolutionary France, 1770–1800*, trans. Charlotte Mandell (Stanford, CA: Stanford University Press, 1997), 76–128; and Bastid, *Sieyès*, 329–39.

10. On Sieyès's idea of representation, see Baker, "Sieyès," 313–23; Keith Michael Baker, *Inventing the French Revolution: Essays on French Political Culture in the Eighteenth Century* (Cambridge: Cambridge University Press, 1990), 244–50; Michael Sonenscher, "Introduction," in Emmanuel-Joseph Sieyès, *Political Writings: Including the Debate between Sieyès and Tom Paine in 1791*, ed. and trans. Michael Sonenscher (Indianapolis: Hackett, 2003); and Michael Sonenscher, *Before the Deluge: Public Debt, Inequality, and the Intellectual Origins of the French Revolution* (Princeton, NJ: Princeton University Press, 2007), 67–94; and Sewell, *Rhetoric*. On the general history of political ideas of representation, see Monica Brito Vieira and David Runciman, *Representation* (Cambridge: Polity, 2008).

11. Abbé Emmanuel-Joseph Sieyès, *Qu'est-ce que le Tiers État?* (1789), ed. Roberto Zapperi (Geneva: Droz, 1970), 139. Also see Abbé Emmanuel-Joseph Sieyès, *Observations sur la rapport du comité de Constitution, concernant la nouvelle organisation de la France* (Versailles, 1789), 19–20; and Abbé Emmanuel-Joseph Sieyès, *Préliminaire de la Constitution: Reconnoissance et exposition raisonnée des droits de l'homme et du citoyen* (n.p., 1789), 37. Sieyès excluded nonnaturalized foreigners while making the point that they were actually more worthy of some form of inclusion than the privileged. Sieyès, *Qu'est-ce que le Tiers État?*, 125, 211.

12. See Bredin, *Sieyès*, 13–17.

13. Bredin, 54.

14. Abbé Emmanuel-Joseph Sieyès, "Citoyens, Eligibles, Electeurs," AN, 284 AP 3, dossier 2, cahier 3.

15. Sieyès, "Esclaves d'une espèce qui ait moins de besoins"; and Sieyès, "Esclavage," in *Écrits Politiques*, 76. On Sièyes and the Society, see Marcel Dorigny and Bernard Gainot, eds., *La Société des amis des noirs 1788–1799: Contributions à l'histoire de l'abolition de l'esclavage* (Paris: Éditions UNESCO, 1998).

16. Sieyès, *Préliminaire de la Constitution*, 15.

17. Germaine de Staël quoted in Bredin, *Sieyès*, 15.

18. Germaine de Staël quoted in Bredin, 15.

19. Sieyès own perspective on these issues is best captured by his manuscript inquiry into force as an issue in physiology, cognition, chemistry, and natural philosophy; Sieyès, "Questions et recherches sur forces simples," AN, 284 AP 5, dossier 3, cahier 3, in *Des manuscrits*, 2:599–697.

20. Sieyès, "Le grand cahier métaphysique," in *Des manuscrits*, 1:80. Also see the five pages of notes from 1770s included at the end of Sieyès, "Questions et recherches sur forces simples," 2:693–97.

21. Sieyès discusses Buffon and Delisle de Sales in a manuscript in AN, 284 AP 2, dossier 3, cahier 1; also published by Quiviger, *Le principe*, 391–92. The additional references are in bibliographies in Sieyès, *Des manuscrits*, vol. 2, esp. 120, 123, 146, 147, 174–75, 185, and 282.

22. See AN, 284 AP 5, dossier 3.

23. Sieyès, "Questions et recherches sur forces simples," 2:643.

24. See the similar observation in Bastid, *Sieyès et sa pensée*, 338.

25. Sieyès, "Questions et recherches sur forces simples," 2:630. Also see Sieyès, "Analogie entre l'action et la réaction, Distribution de la force, action, et réaction," in 284 AP 2, dossier 1, cited in Sieyès, *Des manuscrits*, 2:629–30n81.

26. Sieyès, "Questions et recherches sur forces simples," 2:641, 644.

27. Sieyès, 2:646n91.

28. Sieyès, 2:647.

29. On Fontenelle and Voltaire, see Hans Blumenberg, *Shipwreck with Spectator: Paradigm of a Metaphor for Existence*, trans. Steven Rendall (Cambridge, MA: MIT Press, 2009), 32–38.

30. Gottfried Wilhelm Leibniz, *The Principles of Philosophy, or the Monadology* (1714), in *Philosophical Essays*, ed. and trans. Roger Ariew and Daniel Garber (Indianapolis: Hackett, 1989), 222. On Sieyès and Leibniz, see Quiviger, *Le principe.*

31. Sieyès, "Questions et recherches sur forces simples," 2:647.

32. Sieyès, "Analyse des actes concourant à la cognition," AN, 284 AP 5, dossier 3, quoted and translated in Forsyth, *Reason and Revolution*, 46. On Sieyès's ideas of the self and their context, see Jan Goldstein, *The Post-Revolutionary Self: Politics and Psyche in France, 1750–1850* (Cambridge, MA: Harvard University Press, 2005), 122–29.

33. Sieyès, "Analyse des actes," quoted and translated in Forsyth, *Reason and Revolution*, 45.

34. Sieyès, "Analyse des actes," quoted and translated in Forsyth, *Reason and Revolution*, 45–46.

35. Sieyès, "Analyse des actes," quoted and translated in Forsyth, *Reason and Revolution*, 46.

36. See Marie-François-Xavier Bichat, *Recherches physiologiques sur la vie et la mort* (Paris: Brosson, Gabon, Year VIII [1800]). On Bichat, see Elizabeth Haigh, *Xavier Bichat and the Medical Theory of Eighteenth Century* (London: Wellcome Institute of the History of Medicine, 1984); and François Duchesneau, *La physiologie des Lumières: Empirisme, modèles et théories* (The Hague: M. Nijhoff, 1982), 431–76.

37. Anthelme-Balthasar Richerand, *Nouveaux éléments de physiologie* (Paris: Year IX [1801]). On Richerand, see Roselyne Rey, *Naissance et développement du vitalisme en France de la deuxième moitié du 18ᵉ siècle à la fin du Premier Empire* (Oxford: Voltaire Foundation, 2000), 373–84; Martin S. Staum, *Cabanis: Enlightenment and Medical Philosophy in the French Revolution* (Princeton, NJ: Princeton University Press, 1980), 251–53; Elizabeth A. Williams, *The Physical and the Moral: Anthropology, Physiology, and Philosophical Medicine in France, 1750–1850* (Cambridge: Cambridge University Press, 1994), 134–36.

38. Théophile Bordeu, *Œuvres complètes de Bordeu*, ed. Anthelme-Balthasar Richerand, 2 vols. (Paris: Crapelet, 1818). This work includes Richerand's "Notices sur la vie et les ouvrages de Bordeu."

39. Sieyès commented on the sixth edition of Richerand's *Nouveaux éléments* (1814) and the third edition of Cabanis's *Rapports* (1815). See Sieyès, *Des manuscrits*, 2:581.

40. Abbé Emmanuel-Joseph Sieyès, *Vues sur les moyens d'exécution dont les Représentans de la France pourront disposer en 1789* (n.p., 1789), 3.

41. On Sieyès and this aspect of Hobbes, see Murray Forsyth, "Thomas Hobbes and the Constituent Power of the People," *Political Studies* 29, no. 2 (1981): 191–203.

42. Abbé Emmanuel-Joseph Sieyès, *Dire de l'abbé Sieyes sur la question du veto royal à la séance du 7 septembre 1789*, in *Écrits politiques*, 237.

43. Sieyès, *Qu'est-ce que le Tiers État?*, 213. Also see quotation of Sieyès on unity and method in Forsyth, *Reason and Revolution*, 27.

44. Sieyès, *Qu'est-ce que le Tiers État?*, 213.

45. For Sieyès's reproduction of a *tableau œconomique* of Quesnay's, see Sieyès, *Des manuscrits*, 1:266. For some of his graphic representations, see Sieyès, *Des manuscrits*, 1:349–50, 373–75, 405–6, and 2:529–40.

46. Sieyès, *Qu'est-ce que le Tiers État?*, 214.

47. Sieyès, 214.

48. Sieyès, 214.

49. Sieyès, 215.

50. Sieyès, 214–15.

51. Sieyès, "Représentation du tout n'a rien au-dessus," AN, 284 AP 5, dossier 1, cahier 2, in *Des manuscrits*, 1:464.

52. Sieyès, "Base et fin de la société = respect de la liberté individuelle," AN, 284 AP 5, dossier 1, cahier 3, in *Des manuscrits*, 1:470; and Sieyès, "Contre la démocratie monacle au 1er degré," AN, 284 AP 5, dossier 1, cahier 11, in *Des manuscrits*, 2:553.

53. Sieyès, "Contre la démocratie monacle au 1er degré," AP2:553.

54. Sieyès, "Représentation du tout n'a rien au-dessus," AP1:464.

55. Sieyès, AP1:464.

56. Sieyès, AP1:463.

57. On the different idea of virtual representation as something that could be achieved through public opinion, see the discussion of Malesherbes in Paul Friedland, *Political Actors: Representative Bodies and Theatricality in the Age of Revolution* (Ithaca, NY: Cornell University Press, 2002), 72–79. On the different principle of virtual representation in eighteenth-century England, see Paul Langford, "Property and 'Virtual Representation' in Eighteenth-Century England," *Historical Journal* 31, no. 1 (1988): 83–115.

58. Sieyès, *Qu'est-ce que le Tiers État?*, 180.

59. Sieyès, 178.

60. Sieyès, "Représentation du tout, n'a rien au-dessus," AP1:463.

61. Sieyès, AP2:463.

62. On this element of abandon, and its context, see Charly Coleman, *The Virtues of Abandon: An Anti-individualist History of the French Enlightenment* (Stanford, CA: Stanford University Press, 2014).

63. Sieyès, *Dire de l'abbé Sieyes sur la question du veto royal*, 234.

64. Sieyès, 234.

65. Sieyès, 234.

66. On his organic metaphors as sublimations or secularizations of theological and theologicopolitical concepts, see Marcel Gauchet, *La Révolution des droits de l'homme* (Paris: Gallimard, 1989), xviii–xix; and de Baecque, *Body Politic*, 100–101.

67. Sieyès, "Les nations exemptes de décadence," AN, 284 AP 3, dossier 2, cahiers 1; in Sieyès, *Des manuscrits*, 2:430.

68. Sieyès, *Qu'est-ce que le Tiers État?*, 180.

69. On renewal by thirds and its importance to Sieyès organic vision, see de Baecque, *Body Politic*.

70. Emmanuel-Joseph Sieyès, *Observations de Sieyès, sur les attributions et l'organisation du Jury Constitutionaire proposed le 2 thermidor* (Year III [1795]), 11.

71. Sieyès, 11.

72. Sieyès, 11.

73. Sieyès, "La loi," in *Des manuscrits*, 2:418.

74. Sieyès, *Observations sur la rapport*, 2.

75. Abbé Emmanuel-Joseph Sieyès, *Quelques idées de Constitution applicables à la ville de Paris en juillet 1789* (Versailles, September 14, 1789), 4.

76. Sieyès, 4.

77. Sieyès, 4. Also see Sieyès, "Société primaires," in *Des manuscrits*, 1:403.

78. See Forsyth, *Reason and Revolution*, 183; Andrew Jainchill, *Reimagining Politics after the Terror: The Republican Origins of French Liberalism* (Ithaca, NY: Cornell University Press, 2008), 41; and Marcel Gauchet, *La Révolution des pouvoirs: La souveraineté, le people et la representation, 1789–1799* (Paris: Gallimard, 1995), 159–78.

79. Sieyès, *Des manuscrits*, 2:533. Also see Sieyès, "Contreforces," 284 AP 5, dossier 1, cahier 7, included in Quiviger, *Le principe*, 435.

80. Sieyès, *Essai sur les privilèges*, 99; also see 104.

81. On Sieyès's ideas about labor and laborers, see Sewell, *Rhetoric*, 145–84.

82. See pages 2 and 6 of Abbé Emmanuel-Joseph Sieyès, "Délinémants politiques," AN, 284 AP 2, dossier 15, cahier 1, in Sieyès, in *Des manuscrits*, 1:199–205. Sieyès gives multiple names to some of the classes and subclasses. On Sieyès's terminology and obsessive creation of new terms, see Guilhaumou, *Sieyès et l'order de la langue*.

83. See William H. Sewell Jr., "Le Citoyen / La Citoyenne: Activity, Passivity, and the Revolutionary Concept of Citizenship," in *The French Revolution and the Creation of Modern Political Culture*, ed. Colin Lucas (New York: Pergamon, 1988), 2:105–23. On the various limitations on enfranchisement, see Patrice Gueniffey, "Suffrage," in Furet and Ozouf, *Critical Dictionary of the French Revolution*, 571–81; and Isser Woloch, *The New Regime* (New York: W. W. Norton, 1994), 60–68. On internal enemies and limitations on citizenship during the Terror, see Anne Simonin, *Le déshonneur dans la République: Une histoire de l'indignité, 1791–1958* (Paris: Grasset, 2008), 263–360.

84. Sieyès, *Qu'est-ce que le Tiers État?*, 143–44.

85. Sieyès, *Dire de l'abbé Sieyes sur la question du veto royal*, 236.

86. Sieyès, 236; Abbé Emmanuel-Joseph Sieyès, "La Nation," in *Écrits politiques*, 89; Sieyès, "Esclaves d'une espèce"; and Sieyès, "Citoyens, Eligibles, Electeurs."

87. Sieyès, "Grèce. Citoyen—Homme," in *Écrits politiques*, 81.

88. Sicyès, "Grèce. Citoyen—Homme," 81.

89. A search of "bête humaine" (and its variants) in the ARTFL-FRANTEXT database of historical French books results in only one occurrence in the eighteenth century (in 1795) and twenty occurrences in the nineteenth century, all of those appearing after 1851. Searches in Google Books show similar results.

90. Sieyès, "Citoyens, Eligibles, Electeurs."

91. See Sieyès, *Observations sur la rapport*, 19–20. Also, see Sieyès, *Qu'est-ce que le Tiers État?*, 139.

92. See Sonenscher, "Introduction," lviii; and Quiviger, *Le principe*, 118n158.

93. For the only significant analysis, see Sewell, *Rhetoric*, 153–58. For brief mentions of the document, see Harvey Mitchell, *America after Tocqueville: Democracy against Difference* (Cambridge: Cambridge University Press, 2002), 39; Laurent Dubois, *A Colony of Citizens: Revolution and Slave Emancipation in the French Caribbean, 1787–1804* (Chapel Hill: University of North Carolina Press, 2004), 175–76; and Pierre Serna, *Commes des bêtes: Histoire politique de l'animal en Révolution (1750–1840)* (Paris: Fayard, 2017), 324–25.

94. Sieyès, "Institution: L'homme triple," in *Des manuscrits*, 2:563.

95. Sieyès quoted in Martin S. Staum, *Minerva's Message: Stabilizing the French Revolution* (Montreal: McGill-Queen's University Press, 1996), 108. On friendship with Cabanis, see Bastid, *Sieyès et sa pensée*, 109; and Sieyès, *Des manuscrits*, 1:54.

96. On improving domestic animals, see Sieyès, "Suite du projet décret pour l'Establissement de l'Instruction Nationale," *Journal d'instruction sociale* 5 (July 6, 1793): 151.

97. Sieyès, *Des manuscrits*, 2:147, 185–86.

98. Quiviger, *Le principe*, 391–92.

99. Sieyès, *Des manuscrits*, 2:174–75.

100. Both men were core members of the Society of 1789. See Keith Michael Baker, "Politics and Social Science in Eighteenth-Century France: The Société de 1789," in J. F. Bosher, ed., *French Government and Society, 1500–1800: Essays in Memory of Alfred Cobban* (London: Athlone, 1973), 203–30.

101. See Robert Wokler, "The Ape Debates in Enlightenment Anthropology," *SVEC* 192 (1980): 1164–75; Claude Blanckaert, "Premier des singes ou dernier des hommes? Les métamorphoses de l'homme-singe aux XVII–XVIII siècles," *Alliage* 7–8 (1991): 113–29; Londa Schiebinger, *Nature's Body: Gender in the Making of Modern Science* (Boston: Beacon, 1993); Raymond Corbey and Bert Theunissen, eds., *Ape, Man, Apeman: Changing Views since 1600* (Leiden: Leiden University, 1995); and Wulf D. Hund, Charles W. Mills, and Silvia Sebastiani, eds., *Simianization: Apes, Gender, Class, and Race* (Zurich: LIT Verlag, 2015).

102. Buffon, "Nomenclature des singes," in *HN* 14 (1766), 31, 50–51.

103. Jean-Baptiste-Claude Delisle de Sales, *Essai philosophique sur le corps humain, pour server de suite à la philosophie de la nature* (Amsterdam: Arkstée & Merkus, 1774), 2:386.

104. J.-P. Brissot, *Théorie des loix criminelles* (Berlin, 1781), 1:243–44.

105. Louis E. Robbins, *Elephant Slaves and Pampered Parrots: Exotic Animals in Eighteenth-Century Paris* (Baltimore: Johns Hopkins University Press, 2002), 131.

106. Robbins, 79, 131. Also see Schiebinger, *Nature's Body*, 85; and G. S. Rousseau, *Enlightenment Crossings: Pre- and Post-modern Discourses, Anthropological* (Manchester: Manchester University Press, 1991), 198–209.

107. Buffon, "Les orang-outangs, ou Le pongo et le jocko," in *HN* 14 (1766), 53–54.

108. Voltaire, *Dictionnaire philosophique* (1764), in *Les Œuvres complètes de Voltaire*, hereafter *OC*, ed. Christiane Mervaud et al. (Oxford: Voltaire Foundation, 1994), 35:517–18. Voltaire is playing on the ancient description of man as a "featherless biped capable of speech and reason." See Lynn Festa, "Humanity without Feathers," *Humanity* 1, no. 1 (Fall 2010): 3–27.

109. Diderot, *Le rêve de d'Alembert*, in *OP*, 383–84.

110. Restif de la Bretonne, *Lettre d'un singe*, appended to *La découverte australe*. On the social interaction of Restif de la Bretonne and Sieyès, see David Coward, *The Philosophy of Restif de la Bretonne* (Oxford: Voltaire Foundation, 1991), 765–66. For Sieyès quoting a work by Restif de la Bretonne, see Sieyès, *Des manuscrits*, 1:250. For another strange mix of heterodox philosophy and a fictional treatment of sexual reproduction between humans and orangutans, see Jacques-Antoine Grignon des Bureaux, *Rêveries métaphysiques*, ed. Sylvain Matton (Paris: Honoré Champion, 2012).

111. Mirabeau claimed to read Buffon daily. He eventually bought a large portion of Buffon's library after the naturalist's death. On Mirabeau's purchase, see *Catalogue des livres de la bibliothèque de feu M. Mirabeau l'aîné* (Paris: Rozet and Belin, 1791), iii. On Mirabeau's reading, see Maëlle Levacher, *Buffon et ses lecteurs: Les complicités de "l'Histoire naturelle"* (Paris: Classiques Garnier, 2011), 189–90.

112. Honoré-Gabriel de Riqueti, comte de Mirabeau, *Erotika biblion* (1783), in *Œuvres érotiques* (Paris: Fayard, 1984), 572–73.

113. See Kirill Rossiianov, "Beyond Species: Il'ya Ivanov and His Experiments on Cross-Breeding Humans with Anthropoid Apes," *Science in Context* 15, no. 2 (June 2002): 277–316.

114. Buffon, "Le cochon, le cochon de Siam et le sanglier," in *HN* (1755), 5:102.

115. They were involved in a number of projects, including the Society of 1789 and coediting *Journal d'instruction sociale*. See Keith Michael Baker, *Condorcet: From Natural Philosophy to Social Mathematics* (Chicago: University of Chicago Press, 1975); and Jacques Guilhaumou, "Condorcet-Sieyès: Une amitié intellectuelle," in *Condorcet: Homme des Lumières et de la Révolution*, ed. Anne-Marie Chouillet and Pierre Crépel (Fontenay-aux-Roses: ENS Éditions, 1997), 223–34.

116. Condorcet, "Sur les laines," 17.

117. Condorcet's editorial footnote in Voltaire, *Essai sur les mœurs*, in *OC* (1784), 18:285–86. Condorcet's note is also included in Condorcet, "Espèces," in "Notes sur Voltaire," in *Œuvres complètes de Condorcet* (Paris: Henrichs et al., Year XIII [1804]), hereafter *OC*, 4:403.

118. Condorcet, in Voltaire, *Essai sur les mœurs*, 285–86.

119. On Kant's "ethical turn" and the three phases of revisions, see John H. Zammito, *Genesis of Kant's Critique of Judgment* (Chicago: University of Chicago Press, 1992), 3–8,

263–68. On Kant's political thought in the 1790s, see Frederick Beiser, *Enlightenment, Revolution, Romanticism: The Genesis of Modern German Political Thought, 1790–1800* (Cambridge, MA: Harvard University Press, 1992), 27–56.

120. Beiser, *Enlightenment, Revolution, Romanticism*, 37.

121. Immanuel Kant, *Critique of the Power of Judgment* (1790), ed. Paul Guyer, trans. Paul Guyer and Eric Matthews (New York: Cambridge University Press, 2000), 246–47.

122. On Sieyès and the German-speaking lands, see Marcelle Adler-Bresse, *Sieyès et le monde allemand* (Lille: Atelier reproduction des thèses, Université des Lille III, 1977); and Jacques Droz, *L'Allemagne et la Révolution française* (Paris: Presses Universitaires de France, 1949).

123. On the relationship between the political philosophies of Sieyès and Kant, see Gareth Steadman Jones, "Kant, the French Revolution, and the Definition of a Republic," in *The Invention of the Modern Republic*, ed. Biancamaria Fontana (Cambridge: Cambridge University Press, 1994), 154–72. On Kant, organization, and the life sciences, see James L. Larson, "Vital Forces: Regulative Principles or Constitutive Agents? A Strategy in German Physiology, 1760–1802," *Isis* 70, no. 2 (June 1979): 235–49; Timothy Lenoir, "Kant, Blumenbach, and Vital Materialism in German Biology," *Isis* 71, no. 1 (March 1980): 77–108; Zammito, *Genesis*, 189–227; Philippe Huneman, *Métaphysique et biologie: Kant et la constitution du concept d'organisme* (Paris: Éditions Kimé, 2008); and John H. Zammito, *The Gestation of German Biology: Philosophy and Physiology from Stahl to Schelling* (Chicago: University of Chicago Press, 2018).

124. See François Azouvi and Dominque Bourel, eds., *De Königsberg à Paris: La réception de Kant en France (1788–1804)* (Paris: Vrin, 1991).

125. Constantin-François Volney, *Leçons d'histoire prononcées à l'École Normale* (1795; 1826), in *Œuvres* (Paris: Fayard, 1989), 1:572; Sieyès, "Loi organique de l'ordre politique en France," AN, 284 AP 5, dossier 2, cahier 4, also in Quiviger, *Le principe*, 400–410; Pierre-Louis Roederer, *Cours d'organisation social*, in *Œuvres* (Paris: Firmin Didot, 1859), 8:129–305.

126. See, for example, the political sense of "organisation" being included along with the physiological sense in the *Dictionaire de l'Académie française* between the fourth edition (Paris: Bernard Brunet, 1762) and the fifth edition (Paris: J. J. Smits, 1798).

CHAPTER SIX

1. Marie-Jean-Antoine-Nicolas de Caritat de Condorcet, "Sur l'instruction publique," in *OC*, 9:382, emphasis in original.

2. Condorcet, 382, emphasis in original.

3. On the French Revolution and time, See Reinhart Koselleck, *Futures Past: On the Semantics of Historical Time*, trans. Keith Tribe (Cambridge, MA: MIT Press, 1985); Lynn Hunt, "The World We Have Gained: The Future of the French Revolution," *American Historical Review* 108, no. 1 (February 2003): 1–19; and Peter Fritzsche, *Stranded in the Present: Modern Time and the Melancholy of History* (Cambridge, MA.: Harvard University Press, 2004); and William Max Nelson, *The Time of Enlightenment: Constructing the Future in France, 1750 to Year One* (Toronto: University of Toronto Press, 2021), 121–48.

4. See David A. Bell, *The Cult of the Nation in France: Inventing Nationalism, 1680–1800* (Cambridge, MA: Harvard University Press, 2003), 154–59.

5. Nicolas Ruault, *Gazette d'un Parisien sous la Révolution: Lettre à son frère, 1783–1796*, ed. Anne Vassal (Paris: Perrin, 1976), 160.

6. Maximilien Robespierre, "Sur les rapports des idées religieuses et morales avec les principes républicains, et sur les fêtes nationales (18 floréal Year II [May 7, 1794]), in *Œuvres de Maximilien Robespierre*, ed. Marc Bouloiseau and Albert Soboul (Paris: Presses Universitaires de France, 1967), 10:444–45.

7. Jean-Antoine-Joseph Debry, *Discours sur les fondemens de la morale publique* (Paris, 1794), 18. Also see Andrew Jainchill, *Reimagining Politics after the Terror: The Republican Origins of French Liberalism* (Ithaca, NY: Cornell University Press, 2008), 62–65.

8. Robespierre in the "Suite de la discussion sur l'instruction publique" in the National Convention on August 13, 1793, in *Procès-verbaux du Comité d'instruction publique de la Convention nationale*, ed. James Guillaume (Paris: Imprimerie nationale, 1891–1958), 2:278.

9. On Cabanis, see Martin S. Staum, *Cabanis: Enlightenment and Medical Philosophy in the French Revolution* (Princeton, NJ: Princeton University Press, 1980); Mariana Saad, *Cabanis: Comprendre l'homme pour changer le monde* (Paris: Classique Garner, 2016); Jean-Luc Chappey, *La Société des observateurs de l'homme: Des anthropologues au temps de Bonaparte* (Paris: Société des études robespierristes, 2002), 57; and Martin S. Staum, *Minerva's Message: Stabilizing the French Revolution* (Montreal: McGill-Queen's University Press, 1996).

10. Pierre-Jean-Georges Cabanis, *Coup d'œil sur les révolutions et sur la réforme de la médicine* (Year XII [1804]), in *OP*, 2:78.

11. Cabanis, 2:78.

12. Pierre Rosanvallon, *Democracy Past and Future*, ed. Samuel Moyn (New York: Columbia University Press, 2006), 82.

13. On regeneration, see Mona Ozouf, *L'homme régénéré: Essais sur la Révolution française* (Paris: Gallimard, 1989); and Antoine de Baecque, *The Body Politic: Corporeal Metaphor in Revolutionary France, 1770–1800*, trans. Charlotte Mandell (Stanford, CA: Stanford University Press, 1997), 131–56; Bell, *Cult of the Nation*; and Jainchill, *Reimagining Politics*, 62–107.

14. Mirabeau, "Premiers discours: De l'instruction publique" (1791), in Bronislaw Baczko, ed., *Une éducation pour la democratie* (Geneva: Droz, 2000), 73. While Mirabeau was listed as the author, it may have been written or drafted by Cabanis, one of his assistants at the time. Staum, *Cabanis*, 125.

15. Jacques-Nicolas Billaud-Varenne, *Principes régénérateurs du système social* (Paris: R. Vatar, pluviôse Year III [1795]; Paris: Publications de la Sorbonne, 1992), 90, 101–2.

16. Antoine-Louis-Claude Destutt de Tracy, "Rapport des citoyens Cabanis, Ginguené, Réveillère-Lépeaux, Danou, et Destutt-Tracy . . . ," in François-Pierre Gontier Maine de Biran, *Influence de l'habitude sur la faculté de penser* (Paris: Presses Universitaires de France, 1954), 210.

17. See Bronislaw Baczko, ed., *Une education pour la démocratie: Textes et projets de l'époque révolutionnaire* (Paris: Garnier, 1982); and Mona Ozouf, *L'école de la France: Essais sur la Révolution, l'utopie et l'enseignement* (Paris: Gallimard, 1984).

18. Maximilien Robespierre presenting Michel Lepeltier's plan for education reform, "Plan d'éducation nationale de Michel Lepeltier, présenté à Convention National par Maximilien Robespierre, au nom de la commission d'instruction publique" (July 13, 1793), in *Procès-verbaux du Comité d'instruction publique de la Convention nationale*, ed. James Guillaume (Paris: Imprimerie nationale, 1891–1958), 2:45.

19. For instance, Pierre-Louis Roederer quoted Pascal in "Imitation et l'habitude," *Journal d'économie publique, de morale et de politique* 2, no. 18 (30 pluviôse Year V [1797]): 401–3.

20. Blaise Pascal, *Pensées*, trans. A. J. Krailsheimer (New York: Penguin Books, 1995), 248.

21. Pascal, 247.

22. Pascal, 247.

23. On French sensationism, see John C. O'Neal, *The Authority of Experience: Sensationist Theory in the French Enlightenment* (University Park: Pennsylvania State University Press, 1996).

24. Rousseau, *Émile*, in *OC*, 4:248.

25. Rousseau, 4:282.

26. See Laurence L. Bongie, "Hume and Skepticism in Late Eighteenth-Century France," in *The Skeptical Tradition around 1800: Skepticism in Philosophy, Science, and Society*, ed. Johan van der Zande and Richard Popkin (Boston: Kluwer Academic, 1998), 15–16; and Laurence L. Bongie, "Hume 'Philosophe' and Philosopher in Eighteenth–Century France," *French Studies* 16 (1961): 213–27.

27. Abbé Etienne Bonnot de Condillac, *Traité des animaux* (1755), in *Œuvres philosophiques de Condillac*, ed. Georges Le Roy (Paris: Presses Universitaires de France, 1947), 1:376b.

28. Condillac, 1:363a.

29. Condillac, 1:363a.

30. Condillac, 1:364a.

31. Adrien-Marie Legendre et al. *L'Agence temporaire des poids et mesures aux citoyens rédactuers de la Feuille du Cultivateur* (Paris: Imprimerie de la République, Year III [1794–95]), 9, quoted and translated in Ken Alder, "A Revolution to Measure: The Political Economy of the Metric System in France," in *Values of Precision*, ed. M. Norton Wise (Princeton, NJ: Princeton University Press, 1995), 58.

32. Abbé Henri Grégoire, *Rapports fait au Conseil de Cinq-Cents sur les sceaux de la République* (n.p., 1796), 3.

33. Grégoire, 3.

34. Grégoire, 3.

35. Agence temporaire, *Notions élémentaires sur les nouvelles mesures* (Paris: Imprimerie de la République, Year IV [1795]), 10, quoted and translated in Alder, "Revolution to Measure," 56.

36. On the metric remaking of "the mentality of citizens," see Alder, "Revolution to Measure," 56; and Ken Alder, *The Measure of All Things: The Seven-Year Odyssey and Hidden Error That Transformed the World* (New York: Free Press, 2002), 132–38.

37. On Lindet's report, see Bronislaw Baczko, *Ending the Terror: The Revolution after Robespierre*, trans. Michel Petheram (New York: Cambridge University Press and Editions de la Maison des Sciences de l'Homme, 1994), 115–35. On historical forgetting, see Ozouf, "Thermidor ou Le travail de l'oubli," in *L'école de la France*, 91–108.

38. Jean-Baptiste Say, *Olbie, ou Essai sur les moyens de réformer les mœurs d'une nation* (Paris: Deterville, Year VIII [1800]), 15n1.

39. Say, 15.

40. See Staum, *Minerva's Message*, 28, 69–70, 110–13, 176. On the Idéologues, see Sergio Moravia, *Il pensiero degli Idéologues* (Florence: La nuova Italia, 1974); Georges Gusdorf, *La conscience révolutionnaire, les Idéologues* (Paris: Payot, 1978); and Chappey, *La Société des observateurs de l'homme*.

41. Staum, *Minerva's Message*, 69–70, 110–13, 245.

42. See François Azouvi, *Maine de Biran: La science de l'homme* (Paris: Vrin, 1995).

43. Maurice Merleau-Ponty, *L'union de l'âme et du corps chez Malebranche, Biran et Bergson: Notes prises au cours de Maurice Merleau-Ponty* (Paris: Vrin, 1968).

44. François-Pierre Gontier Maine de Biran, *Influence de l'habitude sur la faculté de penser* (Paris: Presses Universitaires de France, 1954), 7.

45. Pierre-Louis Roederer, "Imitation et l'habitude," *Journal d'économie publique, de morale et de politique* 2, no. 18 (30 pluviôse Year V [1797]): 410.

46. Antoine-Louis-Claude Destutt de Tracy, *Projet d'éléments d'idéologie* (Paris: Didot, Year IX [1801]), 242, 250.

47. Antoine-Louis-Claude Destutt de Tracy, "Extrait raisonné de l'Ideologie, servant de table analytique" (1804), in *Éléments d'Idéologie*, ed. Henri Gouhier (Paris: Vrin, 1970), 1:415.

48. Destutt de Tracy, *Projet d'éléments d'idéologie*, 244–45.

49. Jean-Louis Alibert, "Du pouvoir de l'habitude dans l'état de santé et de maladie," *Mémoires de la Société médicale d'emulation* 1 (Year VI [1798]), 396, 397.

50. Pierre-Jean-Georges Cabanis, *Rapports du physique et du moral de l'homme*, in *OP*, 394.

51. On Condorcet, see Keith Michael Baker, *Condorcet: From Natural Philosophy to Social Mathematics* (Chicago: University of Chicago Press, 1975).

52. On the Société de 1789, see Keith Michael Baker, "Politics and Social Science in Eighteenth-Century France," in *French Government and Society (1500–1800): Essays in Memory of Alfred Cobban*, ed. J. F. Bosher (London: Athlone, 1973), 108–30.

53. Marie-Jean-Antoine-Nicolas de Caritat de Condorcet, "The Nature and Purpose of Public Instruction" (1791), in *Selected Writings*, ed. and trans. Keith Michael Baker (Indianapolis: Bobbs-Merrill, 1976), 113.

54. Condorcet, 113.

55. Condorcet, 113.

56. Condorcet, 113.

57. See Mary Terrall, "Material Impressions: Conception, Sensibility, and Inheritance," in *Vital Matters: Eighteenth-Century Views on Conception, Life, and Death*, ed. Helen Deutsch and Mary Terrall (Toronto: University of Toronto Press, 2012), 121n40.

58. Charles-Georges Le Roy, *Lettres sur les animaux*, ed. Elizabeth Anderson (Oxford: Voltaire Foundation, 1994), 7–14, 27–28, 170–71.

59. On Diderot's dissent, see Timo Kaitaro, *Diderot's Holism: Philosophical Antireductionism and Its Medical Background* (New York: Peter Lang, 1997), 134–37.

60. Marie-Jean-Antoine-Nicolas de Caritat de Condorcet, *Tableau historique des progress de l'esprit humain: Projets, esquisse, fragments, et notes (1772–1794)*, ed. Jean-Pierre Schandeler, Pierre Crépel, et al. (Paris: Institut national d'études démographiques, 2004).

61. See Condorcet's notes, "Fragment 9," included in Condorcet, 889–93.

62. Marie-Jean-Antoine-Nicolas Caritat, marquis de Condorcet, "Sur les laines," in *Histoire de l'Académie Royale des Sciences* (Paris, 1780 [presented in 1777]), 16–17.

63. Condorcet, 17.

64. Condorcet, "Sketch," in *Selected Writings*, 280.

65. Condorcet, 280–81.

66. See Staum, *Cabanis*.

67. See Cabanis, *OP*, 2:549.

68. Pierre-Jean-Georges Cabanis, "Lettre sur un passage de la *Décade philosophique* et en général sur la philosophie de l'esprit humain," in *La Décade philosophique, littéraire et politique* 21 (30 gérminal Year VII), 149–59, reprinted in Cabanis, *OP*, 2:513.

69. Cabanis, *Rapports*, 356.

70. Cabanis, 356. See Buffon, "De la nature: Seconde vue," in *HN* (1764), 13:i–xx.

71. Cabanis, *Rapports*, 356.

72. Cabanis, 356.

73. Cabanis, 356.

74. Cabanis, 357.

75. Pierre-Jean-Georges Cabanis "Quelques considérations sur l'organisation sociale en général et particulièrement sur la nouvelle constitution" (Year VIII [1799]), in *OP*, 2:465.

76. Cabanis, *Rapports*, 578.

77. Cabanis, *Coup d'œil*, 77.

78. Cabanis, 210.

79. Cabanis, 211.

80. See Clare Carlisle, *On Habit* (London: Routledge, 2014); and Tom Sparrow and Adam Hutchinson, eds., *A History of Habit: From Aristotle to Bourdieu* (New York: Lexington Books, 2013). See the introduction and commentary in Félix Ravaisson, *Of Habit*, ed. Clare Carlisle and Mark Sinclair (London: Bloomsbury, 2008); and the edited volume with a selection from Maine de Biran, *The Relationship between the Physical and the Moral in Man*, ed. Darian Meacham and Joseph Spadola (London: Bloomsbury, 2016).

81. Tony Bennett, Francis Dodsworth, Greg Noble, Mary Poovey, and Megan Watkins, "Habit and Habituation: Governance and the Social," *Body and Society* 19, nos. 2–3 (2013): 3–29; and see the rest of this special issue on habit.

82. See, for example, Gusdorf, *La conscience révolutionnaire, les Idéologues*; Moravia, *Il pensiero degli Idéologues*; and Staum, *Minerva's Message*.

83. On Lamarck and his scientific contributions, see François Jacob, *Logic of Life: A History of Heredity*, trans. Betty E. Spillman (Princeton, NJ: Princeton University Press, 1973); Richard W. Burkhardt Jr., *The Spirit of System: Lamarck and Evolutionary Biology* (Cambridge, MA: Harvard University Press, 1977); L. J. Jordanova, *Lamarck* (Oxford: Oxford University Press, 1984); Pietro Corsi et al., eds., *Lamarck, philosophe de la nature* (Paris: Presses Universitaires de France, 2006); and Goulven Laurent, *Jean-Baptiste Lamarck, 1744–1829* (Paris: Éditions du CTHS, 1997).

84. Kyla Schuller, *The Biopolitics of Feeling: Race, Sex, and Science in the Nineteenth Century* (Durham, NC: Duke University Press, 2017), 8–9, 24–25, 35–36, 46–49. On malleable bodies and impressibility in twentieth-century biopolitics, see Kyle Schuller and Jules Gill-Peterson, eds., "The Biopolitics of Plasticity," special issue, *Social Text* 38, no. 2 (June 2020).

85. Jean-Baptiste Lamarck, *Philosophie zoologique, ou Exposition* . . . (Paris: Dentu, 1809).

CHAPTER SEVEN

1. Pierre Guyomar, *La partisan de l'égalité politique entre les individus, ou Problème très-important de l'égalité en droits et de l'inégalité en fait* (Imprimerie nationale, 1793), 3. Reprinted as an appendix to the debate of April 29, 1793, in *Archives parlémentaires*, vol. 63, 591–99.

2. On Guyomar, see Bernard Gainot, "Pierre Guyomar et la revendication démocratique dans le débat autour de la constitution de l'an III," in *1795, Pour une République sans Révolution*, ed. Roger Dupuy and Marcel Morabito (Riennes: Presses Universitaires de Rennes, 1996), 261–73; Léon Dubreuil, "Révolutionnaires de Basse-Bretagne: Le conventionnel Pierre Guyomar," *Annales de Bretagne* 34, no. 2 (1919): 168–87, and no. 3 (1919): 298–318.

3. Guyomar, *La partisan*, 4. On the analogy of enslaved people and free women in the Age of Revolutions, see Denise Z. Davidson, "Feminism and Abolitionism: Transatlantic Trajectories," in Suzanne Desan, Lynn Hunt, and William Max Nelson, eds., *The French Revolution in Global Perspective* (Ithaca, NY: Cornell University Press, 2013), 101–10.

4. On Guyomar's more prominent political role after the Terror, see Gainot, "Pierre Guyomar."

5. Hannah Arendt, *The Origins of Totalitarianism* (New York: Harcourt, Brace, 1951), 289, 297.

6. Arendt, 295, 296.

7. Arendt, 298, 296.

8. Arendt, 295.

9. On natality, see Hannah Arendt, *The Human Condition* (1958), 2nd ed. (Chicago: University of Chicago Press, 1998).

10. On the genealogy of *das bloße Leben,* see Nitzan Lebovic, *The Philosophy of Life and Death: Ludwig Klages and the Rise of Nazi Biopolitics* (New York: Palgrave Macmillan, 2013).

11. Giorgio Agamben, *Homo Sacer: Sovereign Power and Bare Life,* trans. Daniel Heller-Roazen (Stanford, CA: Stanford University Press, 1998), 127.

12. Agamben, 127.

13. Agamben, 128.

14. Agamben, 129.

15. Agamben, 131.

16. Agamben, 131.

17. Agamben, 166.

18. Agamben, 129.

19. For variants of the phrase, see Guyomar, *La partisan,* 4, 12; and see the speech of Jean-Denis Lanjuinais on April 29, 1793 in *Archives parlémentaires,* 63:562, 564.

20. Neither textual research nor the ARTFL-FRANTEXT database indicates any occurrences of "member(s) du souverain" before Rousseau's *Social Contract;* and neither do searches for variants in Google Books turn up any earlier uses.

21. Thomas Hobbes, *Leviathan* (1651), ed. Noel Malcolm, vol. 2 (Oxford: Oxford University Press, 2012), 249.

22. Keith Michael Baker, "Sovereignty," in *A Critical Dictionary of the French Revolution,* ed. François Furet and Mona Ozouf, trans. Arthur Goldhammer (Cambridge, MA: Harvard University Press, 1989), 848–49. Also see Keith Michael Baker, *Inventing the French Revolution: Essays on French Political Culture in the Eighteenth Century* (New York: Cambridge University Press, 1990).

23. Guyomar, *La partisan,* 14, 20.

24. Guyomar, *La partisan,* did, however, qualify women's active participation in politics, arguing that they should vote in the primary assemblies. He did not call for them to be made eligible for election.

25. Guyomar, 1–2.

26. Guyomar, 2.

27. Guyomar, 9, 20, 2.

28. Guyomar, 2.

29. Guyomar, 2.

30. Guyomar, 2.

31. For the language of "reciprocal incorporation," see Timothy Campbell and Adam Sitze, "Introduction," in *Biopolitics: A Reader* (Durham, NC: Duke University Press, 2013), 2.

32. On self-evidence and the rights of man and citizen, see Lynn Hunt, *Inventing Human Rights: A History* (New York: W. W. Norton, 2007); Kate E. Tunstall, ed., *Self-*

Evident Truths? Human Rights and the Enlightenment (London: Bloomsbury, 2012); and Dan Edelstein, *On the Spirit of Rights* (Chicago: University of Chicago Press, 2018).

33. On "dissensus" (that is, the "dispute about what is given") and the rights of man, see Jacques Rancière, "Who Is the Subject of the Rights of Man," *South Atlantic Quarterly* 103, nos. 2–3 (Spring/Summer 2004): 297–310.

34. On contemporary "biological citizenship," see Adriana Petryna, *Life Exposed: Biological Citizens after Chernobyl* (Princeton, NJ: Princeton University Press, 2002); and Nikolas Rose and Carlos Novas, "Biological Citizenship," in *Global Assemblages: Technology, Politics, and Ethics as Anthropological Problems*, ed. Aihwa Ong and Stephen J. Collier (Malden, MA: Wiley, 2005), 439–63; and Nikolas Rose, *The Politics of Life Itself: Biomedicine, Power, and Subjectivity in the Twenty-First Century* (Princeton, NJ: Princeton University Press, 2007).

35. Arendt, *Origins of Totalitarianism*, 294; and Hannah Arendt, "'The Rights of Man: What Are They?," *Modern Review* 3, no. 1 (Summer 1949): 24–37. Also see Seyla Benhabib, *The Reluctant Modernism of Hannah Arendt* (Thousand Oaks, CA: Sage, 1996); and Stephanie DeGooyer, Alastair Hunt, Lida Maxwell, and Samuel Moyn, *The Right to Have Rights* (London: Verso, 2018), particularly Alastair Hunt's discussion of Arendt, rights, and biopolitics, 75–102.

36. Eugen Weber, *Peasants into Frenchmen: The Modernity of Rural France, 1870–1914* (Stanford, CA: Stanford University Press, 1976).

37. François-René de Chateaubriand, *Memoires d'outre-tombe* (Paris: Gallimard, 1997), 1:428.

38. On Chateaubriand and the slave trade, see Georges Collas, *Réné-Auguste de Chateaubriand, comte de Combourg, 1718–1786, un cadet de Bretagne au 18ᵉ Siècle* (Paris: A. G. Nizet, 1949); and Jean Mettas, *Répertoire des expéditions négrières Françaises au XVIIIᵉ Siècle* (Paris: Société française d'histoire d'outre-mer, 1978), 1:408.

39. Arthur Young, *Travels in France, during the Years 1787, 1788, 1789*, 3rd ed., ed. M. Betham-Edwards (London: G. Bell, 1890), 123.

40. See Michèle Duchet, *Anthropologie et histoire au siècle des Lumières* (Paris: Albin Michel, 1995), 307–8, 312–13.

41. Seigneur de Montbrun quoted in Mona Ozouf, *Festivals and the French Revolution*, trans. Alan Sheridan (Cambridge, MA: Harvard University Press, 1988), 236. For the letter to Paris, see A. Gazier, ed., *Lettres à Grégoire sur les patois de France, 1790–1794* (Paris, 1880; reprinted Geneva: Slatkine, 1969), 84–85.

42. Sylvain Maréchal, *Correctif à la Révolution* (Paris, 1793), 265–66.

43. Joseph-Marie Lequinio, *Voyage dans le Jura* (Paris, Year IX [1800]), 1:10–12.

44. On the importance in post-Revolutionary France, see Stéphane Gerson, "Parisian Litterateurs, Provincial Journeys and the Construction of National Unity in Post-Revolutionary France," *Past and Present* 151 (May 1996): 141–73.

45. Michel Vovelle, *De la cave au grenier: Un itinéraire en Provence au XVIIIᵉ siècle* (Québec: S. Fleury, 1980), 407–35; Marie-Noëlle Bourguet, *Déchiffrer la France: La statistique département à l'époque napoléonienne* (Paris: Éditions des archives contemporaines, 1989), 21–46; Daniel Roche, *France in the Enlightenment*, trans. Arthur Goldhammer (Cambridge, MA: Harvard University Press, 1998), 11–40; and Amy S.

Wyngaard, *From Savage to Citizen: The Invention of the Peasant in the French Enlightenment* (Newark: University of Delaware Press, 2004), 151–71. On the vague and clichéd nature of the earlier information, see Marie-Noëlle Bourguet, *Déchiffrer la France: La statistique départementale à l'époque napoléonienne* (Paris: Éditions des archives contemporaines, 1989), 27–28; and André Burguière, "Monarchical Centralization and the Birth of Social Sciences: Voyagers and Statisticians in Search of France at the End of the Eighteenth Century," in Robert M. Schwartz and Robert A. Schneider, eds., *Tocqueville and Beyond: Essays in Honor of David D. Bien* (Newark: University of Delaware Press, 2003), 228–29.

46. Wyngaard, *From Savage to Citizen*, 162.

47. C. Dralet, *Plan détaillé topographique, suivi de la topographie du département du Gers* (Paris, Year IX [1800–1801]), 19.

48. See Constantin-François Volney, *Questions de statistique à l'usage des voyageurs* (1795), in *Œuvres* (Paris: Fayard, 1989), 1:673; and the works of Degérando and Cuvier in *Aux origines de l'anthropologie française: Les mémoires de la Société des observateurs de l'homme en l'an VIII*, ed. Jean Copans and Jean Jamin (Paris: Sycomore, 1978), 129–69, 173–76.

49. On François de Neufchâteau's radicalization, see James Livesey, "A Revolutionary Career? François de Neufchâteau Does Well by Doing Good, 1774–1794," *French History* 18, no. 2 (2004): 186–92. On his life and career, see James Livesey, "An Agent of Enlightenment in the French Revolution: Nicolas-Louis François de Neufchâteau, 1752–1800" (PhD diss., Harvard University, 1994); and Dominique Margairaz, *François de Neufchâteau: Biographie intellectuelle* (Paris: Publications de la Sorbonne, 2005).

50. De Marbois to François de Neufchâteau, Port-au-Prince, February 15, 1787, AN, 27 AP 11 (2), quoted in Livesey, "Revolutionary Career?," 191.

51. On the colonies and the 286 censuses, see J. Dupâquier and E. Vilquin, "Le pouvoir royal et la statistique démographique," in *Pour la histoire de la statistique*, 2 vols. (Paris: INSEE, 1978), 1:83–101. On the colonies and the nominative census, see Robert Bradley Scafe, "The Measure of Greatness: Population and the Census under Louis XIV" (PhD diss., Stanford University, 2005), 116–52. On censuses in early eighteenth-century Louisiana, see Shannon Lee Dawdy, *Building the Devil's Empire: French Colonial New Orleans* (Chicago: University of Chicago Press, 2008), 153–58. On the 1763 census in Martinique, see Fanny Malègue, "Compter les hommes, ou La normalité retrouvée?," *Mélanges de l'École française de Rome* 132, no. 1 (2020): 73–83.

52. Nicolas-Louis François de Neufchâteau, *Les études du magistrat, discours prononcé à la réntrée du Conseil Supérieur du Cap, le jeudi 5 octobre 1786* (Cap Français, 1786), 58.

53. See the exemption for enslaved people filled out by François de Neufchâteau on April 1, 1786, in 27 AP 12, dossier 1, AN.

54. Nicolas-Louis François de Neufchâteau, *Mémoire en forme de discours sur la disette du numéraire à Saint-Domingue, et sur les moyens d'y remédier* (Cap François, 1788), 70.

55. See the tables appended to François de Neufchâteau, *Mémoire en forme de discours*, n.p.

56. François de Neufchâteau, *Mémoire en forme de discours*.

57. On the grand statistical project and its significance, see Jean-Claude Perrot and Stuart J. Woolf, *State and Statistics in France, 1789–1815* (New York: Harwood Academic Publishers, 1984); and Bourguet, *Déchiffrer la France.*

58. Nicolas-Louis François de Neufchâteau, *Recueil des lettres circulaires, instructions, programmes, discours, et autres actes publics, émanés du Cen François (de Neufchâteau), pendant ses deux exercices du Ministère de l'intérieur*, 3 vols. (1799–1802), 2:166.

59. On the Society of the Observers of Man, see Chappey, *La Société des observateurs de l'homme.*

60. Degérando, "Considérations sur les diverses méthods," in Copans and Jamin, *Aux origines de l'anthropologie française*, 128.

61. On Degérando and the Society of the Observers of Man in the history of anthropology, see George W. Stocking Jr., *Race, Culture, and Evolution: Essays in the History of Anthropology* (Chicago: University of Chicago Press, 1982), 13–41; Chappey, *La Société des observateurs de l'homme*; and Jean-Luc Chappey, Carole Christen, and Igor Moullier, eds., *Joseph-Marie de Gérando (1772–1842): Connaître et réformer la société* (Rennes: Presses Universitaires de Rennes, 2014).

62. On François de Neufchâteau's role in the grand statistical project, see Perrot and Woolf, *State and Statistics*; and Bourguet, *Déchiffrer la France.*

63. On the "patois," the past, regeneration, and the civilizing mission, see *Une politique de la langue: La Révolution française et les patois: L'Enquête de Grégoire*, ed. Michel de Certeau, Dominique Julia, and Jacques Revel (Paris: Gallimard, 1975): 160–69; and David A. Bell, *The Cult of the Nation in France: Inventing Nationalism, 1680–1800* (Cambridge, MA: Harvard University Press, 2003), 169–217. On revolutionary regeneration and a "civilizing mission," see Jean-Luc Chappey et al., eds., *Pour qoui faire la Révolution* (Marseille: Agone, 2012), 117.

64. On the development of internal voyageurs in France, see Mona Ozouf, *L'école de la France: Essais sur la Révolution, l'utopie et l'enseignement* (Paris: Gallimard, 1984), 27–54, 351–79; Mona Ozouf, *Festivals and the French Revolution*, 217–23; Gerson, "Parisian Litterateurs"; and Burguière, "Monarchical Centralization," 226–42.

65. Louis-François Jauffret, "Introduction aux mémoires de la Société des observateurs de l'homme," in Copans and Jamin, *Aux origines de l'anthropologie française*, 74.

66. Louis-François Jauffret, "Introduction," in Copans and Jamin, *Aux origines de l'anthropologie française*, 78.

67. On "internal colonization" during the Revolution and the nineteenth century, see Weber, *Peasants into Frenchmen*, 3–23, 485–96; and de Certeau et al., *Une politique de la langue.*

68. See, for example, the work of Paul Broca's student Réne Collignon, *Anthropologie de la France: Dordogne, Charente, Corrèze, Creuse, Haute-Vienne* (Paris: Société d'anthropologie de Paris, 1894). On Broca and his students in the development of race and physical anthropology, see Martin Staum, *Labeling People: French Scholars on Society, Race, and Empire* (Montreal: McGill-Queen's University Press, 2003); Claude Blanckaert, *De la race è l'évolution: Paul Broca et l'anthropologie française, 1850–1900* (Paris: Harmattan, 2009); and Martin S. Staum, *Nature and Nurture in French Social Sciences, 1859–1914 and Beyond* (Montreal: McGill-Queen's University Press, 2011).

69. See Collignon, *Anthropologie de la France*. On cephalic index and eugenic practices, as in the work of Georges Vacher de Lapouge, see Sean Quinlan, "Racial Imagery of Degeneration and Depopulation: Georges Vacher de Lapouge and 'Anthroposociology' in Fin-de-Siècle France," *History of European Ideas* 24, no. 6 (1998): 393–413; and Staum, *Nature and Nurture*.

70. See Alice L. Conklin, *A Mission to Civilize: The Republican Idea of Empire in France and West Africa, 1895–1930* (Stanford, CA: Stanford University Press, 1997).

71. Jacques-Louis Moreau de la Sarthe, "Considérations sur quelques traces de l'état sauvage chez les peuples policés" (1801), in *La Décade philosophique, littéraire, et politique* 35 (Year XII, 4me trimestre, 20 fructidor [September 7, 1804]): 452. On the *métis* and the Breton, see Emmanuelle Saada, *Empire's Children: Race, Filiation, and Citizenship in the French Colonies* (Chicago: University of Chicago Press, 2012), 13.

72. On the racial census under Hugues, see Laurent Dubois, *A Colony of Citizens: Revolution and Slave Emancipation in the French Caribbean, 1787–1804* (Chapel Hill: University of North Carolina Press, 2004), 262–66. On Moreau de Jonnès more generally, see Peter Hulme, "Black, Yellow, and White on St. Vincent: Moreau de Jonnès Carib Ethnography," in *The Global Eighteenth Century*, ed. Felicity A. Nussbaum (Baltimore: Johns Hopkins University Press, 2003), 182–94. On his statistical work, see Joshua Cole, *The Law of Large Numbers: Population, Politics, and Gender in Nineteenth-Century France* (Ithaca, NY: Cornell University Press, 2000); and Libby Schweber, *Disciplining Statistics: Demography and Vital Statistics in France and England, 1830–1885* (Durham, NC: Duke University Press, 2006).

73. Alexandre Moreau de Jonnès, *Ethnogénie caucasienne: Recherches sur la formation et le lieu d'origine des peuples éthiopiens, chaldéens, syriens, hindous, perses, hébreux, grecs, celtes, arabes, etc.* (Paris: Joël Cherbuliez, 1861); and *Notice des travaux de Alexandre Moreau de Jonnès* (Paris: Migneret, 1821).

74. Paul Rabinow, *French Modern: Norms and Forms of the Social Environment* (Chicago: University of Chicago Press, 1989), 130–38; Stuart M. Persell, "The Revival of Buffon in the Early Third Republic," *Biography* 14, no. 1 (Winter 1991): 12–24; and Damien Deschamps, "Les sources scientifiques et la politique indochinoise de Jean-Louis de Lanessan, 1891–1894," in *Viêt Nam, sources et approches: Actes de deuxième colloque international Euroviet*, ed. Phillipe Le Fallier and Jean-Marie Mancini (Aix-en-Provence: Publications de l'Université de Provence), 279–92. Also see Carole Reynaud Paligot, *La république raciale: Paradigme racial et idéologie républicaine, 1860–1930* (Paris: Presses Universitaires de France, 2006).

75. Staum, *Nature and Nurture*, 185.

76. Claude Blanckaert, "Of Monstrous Métis? Hybridity, Fear of Miscegenation, and Patriotism from Buffon to Paul Broca," in *The Color of Liberty: Histories of Race in France*, ed. Sue Peabody and Tyler Stovall (Durham, NC: Duke University Press, 2003), 42–70.

77. For a sophisticated approach to Grégoire's eclectic beliefs, see Alyssa Goldstein Sepinwall, *The Abbé Grégoire and the French Revolution: The Making of Modern Universalism* (Berkeley: University of California Press, 2005). Also see Ruth F. Necheles, *The Abbé Grégoire, 1787–1831: The Odyssey of an Egalitarian* (Westport, CT: Greenwood, 1971).

78. Abbé Henri Grégoire, *Rapport sur les destructions opérées par le vandalisme, et sur les moyens de le réprimer: Séance du 14 fructidor, l'an second de la République une et indivisible* (Paris, 1794), 22.

79. Abbé Henri Grégoire, *Rapport sur l'ouverture d'un concours pour les livres élémentaires de la première éducation: Séance du 3 pluviôse, l'an second de la République une et indivisible*, in *Procès-verbaux du Comité d'instruction publique de la Convention nationale*, ed. James Guillaume (Paris: Imprimerie nationale, 1891–1958), 3:365.

80. Grégoire, 365. Also see Abbé Henri Grégoire, *Sur les moyens d'améliorer l'agriculture en France*, in Guillaume, *Procès-verbaux du Comité d'instruction publique de la Convention nationale*, 2:472; and Abbé Henri Grégoire, "Réflexions extraites d'un ouvrage du citoyen Grégoire sur les moyens de perfectionner les sciences politiques," in *Mémoires de l'Institut national des sciences et des arts: Sciences morales et politiques* 1 (1798): 554.

81. See Sepinwall, *Abbé Grégoire*, 25–34.

82. *Statuts généraux de la Société des philantropes* [of Nancy], *rédigés dans les comices de 1776* (n.p., n.d.; reprint ed., n.p. 1932), 3, 43, 45.

83. He refers to Linnaeus, Bexon (a collaborator of Buffon), Lavater, Legrand d'Aussy, Cambry, and Papon, among others; Abbé Henri Grégoire, "Promenade dans les Vosges," ed. A. Benoît, in *Annales de Société d'émulation du département des Vosges* 71 (1895): 227–30, 270, 273. Also see the reprinted excerpt recounting another trip, "Voyages de l'abbé Grégoire dans les Vosges," in Louis Jouve, ed., *Voyages anciens et modernes dans les Vosges: Promenades, descriptions, souvenirs, lettres, etc., 1500–1870* (Épinal: Durand, 1881), 87–99.

84. Abbé Henri Grégoire, *Essai sur la régénération physique, morale et politique des Juifs: Ouvrage couronné par la Société Royale des Sciences et des Arts de Metz, le 23 août 1788* (1788; Paris: Flammarion, 1988), 75. On Grégoire's *Essai*, see Sepinwall, *Abbé Grégoire*, 56–77.

85. Grégoire, *Essai sur la régénération physique*, 72–78; and Charles-Augustin Vandermonde, *Essai sur la manière de perfectionner l'espèce humaine*, 2 vols. (Paris: Vincent, 1756), 1:112–13.

86. Sepinwall, *Abbé Grégoire*, 95–96, 193.

87. Abbé Henri Grégoire, *Lettre aux philantropes, sur les malheurs, les droits et les reclamations des Gens de couleur de Saint-Domingue, et des aurtres iles françoises de l'Amériques* (Paris: Belin, 1790), 4. Grégoire cites the *Encyclopédie* but clearly was referring to the article by AA [Guillaume-Leonard de Bellecombe], "Mulâtre," in *Nouveau dictionnaire pour servir de supplément aux dictionnaires des sciences, des arts, et des métiers*, ed. Jean-Baptiste-René Robinet (Paris: Panckoucke, 1777), 3:973–74.

88. Abbé Henri Grégoire, *Considérations sur le mariage et le divorce, adressées aux citoyens d'Haïti* (Paris: Baudouin Frères, 1823), 14.

89. Julien-Joseph Virey, *L'art de perfectionner l'homme, ou De la médicine sprituelle et morale*, 2 vols. (Paris: Deterville, 1808); and François-Emmanuel Fodéré, *Les lois éclairées par les sciences physiques, ou Traité de médecin-légale et d'hygiène publique*, 3 vols. (Paris: Ceterville, 1799). On Millot and Mahon, see Anne Carol, *Histoire de l'eugénisme en France: Les médecins et la procréation, XIXᵉ–XXᵉ siècle* (Paris: Seuil, 1995), 23–26; Sean M. Quinlan, *The Great Nation in Decline: Sex, Modernity and Health Crises*

in Revolutionary France, c. 1750–1850 (Aldershot: Ashgate, 2007), 138–40, 149–52; and Michael E. Winston, *From Perfectibility to Perversion: Meliorism in Eighteenth-Century France* (New York: Peter Lang, 2005), 143–44.

90. Louis-Joseph-Marie Robert, *Nouvel essai sur la mégalantropogénésie, ou L'art de faire des enfants d'esprit, qui deviennent de grands hommes: Suivi des traits physiognomiques propres à les faire reconnoître, décrits par Aristote, Porta, et Lavater, avec des notes additionelles de l'autuer*, 2nd ed. (Paris: Le Normant, Year XI [1803]). The first edition was published in Year X [1801] and soon followed by the second edition. On Robert, see Carol, *Histoire de l'eugénisme*, 20–23; and Sean M. Quinlan, "Physical and Moral Regeneration after the Terror: Medical Culture, Sensibility and Family Politics in France, 1794–1804," *Social History* 29, no. 2 (May 2004): 139–64.

91. Robert, *Nouvel essai*, i.

92. Winston, *Perfectibility to Perversion*, 148–50.

93. Winston, 149.

94. Robert, *Nouvel essai*, 1. Robert was not a strict Buffonian on questions of generation; see Robert, 53.

95. Robert, 150–51.

96. Robert included reviews in the second edition. See Winston, *Perfectibility to Perversion*.

97. Louis-Joseph-Marie Robert, *De l'influence de la Révolution française sur la population* (Paris: Allut et Crochard, Year XI [1802]).

98. Jean Burdin, *Cours d'études médicales, ou Exposition de la structure de l'homme comparée à celle des animaux; de l'histoire de ses maladies; des connaissances acquises sur l'action régulière de ses organes, etc. etc.* (Paris: Duprat and Letellier, 1803).

99. Burdin, 3:238.

100. Burdin, 3:239.

101. Burdin, 3:241.

102. Burdin, 3:240–41.

103. For a list of members, see Rey, *Naissance*, 413–36.

104. Henri Saint-Simon, "Mémoire sur la science de l'homme" (1813), in *Œuvres complètes*, ed. Juliette Grange, Pierre Musso, Philippe Régnier, and Franck Yonnet (Paris: Presses Universitaires de France, 2012), 2:1079–90. On Burdin and the Société médicale d'émulation, see Williams, *Physical and the Moral*, 78 and 92.

105. On Burdin and Saint-Simon, see Frank Manuel, *The New World of Henri Saint-Simon* (Cambridge, MA: Harvard University Press, 1956). Also see Johan Heilbron, *The Rise of Social Theory* (Minneapolis: University of Minnesota Press, 1995), 186.

106. Auguste Comte, *Cours de philosophie positive*, ed. Michel Serres, François Dagonet, and Allal Sinaceur (Paris: Harmattan, 1975).

107. Auguste Comte, *Système de politique positive, ou Traité de sociologie instituant la religion de l'humanité*, 4 vols. (Paris: Carilian-Goeury 1851–54).

108. See Claude Blanckaert, *La nature de la société: Organicisme et sciences sociales au XIXᵉ siècle* (Paris: Harmattan, 2004); and Dominique Guillo, *Les figures de l'organisa-*

tion: Sciences de la vie et sciences sociales au XIXe siècle (Paris: Presses Universitaires de France, 2003).

109. Auguste Comte, *Discours sur l'ensemble du positivisme* (Paris: Flammarion, 1998), 356–58.

110. Comte, *Système*, 1:618.

111. See Mauro Bertani, "Sur le généalogie du bio-pouvoir," in *Lectures de Michael Foucault*, vol. 1, *À propos de "Il faut défendre la société,"* ed. Jean-Claude Zancarini (Lyon: ENS Éditions, 2001), 19; and Antonella Cutro, *Michel Foucault tecnica e vita: Bio-politica e filosofia del bios* (Napoli: Bibliopolis, 2004), 65.

112. Comte, *Système*, 619.

113. Comte, 619.

114. On Comte and Montpellier school, see Georges Canguilhem, *A Vital Rationalist: Selected Writings from Georges Canguilhem*, ed. François Delaporte, trans. Arthur Goldhammer (New York: Zone Books, 1994), 237–61. On Comte and organization, see Guillo, *Les figures de l'organisation*; and Heilbron, *Rise of Social Theory*.

115. Pierre Lafitte, *Plan d'un course de biologie d'après Auguste Comte* (Paris: La Revue Occidentale, 1883), 34. Lafitte also associated Buffon with biocracy; see Pierre Lafitte, "Diderot et son siècle," *La revue occidentale philosophique, sociale, politique* 12 (1884): 289.

116. On Toulouse, his idea of biocracy, and the argument that it was a radicalization of the positivist concept, see Michel Huteau, *Psychologie, psychiatrie et société sous la troisième république: La biocratie d'Édouard Toulouse (1865–1947)* (Paris: L'Harmattan, 2002), 9, 49–66. On Toulouse and eugenics, also see Carol, *Histoire de l'eugénisme*; and William H. Schneider, *Quality and Quantity: The Quest for Biological Regeneration in Twentieth-Century France* (New York: Cambridge University Press, 1990), 181–84.

117. Richard C. Keller, *Colonial Madness: Psychiatry in French North Africa* (Chicago: University of Chicago Press, 2007), 55, quoting Édouard Toulouse, "Problème de la prophylaxie mentale" (1929). Keller compares Toulouse's conception of biocracy to biopolitics, 54–55.

118. Mary Pickering, *Auguste Comte: An Intellectual Biography* (Cambridge: Cambridge University Press, 2009), 3:326–27, 339, 354; and Jean-François Braunstein, *Philosophie de la médecine d'Auguste Comte: Vaches carnivores, Vierge Mère et morts vivants* (Paris: Presses Universitaires de France, 2009).

119. See Carol, *Histoire de l'eugénisme*, 69–70. On anthroposociology, see Quinlan, "Racial Imagery."

120. Rudolph Kjellén, *Staten som Lifsform* (Stockholm: Hugo Gebers Forlag, 1916). On Kjellén and biopolitics, see Roberto Esposito, *Bíos: Biopolitics and Philosophy*, trans. Timothy Campbell (Minneapolis: University of Minnesota Press, 2008), 16–17; Thomas Lemke, *Biopolitics: An Advanced Introduction* (New York: New York University Press, 2011), 9–10; and Markus Gunneflo, "Rudolph Kjellén and Nordic Biopolitics before the Welfare State," *Retfærd* 38 (Fall 2015): 24–39.

CONCLUSION

1. Cassirer published his work in 1932, not long before fleeing Germany. Hazard published his first book on the Enlightenment as the Nazis took power, and he wrote his second in Nazi-occupied France. A student of Hazard, Venturi fled Paris before the occupation, returning to Italy and fighting with the antifascist resistance. Peter Gay's family was forced to flee Nazi Germany when he was still a boy. Lynn Hunt with Margaret Jacob, "Enlightenment Studies," in *Encyclopedia of the Enlightenment*, ed. Alan Kors (New York: Oxford University Press, 2003).

2. Peter Gay, *The Enlightenment: An Interpretation*, vol. 2, *The Science of Freedom* (New York: Alfred A. Knopf, 1969), 3.

3. See Carl Becker, *The Heavenly City of the Eighteenth-Century Philosophers* (New Haven, CT: Yale University Press, 1932); Isaiah Berlin, *The Age of Enlightenment: The Eighteenth-Century Philosophers* (Oxford: Oxford University Press, 1979); George Mosse, *Towards the Final Solution: A History of European Racism* (New York: H. Fertig, 1978); and Max Horkheimer and Theodor W. Adorno, *Dialectic of Enlightenment*, trans. John Cumming (New York: Herder and Herder, 1972). For a representative postmodern critique, see John Gray, *Enlightenment's Wake: Politics and Culture at the Close of the Modern Age* (New York: Routledge, 1995). For a classic postcolonial critique, see Robert Young, *White Mythologies: Writing History and the West* (New York: Routledge, 1990).

4. Naomi Schor, *Bad Objects: Essays Popular and Unpopular* (Durham, NC: Duke University Press, 1995), 3.

5. On the "blackmail of Enlightenment," see Michel Foucault, "What Is Enlightenment?," in Foucault, *Ethics: Subjectivity and Truth*, ed. Paul Rabinow, trans. Robert Hurley et al. (New York: New Press, 1997).

6. See Jonathan Israel, *Radical Enlightenment: Philosophy and the Making of Modernity, 1650–1750* (New York: Oxford University Press, 2001); Stephen Eric Bronner, *Reclaiming the Enlightenment: Toward a Politics of Radical Engagement* (New York: Columbia University Press, 2004); Louis Dupré, *The Enlightenment and the Intellectual Foundations of Modern Culture* (New Haven, CT: Yale University Press, 2004); Jonathan Israel, *Enlightenment Contested* (New York: Oxford University Press, 2006); Tzvetan Todorov, *In Defence of the Enlightenment* (London: Atlantic Books, 2009); Zeev Sternhell, *The Anti-Enlightenment Tradition*, trans. David Maisel (New Haven, CT: Yale University Press, 2010); and Jonathan Israel, *Democratic Enlightenment* (New York: Oxford University Press, 2013). One of the most eccentric and selective defenses is Gertrude Himmelfarb, *The Roads to Modernity: The British, French, and American Enlightenments* (New York: Knopf, 2004).

7. Israel, *Enlightenment Contested*, 869, emphasis in the original; also see v, 870; and Jonathan Israel, "Enlightenment! Which Enlightenment?," *Journal of the History of Ideas* 67, no. 3 (July 2006): 524.

8. Israel, *Enlightenment Contested*, 869.

9. For an influential, and misguided, formulation of the clash of civilizations, see Samuel P. Huntington, *The Clash of Civilizations and the Remaking of the World Order* (New York: Simon and Schuster, 1996). For critiques, see Edward W. Said, "The Clash of Ignorance," *Nation*, October 22, 2001, 11–13; and Hugh Gusterson, "The Seven

Deadly Sins of Samuel Huntington," in *Why America's Top Pundits Are Wrong: Anthropologists Talk Back*, ed. Catherine Besteman and Hugh Gusterson (Berkeley: University of California Press, 2005), 24–42.

10. Jonathan Israel quoted by Yoram Stein, "Vrij individu boven godsdienstvrijheid: Radicale Verlichting," *Trouw*, May 6, 2005, quoted in Ian Buruma, *Murder in Amsterdam: Liberal Europe, Islam, and the Limits of Tolerance* (New York: Penguin, 2006), 24. Also see Buruma for more on Hirsi Ali, her embrace of the Enlightenment, including Spinoza, and the political and cultural context of Israel's claim.

11. Horkheimer and Adorno, *Dialectic of Enlightenment*, 6.

12. The phrase *bon à penser* (good to think [with]) was first used in Claude Lévi-Strauss, *Totemism*, trans. Rodney Needham (Boston: Beacon, 1963), 89. Of course, the Enlightenment is itself a historical object created and re-created since the eighteenth century. See James Schmidt, ed., *What Is Enlightenment? Eighteenth-Century Answers and Twentieth-Century Questions* (Berkeley: University of California Press, 1996); James Schmidt, "Inventing the Enlightenment: Anti-Jacobins, British Hegelians, and the Oxford English Dictionary," *Journal of the History of Ideas* 64, no. 3 (July 2003): 421–43; James Schmidt, "What Enlightenment Was, What It Still Might Be, and Why Kant May Have Been Right after All," *American Behavioral Scientist* 49, no. 5 (January 2006): 647–63; Darrin M. McMahon, *Enemies of the Enlightenment: The French Counter-Enlightenment and the Making of Modernity* (New York: Oxford University, 2001); Daniel Brewer, *The Enlightenment Past: Reconstructing Eighteenth-Century French Thought* (New York: Cambridge University Press, 2008); and Antoine Lilti, *L'Héritage des Lumières: Ambivalences de la modernité* (Paris: Gallimard/Seuil, 2019).

13. See Siep Stuurman, "How to Write a History of Equality," *Leidschrift* 19, no. 3 (December 2004): 23–38; Siep Stuurman, *François Poulain de la Barre and the Invention of Modern Equality* (Cambridge, MA: Harvard University Press, 2004); and Siep Stuurman, *The Invention of Humanity: Equality and Cultural Difference in World History* (Cambridge, MA: Harvard University Press, 2017). Also see Étienne Balibar, *Equaliberty: Political Essays*, trans. James Ingram (Durham, NC: Duke University Press, 2014); Étienne Balibar, *Citizen Subject: Foundations for Political Anthropology*, trans. Steven Miller (New York: Fordham University Press, 2017); and Étienne Balibar, *Citizenship*, trans. Thomas Scott-Railton (Cambridge: Polity, 2015).

Index